Banking, International Capital Flows and Growth in Europe

Financial Markets, Savings and Monetary Integration in a World with Uncertain Convergence

Paul J. J. Welfens · Holger C. Wolf (Eds.)

Banking, International Capital Flows and Growth in Europe

Financial Markets, Savings and Monetary Integration in a World with Uncertain Convergence

With 22 Figures
and 63 Tables

Springer

Professor Dr. Paul J. J. Welfens
University of Potsdam
European Institute for International Economic Relations
August-Bebel-Str. 89
14482 Potsdam
Germany

Professor Holger C. Wolf
New York University
Leonard N. Stern School of Business
Management Education Center
44 West 4th Street, Suite 7-78
New York, NY 10012-1126
USA

ISBN 978-3-642-63823-7

Cataloging-in-Publication Data applied for

Die Deutsche Bibliothek - CIP-Einheitsaufuahme

Banking, international capital flows and growth in Europe:
financia\ markets, savings and monetary integration in a world with
uncertain convergence ; with 63 tables/ Paul J. Welfens ; Holger
C. Wolf (ed.). - Berlin; Heidelberg; New York; Barcelona;
Budapest ; Hong Kong ; London ; Milan ; Paris ; Santa Clara ;
Singapore; Tokyo: Springer, 1997
ISBN 978-3-642-63823-7 ISBN 978-3-642-59030-6 (eBook)
DOI 10.1007/978-3-642-59030-6

Hardcover-Design: Erich Kirchner, Heidelberg

SPIN 10633198 42/2202-5 4 3 2 1 0 - Printed on acid-free paper

This conference volume is dedicated to the late *WOLFRAM ENGELS* who was not only a leading German economist (specializing in banking) at the University of Frankfurt but also for many years a critical voice in the Wirtschaftswoche, Germany's leading economic weekly magazine. Rather poor links between the academic world and the political class in Germany have at times contributed to striking misconceptions, most notably as regards the problems of economic and monetary unification, strongly underestimated by government. *WOLFRAM ENGELS* did much to bridge this gap, his voice will be missed.

Table of Contents

Introduction

Paul J.J. Welfens and Holger C. Wolf

While the economies of Asia and, more recently, South as well as North America have enjoyed sustained high growth, the growth performance of western Europe and in particular continental Europe has been rather modest. Coupled with sizable improvements in labor productivity and - at best - steady capital productivity, growth proved insufficient to sustain employment levels, much less to replicate the US job creation success.

Relative inflation performance has been much better: in the run-up to European Monetary Union inflation rates have dramatically converged towards the lower end of the distribution while risk premia on formerly high inflation economies have fallen. Yet, looking forward, the undoubted success in achieving price stability is mitigated by the lackluster growth - and in particular employment - performance. Indeed, the relative little attention paid to initiatives directed at raising economic growth is startling, not only in the light of the US policy record but also in light of the remarkable rebound of those European economies which have aggressively tackled the structural problems, most prominently the UK and Ireland.

Economic growth is even more important in eastern Europe where rising aspiration levels of the population need to be satisfied and a potential political backlash avoided. Longer-term integration of the post-socialist economies into the European Union requires a convergence of relative income levels, and hence again relatively fast growth in the East. Much like the gradual division of western Europe into an - as yet small - group of countries willing to tackle difficult fiscal and labor market issues which are required for a return to robust growth and the - as yet larger - group of countries preferring to tinker at the edges, the recent experience in eastern Europe is quite diverse, ranging from the rather dynamic Visegrad group - Poland,

Czech Republic, Slovak Republic, Hungary and Slovenia - likely to achieve growth rates around five percent in the medium term - to the latecomers still on the downward part of the transition J-curve.

Looking forward, will the whole of Europe experience a period of renewed growth? The essays collected in this volume suggest that the answer to this question will importantly depend on the evolution of the financial sector and that, furthermore, as banks, stock markets and other financial institutions respond to the single market dynamics, financial sector efficiency will increasingly be a European rather than a narrowly national issue.

It is well known of course that the process of international financial integration has dramatically accelerated since the 1970s, beginning with the recycling of petro dollars, continuing with public-public sector lending and, in the last decade, an increasing volume of private-to-private flows, both in portfolio investment flows and in foreign direct investment. A large part of the increased integration was accounted for by sharply improved access of emerging markets: the leading thirty emerging economies, including many from eastern Europe and Asia, had a combined current account deficit of $107bn in 1996 - up from 80bn in 1995 - and will have a deficit of $150bn in 1997. This will be close to 3 percent of the groups' GDP. Well used, capital inflows of this magnitude stand to significantly boost growth performance: rising foreign direct investment flows raises world growth due to a more efficient allocation of capital and the faster dissemination of technical know-how, while portfolio flows sever the dependence of domestic investment on domestic savings and permit greater risk diversification in both recipient and source countries.

Yet integration among mature markets has also accelerated in the wake of further decontrol of financial markets. While Europe has participated in the process on the banking side, she substantially lags behind on the equity side, again with the partial exception of the United Kingdom. Continental Europeans remain notoriously reluctant to invest even in domestic, let alone in foreign equities, foregoing the benefits of international risk diversification and, more importantly, forestalling the emergence of a dynamic NASDAQ style market for new enterprises. As much of the employment growth in the United States - particularly of high wage jobs - is accounted for by new firms, the dormant nature of continental European markets (recent efforts in Germany notwithstanding) is worrisome. Looking forward, the ability of Europe to not only improve the efficiency of national financial systems, but also to integrate them into world capital market will be a major factor in determining whether Europe can rekindle its economic dynamism.

The analysis of **Paul Welfens** shows that the process is well underway on the banking side: banking business is changing in many respects as a more integrated EU financial market is emerging and as EMU is approaching. Continental Europe's industry has of course traditionally been dominated by bank finance, and strong banking systems will provide a growth impetus. However, as mentioned above, the traditional bank-financing model might be less appropriate in a future driven by high technology competition. Instead venture capital and stock markets, which are the natural source for financing risky investments and innovations, assume center stage. Development of equity markets is also a key aspect in the transition from the pay-as-you-go social security systems of the present - increasingly viewed as unsustainable on current demographic and growth trends - to fully funded systems.

The experience of the Anglo-Saxon countries - as well as many of the leading emerging markets, notably Chile - suggests that vibrant equity markets can stimulate savings, discipline managers and, more importantly, channel resources to high growth areas which are difficult to finance through collateralized bank loans. The efficiency gains of course depend on whether hostile takeovers are allowed and disclosure rules are strict. In both regards much is left to be desired in both France and Germany: hostile takeovers are a rare exception, and indeed are not infrequently scuttled by the government, disclosure requirements, even where mandated, rarely have the bite to ensure compliance. This has serious consequences: the stock market capitalization to GDP ratio in Germany (as well as in France and Italy) remains well below the levels of the US, the UK, Switzerland, Sweden and even the more liquid emerging stock markets, for instance Mexico and Thailand. While a more prominent role of bank financing partly substitutes for the lack of equity finance, Germany's falling capital productivity and the capital productivity gap vis-à-vis the US suggest that this substitution is far from perfect, and that the stock market underdevelopment has not been without costs. Looking forward, Welfens argues, that the development of liquid and efficient capital markets, and in particular equity and venture capital markets, is a cornerstone for addressing the unemployment issue. Neither high-technology firms nor service firms, the two main engines of employment growth, boast the ready collateral required for bank loans. The absence of alternative capital markets for upstarts, therefore, places Europe at a distinct disadvantage both in terms of the technology race and in terms of employment creation. The efficiency of the financial sector will likewise be a key feature in determining the success of the transition economies of eastern Europe. Improvements in financial systems are required partly to reverse capital outflows, and thus both to replenish the decimated working capital of existing firms and to finance the creation and expansion of new firms. Welfens argues that establishing adequate prudential supervision, monetary stabilization and a solution to the overhang of inherited debt in state-owned firms are necessary first steps on this road.

The evolution of prudential supervision in the EU in stage III of monetary union will be an important element in the pursuit of efficiency gains. Increased competition in integrated financial markets potentially poses new risks, particularly for poorly capitalized banks, including several state-owned banks. The adoption of legal provisions which ensure the protection of depositors and investors as well as the stability of the whole financial system are thus crucial for sustaining confidence in the stability of the financial system, which in turn is a prerequisite for generating and efficiently allocating savings. Yet care must be taken to avoid over-regulation, which could undermine competition among banks and brokers and thereby lower allocative efficiency. In a similar vein, deposit insurance clearly is an important issue for an integrated EU loan market, yet broad-based unconditional insurance creates well-known problems. Looking forward, the harmonization of prudential regulation - currently still largely undertaken in the national ministries of finance - will assume an increasingly important role, following the progress achieved by the Bank of International Settlements in the area of capital adequacy. In his comments on Welfen's paper, **Uwe Volmer** expresses confidence in the stability of financial markets, though he is more skeptical about the likelihood and impact of European Monetary Union.

Johannes Priesemann presents a broad legal and economic perspective of supervision in European Monetary Union. He points out that in some countries monetary policy and prudential supervision of banks are organized jointly while in others separately. These different national systems make effective and efficient supervision rather difficult. The European System of Central Banks and the European Central Bank certainly will be interested in a stable financial system in the EU. However, there is no obligation in the Maastricht Treaty requiring national supervisors to cooperate with the ESCB and the ECB, Priesemann argues that this commission might turn out to be a major deficiency of the blueprint for monetary union. In her comments on Priesemann' paper **Sydney Key** points to the experiences of the US and takes a closer look at the EC approach to regulation and supervision of financial institutions. She highlights the crucial issues in prudential supervision from a transatlantic perspective and suggests that compared to the US and former national systems in the EU countries the future ESCB will be subject to weak political accountability.

Difficult problems in the emergence of a viable banking system are encountered in Russia. After years of hyperinflation, fraud and liquidity problems in the banking sector, Russia's financial system has achieved some stability. However, if sustained economic growth cannot be achieved (in 1996 GDP growth was -6%, much in contrast to optimistic predictions by many observers) banks will face renewed problems since their balance sheets are a mirror of problems in the real sphere. In his analysis of the Russian banking sector, **Evgeny Gavrilenkov** argues that monetary and budgetary problems are intertwined - sometimes in strange ways, witness the special role of the energy sector and especially Gazprom. It is obvious that problems in macroeconomic stabilization and lack of confidence - resulting from the experience with hyperinflation, insufficient banking supervision and fraudulent systems - are still impairing the functioning of the Russian banking sector. Foreign investors have a low profile in this sector, which can be put down to various factors. In the 19th century Russia welcomed foreign banks only with some hesitation, though the fear that Russian banks would be dominated by their European counterparts proved unfounded as Russian banks achieved an emancipation process at the turn of the century. Commenting on Gavrilenkov's paper, **Daniel Gros** argues that closer attention should be paid to the design of differentiated bank licenses in order to help control moral hazard problems in the financial system.

Peter Hertner analyzes the historical lessons of foreign banking in eastern Europe, emphasizing that Dutch, German and French banks played a crucial part in developing eastern Europe's financial system, and hence played an important role in trade, investment and public debt financing. British banks are notably absent in the 1990s, matching their low profile at the start of the 20th century. Hertner argues that political stability has been a pre-requisite for generating growth impulses from financial markets. In his comments, **Hans Kernbauer** points out that banks in eastern Europe were often founded as a joint venture by foreign banks (of the credit mobilier type) . He points out that underdeveloped capital markets hindered banks from selling poorly performing industrial shares, while the lack of banking supervision created moral hazard problems, two important lessons for the transition economies.

Miroslaw Bojanczyk analyzes the role of privatization and restructuring of banks in Poland. In his contribution - originally a dinner speech - he shows that the restructuring program was rather complex in Poland. For a fast growing economy like Poland the banking system could become a bottleneck for further economic development. It is obvious that the EBRD played a major role in banking reforms in Poland. Many interesting technical aspects of reforming the Polish banking system are presented.

Timothy Lane's paper is devoted to high public debt and its consequences for investment and growth. He develops a simple model to examine the link between high public debt and investment. His analysis of the endogenous economic growth literature which emphasizes learning-by-doing, constant returns to scale production through innovation, the provision of public infrastructure and externalities from human capital suggests - in the spirit of optimal taxation models - that taxation for physical and human capital should be reduced. This could favor a political strategy for high taxes in the short term and lower tax burdens in the longer term, providing a rationale for front-loaded fiscal adjustment to reduce the debt to a manageable level. Ricardian equivalence is unlikely to affect the argument, Lane argues that neither empirical studies on US data nor international experiences permits an unambiguous conclusion in favor of Ricardian equivalence. Finally, the paper focuses on the political economy of public debt, specifically, on factors raising the riskiness of debt service and hence the risk premium, impairing investment and growth - a problem affecting both OECD countries and eastern Europe.

Stanley Black's comments emphasize the role of debt finance and discuss the high public debt problem in the European Union. The debt-GDP and deficit-GDP convergence criteria of the Maastricht Treaty are ambiguous in some respects since much depends on what is included in the public sector and how pensions are funded. Moreover, assets are ignored. He points to the German constitution which prohibits deficits to exceed public capital spending. If such a rule were combined with the 3 percent deficit-GDP criterion of the Maastricht Treaty, public capital formation could not exceed 3 percent of GDP. The author then turns to intergenerational transfer issues which mainly occur in the context of unfunded government social insurance schemes. From a European perspective the dominance of unfunded mechanisms in social security financing place binding constraints on future net capital accumulation.

Jozef van Brabant analyzes foreign investment, banking, endogenous growth and systemic transformation, arguing that while domestic sources of capital formation are important for economic growth, foreign investment will be of strategic importance for catching-up given the need for modernizing the capital stock and acquiring access to world markets, particularly for small and medium-sized firms. Systemic transformation in the sense of comprehensive and consistent institutional adjustment is crucial if foreign investment is to occur. Van Brabant stresses in particular the importance of financial sector reform, notably effective monitoring of financial institutions. **Volker Clausen** in his comments agrees that eliminating distortions and inefficiencies in domestic financial markets is crucial for economic growth. Hence financial liberalization and the provision of adequate savings incentives are important steps towards economic growth in eastern Europe.

Elmar Koch analyzes capital flows in eastern Europe against the background of the experiences of emerging markets in Latin America and Asia. Growth of Asian NICs was impressive in the early 1990s (and 1980s) partly due to a high national savings rate - reaching a third of GDP compared with a fifth in central Europe, partly due to a less pervasive role of government - with government consumption in Asia some ten percentage points lower than in central Europe, and partly reflecting lower inflation. Koch points out the stark contrast between Latin America, receiving mainly portfolio inflows, and Asia, with a much higher share of FDI inflows with their attendant spillover effects. Post-socialist central European countries have achieved a dramatic capital account turnaround as large capital inflows have substituted the earlier capital outflows; what remains to be seen is whether the inflows are used as effectively as in Asia.

In his comments **Albert Schweinberger** takes into account the special experiences of Asia and argues that generalizations are difficult to make; for instance, initial distortions in eastern Europe were different from those in Asia and Latin America. However, he agrees that mobilizing domestic resources is most important for the growth process. He notes that the impact of foreign direct investment on output crucially depends on whether investment is mainly flowing to the protected sector (FDI will then bring about a fall in the value of output at international prices) or to an exposed tradables sector.

Thomas Gries and **Stefan Jungblut** present an innovative paper on catching-up, capital formation and structural change, showing that convergence between two regions can be characterized by an equilibrium income gap under certain circumstances. This model goes a step beyond the traditional neoclassical view and could stimulate many new approaches in the convergence literature. The investigation of the time path of adjustment shows that the original stock of human capital is important for catching-up. During the catching-up process economies will face permanent pressure to adjust structurally so that resources will have to shift from one sector to the other. Given initial distortions a fast return to full employment is unlikely. Commenting on the paper, **Georg Erber** compares the traditional growth accounting literature with the new model and highlights some of the respective shortcomings. Nevertheless, the new growth convergence model provides valuable new insights.

Holger Wolf analyzes savings, credit markets and economic growth in Europe. The proximity of the EU could stimulate high economic growth in eastern Europe, but an alternative scenario argues that the communist legacy and populist politics will lead to Latin-style inward orientation. Most studies of likely growth in transition economies emphasize the role of a high investment output ratio in achieving favorable scenario. While correct, such investment ratios, given limits on external borrowing, require matching domestic savings. Wolf inquires whether the mobilization of sufficient savings is likely. The analysis is based on a standard consumption model applied to the special features of transition economies, specifically income uncertainty, the evolution of asset returns, the role of pension system and the impact of financial liberalization. Wolf concludes that household savings of the order observed in Asia are unlikely, a consequence of differences in financial system characteristics, economic growth and demographic factors. He likewise concludes that public sector savings are unlikely to fill the gap, leaving re-invested earnings as the major likely source of investment funding. The overall conclusion is that a Latin American scenario for eastern Europe is more likely than a dynamic Asia development. In his comments **Heinrich Matthes** points out that high savings can only be expected if institutional changes are achieved in the transformation process and if stable money and sound finances rank high on the political agenda. Eastern Europe has some opportunities which could lead to a better convergence process than that suggested by the Latin-type scenario.

Edward Graham focuses on US multinational investment in the EU, globalization and economic growth. At the beginning of the 1990s almost half of the US outward foreign investment stock was in Europe. Clearly, high US foreign investment flows favored certain EU countries. US firms contribute about 3 percent to capital formation in Europe. High US foreign direct investment in Europe can be explained by various hypotheses discussed by the author. The most convincing is that rivalry among US-based MNCs and their European-based counterparts stimulates transatlantic foreign direct investment. If FDI and exports go together, as the author suggests, both international investment and trade will increase in the future.

EU countries which suffered from declining US inflows (relative to GDP) stand to face a reduced rate of technology transfer and hence lower economic growth. US foreign investment patterns in the EU could also have a path-finder role in the sense that in oligopolistic markets declining US investment signals to other foreign investors that it is worthwhile looking for new alternative locations. In his comments **Rolf Jungnickel** argues that structural factors play a major role in FDI and expresses doubt that FDI is not replacing exports, though he is optimistic about the position of Germany and Europe.

Jan Stankovsky's article focuses on multinational investment and economic growth in eastern Europe, stressing the differences in the impact of the former across countries and raising the issue of absorption capacity for foreign investment. He points out that while the region is of interest for foreign investors in its own right, foreign investment could also build capacities that would largely serve EU markets and other third country markets, an important element in the decision of foreign investors and one of the explanations for the highly unequal distribution of foreign investment across eastern Europe. **Gabor Hunya** argues that buying into new markets was crucial for early FDI inflows and that only after a period of restructuring foreign investors becoming more interested in existing firms.

A panel on the role of banks in financing economic expansion in eastern Europe concluded that a competitive banking system coupled with a stable central bank policy is crucial for economic growth in the post-socialist countries. **Rezsö Nyers** and **Werner Varga** give their views on the topic.

The papers collected in this volume share the tenet that a resumption of economic growth is a key challenge facing both western and eastern Europe. Increasing integration implies that much of the growth will have to come from a better allocation of resources within the new, broader Europe. This will undoubtedly lead to some new frictions: the southern cone of the EU will have to compete with the likely new members from central Europe, trade patterns will adjust and the pressures for unit labor cost equalization will strengthen. With divergent economic growth rates across EU countries and regions it will be important to establish mechanisms which allow disadvantaged regions to participate in prosperity. While Spain, Portugal and Ireland launched a rather successful catching-up process within the EU, Greece was less successful in the 1980s: the Gini-coefficient of EU regions (at NUTS II level) has increased, showing that convergence at the national level can coincide with divergence at the regional level, a process likely to accelerate in the future. Substantial leeway remains to stimulate growth in the EU, not only by removing obstacles to growth (such as a highly progressive tax system), but also by stimulating R&D and increasing efforts in education and training. The papers in this volume suggest that an additional major growth impetus can be obtained by expanding the role played by stock markets in continental Europe.

Diversified investment funds could provide workers with a second source of income while stock options could motivate managers in established firms and - even more so - new firms. Compared to the US the EU corporate birth rate is notoriously low, significantly impeding new high technology fields which rarely developed without the launch of a wave of new firms. Given reduced capital controls in OECD countries foreign direct investment can be a route to transfer technologies internationally. However, with a serious lack of newcomers in many promising fields in EU countries innovative newcomers from the US and elsewhere have difficulties in finding partners.

The focus of governments on EMU - and the implied importance attached to the reduction of inflation even at the cost of high unemployment - has diverted attention from structural reform. Looking forward, the success of the EURO, if it comes into existence, will however be largely driven by the economic dynamism of Europe - its present starting point from high unemployment and sluggish growth is none to perspicuous in this regard.

This conference was the first international conference organized by the newly established **Institute for International Economic Relations** (EIIW by its German acronym for Europäisches Institut für internationale Wirtschaftsbeziehungen). Given its location in Potsdam with its particular historical connotations, the EIIW offers an ideal location for undertaking research into economic issues in both western and eastern Europe, complementing the strong focus on transatlantic economic relations. It aims to stimulate the dialogue between the academic world and the public not only by organizing conferences for policymakers, business people and economists but also by offering a new Internet Service "Economic Policy Issues" in the near future.

In conclusion, many thanks are due to all the participants for contributing to the success of the conference, to the Volkswagen Stiftung for their generous. financial support, and to the Landeszentralbank in Berlin und Brandenburg. Last but not least, the success of the conference was assured by the excellent assistance in the organization of the conference provided by Katrin Bölke, Marc Brüning, Cornelius Graack, Rainer Hillebrand, Ingmar Lehman and Antje Wenk, and by the invaluable editorial support provided by Alison Sinclair.

Potsdam, February 1997 *Paul J.J. Welfens and Holger C. Wolf*

Part I

Banking in Europe and Growth

A. Banks, Capital Markets, R&D and Economic Growth in Europe

Paul J.J. Welfens

1. Introduction

Economic growth and prosperity go together, although high growth and a deteriorating environment can pose a transitory conflict of interest. The need to maintain natural wealth and human capital has become a major concern of economic policy in western Europe after 1945. While maintaining the stock of real capital via depreciations and reinvestments was considered a natural requirement of capitalism, the concern about the stock of the environment and labor market problems reflects more recent problems. Human capital of many workers in western Europe has been eroded as a consequence of high unemployment which is mainly the result of the two oil price shocks in the 1970s and strong wage pressure with a bias in favor of unskilled workers in EU countries. At the same time technological progress and the shift towards the service industry raised the marginal value product of skilled labor overproportionately - which is one reason why income differentials among workers are growing again in OECD countries (another being the global increase in the unskilled labor supply as a consequence of China's opening up).

Economic growth in western Europe resumed in the 1980s when technological progress, supply-side policy reforms and increases in labor productivity coincided favorably. Labor productivity growth in manufacturing was highest in the UK with 82.1% in the period 1980-94, somewhat ahead of Japan, Belgium, Italy, France, the Netherlands, Sweden and the US which reached 47.9%, trailed by Germany with 42.1%. The strong rise in British productivity is partly due to capital deepening and massive foreign direct investment inflows, but the pole position is clearly overstated since a large gain simply reflects the relative shrinkage of manufacturing in the UK. Japan increased its GDP by 58% between 1980 and 1994; the US recorded 42% and Germany 34% which is in line with the average of all western industrialized countries. Between 1980 and 1994 employment in Germany increased by a meager 6%, in the US by 24% and in Japan by 17% (IDW, 1995). The rise of Japan and Asian NICs as exporters of manufactured goods undermined the competitiveness of industry in the UK, France and the US, which all shifted towards the service society. Since 1965 the growth rate of GDP has been higher in developing countries than in industrialized countries, and this new international growth drift strongly rose in the first half of the 1990s, reflecting the high growth of Latin American and Asian market economies, as well as of China.

Since productivity growth in the EU in the 1980s was higher than output growth, unemployment increased despite strong reductions in labor hours worked. While Spain and Portugal entered the EC in 1986 and were catching up with the EU average per capita income (THOMAS, 1995), Greece was falling behind, so that economic convergence remained a problem in the EU as did the high unemployment rates of the late 1970s, imposing additional financing burdens upon the expanding western European welfare state. This welfare state is facing a crisis in western Europe, partly due to the critically high levels of social security contribution rates, unfavorable demographic developments and, above all, the declining ability of governments to tax the increasingly mobile factor real capital and skilled labor. The question arises to which extent the old traditional welfare state is impairing economic growth in Europe as it disturbs the savings and investment process.

EC growth was weakened in the 1980s by massive net outward foreign direct investment of western Europe. US economic growth in the 1980s was not only fueled by domestic forces but strongly stimulated by EC investment inflows as well as Japanese inflows. US banks financed only part of the investment boom in the US in the 1980s since securitization and financial innovations allowed major multinational companies to directly place commercial papers and bonds in the credit market. The structure of banking in the US changed dramatically in the 1980s and so it did in western Europe with some delay.

More dramatic than the developments in the US and western Europe were the events in eastern Europe in the late 1980s when the socialist systems collapsed. They had always been characterized by high investment output ratios (with Yugoslavia's 40% investment output rate leading the socialist countries in Europe), but the low productivity of capital brought about only modest growth or even stagnation. Eager to modernize the capital stock and to achieve capital deepening transforming economies have begun to privatize firms and banks, to create stock markets and to nurture capital markets. Banks' balances in ex-CMEA countries revealed critical problems as many loans had been made to insolvent or illiquid firms, while depositors were reluctant to engage in long-term bank deposits. Poland, Latvia and Russia had banking scandals in connection with fraud schemes (Ponzi games were organized in Russia) so that confidence of the public in the new two-tier banking system was difficult to establish. Currency substitution and capital flight were common transformation problems in the ex-CMEA area, except for the Czech Republic.

Banks have always played a key role for economic growth of industrialized countries. In the course of a booming expansion in the 19th century the banking community and the newly created stock markets in Europe faced speculative bubbles and frauds until the banking community's self-established rules and national prudential supervision created sustained confidence and stimulated savings until the Great Depression (1917 in Russia). In Europe private savings were channeled efficiently into investments and contributed to a dramatic increase in western Europe's standard of living. Indeed the core of capitalism are the capital markets and the international financial flows which allow countries with a relatively high marginal product of capital to temporarily grow faster than domestic savings would allow. International capital flows also create international liquidity under certain conditions, such as the presence of a competitive private banking system.

The creation of the single market in the EU and the envisaged monetary union will create a very competitive EU banking system. Could EMU become a major source of international liquidity and could EU banks benefit from such a development? While facing increased competition in the single market and less profitable credit business, banks benefited from their greater role as service providers. The financial industry's share of employment and value-added increased in OECD countries in the 1970s and 1980s, thereby directly contributing to economic growth (SCHINASI and HARGRAVES, 1992).

Both new investment and reinvestment can be undertaken in a way that generate high income per period, but the time span over which capital can be used is, of course, also essential for the consumption expansion path. The absence of capital markets impoverished people in eastern Germany more in terms of relative wealth positions than in terms of relative income positions: for example east Germany's productivity was 50% of west Germany's in 1950 and its per capita income was 30% in 1989, but its per capita wealth was less than 20% of west Germany's in the year of German unification (WELFENS, 1996a). With the economic and political opening up of the ex-CMEA countries the consumption aspiration levels as well as individual wealth targets are rising and will move close to West European standards. This implies in a Metzler-type savings function (METZLER, 1951) that the perceived large gap between the initial wealth position and the desired wealth target will generate a high savings rate.

The creation of stock markets, the privatization of banks and economic opening up, associated with gains from trade and foreign direct investment, create new opportunities for economic growth in eastern Europe and Russia - the ex-CMEA could become a dynamic area in Europe. At the same time the EU could massively gain from this historical opening up process since it provides new options for cheap imports of labor and skill-intensive intermediate products, new locations for foreign direct investment, new targets for portfolio investment and additional outlets for investment goods and consumer products. So is Europe in for high growth and an economic revival which could strengthen the European position vis-à-vis a stagnating Japan and a US which is facing a sustained twin-deficit in the federal budget and the current account? If western Europe grows at 2-3% p.a. in the late 1990s, will this be sustainable given the many uncertainties of eastern Europe and Russia? Or will EU growth reduce due to internal reasons, namely an unstable monetary integration scheme, high national public deficits, high unemployment rates with a large share of long term unemployed and an unstable banking system in the single market?

Section 2 is devoted to selected issues of the single market dynamics and EMU aspects that are relevant for economic growth. The switch to full capital mobility in stage I of EMU has already deeply affected product and asset markets in the EU, and the creation of a monetary union with at least some major EU member countries would certainly strongly influence financial markets and economic development in the core and the periphery of the monetary union. A special focus is on problems of financial market volatility and macroeconomic aspects of foreign direct investment (FDI). Section 3 focuses on financial markets in the transition process and banks in eastern Europe and Russia. Selected aspects of banking, prudential supervision and foreign direct investment are discussed.

2. Banks and Capital Markets in Western Europe

Western Europe has been affected by three main events in the 1990s, namely the EU single market, the economic opening up of eastern Europe and international impulses from deregulation, financial innovation, securitization and globalization. While the US is already facing a massive decline in traditional banking (EDWARDS and MISHKIN, 1995), western Europe's banking community was still dominating financial intermediation in the 1980s. However, the golden '70s, when banks benefited from petro-dollar recycling, are over. Deregulation and internationalization of financial markets occurred in the 1980s and caused a competition-driven disintermediation from banking systems into securitized money and capital markets. The reduced special role of banks - especially in the wholesale market - encouraged them to shift to high-risk, high-return investments (SCHINASI and HARGRAVES, 1995). The question is whether EU banks can prosper in the 1990s at a time when many banks face additional problems due to global competition and direct or indirect exposure to greater exchange rate volatility. Banks could restrict credit growth which in turn would dampen economic expansion in Europe.

Table A1 Financing Activity on International Capital Markets by Type of Instrument (in bn US$)

				January - April	
	1992	1993	1994	1994	1995
Bonds	333.7	481.0	428.6	154.5	130.8
Equities	23.5	40.7	45.0	16.7	6.9
Syndicated loans	117.9	136.7	236.2	46.0	108.5
Committed back-up facilities	6.7	8.2	4.9	0.6	0.7
A. Total securities and committed facilities	481.8	666.6	714.7	217.8	246.9
Euro-commercial paper programs	28.9	38.4	30.8	6.6	10.6
Medium-term euro-note programs	99.0	113.6	222.1	59.3	82.7
B. Total uncommitted borrowing facilities	127.9	152.0	252.9	65.9	93.3
Grand Total (A + B)	609.7	818.6	967.6	283.7	340.2

Source: OECD (1995), Financial Market Trends, No. 61, June 1995, p. 3.

At the same time one may expect that the removal of capital controls in the EU reinforces downward interest rate convergence in the EMS countries. Since German interest rates fell after the transitory increase during 1990/91 this should lead to lower interest rates in the EU. However, attempts by some EU member countries to defend their exchange rates in the EMS caused short-term interest rates to rise outside Germany. Moreover, uncertainties about stage III of monetary union have an influence on the yield curve so that long-term interest rates are rising. For reasons not fully understood a steeper yield curve should stimulate economic growth.

The volume of facilities arranged on international capital markets in the first quarter of 1995 increased by 20% over 1994 which is mainly due to a sharp rise in syndicated loans which exceeded financing raised through issuance of euro-bonds (Table A1). International equity offerings were reduced in 1994/95. OECD foreign direct investment outflows and FDI inflows continued to rise relative to GNP. This is a tendency that has been observed since 1984.

2.1 International Tendencies in Banking and the Single Market

According to HELLWIG (1994) there were several extraneous tendencies after 1975 which changed international banking significantly:

- Regulated interest rates in the US stimulated attempts to bypass depository institutions with regulated interest rates. Interest fluctuations therefore increased significantly, so that exposure to interest risk became a major problem for banks and other financial institutions.
- OPEC dollar recycling internationalized cross-border activities of banks, while at the same time the disintegration of the Bretton Woods System raised exchange risk inherent in these activities. One may add that the coinciding of the developing countries' foreign debt crisis and the rise of inflation rates worldwide in the decade after 1973 generated a switch to a greater role of debt instruments at flexible interest rates; and it created liquid secondary markets for indebted countries' bonds which are traded at large discounts.
- Innovations in communication and computer technologies decreased barriers to competition due to spatial separation. Transaction costs were reduced and the geographical overlap of markets increased.

- Innovations in risk management techniques enhanced the ability of banks and insurance companies to reallocate risk, so that the scope of intermediation was widened.

The initial impulses for these shifts came from outside the financial system. Deregulation in the US and later in the EC - especially with the single market program - added momentum to this process which brought specific strains (HELLWIG, 1994, p. 6). With the introduction of NOW accounts and money market funds financial innovation assumed a prime role in the competition process. Regulators in the UK and on the continent were finally eager to pick up this new tendency and adopted liberalizing strategies. Lower communication costs and reduced spatial and sectoral barriers caused a massive intensification of competition. This intensified competition was further accentuated by international deregulation (abolition of deposit regulation and asset allocation rules). Overall there was an increase in the risk exposure of banks.

Risks in banking and finance could remain higher in the long term. While net worth of private households - relative to disposable income - increased during the 1980s when gross debts of the private sector sharply rose in OECD countries, asset prices became more volatile and the rise of real estate lending was accompanied by speculative bubbles in several OECD countries (SCHINASI and HARGRAVES, 1992). Remarkable in the context of liberalization and internationalization of banking and rising indebtedness of households and firms is that households' net worth as a ratio of disposable income increased in western European countries (and Japan). These net capital gains will reduce savings in the medium term and thereby stimulate, via rising aggregate demand, economic expansion. If yields remain largely constant, rising net worth will indirectly contribute to higher savings as interest income and dividends will be partly used for future savings. To the extent that rising net worth represents real estate and capital equipment, the private sector can offer higher collateral and thus obtain higher credits to finance consumption, investment and innovation. This would be a virtuous circle in which dynamic financial markets contribute to growth.

An interesting feature is that competition was stimulated by disintermediation. Large multinational companies realized in the 1970s and 1980s that they could benefit from their own credit ratings which were better than those of their banks. International markets provided MNCs with cheap funds, while banks faced less favorable ratings because financial institutions had become subject to increased risk exposure. The mere threat of disintermediation allowed MNCs to put pressure on interest margins. This process is continuing on a global scale and regulators, which for a decade or so were eager to liberalize in an uncoordinated manner, are likely to try to recover lost ground by intensified coordinated regulation. The Basle Committee of Banking Supervision focused on capital adequacy regulation, but the real challenge is risk management of banks, off-balance items and disclosure standards. There are major conflicts in this field as is shown by the failure of WTO to come up with a compromise on trade in financial services.

With margins eroding and the structure of pricing in banking reflecting specific costs of the respective services the banking system no longer enjoys big inframarginal surpluses. Adverse shocks could quickly undermine the stability of the banking systems in OECD countries. To the extent that east European countries are characterized by high foreign indebtedness, transforming economies are indirectly facing a potentially negative spillover from increasing risks in EU financial markets. HELLWIG (1994) concludes with respect to recent crises in OECD financial systems: "They are the systematic consequence of a lack of risk matching in the balance sheets of depository institutions when the risk in question are significant relative to profits. If the intensification of competition in banking and finance continues, we are likely to see more rather than fewer such crises."

Decline of US Banking and Restructuring in Europe

The US banking industry has experienced some decline in the 1980s, especially because Stock Market Mutual Funds and other financial innovations became rather popular after the stock market shocks of 1987 (LITAN, 1994). US banks' share in financial intermediation was only 1/3 of the figure for Japan and Germany in 1994 (BIS, 1996, p. 126). US banks are thus induced to seek more additional business abroad. This might point to similar trends in Europe (KAUFMANN, 1994). There is no doubt that European universal banks will face sharper competition in the context of the single market. The EU's main weakness in financial market development is the insufficient role of stock markets and venture capital. NASDAQ announced plans to help launch an EUDAQ in Brussels in 1996.

The EU has created a single market in which financial services - including insurance services - can be traded freely. There are, however, still barriers to entry in national markets that stem from the existence of state-owned financial intermediaries, restrictions on hostile takeovers, preferences of citizens for national service providers and high sunk costs related to cumulated marketing expenses. State-owned banks in Spain, Italy and France have been earmarked for privatization, where Credit Lyonnais is an extreme case of a poorly managed state bank whose restructuring will be costly for the taxpayer. Takeovers, foreign direct investment and joint ventures have intensified within the private banking community, which seized the opportunities for expansion as several state-owned banks were lining up for privatization in the EU. French, British and Swedish banks faced problems in the early 1990s, although these are dwarfed by the Japanese banking crisis for which Japan's finance ministry suggested a rescue plan at the G-7 meeting in 1995.

2.2 Volatility of Financial Markets and Impact of High Transaction Volumes

Financial markets have shown considerable volatility in the 1970s when flexible exchange rates, deregulation of financial markets (removal of interest rate caps) and high inflation rates coincided. While high inflation rates depress real interest rates, the volatility of the inflation rate is known to raise interest rates, and both contribute to shorter average bond maturities. Historical volatility figures show normal long-term price fluctuations and thereby also allow us to identify unanticipated volatility in the present period. Measuring maximum price swings in absolute or relative terms is an approach to cover price jumps, while the average volatility during a certain period is covered by the variance of yield or price changes. Econometric models as well as option price information can be used to calculate expected volatility. While the fundamentals determine price developments in the long term, short-term price changes can be caused by various impulses.

Analysis of short-term financial market volatility for Germany - based on standard deviation of relative daily price changes which was computed over a moving period of 20 days and extrapolated to yield an annual rate (DEUTSCHE BUNDESBANK, 1996; see Table A2) - showed that the standard deviation of long-term interest rates has slightly increased in the first half of the 1990s and that of short term interest rates has decreased. The standard deviation of the dollar/DM exchange rate remained constant in the two sub-periods 1980-89 and 1990-96, while the variability of the DM/FF exchange rate fell. Annual variability of the German stock market reached 18% and was about twice as high as in the bond market (Bund papers), variability of short-term interest rates reached 13%. Prior to and after the turning point of the interest rate cycle, volatility of the yield on debt securities outstanding was relatively high (except for the high interest rate in the context of German unification in the period of 1991/92).

This indicates that after extended periods of interest rate movements in one direction, rising uncertainty about a possible reversal of the trend stimulates a rise in volatility. In the period of turning points new information carries greater weight - given the increased uncertainty - and hence frequent shifts in financial investments will be observed. Long-term correlation of variability across markets is relatively low. In the short run spillover effects do not show a clear pattern except for the case of turbulent price movements in a market. A turbulent price movement will show high positive correlation effects as might be expected in a period of "excess uncertainty" and reduced confidence - and a higher risk aversion - encouraging investors to seek reduction of risk by substitution: there will be cross-market portfolio shifts into less risky assets. This was observed during the international stock market crash in 1987 and the turbulences in the securities market in 1994. Volatility measures for three-months interest stock markets in the UK and France increased in 1991-95 relative to 1986-90. By contrast interest rate variability in France, Italy and the UK showed no consistent development.

Table A2 Statistics on Longer-Term Volatility in Germany*

Item	Mean daily relative changes in %	Standard deviation in %	Maximum rise per day in %	Maximum fall per day in %	Max. change within a month in %[1]
Yield on debt securities outstanding					
1980-1996	-0.0074	0.60	5.34	-4.73	12.87
1980-1996	-0.0016	0.56	3.09	-4.73	12.87
1990-1996	-0.0165	0.66	5.34	2.82	12.81
Dax					
1980-1996	0.0396	1.12	7.29	-13.71	33.45
1980-1989	0.0513	1.13	7.16	-13.71	33.45
1990-1996	0.0210	1.11	7.29	9.87	21.92
Three-month-fund rate					
1980-1996	-0.0251	0.82	11.78	-12.47	41.76
1980-1989	-0.0051	0.97	11.78	-12.47	41.76
1990-1996	-0.0571	0.48	2.96	4.50	12.08
D-Mark/US$					
1980-1996	-0.0034	0.76	4.06	-5.76	11.68
1980-1989	-0.0005	0.76	3.17	-5.76	11.03
1990-1996	-0.0080	0.76	4.06	-4.51	11.68
D-Mark/French franc					
1980-1996	-0.0093	0.21	1.65	-5.69	6.58
1980-1989	-0.0152	0.22	1.65	-5.69	6.58
1990-1996	-0.0002	0.18	1.42	-2.22	2.75

* Calculated on the basis of daily values for the period from January 2, 1980 to March 29, 1996.

[1] Maximum relative difference between maximum and minimum levels within a month.

Source: DEUTSCHE BUNDESBANK, Monthly Report, April 1996, p. 53.

Table A3 Volatility of Exchange Rates, Interest Rates and Equity Markets

	Exchange rates[1]		Interest rates				Equity markets[2]	
			Overnight		Three-month			
	1986-90	1991-95	1986-90	1991-95	1986-90	1991-95	1986-90	1991-95
	Standard deviation of month-on-month changes							
France	0.7	0.7	0.4	0.8	0.3	0.6	4.6	4.0
Italy	0.7	2.8	0.6	0.9	0.7	0.8	7.6	6.0
United Kingdom	2.4	2.1	0.6	0.4	0.6	0.4	5.5	3.4
Korea	0.8	0.6	0.9	1.3	0.0	0.2	8.9	7.7
Singapore	1.2	1.0	2.5	1.1	0.5	0.5	7.3	4.1

[1] Against the US dollar (emerging market countries) or the Deutsche Mark (Europe).
[2] In US dollar terms.
Source: BIS (1996), 66th Annual Report, Basle , p. 122.

High volatility of financial markets could cause unstable monetary policy, but causation could also run the other way. Monetary policy volatility as well as exchange rate volatility were found to significantly reduce investment growth and the investment-output ratio in some EU countries, most notably in Germany (WELFENS and JUNGMITTAG, 1996). While financial market volatility certainly is useful to some extent, as it reflects the processing of information, policy-induced volatility should be minimized in normal periods.

The increasing importance of institutional investors, which allocate savings internationally, is likely to stimulate higher volatility. The BUNDESBANK (1996, p. 59) notes: "Institutional market participants typically handle large volumes of funds professionally, having a wide range of mostly global investment alternatives at their disposal. Owing to the economies of scale they enjoy it is efficient for institutional investors to devote resources to the procurement and evaluation of information, and to use this as a basis for quick and comparatively frequent portfolio switching. In addition, institutional asset management may be marked by incentives which foster an orientation towards short-term price movements in the market. This is the case, for instance, when portfolio managers' performance is measured continuously in terms of market performance, thus encouraging parallel behavior which reinforces the trend."

Table A4 Cross-Border Transactions in Bonds and Equities*

	1980	1985	1990	1991	1992	1993	1994	1995
	as a percentage of GDP							
United States	9.0	35.1	89.0	95.6	106.6	128.8	131.1	135.5
Japan	7.7	63.0	120.0	91.9	71.8	77.8	60.0	65.7
Germany	7.5	33.4	57.3	55.6	85.2	170.8	159.3	168.3
France	-	21.4	53.6	78.7	121.8	186.8	201.4	178.2
Italy	1.1	4.0	26.6	60.3	92.1	191.9	206.8	250.9
Canada	9.6	26.7	64.4	81.3	113.2	152.9	209.7	192.0

* Gross purchases and sales of securities between residents and non-residents.
Source: BIS, 66th Annual Report, Basle , p. 122.

Table A5 Security Markets (in % of GDP unless otherwise stated)

	Securities outstanding[a]		Equities				Bonds		
			Capitalization		Trading concen-tration[d]	Turn-over[b]	Capitalization		Turn-over[c]
	1990	1994	1990	1995			1990	1994	
USA	203.7	244.5	56.3	94.7	7.4	69.7	108.3	123.4	1460.0[e]
Germany	88.9	132.7	21.6	23.9	61.9	97.8	70.1	85.6	2120.0[e]
Japan	189.5	178.2	99.5	72.1	13.2	32.4	78.0	88.4	250.0[e]
Korea	91.4	105.4	44.0	40.2	12.8	171.6	19.7	24.1[f]	43.0
Taiwan	83.2	134.7	62.3	74.0	23.4	353.5	5.6	13.6	1840.0

[a] Where available, including short-term money market instruments, government bonds, corporate bonds and equities at market value.
[b] Percentage share of the ten most active stocks in the total value traded in 1994. For the United States and Japan, share of total volume traded.
[c] Total value traded as a percentage of average market capitalization in 1994.
[d] 1995.
[e] Government bonds only.
[f] 1993.
Source: BIS, 66th Annual Report, Basle , p. 121.

Cross-border transactions sharply increased after 1980 (Table A4). Foreign investors have played an increasingly important role in the 1980s and early 1990s in the German bond market which strongly grew in volume terms: transactions volumes of non-resident investors increased from DM14.7bn in 1980 to

DM3962.7bn in 1995 (66% of overall turnover). The overall ratio transaction volumes/GDP (transactions in bond and stock markets in Germany) has markedly increased in the 1980s and 1990s. However, securities outstanding - measured by capitalization of equities and bonds relative to GDP - was lower in Germany than in the US or Japan in 1994. Transaction volumes strongly increased in the 1990s in Europe and the US (Table A5).

Given these developments it is not surprising that high monetary growth rates have had a reduced impact on output prices (P). Rising financial market transactions absorbed considerable liquidity. FIELD's (1984) empirical analysis showed for the US in the 1920s that transactions in financial markets absorbed 1/5 of liquidity compared to transactions in goods markets. Since asset value-GDP ratios and (relative) financial market volumes have markedly increased after 1980 in Europe one should consider the following modification of the Fisher equation (where M = stock of money, V = velocity, Y = output, H = price of securities [or stocks], Z= number of bonds [or stocks], i = interest rate):

$$MV(i,Y) = PY + HZ \tag{1}$$

Defining $h = HZ/(PY+HZ)$ and denoting elasticities and growth rates as η and g, respectively, we obtain

$$g_M + \eta_{V,i} g_i + \eta_{V,Y} g_Y = (1-h)(g_P + g_Y) + h(g_H + g_Z) \tag{2}$$

Assuming a constant interest rate i we obtain:

$$g_M + \eta_{V,Y} g_Y - (g_Y + h g_{\frac{HZ}{PY}}) = g_P \tag{3}$$

The inflation rate g_P will, *ceteris paribus*, be reduced if the ratio HZ/PY is increasing, and this could be caused both by domestic and foreign impulses; the latter are important if there are international price spillovers in stock markets and bond markets. From this perspective the US stock market rally 1990-96, which stimulated a boom in stock markets in Europe, contributed to reducing inflation rates in both the US and Europe. Here lies an interesting problem of monetary policy strategy since monetary authorities have to take into account financial market developments when planning a rate of monetary expansion that is consistent with price stability. Following the above approach it is not surprising that relatively high monetary growth rates in Germany and some other OECD countries in the early 1990s did not cause rising inflation.

Speculative Bubbles and Economic Policy Reform

High financial market volatility and excessive price developments - not justified by the fundamentals - undermine macroeconomic stability. The real sector of the economy has to react to financial market impulses, and interest rate and exchange rate movements as well as stock price changes are crucial in this respect. In financial markets there can be even self-fulfilling prophecies based on market actors reacting to "pure expectations" and speculative bubbles are known to be dangerous for the stability of the market system. It is very unlikely that the fundamentals at the stock market change so much that a tripling of real asset values is justified (US stock exchange in 1990 to mid-96), although improving profit prospects in high technology firms were a fundamental impulse for higher stock prices. As the Fed observed in the 1920s when a similar stock market rally occurred, it is difficult to counter such developments via monetary policy. A "time progressive" capital gains tax would be more appropriate to dampen excessive price increases. Such a corporate tax could, for example, tax away 25% (50%) of a doubling (a tripling) of stock prices during one year in order to avoid destabilizing speculative bubbles. The same development over a five year period could be tax-free. Foreigners would be subject to a withholding tax.

2.3 EMU, Single Market Dynamics and Banking

Banks in Western Europe

Western Europe achieved remarkable economic growth after 1945 when growth rates were higher and the standard deviation of the growth rate for major EC countries lower than in the interwar period and the gold standard period 1880-1913 (IMF, 1994, p. 87). However, the EC COMMISSION (1993) noted in its White Paper on "Growth, Competitiveness and Employment" that over the last two decades western Europe's potential rate of growth has shrunk (from 4% to about 2.5% p.a.), the investment ratio has fallen by five percentage points and the competitive position of the EC has worsened in relation to the US and Japan. In 1995 Japan is facing stagnation and a banking crisis whose costs ultimately have to be born by owners and taxpayers, while the EU enjoys a modest upswing which - after overcoming the first transformation stage - has a parallel in the Visegrad countries (Czech Republic, Slovak Republic, Hungary and Poland), much in contrast to Russia, Ukraine and Bulgaria. Poland and Hungary have submitted their membership application to an EU in which industrial enterprises and financial firms are enjoying the stimulus of the EFTA enlargement and EU-induced deregulation in network industries (e.g. telecommunications).

In western Europe banks are subject to four major external impulses (see Figure A1):

(i) Increasing competition in the single market and the removal of capital controls lead to interest rate convergence and more efficient financial markets such that retentions would cease to be the most important source of investment finance and bank-client relations typical of German and French banks would become less relevant.

(ii) At the same time the high volatility of financial markets and the ongoing wave of financial innovations is impressive, especially as regards the expansion of derivates contracts: from \$2.6trillion in 1988 to \$13trillion in 1993, with a market value of outstanding derivatives contracts of some 2% of the total notional value - certainly significant relative to the capital of financial institutions (CROCKETT, 1995, p. 49).

(iii) There is a rising share of intra-EU mergers & acquisitions which is likely to induce a parallel internationalization of banks which as "home banks" often follow multinational companies. Moreover, R&D intensity of manufacturing is increasing which creates new asymmetries between high technology firms and banks. This reinforces the role of stock markets which allow investors to monitor firms constantly (ALLEN, 1993).

(iv) There are the impacts of the EMU project which for low interest countries - such as Germany and the Netherlands - entail the risk of capital losses as the consequence of Euro interest rates in the EMU group which initially were higher than in the *status quo ante*. Moreover, with falling interest rates maturities could increase less than under normal circumstances.

(v) There is the economic opening up of eastern Europe and Russia which is an outside impulse on the EU banking community.

At the same time banks in western Europe are likely to have a strong impact on the transforming economies, namely by exporting financial services, launching foreign direct investment (including joint ventures) and by extending loans to foreign and local firms in eastern Europe and Russia. Since the London Club came to an agreement with Poland and Bulgaria on a debt reduction accord both countries have enjoyed renewed access to the international capital market. Hungary's foreign debt is a serious external constraint and it is not clear whether striving for a debt reduction accord could have improved the situation of Hungary as a transforming economy. Defaulted debt is still a problem for Russia, although in October 1995 the outline of a debt rescheduling package for the $30bn foreign debt owed to some 600 western commercial banks became apparent.

Figure A1 International Environment of Banks in Western Europe

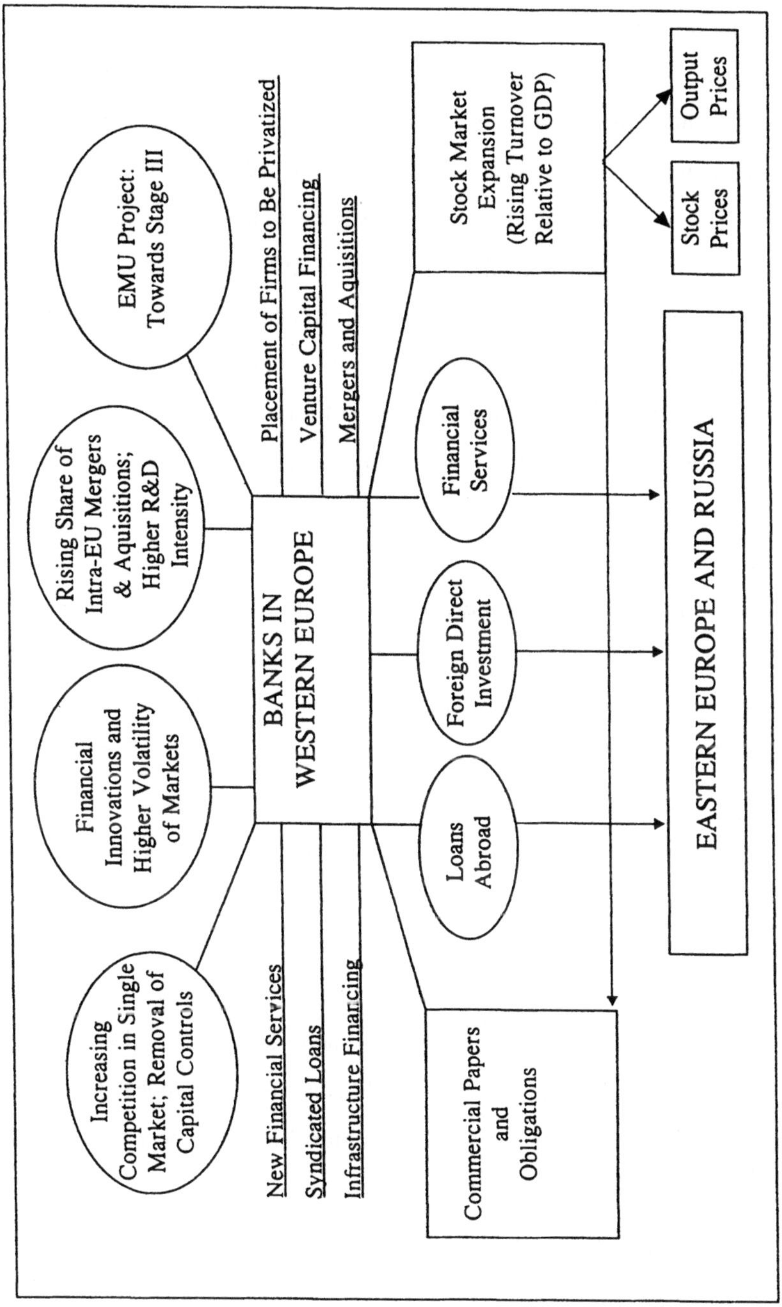

According to this package Russia's defaulted debt would be restructured into new loans of over 25 years with an interest rate of roughly one percentage point above LIBOR, and no principal would have to be repaid over the initial seven year grace period. Whether Russia will finally accept the proposed deal, which does not contain an element of debt forgiveness, is an open question. Russia's foreign debt could pose no major problem if sustained economic growth were to be achieved in the former CIS, but this is uncertain. The Czech Republic is the opposite of the Russian case. For the Czech Republic major capital inflows and hence an upward pressure on the partly convertible currency is a problem. But even in the Czech Republic credit rationing might occur rather than market clearing, namely as a result of asymmetry (reinforced by transition problems) of information between borrowers and lenders. With high and sustained growth one should not rule out that the Czech Republic could become a net capital exporter in the long term, thereby repeating its status of the interwar period.

Banks from western Europe are active foreign investors in the ex-CMEA area despite the fact that most host countries impose restrictions on foreign banks. They are generally accepted if they are partners in a joint venture and thereby contribute to the restructuring of domestic banks. Foreign direct investment of EU banks both in western Europe and in eastern Europe could indeed turn out be excessive as oligopolistic interdependence and managers' aim to maintain market shares in an enlarged market might generate overinvestment in Europe's banking industry. Empirical evidence concerning the wealth effects of US banks' foreign direct investment - with a share in total US FDI rising from 8% in 1970 to 44% in 1991 - is indeed ambiguous (WAHEED and MATHUR, 1995). Some overinvestment of banks in eastern Europe could create a pan-European tendency to compensate prospects of falling margins in traditional loan business by adopting a more aggressive and risky expansion policy.

In the EU increasing competition is taking place under rather favorable conditions since new financial services and increased infrastructure financing -

partly for the creation of EU promoted trans-European networks cofinanced by the EIB - are creating new opportunities for profits for the leading banks. While one may argue that EIB loans, which mainly go to the EU periphery with a less developed financial system, stimulate competition in banking, a critical assessment points out that EIB loans cofinance projects for which the regional or national government in EU member states comes up with subsidized loans such that in effect distortions in capital markets are created (HONOHAN, 1995). EBRD project financing and IFC-sponsored infrastructure projects have increased in the early 1990s. The rise of syndicated loans is indicating an increasing internationalized loan business. Even more interesting is the wave of privatizations in all EU countries and the ongoing mergers & acquisitions which generate large fees for banks. If this would bring about a long-term stock market expansion the bonds market will benefit since leveraged buy-outs and a wave of mergers & acquisitions can be anticipated.

With the EU single market and economic opening up in eastern Europe stimulating the drive of western Europe's firms to improve competitiveness by (relatively) raising R&D expenditures one may expect the marginal product of capital to increase. At the same time prospects for earning Schumpeterian economic rents will improve in the 1990s since the global decline of military R&D shares is intensifying competition in high technology industries. The EU liberalization of public procurement also implies that producer prices are coming under pressure. These developments and the disciplinary effects on monetary and fiscal policy that come from the EMU project and the Maastricht criteria, respectively, will help to restrain inflation in Europe. Nominal inflation rates should thus come down. It is unclear whether or not real interest rates will be falling. If one accepts the hypothesis that massive public deficits in G-10 countries drove up interest rates in the past 35 years and contributed to a fall in the investment-output ratio, one may argue that reinforced fiscal discipline in the EMS will help to bring down interest rates worldwide and to stimulate economic growth. If Germany facing the special burden of unification manages to meet the Maastricht criteria other EU countries can be expected to do so as well.

In the 1990s Germany's firms and banks will be leading investors in both western Europe and eastern Europe because their firm specific advantages favorably join with the macroeconomic phenomenon of an appreciating DM. In the presence of imperfect capital markets bidders from countries with an appreciating currency have improved prospects to obtain loans abroad for a leveraged acquisition (FROOT and STEIN, 1991). Germany's major financial weakness is the low turnover of domestic and foreign stocks at German exchanges, but western Europe as a whole can well compete against the US or Japan since London has reinforced its role as a global financial center in the 1990s. Whether or not a future Euro currency could successfully compete against the so far internationally dominating US dollar will largely depend on a solid development of the EMU area which certainly requires sustained economic growth and stable political conditions. Comparing Germany and the US in 1995, it is remarkable that the average maturity of dollar bonds rose to 8.4 years compared to 5.9 years at the beginning of 1995, while the increase in DM denominated bonds was only from 5.4 to 6.2 years (BANK OF ENGLAND, 1995, p. 241).

Massive EU-wide infrastructure investment, privatizations and liberalizing government procurement will contribute to higher economic growth at the turn of the century. If European financial markets are stable, implying lower transaction costs, one would anticipate an increasing EU growth rate. A rise in the pan-European growth rate is then even more likely since relatively backward transforming economies could record high growth rates as a consequence of rapid technological catching up, foreign direct investment (partly the basis of the former) and rising trade between eastern Europe and the EU. It seems that except for population growth in western Europe and for possible revolutions and coups in eastern Europe all growth characteristics identified by PLOSSER (1992) are present in Europe (see Figure A2 and Table A6). The EU's population growth which is mainly determined by immigration and the potential political instability of eastern Europe and Russia are important caveats. Since industry will only be facing true bankruptcy risk once banks and firms are privatized, the ongoing privatization process in Bulgaria, Romania and Russia will temporarily raise individual firms' cost curve. According to theoretical analysis of GREENWALD and STIGLITZ (1993), firms' cost curves shift upwards with a higher perceived risk and hence higher anticipated bankruptcy costs (see Appendix A1). In the poorly functioning credit markets of transforming economies credit rationing implies that credit growth rather than interest rates are appropriate indicators of the course of monetary policy.

Figure A2 Forces of Economic Growth

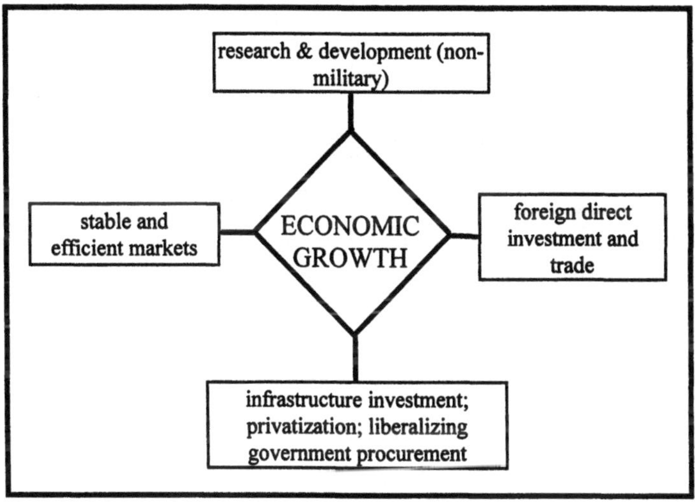

The new growth theory (for a survey see FRATIANNI and HUANG, 1995), which suggests that there can be endogenous growth forces related to positive human capital externalities and technological spillover effects (innovation and learning by doing), implies for eastern Europe that transforming economies will not only benefit from high capital formation but also from investment in human capital and from economic opening up. However, while economic liberalization creates well-known static gains, dynamic losses cannot be ruled out in a model by YOUNG (1991), in which LDCs are shown to be unable to catch up with industrialized countries under certain conditions - a marked contrast to the Solow and Heckscher-Ohlin worlds in which catching up should come with a rise of the capital intensity and economic opening up, respectively.

Table A6 Growth Characteristics of a Cross-Section of Countries

	Overall average n = 97	Slow growth < 0.5% n = 23	Fast growth > 3.5% n = 14	Correlation with GDP growth rate
Real per capita GDP growth 1960-89	2.03%	-0.26%	4.88%	1.00
Investment share of GDP	0.21	0.17	0.26	0.61
Government consumption share of GDP	0.15	0.15	0.14	0.10
Inflation rate	23.00%	42.11%	7.90%	-0.17
Standard deviation of inflation rate	52.38	137.19	5.68	-0.16
Exports as a share of GDP	0.28	0.24	0.35	0.30
Imports as a share of GDP	0.33	0.30	0.40	0.31
Secondary school enrollment rates 1960	0.21	0.06	0.34	0.41
Primary school enrollment rates 1960	0.74	0.44	0.98	0.54
Population growth	2.06%	2.55%	1.26%	-0.36
Revolutions and coups per year	0.20	0.35	0.12	-0.37
Real per capita GDP in 1960	$1840	$889	$1968	0.20

Source: PLOSSER, C. I. (1992), "The Search for Growth", in *Policies in Long-Run Economic Growth,* a symposium sponsored by the Federal Reserve Bank of Kansas.

With the EU convergence criteria forcing governments to reduce the deficit-GDP ratio, banks will intensify competition in the commercial loan business. Since firms face sharp competition in EU goods markets profit margins of EU banks have come under pressure. Banks are forced to unbundle their services and compete with specific services at prices which reflect marginal costs. This implies that unprofitable banks have few reserves if adverse shocks hit the financial market. Risk management becomes more important.

Large infrastructure projects, some guided by the EU Commission, require massive loans. In 1994 the European investment bank was very active in extending loans and financed 4.5% (ECU 18 bill.) of gross capital formation in the EC-12 Community (EIB, 1995). The biggest opportunity for banks is associated with the massive privatization projects envisaged in France, Italy, Spain, Germany and other EU countries; most notably in the field of telecommunications (WELFENS and YARROW, 1996) which is R&D intensive and capital intensive. Intensified competition in telecoms markets leads one to expect that capital-saving innovations will be stimulated such that the marginal product of capital will increase in the communication sector. Moreover, since information is an input in all products and services - especially sophisticated ones - there will be a general market expansion and thus higher economic growth as input prices in information-intensive industries fall. The use of telecoms networks will become much cheaper in the late 1990s in Europe as competition in a liberalized EU market unfolds. Banks themselves will strongly benefit from more advanced and cheaper communication which should facilitate monitoring and trade in financial instruments.

Banks in the EU are facing the challenges of the single market and have started to "go European" in the sense that foreign direct investment and alliances became preferred means of becoming present in the whole EU. Monetary union is reinforcing the incentive among big players to be present in each major market in order to capture first-mover advantages in deposit banking and wholesale-banking in a future post-1999 monetary union. Big banks seem to prefer a quick move towards the third stage of EMU which would bring a single currency for a hard core of EU member countries and economies of scale for large banks. Small banks in Germany and the UK are less keen on EMU since the transition stage at the beginning of stage III of the monetary union imposes additional costs and requires experience with multi-currency accounting in which big internationalized banks have comparative advantages.

EMU pioneer countries should not only fulfill the convergence criteria but declare that convergence criteria will continue to guide fiscal policy. Otherwise there is a danger that governments of EMU countries could raise deficit-GNP ratios while anticipating that part of the induced real interest rate increase will fall on partner EMU countries. Fear of lax fiscal policy in the EMU group could impose capital losses on German and other holders of DM denominated bonds in the transition stage before monetary union (BUNDESVERBAND, 1995): fear of lax fiscal policy will cause a rise of interest rates such that the EMU group would start with interest rates above the former level for DM denominated bonds. Markets' fear of loose fiscal policies of some EMU member countries could also force these countries into high interest policies as a means to defend exchange rates at the desired pre-union level. Even an inverse yield structure could result from this; output growth of EMU member countries would fall in such a scenario.

EMU would mean that the fragmentation of credit markets is markedly reduced within this core of monetary union countries. Less fragmentation of markets implies less scope for swapping operations and therefore a loss in banking service operations. At the same time the EMU area will benefit from reduced transaction costs and thus an expansion of the banks' loan business.

Eliminating exchange rate risk will reduce price risk (danger of unexpected changes in prices) and the creation of an internationally actively traded Euro currency could reduce liquidity risks in EMU. Liquidity risks occur when financial assets cannot be sold quickly, except at big discounts, and these liquidity risks should be lower in an enlarged currency area. Credit risk in the EMU area, i.e. the risk that borrowers will default, could increase since banks will sharply compete to extend loans to new customers in the enlarged currency area. Since transaction costs in financial markets will fall in the EMU area the credit supply curve will shift to the right so that bid-ask-spreads should fall. With a given credit demand curve the implication is a rise in bank loans, lower interest rates for borrowers and higher investment, which could lead to higher economic growth. With respect to the assumption of a given credit demand curve there are three major caveats:

(a) If intra-EU mergers continue and larger EU multinationals are formed securitization will accelerate so that banks will rather compete for expanding financial services than for new loan business - big banks could pick up part of the smaller banks' market shares. Higher economic growth should still result from this development.

(b) The rift between EMU members and non-member EU countries could drive up interest rates in the EMU periphery in the European Union so that exports of EMU countries to other EU countries could fall because of slower growth in the periphery - due to falling exports GDP growth, investment growth and hence the demand for credit could fall. The smaller the EMU core the bigger is the risk that adverse economic developments in the EMU periphery will have serious negative repercussions for the core.

(c) If monetary policies in the EMU countries are more volatile than in the pre-currency union state higher risk premiums and indeed rising transaction costs will prevent an expansionary effect from the loan market.

While reduced transaction costs for EMU countries could reduce real interest rates and raise the investment-output ratio it is unclear whether the incremental capital-output ratio (ICOR) can be reduced so that the growth rate would be stimulated further. ICOR could increase if multinational companies in oligopolistic markets pursue aggressive investment strategies which lead to high excess capacities in industry. MNCs are not so much subject to the discipline of credit markets but enjoy discretion due to imperfect stock markets.

If a future EU currency were at least as stable as the US dollar there would be good prospects for international monetary relations to be shaped by an intensive competition between the dollar and the ECU (or whatever name one will finally chose for the common currency). The Yen could not achieve a sufficient internationalization in the 1980s, and the Japanese stagnation in the mid-1990s in combination with political instability and a major banking crisis further undermines the prospects for the Yen to become a globally leading currency. The currency denomination of foreign trade in Japan's exports and imports was strongly dominated by the dollar in 1975 and still so in 1990 (TAVLAS and OZEKI, 1992). In Germany (and in the US) the national currency dominates international invoicing.

Only a stability-oriented EMU may expect to play a major international role with its new currency (WELFENS, 1995)

2.4 R&D Intensity, Employment and Foreign Direct Investment

A consistent trend in OECD countries is the rise of the R&D expenditures-GNP ratio, which increased from 2% in the 1960s to about 3% in the early 1990s, though it fell slightly in some OECD countries. After the end of the cold war the effective increase in market-oriented R&D expenditures was even higher than indicated by this figure because the US, France and the UK which traditionally had about 50% of R&D expenditures devoted to the military, gradually reduced the share of military expenditures. An increase in product and process innovations should help to improve the international competitiveness of the US and France in the long term - in the UK the impact will be rather small due to the small size of the manufacturing sector. West Germany's firms temporarily neglected international markets and R&D during the first stage of German unification when east German markets offered uncontested outlets for most products, but overall German R&D expenditures are gradually picking up. Interestingly, the growth rate of labor productivity in services matched that of manufacturing industry in the period 1973-92 in Germany, while in the previous decade it was much lower in the service sector. Moreover in the field of mobile services - with mobile service providers or mobile users of services - labor productivity growth already matched that of manufacturing industry in the 1960s and 1970s (KLODT et al., 1994, p. 130). Germany's export position is strongest where its share in international patents are relatively high, i.e. comparative advantages in manufacturing are largely dependent on successful R&D projects.

2.4.1 The High Technology Race and Employment

Capital productivity in continental EU countries - especially in Germany (McKINSEY, 1996) - is apparently lower than in the US. A major reason for this could be the underdeveloped stock markets, venture capitalism and disclosure rules in Germany and other EU countries. With the US, the UK and France focusing their R&D budgets mainly on civilian projects there will be an intensified global high technology race. However, even with many product innovations and a rising product variety in high technology one cannot overlook that market volumes for high technology products are rather limited, except in expanding new markets (e.g. biotechnology, laser technology). Positive employment effects will strongly depend on the creation of new firms, especially in the case of new markets. Adequate incentives for entrepreneurship and venture capitalism are therefore important. In a global market economy with increasing technological competition the role of foreign direct investment - investment of MNCs which traditionally are technology-intensive firms wanting to protect their technology investment abroad - will rise.

With high unemployment rates in the EU there are limited prospects for sustained economic growth as social conflicts destabilize the economic system, the financial burden of high unemployment contribution rates undermine working and saving efforts and, finally, the shortfalls in government revenues contribute to serious deficit problems in several EU countries. For the leading EU countries the southern enlargement of the EU and the economic opening up process requires an expansion in the medium-technology and high-technology sectors. Employment gains were indeed recorded in the advanced-technology sectors (see Table A7).

Venture capital financing is weak in continental Europe. Stocks are still not widely accepted as a safe form of investing savings. The share of people owning stock was relatively high in Sweden, Finland, the US, Japan, Canada, Norway and the UK, with figures in the range of 39% to 22%. But in Switzerland, Germany and Austria it reached only 10, 7 and 4%, respectively, in 1994 (Figure A3). In transforming economies the initial share of people owning stocks is high but is likely to fall since concentration among a few investor groups is to be expected.

Table A7 Technology Intensity[a] and Employment Development in OECD Countries, 1970-1991, (Average Growth Rate p. a., in %)

Country	High Technology Sector	Medium Technology Sector	Low Technology Sector	Producing Sector (all)
Denmark	0.6	0.7	-1.3	-0.6
Germany[b]	0.4	0.5	-1.5	-0.5
France	0.1	-0.8	-1.7	-1.1
UK	-1.4	-2.1	-2.6	-2.2
Italy	0.0	-0.1	-0.4	-0.3
Netherlands	-0.5	-0.4	-1.7	-1.2
USA	0.7	0.2	-0.6	-0.1
Japan	1.9	0.8	-0.3	0.4
OECD-13[c]	0.6 (19.1)	0.0 (29.0)	-0.9 (51.9)	-0.4 (100)

[a] Classification according to the OECD in 1986.
[b] Only the old Länder.
[c] Including Australia, Canada, Finland, Sweden and Norway; in ( ) shares of employees in the industrial sector in 1991, in percent.
Source: OCHEL and PENZKOFER (1995), "Internationale Wettbewerbsfähigkeit und ihre Implikationen für die Europäische FuE-Politik", p. 32.

Figure A3 Share of People Owning Stocks in 1995 (in %)

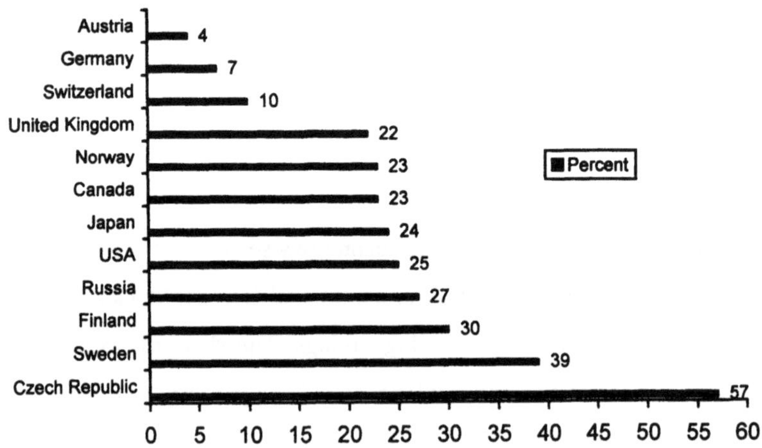

Source: Österreichisches Aktieninstitut

2.4.2 Foreign Direct Investment

Global foreign direct investment (FDI) has dramatically increased after 1985 and reached some $240bn in 1995 (OECD, 1996, p. 38). The FDI dynamics of the 1980s (KLEIN and WELFENS, 1992) accelerated. FDI is closely linked with R&D since international technology trade is mainly within MNCs or between MNCs. More and more firms have become active foreign investors in the 1980s and the range of both host countries and source countries has expanded, most notably after the economic opening up of the transforming postsocialist countries in eastern Europe. In the mid-1990s the Czech Republic and Hungary joined the Asian NICs as source newcomers which find, like more established source countries, an enriched international asset menu for acquisition worldwide since privatization accelerated in the 1990s worldwide. FDI in services outpaced that of manufacturing in OECD countries after 1985. With real capital becoming much more mobile marginal products of capital should equalize faster across countries than in the 1980s. The natural tendency of European managers for overextending the size of firms will be increasingly checked by hostile takeover bids from domestic and foreign rivals as well as rising pressure from stock markets with a higher profile of institutional investors. After US firms were trimmed down in the 1980s leading EU firms are likely to follow suit such that additional jobs can mainly be generated by new firms and growing young firms.

Among the worst problems in FDI analysis are data inconsistencies (OECD, 1996): Japan reported overall FDI inflows of $37mn in 1995, while the US alone reported outflows to Japan of $3.2bn in that year; in the decade after 1984 the OECD area reported investing $72bn in Germany, while the Bundesbank recorded foreign inflows of only $22bn. With foreign investment becoming a crucial international factor of economic interdependency one can recommend that international statistics be harmonized and made consistent quickly. Despite data problems there is little doubt that foreign investment flows are still dominated by eight leading source countries (the "I-8 countries"), namely the US, the UK,

Germany, the Netherlands France, Canada, Switzerland and Japan which accounted in 1980 for 92% of the total outward FDI stock and by 1994 still represented some 84%. The US alone stood for $97bn of outflows. On the host country side Singapore is one of the most impressive countries since for each citizen $20000 of foreign investment were recorded. In absolute terms - calculated on the basis of cumulative flows 1985-94 - the US, the UK, China, France, Spain, Belgium-Luxembourg (distorted by its hub function for holding companies), Canada, Australia, the Netherlands and Singapore were the ten most important host countries. Global FDI outflows reached a record $318bn in 1995.

The FDI stock - with a global figure of $2700bn in 1995 - among Triad members is rather asymmetric and points to regional clusters, except for Japan which is hardly important as a host country (UNCTAD, 1996). Intra-EU investment has increased in the 1990s and so have EU investments in eastern Europe. Russia is almost a white spot on foreign investors' map, mainly because of the lack of political stability and the absence of a strict rule of law.

Introducing foreign direct investment in the IS-LM-BP system changes the traditional analysis for fixed exchange rates to some extent. The first-round impact (balance-of-payments effect) of foreign direct investment inflows shifts the BP curve, which portrays foreign exchange market equilibrium in r-Y-space, downwards [to BP_1 in panel (a) of Figure A4] unless the associated medium-term effect of FDI inflows, namely induced imports (typically capital equipment), immediately dominates. The medium-term effect associated with higher overall investment produces a rightward shift of the IS curve [to IS_1]. Starting for ease of exposition with a zero capital account balance, FDI inflows will cause an excess supply of foreign exchange so that a higher output and hence higher imports of goods are required [point F in panel (a)] to restore equilibrium in the foreign exchange market. The LM curve, portraying long-term money market equilibrium, will shift in the long run to the left [to LM_1 in panel (a)]. This assumes that the medium-term demand for money depends on the production potential which will be raised by foreign direct investment inflows (via technology transfer and, in the case of greenfield investment, via a higher capital stock).

Figure A4 Foreign Direct Investment in the IS-LM-BP Model

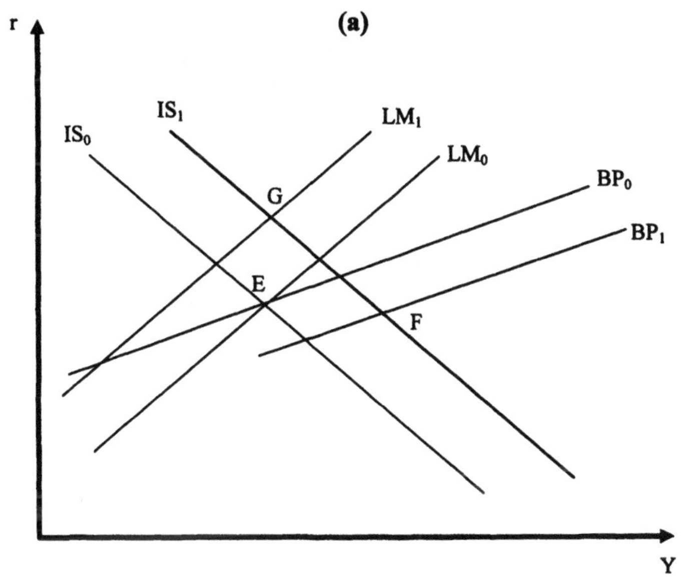

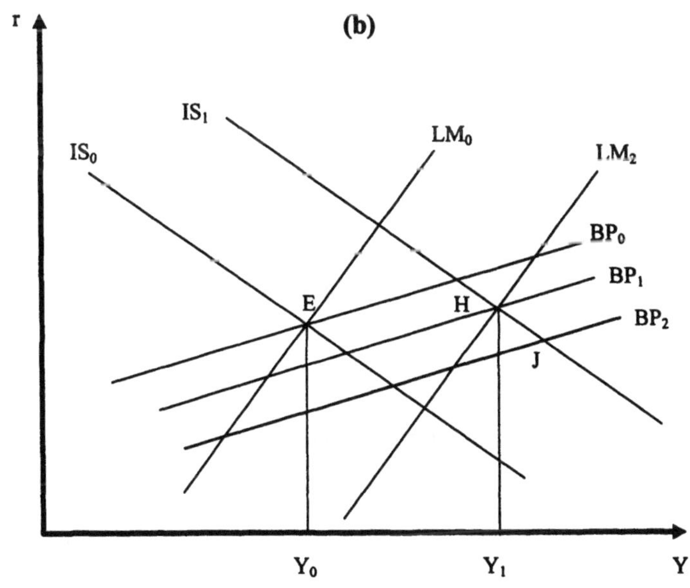

However, if the central bank allows the money stock to expand in proportion to the production potential, the LM curve will ultimately shift to the right [to LM_2 in panel (b)], possibly supported by a fall in the price level following FDI-induced productivity gains. Furthermore, in the long-term the IS curve will shift to the right [to IS_2 in panel (b)] for three reasons: (i) a rise in consumption due to the higher permanent income - especially wage income - associated with foreign direct inflows; (ii) a rise in overall investment, assuming greenfield investment; (iii) a rise in net exports based on foreign direct investment, which will also shift the BP curve downwards to BP_2.

Investment I is the sum of domestic investment I^h and foreign investment inflows I^f. In the simple case of an exogenous foreign direct investment inflow the equilibrium condition for the goods market can be written as:

$$Y_t = C_t(\alpha Y_t + (1-\alpha)Y_{t+1}) + I_t^h(r) + I_t^f + G_t + X_t(q, Y_t^*) - \frac{1}{q} X_t^*(q, Y_t, \Sigma I_t^f) \qquad (4)$$

Exports X depend on the terms of trade q and output abroad Y^* (* denote foreign variables), while imports X^* will depend on q, domestic output and the stock of foreign investment inflows (ΣI^f). The higher the initial stock of foreign direct investment inflows, the higher will be the import of capital goods. This assumes that (i) the subsidiary has a preference to use the same capital equipment as in the source country with the source country assumed to be a dominant producer of capital equipment, and (ii) to minimize risk investments first occur in industries with a low capital intensity and only later in more capital-intensive, high-technology sectors. Assuming a young host country of FDI, a rising stock of FDI inflows therefore gradually shifts the BP-curve upwards instead of downwards to BP_1 as panel (a) of Figure A4.

This effect could be refined if one takes into account that FDI inflows positively depend on output - a proxy for the economic size of the host country (and profits). Net exports of goods are likely to depend negatively on foreign direct investment inflows in the medium run, only in the very long run subsidiaries of foreign multinationals are likely to contribute to net exports (e.g. the case of Korea in the 1980s when it already was an established "mature" host country) which implies that the BP curve becomes flatter over time: for a given increase in domestic output the required rise in interest rates necessary to attract sufficient portfolio capital inflows has reduced. The presence of foreign investors - and this is a stock effect - is likely to influence the interest elasticity of overall investment, the interest elasticity of the demand for money and the elasticity of the export and import function as well as the interest elasticity of international capital flows. While currency substitution in OECD countries is rare, a higher FDI stock in other countries will contribute to a reduction in money demand.

Given a Cobb-Douglas production function and the marginal product rule of factor rewards, and assuming that overall long-term investment is proportional to Y, the long-run equilibrium in the goods market (with $\gamma = G/Y$) is given by the following equation:

$$rK + [1-\beta]Y = [c+\gamma]Y + aY + X(q,Y) - \frac{1}{q}X^*(K^*,q,Y^*) \qquad (5)$$

where β = production elasticity of capital, $K = H + K^*$, H = home stock of capital, K^* = stock of inward FDI and K = overall capital stock. In a technologically diversified world the stock of inward FDI will also raise the overall level of productivity, namely both by capital-embodied technological progress and by positive technological spillover effects. Given an exogenous labor supply L equation (5) determines full employment income as a function of H, K^* and the parameters.

3. Banking, Capital Markets and Economic Growth in Eastern Europe and Russia

Many transforming post-socialist economies are trying to emulate the growth patterns and developments strategies of Newly Industrializing Countries, which are, however, characterized by divergent strategies. Economic growth in emerging markets in Asia is based on smooth financing of investment projects and technological catching up. Stock markets play a major role in this respect. Thus, the relative size of the stock market (in terms of market capitalization) in Chile, Hongkong, Malaysia and Singapore was as high as in the US and the UK; in Mexico and Korea the stock market capitalization was higher than in Germany or France in 1994 (BIS, 1995, p. 165). In eastern Europe stock markets have been created and in some countries have - together with liquid markets - become a decisive tool for economic growth. However, the banking system in most ex-CMEA countries is facing major problems as bad loans, lack of experience and increasing international competition require restructuring of most banks. Both access to equity capital and access to loans is difficult for many firms. Small firms often do not have access to either capital source and hence cannot prosper.

Systemic transformation of post-socialist countries in the ex-CMEA area is a complex challenge which involves institutional innovations, macroeconomic stabilization, structural change and supply-side shifts as well as a new role for the state. People in eastern Europe and Russia are not interested in the market economy for its own sake but expect rapid economic improvements and long-term catching up with the prosperous EU.

Systemic transformation in the Visegrad countries has made considerable progress in the first half of the 1990s. Except for Hungary, which is facing slow economic growth because of a balance of payments crisis and massive debt problems, the Visegrad countries are recording high economic growth of 5-6%. This is rather impressive at first sight. However, for the majority of the population this is unlikely to bring about a major improvement in personal welfare because one may assume that the top income quintile will record income growth rates of about 20% which alone would imply an aggregate growth rate of 4%. On the one hand this explains why Visegrad countries have experienced a revival of socialist parties, on the other hand this points to the need to generate even higher growth rates (7% or more) if the majority of the population is to politically support the transformation process. A critically high growth rate is needed not least because a considerable part of the population is facing new uncertainties in the form of unemployment risk, price shift risks (e.g. in the field of rents) and capital losses - the latter in the context of newly acquired shares in privatized firms. From a portfolio-theoretical point of view such additional risks require sufficient compensation through higher real income and improved quality of goods and services, otherwise the utility level will fall as a consequence of systemic transition. Moreover, one can argue that economic opening up has rendered a large part of the capital stock obsolete, which leads to the question of welfare-increasing protectionism. This question is most important for Russia, but less so for the Visegrad countries.

3.1 Banking in Transforming Economies

Role of Banks and Economic Growth in Eastern Europe and Russia

Banks were important catalysts of economic growth in industrialization, but in the second half of the 20th century their role as an intermediary between firms and households is diminishing in importance in both western Europe and the US. One may raise the question whether banks in eastern Europe are not enjoying a special and more important role than in western Europe. If this were true one may expect west European and US banks to aggressively aim at conquering east European markets. Banks from OECD countries will aim at eastern Europe under their own initiative or they will follow firms of their parent company market which are investing in transforming economies. In eastern Europe foreign investors are facing investment barriers, one of which consists of restrictions to borrow abroad.

Following HELLWIG (1994) and TOBIN (1965) banks are part of the system of financial intermediation, where financial intermediaries represent institutions that hold the primary securities issued by firms, financing themselves by issuing "own securities" which are sold to private households. Firms issue debt and equity. Households which want demand deposits and life insurance policies use the service of intermediaries. Financial intermediaries link households and firms by issuing deposits or insurance policies and use the proceeds to acquire stakes in firms' shares and debt certificates. A more complicated and realistic picture is one where households acquiring real estate are also among the issuers of primary securities, where firms invest in financial securities or machines, and where financial intermediaries hold each others securities. Netting out all financial relations among the intermediaries we get the transformation of primary securities, issued by holders of real assets, into the "final" securities, held by households. Following this characteristic of the banking sector HELLWIG (1994) raised the illustrative question why intermediation is really needed (firms could issue demand deposits themselves and private households could hold firms' shares to a very large extent). It is obvious that banks do not have a role in the frictionless Arrow-Debreu world in which a general competitive equilibrium would be characterized by (i) full diversification of all diversifiable risks and (ii) efficient sharing of all non-diversifiable risks. Hence frictions impairing the functioning of perfect markets must be the reason why direct finance is unattractive or impossible, and these frictions are particularly a problem in transforming economies. Financial intermediation allows society to overcome the frictions. Big firms facing booming markets might decide to create a bank themselves, and this was indeed the case in the US in the 19th century. It is again the case in Russia in the 1990s, although it remains unclear whether management and monitoring skills are adequate in Russian banks which face a highly inflationary environment with firms not competing on a level playing field.

Referring to the standard literature there are three kinds of important frictions which explain the usefulness of banks:

- Indivisibilities and other nonconvexities - including fixed transaction costs - which imply limits for risk diversification through direct finance. This is not special to eastern Europe and Russia.

- Spatial separation of agents restricts the scope of obtaining insurance of individual liquidity needs via direct market participation. Households face individual risk about the time incidence of consumption needs. This represents risk that could in principle be insured away. Since the necessary resource transfer between consumers is impossible or extremely costly if consumers are spatially separated at the time when they learn about their liquidity requirements, intermediation is useful. An intermediary who is accessible and provides liquidity to different agents can reduce the problem and profit from diversification gains across consumers and economies of scale. Given the underdeveloped infrastructure, the newly emerging networks of firms and their suppliers, as well as politico-economic instability, intermediation will yield particular gains in transforming economies.
- Asymmetric information and moral hazard cause agency costs which reduce the scope for direct finance, and intermediation reduces these agency costs of finance via devices that allow monitoring (with scale economies) and controlling the final borrower, the firm. In eastern Europe the existence of asymmetric information and moral hazard problems ("incentives to cheat with respect to providing true information") are very important so that banks could play an extremely important role during transition. The share of non-performing loans exceeded 10% in transforming economies in the period 1992-95 (see Table A8). Unfortunately, banks themselves are part of the problem since initially most of them were state-owned banks with no skilled personnel for evaluating investment projects under the competitive conditions of a market economy. Bankruptcy laws were adopted only in 1992/93 in transforming economies and such laws are still not enacted in Russia so that the scope for the necessary recapitalization of banks is unclear at present.

Table A8 Non-Performing Bank Loans in Transforming Economies (% of total loans)

	1991	1992	1993	1994	1995
Albania	...	...	14	27	31
Bulgaria	...	...	...	50	...
Czech Republic	...	19	24	38	38[a]
Georgia	...	...	...	25	38[b]
Hungary[c]	8	10	23	21	...
Kazakstan	...	...	...	...	40
Latvia	...	...	...	33	...
Poland	16	...	...	...	...
Russia	...	...	12	31	39

[a] September 1995.
[b] June 1995
[c] In % of domestic credit.
Source: IMF, *World Economic Outlook*, April 1996, table 24, based on national authorities, IMF estimates and M. S. Borish, M. F. Long and M. Noel, "Restructuring Banks and Enterprises: Recent Lessons from Transition Countries", World Bank Discussion Paper No. 275, January 1995.

Corporate Governance and Privatization

Effective corporate governance can reduce the risks a bank is facing when extending loans to a firm. The control over assets and business decisions in firms is shared by internal and external bodies in a market economy. Internally it is done by corporate boards and employees or their representatives. But on the one hand employee ownership programs popular in most transforming economies have trapped many employees of poorly managed companies, while on the other hand disperse ownership creates the problem of a lack of strategic investors and effective governance. In the Czech voucher privatization and the Polish mass privatization program this problem is partly visible. An important feature of the two rounds of Czech mass privatization was that a liquid asset market emerged whose capitalization jumped from $12bn to 20bn in 1995 (after wave II). However, in the Czech Republic investment funds are often owned by the leading state-owned banks which want to gain credit business and not undertake market-oriented restructuring. Paradoxically, these banks therefore contribute to the lack of corporate governance in industry. Hence, the key to banking sector reform is privatization including strategic foreign investors - a strategy finally accepted in Hungary and Poland in 1995/96.

Firms are controlled externally by markets for debt, i.e. creditors and the threat of bankruptcy which is not credible as long as banks and firms are largely state-owned. In addition to this there is the market for corporate control whose functioning requires the possibility of hostile takeovers, a large pool of skilled managers and an efficient use of proxy voting through private banks exercising ownership rights of individual investors. Hostile takeovers are uncommon in the whole of continental Europe, the pool of managers is narrow and many banks are not yet privatized in eastern Europe, so that corporate governance is weak from this perspective. Finally the firm is indirectly controlled through goods markets in which competitors' attempts to raise market shares forces the firm to undertake rationalization investment or launch product innovations. Competition is strong in the tradables sector in all small ex-CMEA countries. However, it is weak in these countries' non-tradables market where only tough domestic competition policy, dismemberment of large firms and support for the creation of new firms would create strong competitive pressure.

In a big country such as Russia - with heavy supply-side distortions and considerable learning time required by firms with a potential to survive - rapid import liberalization in the tradables sectors is largely not creating a positive response since domestic firms are facing such an overwhelming pressure from imports and have so little experience in restructuring. Hence import competition is mainly killing domestic competition rather than contributing to overall competition. Export promotion which is helpful for stimulating competition in the tradables sector is - in contrast to the case of the Visegrad countries - also not working in Russia since its exports are dominated by natural resources.

High economic growth will be achieved only if universal banks are successful in both their role as stock owners and in extending loans, while pricing risk adequately. Diversified ownership and a seat in company supervisory boards will help banks to monitor firms and their management, respectively. However, one should be aware that banks in eastern Europe and Russia are rather inexperienced in this role, that corruption could erode the banks' monitoring function and that moral hazard resulting from deposit insurance could be considerable (ROSTOWSKI, 1995, p. 27). This does not mean that deposit insurance should be neglected as was the case in several transforming economies, including the Czech Republic where it was only introduced after three banks nearly failed.

CORBETT and MAYER (1992) argued that German-type universal banks, which would have large equity stakes in non-financial firms, enjoy the insight of supervisory board representation and give credits to firms with future profits, would be useful for eastern Europe. This argument could be valid in countries which accept foreign banks as partners so that a fast transfer of expertise would be achieved. An east European revival of the argument of GERSCHENKRON (1968), that universal banks can partly substitute for intra-firm entrepreneurship, seems realistic in the long term under an appropriate open door policy for foreign banks. These, however, are not quite welcome in eastern Europe. Privatization and foreign direct investment are keys for systemic transformation (JASINSKI and WELFENS, 1994), but apparently foreign investors in the manufacturing sector are less of a sensitive political issue than foreign banks are. In countries in which investment funds play a strong role because of a two-stage privatization process, e.g. the ex-CSFR, Poland and Romania after the recent mass privatization program, the role of universal banks is less important than in countries which favored other forms of privatization. With high foreign direct investment inflows in the first half of the 1990s Hungary enjoyed an external impulse for growth, but these very inflows apparently reduced government's attention to the banking system, whose fragility then negatively compensated for the positive external stimulus. This is a special form of a winner's curse (here related to foreign direct investment inflows).

At the bottom line there is a mixed picture of corporate governance, namely a positive one in the Visegrad countries, with some caveats in Hungary because of banks' problems and lack of privatization and a clearly negative one in Russia. Bulgaria and Romania which established a stock exchange only in 1995 are not yet in a position which allows clear judgment.

Portfolio Perspective of Transformation

Saving in eastern Europe can be mobilized if (1) the financial system is stable, (2) interest rates are high and (3) per capita incomes are increasing. The latter two conditions might not be met: in countries where investment is falling production capacities are underutilized and investment then falls further along with real income, so that a negative Keynesian multiplier chain can prevent that sufficient saving is available. Moreover, if declining economic activity is associated with rising politico-economic instability a large part of the already diminished savings could be transferred abroad, mostly as part of capital flight. The Ukraine and Russia are two transforming countries in which such developments occurred in the early 1990s. Banks in the UK, Switzerland and Germany benefit from the inflow of capital from eastern Europe, while eastern Europe is paying the triple price of falling exchange rates, increasing interest rates and rising external indebtedness.

Figure A5 Portfolio Perspective of Transformation and Economic Growth

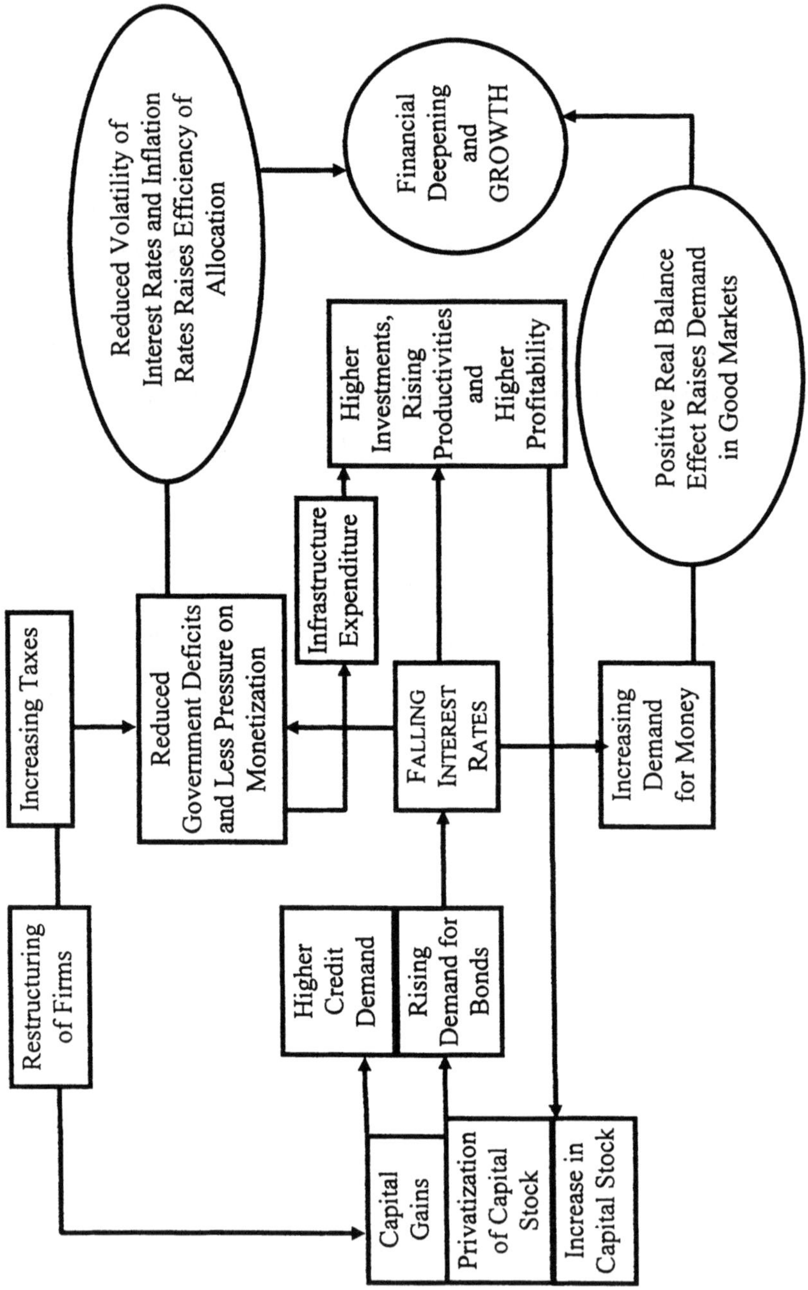

Prudential Supervision, Capital Account Liberalization and Catching Up

Since eastern Europe's domestic saving mainly has to finance investment, as many countries face foreign debt and current account problems, it is important that a sound financial system provides a safe outlet for domestic savings. High economic growth could be achieved if a competitive banking system were to finance aggressive, but well-founded investment plans of firms. A very competitive banking system with limited regulation and thus low costs of capital would be conducive to economic growth. However, in the short run governments will be less interested in a competitive banking system which would operate with narrow margins and face considerable risk of debtor default. Rather governments are likely to apply restrictions in the form of regulations so that failure rates among banks would be minimal and stability of the financial system be maintained in the short run (BOOT and VAN WIJNBERGEN, 1995). There have been, however, many banking collapses in transforming economies. Adoption of the Basle guidelines which require an 8% ratio of core capital to risk-bearing assets helped to increase long term stability; in most countries recapitalization of banks and mergers of banks became necessary in this context. The low intensity of competition resulting from regional and functional specialization (typical of socialist countries) can only gradually be overcome as new commercial banks emerge.

Given the restrictions imposed on competition in transforming economies' banking systems it would be dangerous to fully liberalize the capital account. In a situation in which western Europe is deregulating the banking system and short-term interest rates - including yields of money market funds - are increasing, it would be dangerous to fully liberalize the capital account. Domestic banks in eastern Europe would come under pressure to finance more risky investment with a higher expected return on investment, and if only one major bank would then face difficulties from adverse developments among its clients the whole banking system could face instability and a central bank pursuing an expansive inflationary policy would in effect undermine much of the early transformation progress. Sustainable transformation would be endangered by early capital account liberalization, and this in turn implies that marginal products of capital will differ considerably between eastern Europe and western Europe (high profit rates in eastern Europe could indeed be invoked by nationalist parties as an argument to fend off foreign multinationals). This aspect, and possibly not so much the Maastricht convergence criteria, is the most important barrier for Visegrad countries to quickly join the EU, which would certainly require that the principle of free capital flows and free financial services be fully implemented. The Europe treaties stipulate almost full external liberalization after a ten year transformation period.

Learning from NICs and Catching Up

State-owned banks and firms in upstream markets were part of the interventionist approach to development used in Korea and Taiwan in the 1960s when investment and thereby growth was stimulated by government policy. However, while Korea and Taiwan were characterized by rather equitable income distribution and lack of powerful companies that could have distorted government intervention towards non-productive strategies and rent-seeking, eastern Europe and Russia are characterized by an increasingly skewed income distribution and big powerful firms. Government intervention cannot be prudent under such circumstances, and this holds all the more since political instability is typical of most of the ex-CMEA area. Consequently, capital markets and banks are all the more important for economic growth.

ALLEN (1993) has emphasized that stock markets provide continuous checking on managerial decisions which is particularly valuable if new technologies are used. Therefore advanced countries should rely more on stock-based financial systems than less developed ones. This is an argument for eastern Europe with its pool of medium technology producers to rely more on banks than on stock markets. By contrast, Russia - eager to remain a high technology country - should rely on stock markets (a similar argument applies to the leading EU countries). A major caveat is that speculative bubbles in stock markets could play a considerable and very destabilizing role, especially if monetary policy is unstable. In industries with standard technology, such as utilities, bank financing could play a large role. High debt and payout ratios are optimal, whereas high-technology firms need conservative debt and dividend policies so that they can finance risky R&D projects with retained earnings. It is, however, unclear to which extent universal banks' ownership of high-tech firms is compatible which high debt ratios (Japan, Germany).

BLACK and MOERSCH (1995) have shown that the Visegrad countries would record high growth rates if they could adopt western Europe's production function. This sounds as if the Asian NIC miracle could have a parallel development in eastern Europe. MADDISON (1991) argued that economic catching up in Asia is not mysterious since growth of labor and capital inputs as well as the advancing knowledge embodied in human and physical capital had its impact. However, in eastern Europe and Russia there is exactly the problem how to achieve high rates of efficient capital formation and how working efforts can be increased in an environment that is characterized by both the distortions of the past command economy and those of the new capitalist shadow economy. Rapid catching up in the Visegrad countries is only a potential adjustment trajectory, where internal political stability and external stability - i.e. a successful transformation process in the Ukraine and Russia - are necessary conditions for any sustaining catching-up process in the long term.

3.2 Role of Banks for New Private Firms

Credit Rationing and the Loan Market

Newly created firms are urgently needed in post-socialist countries in order to correct the distorted skewed distribution of firm size in ex-CMEA countries. Among the many problems faced by newcomers in eastern Europe there are two specially important ones. Firstly, land is often not offered to new firms by the local communities, which instead prefer to speculate with land available for investors - sometimes this is hidden behind the declared intention that the local authorities want to avoid excessive speculation by private developers. Secondly, credit is often not available to small firms since the large banks prefer to extend loans to large companies, which they consider as a rather safe bet because politicians will not allow big firms to go bankrupt. This reluctance to extend loans to small companies - with ample evidence in Poland and other countries - can be reinforced by apparent uncertainty which banks perceive when new borrowers want to obtain loans. Theoretical analysis underlines this point (STIGLITZ and WEISS, 1981). One solution to the problem is to create special banks for the small and medium enterprises. This could be a state owned development bank or one might consider the German Industriekreditbank model which is owned by major companies but mainly extends loans to medium-sized firms. Indeed large companies should have an active interest in nurturing innovative and efficient suppliers, which large players later might acquire in order to rejuvenate themselves. Finally, several big companies could create a joint bank with a strong focus on venture capital financing, which would allow innovation projects to be monitored and the winners to be picked in a later takeover strategy.

Privatization, Capital Gains and Opening up

From a portfolio perspective real capital and financial wealth (money plus bonds) are complementary. If privatization is organized in a way that - in connection with increasing competition - resources are employed in a more productive use and hence profits increase, the real value of machinery and equipment will increase. Indeed, switching to a market economy should in the first privatization stages entail positive network effects as more efficient privatized suppliers and competitors generate positive spill-over effects on already existing firms. Often state-owned firms will benefit, too - especially if soft budget constraints are eliminated - such that distinguishing between primary and secondary efficiency gains from privatization might be difficult. Since banks and governments are issuing interest-bearing debt instruments, a successful privatization strategy resulting in real capital gains will increase the demand for bonds and thereby reduce real interest rates. For east European governments this should provide an incentive to organize privatization swiftly and in a way which nurtures capital markets. Only the ex-CSFR's voucher approach is convincing in this respect, while the Russian approach of widely used employee ownership programs (often giving 51% of a company to employees) is counterproductive: while working efforts might be slightly stimulated by employee ownership programs there is no risk-pooling element in the Russian approach, which in turn reduces the liquidity of stocks and weakens inter-sectoral and regional labor mobility. This mobility would be much needed to reallocate labor towards the most productive use such that the market value of real capital would be raised, productivity increased and growth promoted.

While capital account liberalization is controversial as an early step in liberalization in developing and in transforming economies, current account liberalization is widely recommended as an early step. Import competition and the incentive to increase exports will raise the efficiency of resource allocation. Economic opening up is indeed generally recommended in textbook approaches as a strategy which makes both countries better off in a two-country world. Except for the case of immiserizing growth there is no exception from this insight. But even from a static view there exists an exception (Appendix A2).

3.3 Russia as a Special Case?

In Russia the view is widely held that the rich natural resources could be a prime source for economic development and that therefore state banks' loans should be used primarily for the exploration, mining and export of natural resources. While it is true that a dynamic natural resource sector can generate high export proceeds, it is clear that endogenous growth will not be supported much by the natural resource sector which is quite capital intensive and uses mostly standardized technology and equipment. Positive technology spillovers effects will hardly occur. Export-driven endogenous growth could only be expected from rising exports of machinery, transportation equipment and sophisticated consumer goods, for which in turn domestic markets still have to be developed.

Natural resource endowment has declined in importance for economic growth and high income since technological progress and economic growth require skilled employees and sophisticated equipment as crucial production factors. The value of land and minerals was 60% of the value of all tangible assets in 1688 in Great Britain but only 15% in 1977 and since asset-income ratios have increased, natural resources' importance relative to income declined even more strongly than indicated by these figures. In 1870, Australia which has rich natural resources had twice the per capita income of Switzerland which is a resource poor country (WORLD BANK, 1989, p. 26). In 1990 Switzerland's per capita income was 50% above that of Australia. Japan and Germany as well as Korea and Singapore are further examples of rich countries with a poor endowment in natural resources. The decisive difference between poor and rich countries is not the endowment in natural resources but the efficiency with which these countries use national and external (imported) resources. Financial markets and banks are the pillars of efficient resource use in market economies.

One major difference to economic catching up in the 1960s and the 1990s is that the R&D intensity of output has increased in all industrialized countries. R&D ventures are risky and their financing requires either sophisticated venture capital markets, internal funds from an affluent parent company - as in the case of MNCs - or sufficient retained earnings. Banks typically are reluctant to provide funds for innovations, especially if the companies involved lack reputation or if they are newly founded firms, which applies to Russia and other transforming countries of the ex-CMEA area. Considering the risk involved in innovations, banks will come up with loans for innovative projects and investments only if sufficient equity capital is available or if collateral can easily be offered by the firm.

Since markets for lands are underdeveloped in ex-CMEA countries in general and in Russia in particular, where the idea of private land property is rather unpopular, it is often difficult for firms to mobilize collateral for bank credits. Therefore healthy profits and government R&D subsidies would be required in Russia if firms are to upgrade their product assortment and to move up the technological ladder. However, profits are still unpopular in Russia and the decisive distinction between static profits and Schumpeterian economic rents is not well understood. If temporarily high profits for entrepreneurs are not acceptable for political or social reasons in Russia, economic catching up will not be feasible. The alternative route for technological catching up in Russia would be to attract massive foreign direct investment. The Russian government's aim is to attract about 10% of the some $250bn p.a. in foreign direct investment worldwide, so that overall domestic investment can be increased and growth be achieved. Given the political instability, poor infrastructure and instability of the economic situation this goal is rather illusory. However, the OECD is expecting first-time growth in post-socialist Russia in 1996. This would require a high domestic saving rate and a high marginal product of capital which is unlikely given inefficient privatization, the poorly functioning capital markets and recurrent banking crises. Real income of higher income groups increased by about 30% in 1994 in Russia, while that of the poorer strata increased by only 5% (UNECE, 1995, p. 93) so that the average savings rate of private households might increase. Rising inequality could distort government policies towards redistributive interventions which weaken economic growth. Thus it is doubtful that high economic growth can be achieved. Having recorded distortionary high negative real interest rates in 1993/94 and very high positive rates in 1995, it is only in 1996 that a one-digit real interest rate was observed.

Russia is facing problems that are in many ways similar to those in Germany in the Weimar Republic. Given the extreme problems in Russia and the enormous international changes in the world economy there is the danger that economic and political instability in Russia would undermine the whole of western Europe. A success-promising catching-up strategy in Russia will require strong domestic competition, conversion, macroeconomic stabilization and some selective tariff protectionism with a pre-announced strategy of tariff reductions in the long term (WELFENS, 1996b).

3.4 Conclusions

The analysis has shown that the EU will have a much more competitive banking system in the future. On the hand this is likely to reduce real interest rates, on the other hand financial market instability could become a greater risk in Europe as the banking system - with a few state players left - has to cope with narrow profit margins that leaves the system more fragile than in the past. At the same time banks will benefit from massive infrastructure investment and privatization of state-owned firms in Europe. The role of stock markets and FDI will increase in Europe.

It was also shown that banks are facing some problems in the EU but that the overall development of financial intermediaries is favorable. Since profit margins are coming down the stability of the banking system depends critically on supervision and standards. With ongoing mergers & acquisitions in the single market EU multinationals are getting larger and thus should find new options for bypassing banks. While banks will face reduced options for financing government deficits they are likely to find new loan markets for infrastructure projects. Large EU infrastructure projects which are largely cofinanced by the European investment bank open up new markets for banks, however they also create new risks (e.g. the Chunnel project).

In eastern Europe, Poland and the Czech Republic were largely successful in restructuring the banking sector and also benefit from radical early steps towards a market economy and the existing memory of the market economy in the population.

At the other extreme in Russia the situation is extremely difficult, since the memory of the market economy is dead after 70 years of a command economy and since Russia suffers from declining investment, output, employment and tax proceeds. A viable banking system plus a functional venture capital system are needed in transforming economies. Firm internal capital markets in big companies can allocate funds efficiently only if both the internal governance structure and the market allocation process can effectively be decentralized. Banks in western Europe will be involved in the east European transformation process via lending, portfolio investment and direct investment. The EBRD and the EU would be wise to support the transition process.

The expansion of stock markets, nurtured by privatization programs in western Europe and eastern Europe, is a common feature of the whole continent. Major infrastructure projects in the whole of Europe will generate rising fees and increasing opportunities for syndicated loans. High and growing foreign debt of transforming economies links Europe's two former blocs. With increasing competition in the single market and pressure on privatized banks and insurance companies in several EU countries to achieve competitive yields, interest rates are increasing for short term instruments; the impact on average maturities and the yield curve is unclear. Facing intensified competition and financial innovation industrial firms might find it easier to borrow at low costs which would stimulate economic growth. The tendency towards an increasingly knowledge-based society with high R&D-sales ratios could mean that financing via equity issues becomes increasingly important. This could also apply to Russia.

A crucial development since 1985 is the rapid rise of foreign direct investment which intensifies locational competition worldwide. FDI in the service sector outpaced that of the manufacturing industry. Given the fact that capital intensity of the service industry is lower than in manufacturing even a modest investment-output ratio (such as in the US) can generate high economic growth; an implicit assumption is that software innovations and investments contribute particularly to productivity growth in the service economy.

Eastern Europe faces massive problems in the banking industry and could become a leader in the expansion of stock markets in Europe. Russia is a special problem which could generate negative spillovers for the whole of Europe (TILLY and WELFENS, 1995). Financial markets with their increased volatility remain the natural Achilles heel of capitalist systems, especially since political instability will remain a major problem in Europe.

Appendix A1 The Greenwald-Stiglitz Approach

In the model of GREENWALD and STIGLITZ (1993) firms use circulating capital inputs. These inputs have to be paid for before output can be sold at prices which at first are uncertain. firms maximize the net (of bankruptcy costs) expected value v of equity at the end of the period and taking into account that end of period equity is given by:

(A1) $$v(q_t) = p_t q_t - (1 + r_t) b_t$$

where b is the firm's borrowing, p the expected price and r the cost of borrowing. Bankruptcy will occur if the value of debt exceeds the value of sales, i.e. the end of period equity is negative. Firms incur debt to finance purchases of labor, where employment n is an increasing function of output: $n = f(q)$. The wage rate is w. Borrowing will be reduced if equity funds are available to the firms from the previous period. Hence at the beginning of the period debt is given by:

(A2) $$b_t = w_t f(q_t) - v_{t-1}$$

The representative manager of each firms maximizes:

(A3) $$v_t - (1 + r_t)[w_t f(q_t) - v_{t-1}] - h(q_t) P_B$$

where the expected price P is set at unity and the cost of bankruptcy $h(q)$ is an increasing function of output: the cost of bankruptcy is rising with the scale of the firm (in contrast to this assumption of Greenwald and Stiglitz managers in eastern Europe's big firms might indeed speculate that big firms are more likely to obtain financial support than small firms). The probability of bankruptcy is $P_B = F(u_t)$, where u_t is the price below which the firm will go bankrupt. Profit maximization of equation (3) yields the condition:

(A4) $$1 - (1 + r_t) w_t f' + z_t = 0$$

where z_t is the marginal bankruptcy cost of the firm. Only with $z_t = 0$ does one get the traditional textbook condition that output will be raised until marginal costs equal price. As z_t is positive the equilibrium level of output will be reduced, i.e. the effective marginal cost curve shifts upwards. One can also show that labor markets are affected by the perceived bankruptcy risk which in turn has implications for the transmission process of monetary policy (DIMSDALE, 1994). The aggregate labor demand curve is shifted to the left by a fall in equity levels v_t, a rise in perceived risk u, and an increase in the dispersion of equity.

Appendix A2 Opening Up and Wealth Effects

Economic opening up is welfare increasing in every textbook model, except for immiserizing growth. If wealth directly enters the utility function one might consider at least one counter-example, which is related to the relative price of investment goods and the price of capital, respectively. The budget line BB_0 in (q_2,q_1) space has the slope p_1/p_2. Let us assume that good 1 is (also) an investment good and that after economic opening up the slope of the budget line would increase so that the relative price of investment is increasing. If the price of investment goods and that of the stock of capital had been initially identical and some investment had been undertaken in this initial equilibrium, it is clear that firms will temporarily reduce investment which leads to an underutilization of the capital stock, falling profits and hence a falling relative price of the stock of capital. This capital loss would have to be offset by a sufficiently strong increase in consumption if the representative individual - owning stocks - is to maintain his initial (autarchy) utility level. To put it differently, eastern Europe economic opening up will have different welfare results depending on whether the relative price of investment falls or increases, while the textbook models treat both cases as identical. With respect to stimulating economic growth, a relative fall in the price of investment goods (BB_2) would be the more desirable effect and possibly higher learning economies (shifting out the production frontier line) will be realized since - given the existing price of the stock of capital (i.e. the equity price level) - new investment will thus be stimulated. Standard textbooks models suggest that economic opening up is welfare increasing regardless whether the new budget line is steeper or flatter than BB_0. This analysis does not suggest that current account liberalization should be postponed on a broad scale, but it points to the problem that opening up could entail capital gains or capital losses, which should be taken into account in the transformation strategy. If capital losses are anticipated current account liberalization should come before privatization and the government should certainly not request wage restraint from workers as a price for employee ownership programs. If capital losses - instead of typically expected capital gains - are realized workers will be disappointed and policymakers' reputation undermined.

Figure A6 Economic Opening Up and Alternative Wealth Effects

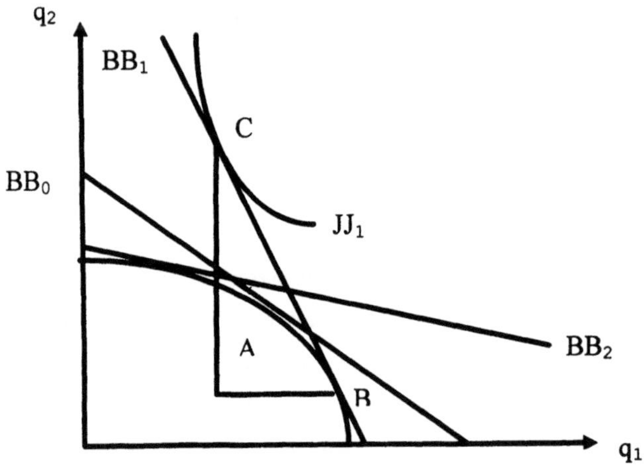

Appendix A4 Labor Hours and Productivity in the Manufacturing Industry

Figure A7 Effective Labor Hours in the Manufacturing Industry

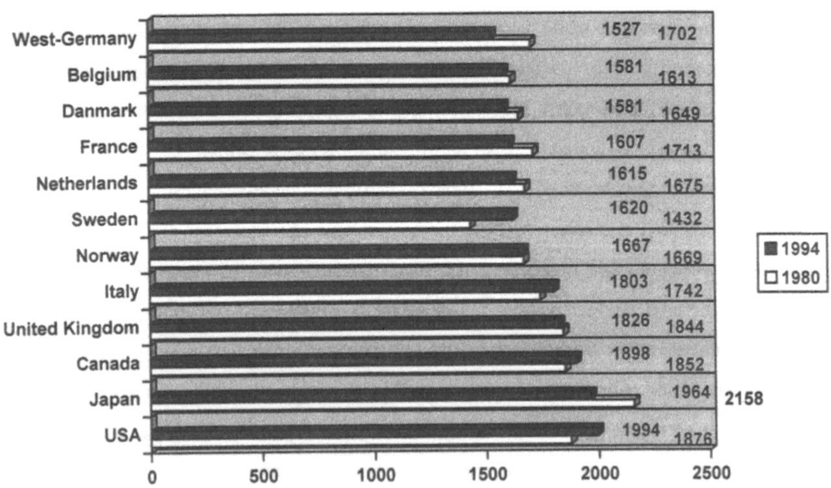

Source: U.S. Department of Labor.

Figure A8 Labor Productivity Growth in the Manufacturing Industry, 1980-1994

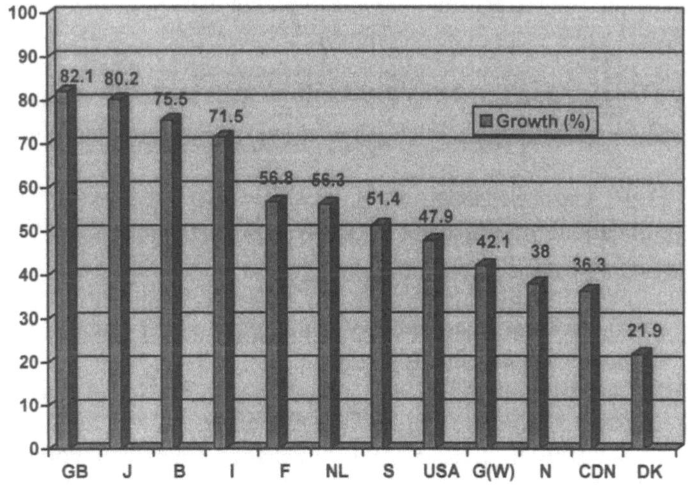

Source: For both figures U.S. Department of Labour.

References

ALLEN, F. (1993), "Stock Markets and Resource Allocation," in MAYER, C. P. and VIVES, X. (eds.), *Capital Markets and Financial Intermediation*, Cambridge University Press, Cambridge.

BANK OF ENGLAND (1995), *Quarterly Bulletin*, Vol. 35, London.

BIS - Bank of International Settlements (1995), *65. Jahresbericht*, Basle.

BIS - Bank of International Settlements (1996), *66th Annual Report*, Basle.

BLACK, S. W. and MOERSCH, M. (1995), "Investment and its Financing During the Transition in Central and Eastern Europe," Paper presented at AICGS conference 'Europe's Economy Looks East', Washington D.C., May 15-16, 1995.

BOOT, A. W. A. and VAN WIJNBERGEN, S. (1995), "Financial Sector Design, Regulation and Deposit Insurance in Eastern Europe," in ROSTOWSKI, J. (ed.), *Banking Reform in Central Europe and the Former Soviet Union*, Central European University Press, Budapest, 42-57.

BUNDESVERBAND deutscher Banken (1995), "Auswirkungen der Europäischen Wirtschafts- und Währungsunion auf die Finanzmärkte," Mimeo, Bonn.

CORBETT, J. and MAYER, C. (1992), "Financial Reform in Eastern Europe: Progress with the Wrong Model," *Oxford Review of Economic Policy*, Vol. 8.

CROCKETT, A. (1995), "Financial Innovation: Macro-Economic and Macro-Prudential Consequences," *Kredit und Kapital*, Vol. 28, 46-61.

DEUTSCHE BUNDESBANK (1996), "Finanzmarktvolatilität und ihre Auswirkungen auf die Geldpolitik," *Monatsberichte der Deutschen Bundesbank*, April, 53-70.

DIMSDALE, N. (1994), "Banks, Capital Markets, and the Monetary Transmission Mechanism," *Oxford Review of Economic Policy*, Vol. 10, No. 4, 34-48.

EC COMMISSION (1993), *Growth, Competitiveness, Employment*, White Paper, Brussels.

EDWARDS, F. R. and MISHKIN, F. S. (1995), "The Decline of Traditional Banking: Implications for Financial Stability and Regulatory Policy," *Federal Reserve Bank of New York Economic Policy Review*, July 1995, 27-45.

EIB - European Investment Bank (1995), *Annual Report*, Luxembourg.

FIELD, A.J. (1984), "A New Interpretation of the Onset of the Great Depression," *Journal of Economic History*, 44, 489-498.

FRATIANNI, M. and HUANG, H. (1995), "New Growth Theory: A Survey from a Policy Perspective," *Kredit und Kapital*, Vol. 28, 62-86.

FROOT, K. A. and STEIN, J. C. (1991), "Exchange Rates and Foreign Direct Investment. An Imperfect Capital Markets Approach," *Quarterly Journal of Economics*, November, 1191-1217.

GERSCHENKRON, A. (1962), *Economic Backwardness in Historical Perspective*, Cambridge, Mass.

GERSCHENKRON, A. (1968), *Continuity in History and Other Essays*, Harvard University Press, Cambridge.

GREENWALD, B. and STIGLITZ, J. E. (1993), "Financial Market Imperfections and Business Cycles," *Quarterly Journal of Economics*, Vol. 108, 77-114.

HELLWIG, M. (1994), "Banking and Finance at the End of the Twentieth Century," Wirtschaftswissenschaftliches Zentrum der Universität Basel, Mimeo.

HONOHAN, P. (1995), "The Public Policy Role of the European Investment Bank within the EU," *Journal of Common Market Studies*, Vol. 33, 315-330.

IMF - International Monetary Fund (1994), *World Economic Outlook*, October 1984, Washington DC.

INSTITUT DER DEUTSCHEN WIRTSCHAFT (IDW), IWD-Mitteilungen, Nr. 39, Cologne.

JASINSKI, P. and WELFENS, P. J. J. (1994), *Privatization and Foreign Direct Investment in Transforming Economies*, Dartmouth, Aldershot.

KAUFMANN, H. (1994), "Structural Changes in the Financial Markets: Economic and Policy Significance," *Economic Review of the Federal Reserve Bank of Kansas City*, 2nd quarter.

KLEIN, M.W. and WELFENS, P.J.J. (1992), *Multinationals in the New Europe and Global Trade*, Springer, Heidelberg.

KLODT, H. et al. (1994), *Standort Deutschland: Strukturelle Herausforderungen im neuen Europa*, Mohr, Tübingen.

LITAN, R. E. (1994), "Financial Regulation," in FELDSTEIN, M. (ed.), *American Economic Policy in the 1980s*, University of Chicago Press, Chicago.
MADDISON, A. (1991), "Postwar Growth and Slowdown: A Global View," in GAHLEN, B., HESSE, H. and RAMSER, H. J. (eds.), *Wachstumstheorie und Wachstumspolitik. Ein Neuer Anlauf*, Mohr, Tübingen, 23-41.
McKINSEY (1996), *Capital Productivity*, Washington D.C.
METZLER, L. A. (1951), "Wealth, saving and the rate of interest," *Journal of Political Economy*, Vol. 59, 93-116.
OCHEL, W. und PENZKOFER, H. (1995), "Internationale Wettbewerbsfähigkeit und ihre Implikationen für die Europäische FuE-Politik," Mimeo, Ifo-Institut, München.
OECD (1993), *Transformation of the Banking System*, Paris.
OECD (1996), *Financial Market Trends*, No. 61, Paris.
PLOSSER, C. I. (1992), "The Search for Growth," in *Policies in Long-Run Economic Growth*, Federal Reserve Bank of Kansas.
ROSTOWSKI, J. (1995), "The Banking System, Credit and the Real Sector in Transition Economies," in ROSTOWSKI, J. (ed.), *Banking Reform in Central Europe and the Former Soviet Union*, Central European University Press, Budapest, 16-41.
SCHINASI, G. and HARGRAVES, M. (1995), "'Boom and Bust' in Asset Markets in the 1980s: Causes and Consequences," IMF Staff Studies for the World Economic Outlook, Washington DC, 1-27.
SCHRÖDER, K. (1995), "Banking Reforms in East Central Europe," *Intereconomics*, Vol. 30, 133 - 195.
STIGLITZ, J. and WEISS, A. (1981), Credit Rationing in Markets with Imperfect Information, *American Economic Review*, Vol. 71, 393-410.
TAVLAS, G. S. and OZEKI, Y. (1992), "The Internationalization of Currencies: An Appraisal of the Japanese Yen," IMF Occasional Paper No. 90.
THOMAS, I. P. (1995), "Konvergenz und Divergenz in der Europäischen Union - Theoretischer Überblick, empirische Evidenz und wirtschaftspolitische Implikationen," April.
TILLY, R. and WELFENS, P. J. J. (1995) (eds.), *European Economic Integration as a Challenge to Industry and Government*, Springer, New York.
TOBIN, J. (1965), Money and Economic Growth, *Econometrica*, Vol.33, 671-684.
UNCTAD (1995), *World Investment Report 1995*, Geneva.
UNECE (1995), *Economic Survey of Europe in 1994-1995*, Geneva.
WAHEED, A. and MATHUR, I. (1995), "Wealth Effects of Foreign Expansion by U.S. Banks," *Journal of Banking & Finance*, Vol. 19, 823-842.
WELFENS, P. J. J. (1992), *Market-oriented Systemic Transformations in Eastern Europe*, Springer, New York.
WELFENS, P. J. J. (1995), *European Monetary Integration*, 3rd revised and enlarged edition, Springer, New York.
WELFENS, P. J. J. (ed.) (1996a), *Economic Aspects of German Unification*, 2nd, revised and enlarged edition, Springer, Heidelberg and New York.

WELFENS, P. J. J. (1996b), "Wettbewerbs- und Strukturpolitik im Transformationsprozeß: Analyse, Politikoptionen und Implikationen in Rußland," in GÖTZ, R. and GRINBERG, R. (eds.), *Strukturpolitik in Rußland: Materialien einer Konferenz*, Bundesinstitut für ostwissenschaftliche und internationale Studien, Sonderveröffentlichung, August.

WELFENS, P. J. J. and JUNGMITTAG, A. (1996), "The Political Economy of EMU and Stabilization Policy," paper presented at the international conference 'European Monetary Union: Transition, International Impacts and Policy Options', EIIW, Potsdam, 25.-26. April 1996.

WELFENS, P. J. J. and YARROW, G. (eds.) (1996), *Telecommunications and Energy in Systemic Transformation*, Springer, Heidelberg and New York.

WORLD BANK (1989), *World Development Report 1989*, Oxford University Press for the World Bank, Washington, D.C.

YOUNG, A. (1991), "Learning By Doing and the Dynamic Effect of Trade," *Quarterly Journal of Economics*, Vol. 106, 369-405.

Comments on
Banks, Capital Markets, R&D and Economic Growth in Europe

Uwe Vollmer

In his paper, Paul Welfens surveys the contributions of the banking system and of capital markets to the development of R&D activities and economic growth in Europe. His analysis proceeds in two steps. In the first part, he concentrates on the economic growth process in western Europe. Here, he states some common tendencies in the international banking industry such as innovation, securitization, globalization and disintermediation, considers the influence of the European Monetary Union on banking, describes R&D activities and the growth process in Europe and investigates the consequences of the social security network on the savings process in western Europe. In the second part of the paper, Paul Welfens discusses the role of banking, financial markets and foreign direct investments in the process of systemic transformation in post-socialist European economies, especially the Visegrad countries and Russia. Here he stresses the catalyst functions of banks for economic growth in eastern Europe and Russia, considers the role of banks in providing venture capital for new private firms and finally discusses the special situation of Russia compared to the other eastern European economies in systemic transformation. The paper is full of detailed empirical information about the growth process and R&D activities in both parts of Europe. I will not comment on these details, but, instead, will concentrate on three remarks of which the first two concern the role of banking in western Europe's growth process, while the third applies to the eastern European growth and transformation process.

1. The paper claims that financial markets are the "Achilles heel of capitalist systems" and that "supervision and standards", i.e. state regulations are needed to guarantee the stability of the banking system. I do not subscribe to this point of

view; on the contrary, I believe that western European countries do not suffer from too much competition and laisser faire, but instead from too much regulation and state intervention. This also applies to the banking system where state sponsored central banks force commercial banks to hold fractional reserves, act as "lenders of last resort" and severely regulate decisions in the banking community. These regulations are often justified on natural monopoly grounds (due to economies of scale in banking from reserve holdings) and on grounds of banking panics (due to "contagion effects" which cause single bank failures to trigger system-wide bank runs). However, the argument that banking suffers from a tendency towards natural monopoly is not supported by empirical evidence, and unregulated banking systems have scarcely suffered from nationwide bank runs (DOWD, 1992, pp. 388-390; SCHULER, 1992, pp. 15ff.). In fact, at least for most European countries, these arguments have not been the central motive for state intervention in the banking business. Instead, the main reasons have been plain fiscal motives and the interest of the state to nationalize monopoly rents from the production of money (SCHULER, 1992, pp.40-43). Furthermore, we have some historical evidence about the beneficial impact of unregulated competition on economic growth: one prominent example is the Free Banking era of 18th and 19th century Scotland where competitive banking caused a sustained economic growth process and a catching up with neighboring England (WHITE, 1991).

2. The paper takes a rather favorable view on the potential impact of the European Monetary Union on economic growth in Europe. I agree as for the beneficial consequences of the opening up of financial markets, of the reduction of transaction costs, and of the abolishment of exchange rate risks. But in my opinion these arguments do not tell the whole story because they neglect some potential risks that European Monetary Union poses for economic growth: transaction costs savings due to the use of one currency have to be weighed against additional transaction costs arising from the replacement of national currencies with the new artificial European currency. Absolutely fixed exchange rates might cause additional

unemployment if national economies are hit by asymmetric real macroeconomic shocks and real wages are not perfectly flexible. The board of governors of the new European Central Bank might follow a more accommodating monetary policy and therefore produce a higher and more unstable inflation rate than some of the now existing national central banks. This, too, will reduce the European growth rate since in the long run inflation rates have inhibiting effects on national growth rates (HELLER, 1995, pp.281-286). Therefore, it is as yet an open question whether European Monetary Union will enhance or reduce European growth rates, and a lot will depend on the future monetary policy of the European System of Central Banks.

3. My last remark concerns the second part of the paper and the process of systemic transformation in eastern Europe. Here it is stated that it would be dangerous to fully liberalize the capital account. I suppose the reason for this verdict is a fear of extensive capital flight. But as long as international differences in real interest rates reflect differences in the marginal productivity of capital international capital movements are beneficial for both sides, that means for the capital receiving country and for the capital giving country as well. International capital movements are not beneficial if the condition mentioned above is not fulfilled and, for instance, different tax rates drive wedges between the marginal productivity of capital and real interest rates which differ from economy to economy. The result will be a misallocation of real capital (FUKAO and HANAZAKI, 1987, pp.57-73), but the reason for this are different tax policies and not capital movements per se, so the right policy advice might be to embrace tax harmonization and not capital controls. Furthermore, I cannot understand how foreign capital is to be attracted by transforming countries, if a repatriation of investments and profits into the sending country is prohibited by a not fully liberalized capital account.

To sum up, I am more optimistic than Paul Welfens about the potential role of an unregulated banking system for economic growth in Europe and more pessimistic about the probable growth effects of European Monetary Union. After all, a severely regulated banking system (in fact a one-tier banking system) and fixed exchange rates between national currencies were characteristics of the financial systems of socialist economies, and these characteristics might have contributed to the slowdown in economic growth in these countries. In my opinion this experience stands as a warning against too much regulation and intervention in financial markets.

References

DOWD, K. (1992), "Is Banking a Natural Monopoly?" *Kyklos*, Vol. 45, 379-392.

FUKAO, M. and HANAZAKI, M (1987), "Internationalisation of Financial Markets and the Allocation of Capital," *OECD Economic Studies*, Vol. 8, 35-92.

HELLER, D. (1995), "Inflation und Wachstum," *Quartalsheft der Schweizerischen Nationalbank: Geld, Währung und Konjunktur*, Vol. 13, 278-288.

SCHULER, K. (1992), "The World History of Free Banking: An Overview," in DOWD, K. (ed.), *The Experience of Free Banking*, Routledge, London, New York, 7-47.

WHITE, L. H. (1991), "Banking Without a Central Bank: Scotland Before 1844 as a 'Free Banking System'," in CAPIE, F. and WOOD, G. E. (eds.), *Unregulated Banking: Chaos or Order?*, Macmillan, London, 37-62.

B. Policy Options for Prudential Supervision in Stage Three of Monetary Union

Johannes Priesemann

1. Introduction[1]

With the beginning of Stage Three of Monetary Union, Europe will be faced with an unprecedented systemic change in monetary policy. Monetary policy will be carried out by the European System of Central Banks (ESCB), which will be composed of the European Central Bank (ECB) and the national central banks (NCBs) of the Member States. The responsibility for monetary stability will shift from national authorities to a Community institution. What are the consequences of this major systemic shift in the field of monetary policy for the area of prudential supervision? This presentation will deal with this question in the first place from an institutional angle. The discussion is focused on the interrelationship between the authorities responsible for the exercise of prudential supervision and the ESCB.

Following this institutional focus, a first part will elaborate on possible institutional frameworks for prudential supervision and central banks' involvement. In a second part the (few) specific provisions of the Treaty on European Union concerning prudential supervision are looked at in order to identify the institutional framework envisaged by the Treaty.

The term **"prudential supervision"** is used in this presentation in a broad sense. Prudential supervision is understood as the application of specific legislative provisions to enterprises active in the financial sector with the objective of ensuring the protection of customers (depositors, investors, those insured) and the stability of the financial system as a whole. The "toolkit" of the provisions usually covers the licensing of a financial enterprise, the vetting of its managers and shareholders (as well as of the shareholder or "group" structure) and the application of specific rules concerning the financial situation of the enterprises or groups of connected enterprises. In order to use these tools efficiently, supervisors are given far-reaching inspection powers and regularly receive a considerable amount of (confidential) information.

The notion is further understood as comprising the prudential supervision of all types of financial enterprises, i.e. credit institutions, investment firms and insurance undertakings. This breadth with respect to business activity is chosen for two reasons. Firstly, the borderlines of financial business are becoming more and more blurred. In Europe there are significant groups active in all three financial sectors ("financial conglomerates") and in some countries (e.g. Denmark, Norway and Sweden) the supervision of all three types of undertakings is combined in one authority. This should not be ignored. Secondly, the broad use of the term in this presentation reflects its use in the Treaty on European Union. In Article 105 (6) of the Treaty the term "prudential supervision of credit institutions and other financial institutions" includes the prudential supervision of insurance undertakings. As responsibility for the supervision of insurance undertakings will not be given to the ECB, these undertakings had to be explicitly excluded in that provision.

In this context I should like to stress that the provision of liquidity (be it under regular circumstances or in cases of crises at individual institutions or market turmoil, the latter often referred to as "lending of last resort") does not fall within the remit of prudential supervision but rather within monetary policy. Furthermore, market supervision, as opposed to the supervision of individual firms, is left to one side as central banks' involvement remains the exception rather than the rule.

Similarly excluded from the notion of prudential supervision as understood in this paper is the task of payment systems oversight. This task, which is often formally or informally conferred upon central banks, is related to the stability and functioning of a system rather than the safety and soundness of an institution. Consequently, the techniques and approaches of payment systems oversight and of prudential supervision differ. However, in an ideal world both would contribute to systemic stability.

2. Institutional Models for Prudential Supervision and Central Banks' Involvement

2.1 Central Banks and *Banking* Supervision

In defining the institutional setting for prudential supervision, countries have chosen different solutions. These solutions reflect the traditional approaches of public regulation and the nature of the financial system in a country. For instance, it comes as no surprise that until very recently a universal banking country like Germany lacked a specialized investment firms supervisor. One of the most frequently discussed questions in the context of possible institutional frameworks is the form and degree of central bank involvement in *banking* supervision[2] (apart from the question of whether central banking and public prudential supervision is desirable at all[3] - which is left to one side in this presentation because the abolition of central banks and prudential supervision does not appear to be likely, at least in the foreseeable future in Europe). This question is also at the center of interest in the institutional discussion related to the specific tasks of the ESCB.

The argument in the literature concerns in the first place the question of whether or not the central bank should be vested with the task of the exercise of prudential supervision of credit institutions. The traditional arguments for and against a separation of monetary policy functions and *banking supervision* can be briefly summed up as follows:[4]

For an integration:[5]

(i) prudential supervision is a "natural extension" of central banking;

(ii) combination of the two tasks entails economies of scope (use of the same expertise and information to fulfill the two different tasks);

(iii) information is used (and gathered) more efficiently;

(iv) the central bank is responsible for the systemic stability and necessarily involved in crisis management and lender of last resort activities, for which it needs prudential supervisory information;

(v) the central bank's role as payment systems overseer necessitates its involvement in the prudential supervision of the participants in the payment system.

For a separation:

(i) combination of the functions may lead to conflicts of interest because the objectives of the two functions are not necessarily compatible (e.g. favoring the policy objective of maintaining the stability of the financial system may compromise monetary stability);

(ii) failure in the prudential function may undermine the credibility of the central bank in its monetary function;

(iii) combination of functions leads to an overly powerful institution;

(iv) the exercise of public tasks entailing the imposition of sovereign acts (such as licensing) subject to judicial review may be difficult to reconcile with the desired independence of a monetary authority.

Any evaluation of the pros and cons of each argument will necessarily remain judgmental. What is clear, however, is that in the real world the argument is undecided: in a survey on 27 countries GOODHART and SCHOENMAKER (1993)[6] classify fourteen countries as having the monetary and supervisory functions combined and thirteen countries as having the two functions separated. Even the apparently better inflation track record of the countries favoring the separation found by GOODHART and SCHOENMAKER (1993)[7] does not lead them to conclude that the functions should necessarily be separated. Their final conclusion is that "a central bank's involvement in supervision does not necessarily weaken its stance on monetary policy". Other factors, such as a country's banking and financial systems, are viewed as having probably more influence on the conduct of monetary policy.[8]

GOODHART and SCHOENMAKER (1995) confirm the conclusion that "there are no overwhelming arguments for either model".[9] However, based on a survey of bank failures and the funding of rescue measures they identify a tendency for a decreasing central bank involvement in the (organization of the) funding of bank rescues. Assuming the principle that "*he who pays the piper calls the tune*", Goodhart and Schoenmaker identify the type of funding for rescues (central bank and commercial banks versus explicit deposit insurance/government) as a possible major determining factor for the institutional arrangements for prudential supervision. At the same time they acknowledge that even in a separated system there will remain significant central bank involvement in prudential supervision.[10]

I conclude, therefore, that banking supervision *can* be exercised by the central bank but *must* not necessarily be exercised by the central bank. The real practice appears to be more nuanced. A black and white classification of institutional models[11] into the two boxes "separating" and "combining" the monetary and prudential functions might miss some important aspects of central bank involvement in prudential supervision in countries where the two functions are seen as separated.[12] The following section will therefore look at some specific examples of involvement by central banks in banking supervision in "separating countries".

2.2 Examples of the Central Bank's Involvement in Banking Supervision in Countries with Separate Authorities

MICHELACCI (1993) has conducted a comparative analysis of central bank involvement in the supervision of the banking system in nine countries.[13] He concludes that "*even in the countries where an agency different from and independent of the central bank is entrusted with prudential supervisory powers, the central bank keeps responsibilities relating to prudential supervision*".[14] His analysis is based on a split of the supervisory "toolkit" into the elements of "*structural controls, liquidity controls, prudential controls, intervention in banking crises and inspection powers*". In many instances, national legislation or practice requires the separate prudential supervisory agency to cooperate closely with the national central bank.

The same picture evolves from the country reports contained in the report "Banking Supervision in the European Community" of a working group of the ECU Institute under the chairmanship of Jean-Victor Louis (ECU INSTITUTE 1995).[15] In its recommendations the group concludes that "*the examples of Germany, Belgium, Denmark and France, the Member States in which the central banks do not have direct responsibility for prudential supervision, show that close collaboration between the monetary authority and the authority responsible for prudential supervision is essential*".[16]

The involvement of the central bank in prudential supervision in "separating countries" takes the following forms:

- a general obligation for the banking supervisory agency and the NCB to cooperate closely (e.g. Belgium, Germany);
- consultation of the NCB in matters of prudential supervisory rule-making (e.g. Belgium, Germany);
- the collection and evaluation of prudential returns by the NCB and access by the NCB to information collected for banking supervisory purposes (e.g. Belgium, Germany);
- consultation of the NCB by the supervisory agency in cases of individual measures, such as the granting or withdrawal of a license (e.g. Belgium, Germany, Sweden);
- the provision of information, consultation or close cooperation in the case of acute crisis (e.g. Belgium, Germany, Sweden).

It appears that at least Belgium and Germany follow an institutional model in which the central bank is involved in the banking supervisory policy-making, has access to the relevant supervisory information and has its say when individual measures are considered. The final word and responsibility for sovereign acts and prudential rule-making, however, rests with the separate authority and/or parliament. This system can be characterized as ***separation combined with close cooperation***. The central bank is kept informed about the financial situation of the financial institutions, the central bank follows and influences prudential rule-making, and coordination in the crisis management is provided for. Vesting the separate authority with the ultimate responsibility for prudential supervision avoids the central bank's reputation being compromised in the event of failure.

2.3 European Prudential Supervisory Legislation and its Impact on the Institutional Framework in Stage Two of Monetary Union

So far, the discussion has focused on *banking* supervision and on national contexts. This section discusses the impact of EU legislation on the organizational set-up of prudential supervision (including also investment firm and insurance supervision) in Stage Two of Monetary Union.

At the outset the subsidiarity principle (Article 3b of the Treaty on European Union) has to be recalled, according to which the Community shall only act if and so far as the objectives of the proposed action cannot be sufficiently achieved by the Member States. The absence of a centralized authority carrying out specific tasks in the area of prudential supervision at Community level reflects the application of the subsidiarity principle.

The basis for the specific secondary legislation lies in Articles 52 and 59 of the Treaty, which enshrine the freedom of establishment and the freedom to provide services on a cross-border basis. For the secondary prudential legislation, the Community has chosen an approach of minimum harmonization and of mutual recognition of the supervisory practices and of authorization ("single license").[17] Thus, prudential supervision is carried out in all three sectors according to the principle of home-country control. The Member State of establishment of an institution is responsible for the prudential supervision of that institution and all its European branches and cross-border activities.

In the area of *banking* services, the ground has been laid by the Second Banking Co-ordination Directive and a number of specific directives harmonizing the basic rules of prudential supervision in the banking sector (notably the Own Funds Directive, the Solvency Ratio Directive, the Large Exposures Directive and the Directive on the Consolidated Supervision of Credit Institutions). In the sector of *securities* services, a similar result has been achieved through the Investment Services Directive and the Capital Adequacy Directive, which is the specific directive on the prudential standards to be maintained by investment firms (and also by credit institutions carrying out securities business on a significant scale). In the *insurance* sector, the single market has been accomplished by the Third Life and the Third Non-Life Directives.

The Community legislation does not contain specific requirements concerning the institutional set-up of the supervisory authorities. Therefore, different models can be found ranging from one authority competent for all three sectors (e.g. in Denmark), via combinations (banking and investment firm supervision by one agency, insurance supervision by another, like in Belgium), to a separation mirroring the different financial sectors (e.g. in Germany and the United Kingdom).

It should be noted, however, that EU legislation contains certain obligations for cooperation at the EU level. Authorities are obliged to cooperate closely in the supervision of EU branches - cf., for example, Article 7 of the First Banking Co-ordination Directive (77/780/EEC) in the case of banking supervisors, and Article 23 of the Investment Services Directive (93/22/EEC), which applies, under certain conditions, to supervisors of all three sectors.

Under certain circumstances, specific obligations for cooperation and the sharing of information are laid down in the case of credit institutions, investment firms and insurance undertakings operating in a "group" of financial undertakings - cf. Article 7 (4) of the Directive on the Supervision of Credit Institutions on a Consolidated Basis (92/30/EEC) and Article 7 (3), eighth indent, of the Capital Adequacy Directive (93/6/EEC).

However, it has to be recognized that the provisions concerning cooperation may have certain loopholes. For instance: why does Article 7 (3), eighth indent, of the Capital Adequacy Directive not require the sharing of information between the authorities as the Directive on consolidated supervision does? What kind of cooperation applies in the case of an insurance-led group?[18]

Furthermore, EU legislation does not oblige the prudential supervisory authorities to cooperate with the national central banks. Such cooperation is at the Member States' discretion.

To sum up, the situation can be characterized as follows:

- EU legislation leaves the prudential supervision at the national level and leaves the national legislator virtually complete freedom as regards the organizational framework of supervision;
- EU legislation stipulates Union-wide free branching and free provision of services on the basis of home-country control;
- EU legislation stipulates close cooperation between supervisory authorities of the same sector and also, under certain conditions, cross-sectoral cooperation;
- there is no obligation to provide for cooperation between prudential supervisors and national central banks.

3. The Model Envisaged in the Maastricht Treaty

As mentioned in the introduction, the creation of the ESCB will constitute a systemic shift in monetary policy. At the same time, this is a constitutional quantum leap for Europe. The conduct of monetary policy will be assigned to a Community institution. On the other hand, there is no substantial change foreseen for the exercise of prudential supervision, which will continue to be carried out according to the same principles as in Stage Two.

As the ESCB will carry out the central bank functions in the EU, it ensues that it may have, in principle, the same need for cooperation with prudential supervisors as a national central bank. Similarly, all arguments for and against the involvement of the ESCB in prudential supervisory matters will apply as they do at the national level for any national central bank.

The use of prudential supervisory information could be conducive to the day-to-day exercise of monetary policy operations and could also enhance the risk management of the ESCB's balance sheet. In the event of liquidity shortages at individual institutions or in the entire system, speedy access to detailed and up-to-date information may be crucial for decision-making within the ESCB. It should be noted that the ultimate responsibility for the provision of liquidity is reflected in the ESCB's involvement in the operation of payment systems. Article 105 (2) of the Treaty mentions the promotion of the smooth operation of payment systems as one of the basic tasks of the ESCB. Also in this context, access to supervisory information and close cooperation with those responsible for the supervision of the participants in a payment systems may be invaluable assets for the ESCB.

At the same time, the ESCB will have to be aware of the impact of its monetary policy on the financial systems in the participating Member States. As pointed out by SCHOENMAKER (1995),[19] the ECB has to be familiar with the different financial and banking systems in the EU Member States in order to assess the impact of monetary policy measures. Schoenmaker refers in this context to the role the financial structure plays in the monetary transmission channel and stresses the interdependence between monetary and financial stability.

The relationship between the ESCB and prudential supervisors in the third stage will have to reflect these mutual needs and cross-ramifications. The following sections will analyze in some detail the specific Treaty provisions in the light of this need for mutual cooperation.

3.1 Contributions of the ESCB to the Conduct of Prudential Supervision

Article 105 (5) of the Treaty is the basic provision spelling out the tasks of the ESCB in prudential supervision. It obliges the ESCB "*to contribute to the smooth conduct of policies pursued by the competent authorities relating to the prudential supervision of credit institutions and the stability of the financial system*".

The wording of this provision is relatively vague and leaves scope for interpretation. The ECU INSTITUTE (1995) distinguishes between a "modest" and a "bolder" interpretation.[20] According to the modest interpretation, the ESCB's role would be confined to being involved in the prudential (banking) supervisory policy-making. The advice which the ECB may give according to Article 25.1 of the ESCB/ECB Statute in the area of policy-making would be its minimum contribution to prudential supervisory policies. The bolder interpretation would give the ECB more of a coordinating role. Article 105 (5) of the Treaty would also oblige the ESCB to take into account the impact of measures taken in the monetary area on the prudential supervisory policies and, more general, the stability of the financial system.

Article 105 (5) of the Treaty has to be seen as the specific provision which obliges the ESCB to develop an awareness of prudential supervisory and systemic issues and to conduct its policies in full consciousness of these issues. The wording of the provision gives the ESCB the necessary flexibility to develop its contributions to the prudential policies over time in pace with the increasing experience of the functioning of a single monetary policy.[21]

3.2 Contributions of the Prudential Supervisors to the ESCB's Tasks

The Treaty does not provide for any contributions by the prudential supervisors to the ESCB's task. At first sight, this appears to be a clear deficiency of the Treaty. For instance, it seems as if the ESCB will have no access at all to supervisory information. Prudential supervisory authorities are not obliged to cooperate with the ESCB or the ECB.

The Treaty relies in this respect on the existing cooperation at national level between national supervisors and NCBs. This reliance works clearly towards a decentralized operation of the ESCB's tasks. It can be (or is) assumed that at national level all relevant information is available to the NCB. It is, however, a valid question to what extent the ECB and all NCBs dealing with an institution should have access to supervisory information held at national level and whether the national supervisory authorities should not be obliged to cooperate with the ECB.

In this context, the so-called "BCCI Directive"[22] should be borne in mind, which allows the transmission of confidential information from competent (supervisory) authorities to "*central banks and other bodies with a similar function in their capacity as monetary authorities*" and to payment systems overseers. The transmission of such information is left to the discretion of the Member States' competent authorities. Interestingly, the possibility is foreseen for the transmission not only of banking supervisory information but also of confidential information at the disposal of supervisors of investment firms, insurance undertakings and mutual funds.

In summary, it can thus be concluded that the Treaty does not provide for specific contributions of the national prudential supervisory authorities to the tasks of the ESCB. Secondary legislation leaves it to the discretion of the Member States whether and to what extent supervisors and NCBs should cooperate and share information. In my view, there might be a need to revise this situation in the light of experience gathered in Stage Three of Monetary Union, or even before.

3.3 Advisory Functions

The ECB will exercise specific **advisory functions** in the area of prudential supervision. Article 25.1 of the ESCB/ECB Statute entitles the ECB to offer its advice to the Council, the Commission and the competent authorities of the Member States. The subject of the advice is the "*scope and implementation of Community legislation relating to the prudential supervision of credit institutions and to the stability of the financial system*". It can be disputed[23] whether this advisory task is an exhaustive description of the tasks laid down in Article 105 (5) of the Treaty, a specific formulation of the general advisory functions of the ESCB laid down in Article 105 (4), last sub-paragraph of the Treaty, which entitles the ECB to deliver opinions on matters in its field of competence, or (just) one possible contribution of the E(S)CB to the smooth conduct of supervisory policies.

Depending on the answer to the question of whether Article 105 (5) of the Treaty constitutes a "field of competence of the ESB" in the area of prudential supervision, the ECB will have general advisory functions in that area derived from Article 105 (4) of the Treaty in addition to the specific advisory function laid down in Article 25.1 of the Statute. A general advisory function would not be confined to issues related to the "scope and implementation of Community legislation", but also extend to national legislation and questions of a more general nature and on which the Community has not legislated.

3.4 Option to Vest the ECB with Specific Tasks

Article 105 (6) of the Treaty contains an "option" to confer upon the ECB "specific tasks concerning policies relating to the prudential supervision of credit institutions and other financial institutions with the exception of insurance undertakings". The exercise of this option is subject to a strict condition: the Council's decision requires unanimity of all Member States of the European Union (i.e. including those not participating in Monetary Union). In addition, it should be borne in mind that Member States will exercise this option only in the light of the subsidiarity principle. Thus, for political reasons, the likelihood of a shift to a model in which the ECB has specific prudential supervisory tasks appears to be relatively low.

It should further be borne in mind that vesting the ECB with specific prudential supervisory tasks will inevitably raise the issue of its accountability and appeal to court against the sovereign acts it may take in the exercise of these tasks. These institutional implications should not be underestimated.[24]

The ECU INSTITUTE (1995)[25] strongly recommends using the option laid down in Article 105 (6). In addition it suggests[26] four principles in relation to the exercise of prudential supervision: no total liberalization of prudential supervision at Community level, no total centralization, no total decentralization and no status quo. Multinational groups of companies should be subject to exclusive control by a Community system managed by the ECB. On the basis of objective criteria (in order to avoid the risks of "supervisory shopping"), institutions would have the free choice between a Community control and a national supervision system.[27]

SCHOENMAKER (1995)[28] discusses a similar approach, put forward by the Centre for European Policy Studies in 1994, which would also lead to a two-tier structure segregating small to medium-sized banks (supervised and chartered nationally) and large banks (chartered and supervised by the ECB in addition to their national supervision). In addition to the institutional problems linked to accountability, he sees the threat of a competitive deregulation and doubts whether the ECB's staff - being far removed from the national financial centers - could cope with supervising institutions in another Member State. Therefore, he does not assume or suggest that the option laid down in Article 105 (6) of the Treaty will be exercised by the Council in the first years of the Third Stage.

Assuming a lender of last resort function of the ESCB and focusing on its involvement in payment systems, VIVES (1993)[29] suggests that the ECB should have authority in liquidity matters. The ECB would share supervisory powers with the national authorities but would have the primacy. This suggestion, however, would face the same questions as the tiered banking structure involving a central supervisor.

4. Challenges for Supervisors

The focus of this presentation has been on institutional issues. Developments in the financial sector and their possible impact on the exercise and content of prudential supervision[30] have not been looked at. Similarly, the impact of future developments of the supervisory framework is not analyzed in any detail in the foregoing sections. I do not expect that these issues will have an impact on the **institutional** supervisory framework at Community level in the short term. However, in the longer term certain industry and supervisory developments may trigger a discussion of their institutional consequences.

In the first place, it can, for instance, be argued that the increasing importance of **financial conglomerates,**[31] in which enterprises of all three sectors are active in one group, may pose problems which can no longer be addressed by a plethora of supervisors cooperating within and across countries. A merger between the supervisory authorities may be more than just desirable. Consequently, the exclusion of insurance undertakings in Article 105 (6) of the Treaty might have to be reconsidered.[32]

The discussion on how to regulate **derivatives** has been led by both supervisors[33] and central bankers[34] at a global level. The discussion does not only show that derivative products in particular call for international cooperation between supervisors, but is a classic example of the link between prudential supervision (understood as an activity concerned with micro-prudential issues) and central banking (concerned with macro-prudential issues). Issues like the securitization, disintermediation and increasing importance of institutional investors[35] are similarly of interest to central bankers and prudential supervisors alike. Once again, the fact that major financial groups are active not only in different countries but also in different sectors and organized according to a plethora of national supervisory rules may give rise to a call for even stronger internationally integrated supervision. It will have to be seen which role the ESCB and ECB will play in this international discussion.

5. Conclusion

The Maastricht Treaty does not provide for a role for the ESCB or ECB in day-to-day supervision, which remains a national competence. The ESCB has to take account of systemic and prudential supervisory issues and to contribute with its policies to the smooth conduct of the policies in this area pursued by the national authorities at the national level. The provisions of the Treaty give the ESCB the necessary flexibility to identify, in the light of the experience with the single currency, the specific contributions to prudential supervision which might become necessary.

The ECB has an advisory role in the prudential supervisory rule-making and may be vested with specific supervisory tasks in the future. Due to the absence of any obligation for the national supervisors to cooperate with the ESCB and/or the ECB, the framework chosen by the Maastricht Treaty is unique. This lack may work to the disadvantage of the smooth functioning of the system and there may arise a need to revise this situation sooner or later.

I hope to have shown that the discussion of the ideal interplay between central banking and prudential supervision is still open. Neither model, separation or integration, has won the field in literature or in real life. In the Third Stage of Monetary Union, the "quantum leap" in monetary policy is not planned to trigger, for the time being, a similar leap in prudential supervision. The ESCB will start in a unique environment, with the model coming closer to that of the separation of functions with close cooperation. However, amendments to the framework might still be necessary, as the mere possibility of providing information to the ECB (as provided for in the BCCI Directive) might fall short of the needs of the ESCB.

Viewed globally, there are substantial challenges for prudential supervision lying ahead (financial conglomerates, derivatives, securitization and disintermediation), which may trigger the need to reconsider the institutional framework of prudential supervision independently of Monetary Union. These challenges may call for further centralization. Similarly, the "exercise" and possible modification of the option laid down in Article 105 (6) of the Treaty might have to be considered one day.

Endnotes

1 Revised version of a paper presented at the Conference on "Banking, International Capital Flows and Growth in Europe", University of Potsdam, Potsdam, 13th and 14th October 1995. The author is working at the European Monetary Institute on Banking Supervision and Risk Analysis. The author would like to thank the conference participants, notably Ms. Sydney Key, the discussant, and Messrs. E. Philip Davis and Mauro Grande for useful comments. However, any errors are those of the author; likewise, the views expressed are those of the author and not necessarily those of the European Monetary Institute.

2 A rich discussion of this issue is contained in BRUNI (1993).

3 The usefulness of public regulation is questioned notably by the free banking school; see, for example, SELGIN (1989), BENSTON, and the discussion of the arguments against banking regulation in DAVIS (1993).

4 See, for instance, de SWAAN, p. 332; QUINN (1993); GOODHART and SCHOENMAKER in BRUNI (1993), p. 354 ff.; ANGELINI and PASSACANTANDO in BRUNI (1993), p. 453 ff.; SCHOENMAKER (1995); HELLER, p. 269 ff.

5 GREENSPAN (1994) argues strongly in favor of a central bank involvement in banking supervision. He feels (pp. 3,4) that a single regulator would "*inevitably have a long-term bias against risk-taking and innovation*" as he receives no credit for contributions to economic growth. This argument relates the institutional incentive structure of prudential supervision to the degree of innovation and might merit some empirical analysis.

6 Loc. cit., appendix 2, p. 396.

7 In Appendix 2 (loc. cit.) GOODHART and SCHOENMAKER (1993) give average annual inflation rates for twenty-seven countries in the periods from 1980-91 and 1980-87. The figures tend to show lower inflation for the countries classified as "separating" the two functions.

8 Loc. cit. p. 398; this conclusion is apparently shared by QUINN and de SWAAN (loc. cit.).

9 P. 556.

10 P. 555.

[11] The difficulties of making a clear-cut separation can be best demonstrated by the example of the United States, which, though the Federal Reserve Bank has certain supervisory functions, has been classified by GOODHART and SCHOENMAKER (1993) as a "separating" country (loc. cit. Appendix 2). GOODHART and SCHOENMAKER (1995) maintain this classification (Appendix, p. 559) but mention the supervisory functions of the Federal Reserve Board. In their conclusion they ask whether a change from a combined to a separated system would "*make much difference to the practical realities of central banking*" (GOODHART and SCHOENMAKER, 1995, p. 556). I would answer this question in the affirmative as far as the "mud flung" is concerned when failures occur and with a "maybe" with respect to the central bank's involvement in terms of access to information and crisis management.

[12] This aspect is also stressed by GREENSPAN (1994), p. 5.

[13] MICHELACCI (1993); the analysis covers Belgium, France, Germany, Greece, Italy, Japan, Spain, Sweden and the United Kingdom.

[14] Loc. cit. p. 2.

[15] ECU INSTITUTE (1995).

[16] ECU INSTITUTE (1995), p. 69.

[17] The approach is described in further detail in DASSESSE, ISAACS and PENN (1994), p. 25 ff., with further references.

[18] Recently, a proposal has been tabled by the Commission covering, inter alia, this subject: "Proposal for a European Parliament and Council Directive on the supplementary supervision of insurance undertakings in an insurance group" (COM(95) 406 final of 4th October 1995). Article 7 of this proposal suggests a certain cooperation and exchange of information in cases where credit institutions and insurance undertakings are "related undertakings".

[19] SCHOENMAKER (1995), p. 43 ff.

[20] ECU INSTITUTE (1995), p. 45.

[21] KINSELLA in CURRIE and WHITLEY (1994) criticizes this "evolutionary approach", arguing that the supervisory framework chosen in the Maastricht Treaty may lead to a "regulatory deficit". He sees a "compelling need to strengthen and develop the European dimension" of prudential supervision.

[22] Directive 95/26/EEC of 29th June 1995, OJ No. L 168 of 18th July 1995, p. 7 ff.; the relevant provisions, amending the prudential legislation in all three sectors of the financial industry, are laid down in Art. 4 No. 4, 5 and 7 of the Directive.

[23] See, for instance, the discussion of this issue in ECU INSTITUTE (1995), p. 45.

[24] SCHOENMAKER (1995), p. 41, describes the issue of accountability as "thorny" and points to the possible ramifications for the ECB's independence.

[25] ECU INSTITUTE (1995), p. 67.

[26] Loc. cit. p. 51 ff.

[27] Loc. cit. p. 63.

[28] SCHOENMAKER (995), p. 40 ff.

[29] VIVES, in BRUNI (1993), p. 530 ff.

[30] Most eminently: the intensive discussion of the possibility to allow the use of banks' internal models determine supervisory capital requirements for market risk, connected with BASLE COMMITTEE ON BANKING SUPERVISION (1995a and, more specific, 1995b).

[31] In the area of financial conglomerates, a "tripartite" (i.e. including banking, securities and insurance supervisors) group with global representation has elaborated a report: "The Supervision of Financial Conglomerates", BANK FOR INTERNATIONAL SETTLEMENTS, 1995); WEINEL (1996) gives a detailed analysis of regulatory problems.

[32] The working group of the ECU Institute favors both merging supervisory authorities (ECU INSTITUTE, 1995, p. 64) and the abrogation of the words "with the exclusion of insurance undertakings" in Art. 105 (6) of the Treaty.

[33] For an overview see BASLE COMMITTEE ON BANKING SUPERVISION (1994).

[34] Cf., for example, EURO-CURRENCY STANDING COMMITTEE (1994).

[35] For the impact of these issues on monetary policy, see DAVIS (1995), with further references.

References

ANGELINI, P. and PASSACANTANDO, F. (1993), "Central banks' role in the payment system and its relationship with banking supervision," in BRUNI, F. (ed.), *Prudential Regulation, Supervision and Monetary Policy: Theory, International Comparison and the ESCB Role*, Proceedings of the Conference organized by the 'Paolo Baffi' Centre for Monetary and Financial Economics, held at Bocconi University, Milan, February 5th 1993, 453-491.

BANK FOR INTERNATIONAL SETTLEMENTS (1995), *The supervision of Financial Conglomerates*, Basle.

BASLE COMMITTEE ON BANKING SUPERVISION (1994), *Prudential supervision of banks' derivatives activities*, Bank for International Settlements, Basle.

BASLE COMMITTEE ON BANKING SUPERVISION (1995a), *Planned supplement to the Capital Accord to incorporate market risks*, Bank for International Settlements, Basle.

BASLE COMMITTEE ON BANKING SUPERVISION (1995b), *An internal model-based approach to market risk capital requirements*, Bank for International Settlements, Basle.

BENSTON, G. J. (1991), "Does Bank Regulation Produce Stability? Lessons from the United States," in CAPIE, F. and WOOD, G. H. (eds.), *Unregulated Banking, Chaos or Order?*, Macmillan, London.

BRUNI, F. (ed.) (1993), *Prudential Regulation, Supervision and Monetary Policy: Theory, International Comparison and the ESCB Role*, Proceedings of the Conference organized by the 'Paolo Baffi' Centre for Monetary and Financial Economics, held at Bocconi University, Milan, 5th February 1993.

COMMISSION OF THE EUROPEAN COMMUNITIES (1995), "Proposal for a European Parliament and Council Directive on the supplementary supervision of insurance undertakings in an insurance group," document COM(95) 406 final of 4th October 1995, Brussels/Luxembourg, (OJ No. C341 of 19.12.95, p. 16ff.).

CURRIE, D. and WHITLEY, J. (eds.) (1994), *EMU after Maastricht: Transition and Revaluation*, Lothian Foundation Press, London.

DASSESSE, M., ISAACS, S. and PENN, G. (1994), *EC Banking Law*, 2nd edition, Lloyds of London Press, London.

DAVIS, E. P. (1995), "Institutional Investors, Unstable Financial Markets and Monetary Policy," paper presented at the SUERF Conference, Thun, Switzerland, October 1995, also available as Special Paper No. 75, London School of Economics, Financial Markets Group, London, November 1995.

DAVIS, E. P. (1993), "Problems of Banking Regulation - an EC Perspective," Paper presented at the conference on 'Economic Policy Issues in Financial Integration', Helsinki University, 20th-21st September 1993.

ECU INSTITUTE (1995), "Banking Supervision in the European Community - Institutional Aspects," report of a working group of the ECU Institute under the chairmanship of Jean-Victor LOUIS, Brussels 1995.

EURO-CURRENCY STANDING COMMITTEE (1994), *Macroeconomic and Monetary Policy Issues Raised by the Growth of Derivatives Markets*, (Hannoun Report), Bank for International Settlements, Basle.

GOODHART, C. and SCHOENMAKER, D. (1993), "Institutional Separation between supervisory and monetary agencies," in BRUNI, F. (ed.), *Prudential Regulation, Supervision and Monetary Policy: Theory, International Comparison and the ESCB Role*, Proceedings of the Conference organized by the 'Paolo Baffi' Centre for Monetary and Financial Economics, held at Bocconi University, Milan, 5th February 1993, 353-439.

GOODHART, C. and SCHOENMAKER, D. (1995), "Should the functions of monetary policy and banking supervision be separated?," *Oxford Economic Papers*, Vol. 47, 539-560.

GREENSPAN, A. (1994), "Testimony before the Committee on Banking, Housing and Urban Affairs," United States Senate, 2nd March 1994.

HELLER, H. R., "Prudential supervision and monetary policy," in FRENKEL, J. A. and GOLDSTEIN, M. (eds.), *International Financial Policy: Essays in Honour of Jacques J. Polak*, IMF, Washington D.C.

KINSELLA, R. (1994), "The European Central Bank and the Emerging EC 'Regulatory Deficit'," in CURRIE and WHITLEY.

MICHELACCI, C. (1993), "Central bank involvement in the supervision of the banking system and of financial markets: a comparative analysis," Bocconi University, Milan.

QUINN, B. (1993), "The Bank of England's role in prudential supervision," speech given at a Westminster and City Programmes Conference on 'Re-examining City Regulation', London, 24th March 1993.

SCHOENMAKER, D. (1995), "Banking supervision in Stage Three of EMU, The Single Market in Banking: From 1992 to EMU," CEPS Research Report No. 17, Brussels.

SELGIN, G. A. (1989), "Legal Restrictions, Financial Weakening, and the Lender of Last Resort," *Cato Journal*, Vol. 9, No. 2, 427 ff.

de SWAAN, T., "Prudential supervision: a central bank function?," in DE NEDERLANDSCHE BANK (ed.), *Monetary Stability through International Co-operation: Essays in Honour of André Száz.*

VIVES, X. (1993), "The supervisory function of the European System of Central Banks," in BRUNI, F. (ed.), *Prudential Regulation, Supervision and Monetary Policy: Theory, International Comparison and the ESCB Role*, Proceedings of the Conference organized by the 'Paolo Baffi' Centre for Monetary and Financial Economics, held at Bocconi University, Milan, 5th February 1993, 523-532.

WEINEL, M. (1996), "Finanzkonglomerat im Europäischen Binnenmarkt - eine aufsichtsrechtliche Analyse," Gabler, Wiesbaden.

[illegible] (1983), [illegible] ... Stock Market in Berlin ... [illegible] Brussels.

SELGIN, G. A. (1988), The [illegible]

[illegible]

[illegible]

Comments on

Policy Options for Prudential Supervision in Stage Three of Monetary Union

Sydney J. Key[1]

Johannes Priesemann's paper succinctly sets forth the issues regarding prudential supervision and a future European Central Bank (ECB) and European System of Central Banks (ESCB). In keeping with the tradition of solidarity among central bankers, I have no real disagreement with his analysis. In this comment, I would like to supplement the discussion in Mr. Priesemann's paper by addressing three issues.

First, I would like to consider whether, even without a supranational central bank, the EC approach of mutual recognition and home-country control for regulation and supervision of banks might move toward greater harmonization of rules and increased supervisory coordination and to suggest that establishment of the ECB may create additional pressures for such changes, regardless of whether the ECB itself becomes a forum for coordination. Second, I would like to note a further argument in support of a supervisory role for central banks that was set forth by Chairman Greenspan in testimony before the US Congress in 1994. Third, I would like to mention briefly a couple of points about US Federal Reserve Districts and accountability of central banks that may be useful to keep in mind when making comparisons between the ESCB and the US Federal Reserve System.

1. Supervisory Coordination Within the European Community

The EC approach of mutual recognition for financial services provided through branches or across borders is based on harmonization of essential rules and, where harmonization has not occurred or has occurred only in very general terms, on use of *home*-country rules - see Figure b1 (KEY, 1989). This approach goes well beyond the widely used principle of national treatment, which involves the nondiscriminatory application of *host*-country rules. With regard to the separate but related issue of supervisory authority, the EC relies on home-country control, that is, the administration of rules by home-country authorities.

Figure b1 EC Approach to Regulation and Supervision of Financial Institutions

RULES

-- Host-country rules		
-- Home-country rules	}	
	}	**MUTUAL RECOGNITION**
-- Harmonized rules	}	

ADMINISTRATION Of RULES

-- Host-country supervisor		
-- Home-country supervisor	}	**HOME-COUNTRY CONTROL**
-- Supranational entity		

The European Community has been able to rely on home-country rules and supervision because its harmonizing measures are different from what has been achieved beyond the Community in two significant respects. First, they are legally binding as part of the body of supranational EC law, as opposed to informal agreements among, for example, bank supervisors of the major industrial countries. Second, the harmonization within the Community is much broader than that which has been achieved beyond its borders, where the major negotiated harmonization of rules involves the Basle Accord on risk-based capital standards, now expanded to include market risk. Besides capital standards, EC banking legislation also deals with matters such as bank ownership of nonfinancial institutions, bank accounting standards, major shareholders and changes in share ownership, large exposures, consolidated supervision, deposit insurance, and, in future, perhaps bankruptcy rules. (A longstanding Commission proposal with regard to bankruptcy rules for financial institutions has recently been reactivated.) Moreover, harmonizing measures in other areas, such as competition policy and company law, also affect the banking sector.

In addition, within the Community, several existing fora - the Banking Advisory Committee (BAC), the Groupe de Contact, and the Banking Supervisory Subcommittee of the European Monetary Institute (EMI) Council - facilitate cooperation and coordination with regard to bank regulation and supervision and thereby play an important role in making the EC's home-country approach work. (The Banking Supervisory Subcommittee of the EMI Council was formerly a subcommittee of the Committee of Governors of EC Central Banks and, in Stage Three, is likely to become a subcommittee of the Governing Council of the ECB.) To some extent, membership and functions of these groups overlap. Broadly speaking, the BAC deals with policy issues in formulation and implementation of EC financial services legislation, the Groupe de Contact deals with practical supervisory issues, including problems with individual institutions, and the Banking Supervisory Subcommittee focuses on so-called macro-prudential issues, particularly in relation to economic and monetary union (EMU) (see Figure b2).

For example, the Groupe de Contact was the principal forum for work by Community banking supervisors on implementing the practical arrangements for home-country control. Initially, consideration was given to drawing up what would have amounted to a single Communitywide Memorandum of Understanding (MOU) governing the allocation of specific supervisory responsibilities among supervisory authorities of the Member States, but it was decided that it would be preferable to use a network of bilateral MOUs instead. The French-German MOU, which relies heavily on the exchange of information between supervisory authorities, served as a model for many of the other agreements.

Figure b2 Major Coordination Fora in Banking Supervision Relevant to the EC

(Reprinted with permission from VAN DEN BERGH, M., PEARSON, P. and SMITS, R., "Institutional Arrangements," in VAN EMPEL, Martijn and SMITS, René (eds.), *Banking and EC Law: Commentary,* Amsterdam Financial Series, Kluwer Law and Taxation Publishers.)

World-wide

International Conference of Banking Supervisors
(meeting of banking supervision officials from around the world, held every even year)

G10*

Basle Committee on Banking Supervision
- established in 1974
- prepared 1975 'Concordat' (an attribution of supervisory responsibilities with respect to international banks), revised in 1983 (principle of consolidated supervision), supplemented in 1990 with arrangements an information flows between banking supervisory authorities;
- prepared 1988 Basle Capital Adequacy Framework (solvency ratio for international banks);
- adopted 1992 Minimum Standards for supervision of international banking groups and their cross-border establishments.

EC

Banking Advisory Committee[1]
- established in 1977;
- assists Commission in preparing EC banking supervision regulation;
- consists of high-ranking officials from central banks, supervisory agencies (Belgium, Denmark, Germany) and finance departments, plus Commission officials;
- responsible for solvency, liquidity and profitability 'observation ratios' which form(ed) the basis for 'observance ratios' (to be) adopted in EC banking regulation;
- in the same composition but with different organizational and voting arrangements acts as a regulatory committee with respects to technical amendments of EC directives and application of 'reciprocity' rules.

Contact Group[2]
- formed in 1972;
- consists of central bank or supervisory agency officials (plus Commission representative for non-confidential meetings);
- conduit for exchange of information on individual cases;
- conducts surveys on banking regulation with a view to harmonization.

Banking Supervisory Subcommittee of the Committee of Governors of EC Central Banks[3]

- set up in 1990;
- assists Committee of Governors in area of prudential supervision;
- consists or representatives of central banks and supervisory agencies (Belgium, Denmark, Germany); Commission official may participate in meetings;
- set up as part of strengthening of Committee of Governors with a view to Stage One of EMU.

* In area of banking supervision actually 12 countries: USA; Japan; UK; France; Germany; Italy; The Netherlands; Belgium; Luxembourg; Canada; Sweden; Switzerland.

1. Setup by Article 11 of die First Banking Directive (1977). The BAC overlaps the regulatory committee which operates under Article 22 of the Second Banking Directive, Article 9 of the Solvency Ratio Directive, Article 8 of the Own Funds Directive and Article 7 of the Large Exposures Directive.
2. Informally organized; continued functioning acknowledged in final recital of the preamble to the First Banking Directive.
3. The Banking Supervisory Subcommittee was established by the Committee of Governors under Article 5 of Council Decision 64/300/EEC, on cooperation between central banks of the Member States of the EEC (OJ No. 77, 21 May 1964, p. 1206/64), as amended by Decision 90/142/EEC of 12 March 1990 (OJ 1990, No. L78/25).

At present, as part of its work on financial conglomerates, the European Commission is using the BAC, together with similar high-level committees for securities and insurance, to facilitate communication and cooperation among different types of EC supervisors through, for example, joint meetings of the committees. These efforts supplement similar efforts underway beyond the Community under the auspices of the Basle Committee on Banking Supervision, the International Association of Securities Commissions (IOSCO), and the International Association of Insurance Supervisors (IAIS).

Besides establishing the general principle of home-country control, EC legislation regarding bank supervisory policies deals primarily with two areas: first, requirements for information sharing, both among supervisors in different Member States and among supervisors of different types of institutions; and second, requirements for consolidated supervision of banking and investment firms in groups headed by banks, investment firms, or financial holding companies. In general, however, EC legislation does not harmonize supervisory *practices*. For example, there are no Community rules requiring on-site examinations or dealing with the type or frequency of examinations, the qualifications of examiners, or establishing uniform reporting requirements for supervisory purposes. The Second Banking Directive gives home Member State authorities the right to examine branches of their banks in other Member States, but does not require such examinations.

Over the longer run, market developments may necessitate additional harmonizing legislation and/or more formal coordination among EC supervisors in different Member States and for different types of financial institutions. Moreover, establishment of the ECB could generate additional pressures for greater coordination. In particular, significant differences that now exist among Member States in dealing with troubled and failing institutions may become less acceptable. Although EC legislation contains a general requirement that supervisors must ensure that a bank whose capital ratio has declined below the required minimum take appropriate measures to restore it as quickly as possible, there are no specific Community rules governing early intervention as capital ratios decline and virtually no harmonization of policies dealing with the resolution of a failing bank. However, measures taken in support of a bank experiencing difficulties must be consistent with the provisions of the EC Treaty governing state aid. The European Commission examines such measures to determine whether there is an aid component and, if so, whether such aid is compatible with the treaty.

At present, the Deposit-Guarantee Directive is the only EC banking legislation involving harmonization of rules in situations where prudential supervision and regulation have proved an ineffective first line of defense. The directive is a hybrid of the home- and host-country approaches, primarily because the Member States could not agree sufficient harmonization to allow a complete home-country approach. Moreover, deposit-protection schemes, like other elements of the safety net, may involve government subsidization. With regard to the Deposit-Guarantee Directive, however, there appears to have been a political consensus to leave pricing and subsidization issues alone. In its explanatory memorandum for the directive, the Commission noted that it had received assurances from the Member States that the schemes are set up on a sound financial basis. The Commission stated that it did not seem appropriate to prohibit the authorities of the Member States from providing assistance in emergency situations when a scheme's resources had been exhausted. It noted, however, that such assistance is not desirable as a general rule and could not be allowed to conflict with the rules concerning state aid in the EC Treaty.

Although the term "lender of last resort" is not used in the Treaty on European Union, the concept is considered by most, but not all, Member States, to be embodied in the tasks and implementing powers given to the ECB. Serving as a lender of last resort, broadly defined, involves providing liquidity for the banking system and also for individual institutions experiencing difficulties, although some Member States would not accept this broad definition. In theory, the latter type of assistance is provided for illiquid but not insolvent institutions, although in practice this line is blurred. The details of the way in which the ECB would function to control liquidity in the normal conduct of monetary policy - and presumably also in circumstances in which lender of last resort is at issue - are not specified in the Treaty and, at present, are in the process of being worked out under the auspices of the EMI.

One issue to be resolved is whether the ECB would decide whether and under what conditions to lend to a particular institution or whether such decision making would remain at the national level. (In the former case, national central banks would presumably act as agents for the ECB in extending credit.) But whatever approach is used will have to take into account the need to coordinate the decision to lend to a troubled bank with the decision about the method of resolution - a recapitalization (preserving the institution), a reorganization (purchase of assets and assumption of liabilities by another institution), or a liquidation (requiring a deposit-insurance payout) - and also with bank supervisory practices. Beyond the issue of whether the functions of lender of last resort for individual banks and prudential supervision should be combined in a single institution, the need for coordination raises the question of whether these functions should be carried out at the same political level - i.e., national or supranational - in order to facilitate such coordination, or, if not, how such coordination could best be achieved.

In the United States, the dual banking system and multiple federal regulators pose considerable challenges to policy coordination where problem or failing banks are involved. Over time, the various responsible parties have developed good working relationships, which were given a thorough test during the banking difficulties of the 1980s. Within the Federal Reserve System, the Reserve Banks have considerable discretion in their credit decisions, but they must operate within policy guidelines set down by the Board, and there are frequent communications with the Board. All lending to a troubled bank is undertaken in consultation with the Federal Deposit Insurance Corporation (FDIC) and the borrower's primary regulator. Credit extensions are made only if they are in the public interest, and only if they are part of a plan for a prompt resolution of the borrower's difficulties. To discourage prolonged lending to troubled, FDIC-insured banks, the FDIC Improvement Act of 1991 sets limits on provision of Federal Reserve credit to troubled institutions, and any lending beyond these limits may result in financial liability to the FDIC. While the particular arrangements for policy coordination which I have described reflect the features of the US bank regulatory system, they highlight the importance of coordination among central banks and authorities responsible for supervision, licensing, and deposit insurance in dealing with problem or failing banks.

If market and institutional developments require greater supervisory coordination within the European Community, two important issues arise: first, the appropriate *form* of any additional harmonization, e.g., legislation (which would, of course, need to be proposed by the Commission), MOUs among supervisory authorities on a Communitywide or bilateral basis and/or among supervisors of different types of institutions; and second, the appropriate *forum* for additional coordination, e.g., the BAC and Groupe de Contact, the ECB itself, or, what seems virtually out of the question, a new supranational forum.

Is the ECB likely to become the major forum for increased cooperation and coordination among Community supervisors? As Johannes Priesemann explains in his paper, the Maastricht Treaty specifies only advisory and consultative powers for the ECB with regard to bank supervision. An enabling clause would allow other powers to be transferred to the ECB, but such a transfer would require a unanimous decision by the Council of Economic and Finance Ministers and, at present, virtually all Member States oppose transferring additional supervisory powers to the ECB. As Johannes Priesemann noted, some commentators have suggested that the ECB's limited mandate in the field of prudential supervision is nonetheless broad enough to allow it to serve in a coordinating role (ECU INSTITUTE, 1995).

Even if that viewpoint were generally accepted, the issue of the "ins" and the "outs," i.e., the Member States participating and not participating in EMU, could create a serious drawback to using the ECB and its Banking Supervisory Subcommittee as a coordinating forum for prudential supervision. If, as seems virtually certain, not all EC Member States are initial participants in EMU, only a subset of Community banking supervisors might be represented on the subcommittee. The relevant provisions of the treaty and governing statute are open to different interpretations regarding the participation of the "outs" that have not yet been resolved. A further issue would be the role of the ECB and the subcommittee in cross-sectoral supervisory coordination within the Community, which, as I have already mentioned, is now being addressed in the framework of the banking, securities, and insurance advisory committees.

2. A Supervisory Role for Central Banks

In addition to the considerations that have already been mentioned regarding a supervisory role for central banks, I would like to highlight one additional argument in support of such a role that was set forth in testimony by Chairman Greenspan's testimony before the US Senate Banking Committee in 1994 (see attached testimony in Appendix b1).

Chairman Greenspan suggested that a banking regulator without macroeconomic policy responsibility is likely to inhibit prudent risk-taking by banks and thereby limit economic growth and stability. He noted that, because economic growth requires risk-taking, which in turn requires financing, there is a significant policy tradeoff in banking regulation. On the one hand, regulators are concerned about bank failures, their cost to the insurance funds, and their effect on the economy; on the other hand, to finance economic growth banks must take risks. "...[A] single regulator with a narrow view of safety and soundness and with no responsibility for the macroeconomic implications of its decisions would inevitably have a long-term bias against risk-taking and innovation."

Chairman Greenspan also emphasized an argument that Mr. Priesemann has already mentioned, namely, that hands-on involvement in supervision and regulation is necessary for a central bank in order to carry out its macroeconomic responsibilities effectively. Moreover, such involvement, with the concomitant expertise and knowledge of banks, financial markets, and payment systems, increases the ability of the central bank to forestall financial crises and to manage a crisis when it does occur.

In his testimony, Chairman Greenspan also cautioned against establishing a single monolithic federal regulator in the United States. Since the regulators have considerable discretionary powers, a "safety valve is vitally needed to avoid the exercise of arbitrary actions."

3. Comparisons with US Federal Reserve Districts and Accountability of Central Banks

In making comparisons between the US Federal Reserve System and the ESCB, it is useful to keep in mind that Federal Reserve districts are not coterminous with states or any other political unit. By contrast, in the ESCB, national central banks and, in most cases, other supervisory authorities correspond to the political unit of an independent sovereign Member State. The main political accountability of the Federal Reserve System exists at the national level as opposed to the district or state level. By contrast, for the ESCB, as was discussed in the debate on the Maastricht Treaty, it does not appear that there will be a mechanism for democratic political accountability at the Community level comparable to the mechanisms that currently exist for national central banks at the level of the Member State. At the Community level, the European Parliament and the Council of Economic and Finance Ministers will be the primary mechanisms for accountability. However, they will not have the same powers that national governments could now exercise to amend the laws governing the operation of a national central bank; such changes would require amending the treaty. In this regard, I would like to note Richard Cooper's distinction between central bank independence and democratic accountability: While a central bank should have independence from the government that is currently in power, it should not be independent of the political process (COOPER, 1994).

Appendix b1

Testimony by Alan Greenspan, Chairman, Board of Governors of the Federal Reserve System, before the Committee on Banking, Housing, and Urban Affairs, United States Senate (March 2,1994)

Mr. Chairman, I am pleased to appear today before the Senate Banking Committee to give the views of the Federal Reserve Board on proposals to consolidate the banking regulators into a single agency. We have prepared a detailed analysis of such proposals, which I have attached to my statement. My remarks this morning will highlight that analysis.

The proposals to create one federal bank regulator have the clearly stated objectives of reducing the government's costs of regulating and supervising banks, of reducing bankers' costs and burdens from duplicative examination and overlapping supervision, and in general making the supervisory process more efficient and more accountable. The Federal Reserve Board shares these goals, but disagrees with the approach of one regulator for achieving these objectives. However, the Board believes that it is possible to achieve virtually all of these proposals' objectives without creating the risks of one regulator that so trouble us.

In reaching this conclusion, the Board tested various proposals against the fundamental principle that the purpose of regulation is to enhance the capability of the regulated entity to contribute effectively to the nation's long term economic growth and stability. We have concluded that for this to be accomplished four subsidiary principles must be achieved:

- First, there should not be a single monolithic federal regulator.
- Second, every bank should have a choice of federal regulator.
- Third, there should be only one federal regulator for all of the depository institutions in any single banking organization.
- Fourth, the U.S. central bank should continue to have its essential hands-on involvement in supervision and regulation.

A consolidated single regulator would deprive our regulatory structure of what the Board considers to be the current invaluable restraint on any one regulator conducting inflexible, excessively rigid policies. Laws on bank regulation and supervision must be drawn very generally leaving the specifics to agency rulemaking. This vests the agencies with a broad mandate and a not inconsiderable amount of discretionary power. Hence, a safety valve is vitally needed to avoid the exercise of arbitrary actions. A denial of, or severe limitation of, charter choice closes off a safety valve inevitably leading to greater micromanagement of banks and a lessened market for bank credit. We must avoid a regulatory structure that inhibits economic growth.

The present structure provides banks with a method - albeit one neither easily accomplished nor often taken - of shifting their regulator, an effective test that provides a limit on the arbitrary position or excessively rigid posture of any one regulator. The pressure of a potential loss of institutions has inhibited excessive regulation and acted as a countervailing force to the bias of a regulatory agency to overregulate.

The dual banking system and multiple federal regulators have facilitated diversity, inventiveness, and flexibility in our banking system, so important to a market economy subject to rapid change. A single federal regulator would effectively end the dual banking system: it would become an empty shell if a state-chartered entity had no choice of federal regulator or - reflecting a recent FDICIA provision - different asset powers. The dual banking system cannot survive consolidation at the federal level. I, as well as my colleagues on the Board, believe that would be a tragic loss.

In addition to the effective loss of the dual banking system, the single regulator contemplated in current proposals would be disconnected from broad economic policy issues. This is a problem because a regulator that does not have macroeconomic responsibility for its actions is likely to inhibit prudent risk-taking by banks, thus limiting economic growth and stability. The central historic purpose of banking is to take risks through the extension of loans to businesses and others. Economic growth in our system could not occur without risk-taking by entrepreneurs and small and large businesses. Risk-taking requires financing. Thus, either an unwillingness or an inability of lenders to take risks would slow the expansion of our nation's employment and income. This fact creates a significant policy tradeoff in banking regulation, especially because of the government guarantee of bank deposits. On the one hand, regulators are concerned about bank failures and their effects on the economy, as well as their cost to the insurance fund. On the other hand, banks need to take risks to finance growth. Tradeoffs are required, and a swing in either direction can create both short- and long-term problems.

Indeed, a single regulator with a narrow view of safety and soundness and with no responsibility for the macroeconomic implications of its decisions would inevitably have a long-term bias against risk-taking and innovation. It receives no plaudits for contributing to economic growth through facilitating prudent risk-taking, but it is severely criticized for too many bank failures. The incentives are clear.

The Federal Reserve's stabilization objectives cause us to seek to avoid either excessive tightness or ease in our supervisory posture. The former leads inevitably to credit crunches, and the latter to credit policies that contribute, with a lag, to bank losses and failures. This is not to say, as some have advocated, that the Fed itself should be the only regulator. A single regulator Fed would be prone to arbitrary and capricious behavior as would any other single bank regulator. We would thus oppose such an initiative, since as a single regulator we would inevitably drift to increasing day-by-day control of banking institutions who would soon become less innovative and competitive - a severe loss to the nation.

Not only is it important that one of our regulators have macroeconomic responsibility in order to carry out the regulatory function properly, but also our central bank must continue to have hands-on involvement in supervision and regulation in order effectively to carry out its macroeconomic responsibilities. Joint responsibilities make for better supervisory and monetary policy than would result from either a supervisor divorced from economic responsibilities or a macroeconomic policymaker with no involvement in the review of individual bank's operations. Without the hands-on experience of regulation and supervision, and the exposure to the operations of banks and markets provided by such experience, the Federal Reserve's essential knowledge base would atrophy. Its deliberations would become increasingly academic and the nation's central bank would soon resemble an ivory tower rather than an institution necessarily involved with the day-today activities of our economic and financial system. It is our knowledgeable examiners and supervisors - knowledgeable about banks, financial markets, and the payment systems that connect them - that provide the expertise the Fed needs. And the fact is that we simply could not retain such staff if they were not actively involved in the process; reading reports or joining as junior participants in a handful of examinations would not be sufficient.

Some have argued that most foreign central banks are not involved in bank supervision and regulation. In fact, as described in more detail in the attachment, central banks in all but one G-7 country (Canada), in most cases *de jure* but always de facto, are closely involved with the supervision of banks in their countries and internationally. More broadly, the central bank has either total or shared responsibility for bank supervision in three quarters of the nations in the OECD. One example that is frequently used by those that believe that central banks in foreign countries are not involved in supervision is the Bundesbank. The facts are quite the contrary: the Bundesbank has more supervisory staff than the German Federal Banking Supervisory Office, reviews the auditors' reports before the Banking Supervisory Office receives them, and has veto power over certain liquidity and capital regulations of that office. In all industrial countries, either central banks or finance ministries, or both, are involved with supervision because nations have come to understand that bank supervision has economic consequences that are important for stability and economic growth.

Removing the Federal Reserve from supervision and regulation would greatly reduce our ability to forestall financial crises and to manage a crisis once it occurs. In a crisis, the Fed could always flood the market with liquidity through open market operations and discount window loans. But while rapid liquidity creation is often a necessary response to a crisis, supervision and regulation responsibilities give the Fed insight and the authority to use less blunt and more precisely calibrated techniques to manage such crises and, more importantly, to avoid them. The use of such techniques requires both the clout that comes with supervision and regulation and the understanding of the linkages between supervision and regulation and macroeconomic growth and stability.

The Fed is required to play the key role when systemic breakdown threatens. The attachment to my statement provides some detail about Federal Reserve involvement in financial crises over the last decade. As you review it, I request that you consider certain key questions.

Could the Fed without supervisory responsibilities have successfully managed the Mexican debt crisis of 1982, the 1985 collapse of Ohio and Maryland privately insured thrifts, the stock market crash of 1987, or the Drexel failure of 1990?

Would the banking community have been persuaded to respond as they did in each of these cases by a central bank with much more limited authorities to affect events? Would the Fed have been able to play a role in persuading many of the banks to complete the payments necessary to prevent payments gridlock without supervisory knowledge and authority?

Finally, would a single bank regulator with no macroeconomic stabilization responsibilities have given the proper weights to financial market stability and economic growth? Without market expertise, would such a regulator have recognized early enough many of the problems central to resolution of these crises?

In my judgment, the risk that the answer to all of these questions is "no" is too great to take.

There are ways, short of the creation of a single agency, to address the problems in the current regulatory structure and reduce the costs of regulations. The crux of the issue is duplicative examinations of banks. This problem could be eliminated by a regulatory system that maintained two federal regulators, but provided that in general only *one* of those regulators supervised all the depository institutions in any banking organization.

While there are many ways to achieve an improved regulatory structure, one such approach supported by the Federal Reserve Board that could be implemented with a relatively modest series of reforms would contain the following provisions:

- Merge the OCC and the OTS. This organization would become the Federal Banking Commission.
- Remove the FDIC from examining healthy institutions.
- Put all independent national banks, all lead national banks that are part of a holding company, and all thrifts under the purview of the Federal Banking Commission; and put all independent state banks, and all lead state banks in a holding company under the purview of the Federal Reserve.
- Provide that the supervisor of the lead depository in a banking organization also be the supervisor and regulator of all the depository institutions in the organization regardless of the charter class of those affiliates.
- Finally, treat all U.S. activities of foreign banks as now, with adjustments where necessary to reflect the changes in the regulatory structure described above.

The Board has not yet adopted a position on the supervision and regulation of bank holding companies and their nonbank affiliates. There are two broad options, and a strong case can be made for each:

- Under the first option, all holding companies and their nonbank affiliates could remain under the Fed's jurisdiction, continuing to provide uniform rulemaking for competitive equity and a substantial role for the Fed in shaping the financial structure, so useful for stabilization and systemic risk purposes.
- Under the second option, the jurisdiction of virtually all holding companies could be split between the Fed and the FBC on the basis of the charter class of the lead bank. However, for systemic risk reasons, jurisdiction over the holding companies and nonbank affiliates of a modest number of banking organizations that meet certain criteria - such as large size and payment and

foreign activity - would be retained by the Fed, even if the lead bank of the organization had a national charter organization.

Under either option, the number of banking organizations subject to multiple regulators would drop sharply.

Whichever holding company option is selected, the general proposal would have the Fed supervise and regulate state nonmembers, with these banks being a significant addition to our existing regulatory load. This expansion of the Fed's supervisory functions rests solely on the notion that in a two agency structure, it is desirable to have supervision and regulation responsibility defined clearly by charter class in order to preserve the dual banking system. The Board makes no case that responsibility for such banks - that account for almost one-quarter of bank assets - is needed for financial stability and monetary policy purposes. However, responsibility over banks of various sizes and locations, as under our existing authorities, is required if the Fed is to perform its functions effectively.

The Board's approach would achieve essentially all of the benefits of one consolidated regulator while incurring virtually none of its risks. It eliminates duplicate supervision of depositories in a single banking organization and greatly reduces overlapping regulation. It maintains the dual banking system and permits any bank to change federal regulator by changing charter, thus ensuring a set of checks and balances on the arbitrariness of a single regulator. It maintains the healthy process of dynamic tension in bank rulemaking. It maintains the practical knowledge and skill, and the influence and authority, of the central bank, so critical for crisis prevention, crisis management, and monetary policy. It maintains the valuable perspective the central bank brings to supervision. In short, the proposal would avoid an inflexible, single regulator, preserve the dual banking system, assure that an economic perspective is brought to, supervision and regulation, and maintain a strong central bank.

Endnotes

[1] Economist, Division of International Finance, Board of Governors of the Federal Reserve System. The views expressed in this comment are those of the author and should not be interpreted as representing the view of the Board of Governors of the Federal Reserve System or anyone else on its staff.

References

COOPER, R. (1994), "Yes to European monetary unification, but no to the Maastricht Treaty," in STEINHERR, A. (ed.), *30 Years of European Monetary Integration from the Werner Plan to EMU*, Longman, New York, 68-71.

ECU INSTITUTE (1995), *Banking Supervision in the European Community: Institutional Aspects*, Report of a Working Group chaired by Jean-Victor Louis, Institute of European Studies, University of Brussels.

KEY, S. J. (1989), "Mutual Recognition: Integration of the Financial Sector in the European Community," *Federal Reserve Bulletin*, Vol. 75, 591-609.

C. Banking, Privatization and Economic Growth in Russia

Evgeny Gavrilenkov

1. Brief Chronicle of Banking Sector Developments during the Reforms

The banking sector plays a key role in a market economy. It should provide a number of the first and foremost services, such as lending money, fast payment transactions between economic agents, etc. It should also attract and accumulate money, acting as an intermediary between savings and investments. A strong and reliable banking sector is the backbone of a national economy. Thus, the creation of a market-oriented banking system was one of the main targets of the institutional transformation in Russia.

The reforms gave birth to a two-tier banking system: commercial banks and the Central Bank. The idea was to change the payment system and separate finances of the enterprise sector from state finances. The transformation aimed to harden the budget constraints faced by producers, thus making them change their behavioral patterns. Privatization also had this objective.

It was decided to alter the payment system by channeling transactions among enterprises through commercial banks and collection centers of the Central Bank. After receiving the payment order from the seller, money from a purchaser's account with a commercial bank was supposed to be transferred to the local collection center of the Central Bank and then to another local collection center, located in the seller's region. At the end, money went to the seller's account with some other commercial bank. The money, however, was supposed to pass via the Central Bank. This procedure was not computerized and was based on ordinary mailing, so due to enormous paper work it could take up to several months to transfer money from the purchaser to the seller. That was one of the reasons for the sharp arrears crisis that burst out in mid-1992.

On the other hand, as money could remain for a long period of time out of control in the banking system (and no interest was paid), this money could be used as credit resources. Thus, a rapid growth in the number of commercial banks was seen, especially in 1992. Already by December 1992, 1675 commercial banks were operating in Russia: 688 of these were founded on the basis of the former specialized state banks and their branches, while the other commercial banks were newly established. Since 1993 the pace of quantitative growth of the number of banks slowed down following tightening regulation of the banking business. By the end of 1993, 2019 commercial banks were operating, 2517 by the end of 1994 and 2571 by August 1st 1995. Moreover, 315 banks were closed in 1995 for violations of the legislation. The slow-down in growth of the number of banks in 1995 was caused also by tighter fiscal and monetary policies.

Banking business was one of the most profitable activities due to the fact that commercial banks could also find a number of channels to obtain money at a real negative interest rate. In 1992-1993, for instance, the Central Bank of Russia maintained a refinancing interest rate far below the rate of inflation: it varied between 20 percent per annum in January and 80 percent in December 1992. However, by the end of 1993 the Central Bank under pressure from the Finance Minister Boris Fedorov was forced to raise step by step the refinancing rate up to 210 percent per annum: so only since then has it reached positive levels in real terms.

The Central Bank of Russia provides some data characterizing the monetary environment in 1992 and showing that the "soil" for the development of commercial banking was rather fertile (see Table C1). According to the Central Bank the stock of money in Russia increased by 7 times during 1992 and reached nearly 6 trillion roubles at the beginning of 1993. Over this period commercial banks received more than 2.6 trillion roubles from the Central Bank at a real negative interest rate. The

Central Bank has also channeled some 2 trillion roubles to the economy in order to cover the fiscal deficit: the government paid its debts and money was returned back to the banking system remaining in the accounts of state and non-state enterprises.

Table C1 Interest Rates and Inflation in 1992 (in percent per annum)

	January	April	July	October	December
Central Bank's refinancing rate	20	50	80	80	80
Average weighted interest rate on the inter-bank credit market	26.6	46.9	92.3	103.3	114.6
Credits to state enterprises	20.4	37.2	81.8	96.9	95.2
Credits to non-state enterprises	26.4	50.2	97.5	114.5	121.2
Average weighted interest for deposits	14.5	39.1	59.1	71.9	78.1
Memorandum item					
Inflation (times to December 1991)	3.5	7.5	11.1	16.5	26.1

Source: Central Bank and Goskomstat of the Russian Federation.

As can be seen from Table C1, the interest rate for deposits was even below the Central Bank's interest rate. Those who could earn money had little incentives to save. It was quite natural that during the year the share of time and demand deposits in M2 dropped from 46.7 percent on January 1st 1992 to 14.6 percent on January 1st 1993. However, there were few alternatives for savings: hard currency and financial markets were not developed in the country. The appearance of other financial intermediaries, such as investment funds, for instance, could be seen in the fall of 1992, following the privatization process. Table C1 also shows that most profits of the commercial banks in 1992 came from the non-state sector: i.e. from private enterprises and partly from households, as Sberbank (the main holder of household money) operated actively on the inter-bank credit market.

The situation in the banking sector did not change much till the fall of 1993 when the Russian government and monetary authorities turned to tighter fiscal and monetary policies, that resulted in a relative slow-down in inflation from a monthly average of 20-25 percent to 13 percent in December 1993. On this background interest rates in Russia (calculated on a monthly base) reached positive levels in December 1993. Nevertheless, despite a permanent tightening of fiscal and monetary policies commercial banks could still obtain credits from the Central Bank at a real negative interest rate during the whole of 1993. Their net borrowing from the Central Bank increased from 2.6 trillion roubles to 8.7 trillion roubles during 1993. At the same time some 10 trillion roubles was channeled from the Central Bank to the economy cover the fiscal deficit. This money also appeared in commercial banks. Thus, money supply expansion in 1993, as well as in 1992, was a "fertile soil" for further development of commercial banking.

One difference between the 1992 and 1993 performance is essential: in 1993 more money was channeled by the Central Bank to the economy via the government rather than through commercial banks. This shift became more vivid in the fall of 1993, when the Central Bank's refinancing rate moved closer to positive levels. So, already in December 1993 commercial banks practically stopped borrowing money from the Central Bank. The developments in 1994 also show that commercial banks did not need to borrow money from the Central Bank at positive refinancing interest rates while they could obtain enough money "free of charge" from the Central Bank via the government: the budget deficit amounted to some 10 percent of GDP and was covered mainly by money supply expansion. More than 48 trillion roubles was channeled this way during 1994.

This shift between channels of money supply expansion resulted in the shifts in interest rates. When the refinancing interest rate was far below positive levels, interest rates on the inter-bank credit market were above the refinancing interest rate, as the commercial banking sector was largely credited by the Central Bank. However, as the stock of the Central Bank's direct credits to commercial banks decreased, while the share of cheap money channeled to the economy via the government increased, interest rates on the inter-bank credit market dropped below the refinancing rate. This means that the Central Bank has partially lost control over the money supply and over commercial banks, since monetary authorities can count only on the rate of reserves, but not on the refinancing interest rate as a control instrument.

Table C2 Interest Rates in 1995 (in percent per annum)

	Jan	Feb	Mar	Apr	May	Jun
CBR refinancing interest rate	200	200	200	200	195	195*
Inter-bank credit markets						
1 month credits	175.0	145.4	132.9	118.7	76.7	57.0
from 1 month to 3 months credits	190.7	194.0	176.8	147.2	122.2	85.3
more than 3 months credits	173.0	-	-	155.0	140.0	123.0
Average weighted interest rate on the inter-bank credit market	176.9	153.2	137.7	120.6	79.4	58.6
Credit for the enterprises (Moscow region)	189.9	182.4	185.4	179.0	166.8	154.7

* 180 effective June 19th 1995.
Source: Central Bank of Russia, own calculations.

The situation remained the same in 1995, although the reasons for the remaining gap between the refinancing interest rate and market interest rates were different. Table C2 shows the interest rates for various types of credits on credit markets in Russia in 1995. It should be emphasized that the bulk of deals on the inter-bank credit market is closed with short-term (less than 1 month) credits. It can be seen from Table C2 that even in 1995 enterprises could obtain credits at a rate below the CBR's refinancing interest rate. However, the gap between interest rates on the inter-bank credit market and interest rates for enterprises was rather big, allowing the banking sector to accumulate more profits. Moreover, the gap was increasing during 1995, as the stock of government securities issued to cover the fiscal deficit, was growing. So more and more money was absorbed by the government causing serious problems for the real sector.

Concluding this overview, it should be noted that the Russian banking system was established in a cheap money environment. Those banks, that could get better access to money sources (servicing privileged or strong clients, getting privileges in obtaining credits from the Central Bank, etc.) had an advantage over other banks. At any rate, however, the bulk of banks became accustomed to cheap money, and the permanent tightening of fiscal and monetary policies caused many problems for them. In August 1995 for instance, it resulted in the so-called "banking crisis", when interest rates on the inter-bank credit market suddenly jumped up to 1000 percent, threatening the whole banking system in Russia, and forcing the Central Bank to issue additional money in order to resolve the problem. It is expected that the number of banks in Russia will decrease in the near future.

2. The Banking System and the Household Sector

Initially only few commercial banks tried to attract money of households, while the bulk of the banks competed with each other trying to attract money of enterprises. If the banking system is not developed, if banks do not have enough offices, then it is easier to deal with dozens or hundreds enterprises rather than with hundred thousands of people. The bulk of households savings at the beginning of the reforms was deposited in the former state savings bank (Sberbank). In the former system it was the only bank dealing with the general public. So it had a number of branches and offices in every region of Russia. Due to its monopolistic status it could maintain very low interest rates.

The other reason for commercial banks' reluctance to deal with households was that the dual money system, inherited from the planned economy, still dominated Russia at the beginning of reforms. The shortages in supply of new bank notes, that occurred in the first half of 1992, caused dramatic delays in wages which in turn pegged households savings. Thus, it was much easier for the banks to attract non-cash money (money of enterprises) rather than cash (money of households).

The performance of 1993 and 1994 was characterized by a very moderate fiscal policy that resulted in the rapid growth of nominal and real disposable incomes. In 1994, for instance, real disposable incomes increased by 12 percent. Starting in early 1994 each month 15 to 20 percent of households' current incomes were used for savings (they were deposited or spent for purchases of hard currency and equities). Deposits of households increased from 4.1 trillion roubles on January 1st 1994 to nearly 30 trillions in January 1995, i.e. 7.5 times, while the inflation rate was 3.1 times over 1994.

The tendency of rising household savings appeared already at the end of 1993. On the other hand, the share of cash in circulation in M2, which is also household money, has been permanently increasing since 1992. This forced commercial banks to turn to the general public, as the share in M2 of household money was also permanently increasing. In order to attract more savings from households commercial banks raised interest rates more than Sberbank. Table C3 shows the structure of deposits of households in Sberbank and other commercial banks in 1993-1994.

Table C3 Allocation of Household Deposits in Sberbank and Commercial Banks (in percent)

as of:	1.01.93	1.07.93	1.01.94	1.07.94	1.01.95	1.07.95	1.09.95
Total deposits	100	100	100	100	100	100	100
of which:							
Sberbank	90.0	80.2	60.0	42.5	58.6	59.2	60.3
Commercial banks	9.6	18.8	38.7	57.3	41.2	40.6	39.3

Source: Central Bank of Russia.

As can be seen from Table C3 the share of household deposits in commercial banks increased to nearly 60 percent of total deposits from some 10 percent at the beginning of 1993. However, after a number of bankruptcies of commercial banks in the second half of 1994 and especially after "Black Tuesday" households savings again shifted to the more reliable Sberbank. These proportions remained relatively stable till the end of 1995.

Contrary to the early stage of reforms, in 1994-1995 the role of the household sector increased and many banks turned to the population trying to attract money from households. Really, the bulk of money in Russia is households money, including cash in circulation (see Table C4). The share of household deposits in M2 has grown more than threefold since 1993. In 1995 households own almost 70 percent of Russia's rouble money stock. This happened, however, on the background of a tremendous increase in the gap between the poorest and richest social groups (the gap between the poorest and the richest deciles increased from 4.5 in 1991 to 15.1 in 1994). The Gini coefficient in 1993-1995 varied in Russia around 0.4.[1] This means that the bulk of savings is concentrated in the hands of a some small group of the population. Concentration of money, however, has not resulted in growing investment activities, and the banking sector is not acting as an intermediary between savings and investment.

Table C4 Structure of the Aggregate Money Supply in Russia (in percent)

	1.01.1993	1.01.1994	1.01.1995	1.12.1995
M0 (cash in circulation)	24.9	37.0	36.0	36.5
Household deposits	9.8	14.2	27.1	33.3
Other accounts	65.3	48.8	36.9	30.2
M2	100.0	100.0	100.0	100.0

Source: Central Bank of Russia.

3. The Radical Shift in Fiscal Policy, Money and Banking in 1995

Russia's macroeconomic performance in 1995 was greatly influenced by the fiscal policy pursued. This policy originated in the traditional IMF stabilization programs, implemented in various countries. In order to peg inflation in the short run, it was decided to avoid borrowing from the Central Bank and to cover the fiscal deficit mainly by foreign borrowing and the issue of government securities.

Though the Russian government was able to reduce inflation considerably, the stabilization policy was not entirely successful. Inflation in January-August 1995 was practically the same as over the same period in 1994 (see Table C5). In order to move closer to the targeted inflation rate the government decided to use quite a crude but "reliable" method: it fixed energy prices in the fourth quarter of 1995.

Table C5 Price and Money Supply Growth in 1994-1995 (monthly percentage change)

	Jan	Feb	Mar	Apr	May	Jun	Jul	Aug
Consumer prices								
1994	118	111	107	108	107	106	105	105
1995	118	111	109	108.5	107.9	106.7	105.4	104.6
Producer prices in industry								
1994	119	116	110	110	107	108	108	106
1995	122	117	111	115	109	106	107	107
Memorandum item Money supply (M2)								
1994	108.7	107.3	112.4	116.4	114.9	111.3	107	113.2
1995	96.2	108.5	105.1	115.2	112.5	113.6	105.8	105.4

Source: Goskomstat RF, Central Bank of Russia.

The fiscal deficit was reduced in 1995 to less than 3 percent of GDP (compared to some 10 percent in 1994). This is the lowest value since the start of reforms and is comparable to those in most industrial developed countries. Inflation in Russia, however, was still rather high: between December 1995 and December 1994 consumer prices increased 2.3 times, while the rouble money stock increased 2.1

times over this period. Does this not mean that the fiscal deficit should not be considered as the only reason for the rapid growth in money supply and high inflation in Russia?

The tight fiscal policy pursued in the first quarter of 1995 caused a lack of working capital in the economy. But this did not result in a slow-down of inflation. The main reason were hard currency savings accumulated during the previous years. There is no exact information about the stock of hard currency circulating in Russia. However, according to various independent estimates, the rouble money stock at the beginning of the year was at least comparable with the stock of hard currency in the country. Thus, the lack of roubles caused the supply of hard currency on the currency exchange market to increase rapidly by the end of April. This rise was also driven by expanding exports and a positive trade balance. Since May a rapid appreciation of the rouble could be seen, not only in real but also in nominal terms.

In order to avoid a more rapid appreciation of the national currency, that could harm domestic manufacturing, monetary authorities were forced to increase the rouble money supply by purchasing hard currency and thus increasing international reserves. The monthly money supply growth rate in the second quarter varied from 12 to 15 percent, while during January-March the stock of rouble money increased by only 9 percent.

It shows that, as in the previous stages of the reform period in Russia, monetary decisions have been driven by the effects of fiscal policy or by the counteractions of the economy to particular government interventions. Thus, the government was not able to maintain a sustainable growth of the money supply and avoid sharp swings in monetary policy. In the second half of 1992, for instance, the Central Bank of Russia, clearing mutual inter-enterprise debt, was forced to increase the money supply by a monthly range of 20-30 percent, while at the beginning of 1992 money supply growth was limited to a monthly 10-12 percent.

The Russian Government has been widely criticized in the media in Russia for monetarist ideology. However, such criticism can scarcely be taken seriously.

Milton Friedman in his well-known lecture (see FRIEDMAN, 1968) pointed out that the "*monetary authority should guide itself by magnitudes that it can control, not by ones it cannot control*". In this sense inflation is not the best policy target, as "*we cannot predict at all accurately just what effect a particular monetary action will have on the price level and, equally important, just when it will have that effect*". This was said with regard to countries with well-developed markets. In Russia, in contrast, market forces are still not strong enough despite the ongoing privatization process: in Russia uncertainty can be higher than elsewhere. Hence, as shown above, the Russian government could never follow a pure monetarist ideology for a long period of time.

Trying to limit money supply growth in 1995, the government started expansion on financial markets by issuing government bonds. Net issue of such liabilities reached nearly 27 trillion roubles by December 1st 1995. The bulk of these bonds were issued for three months and were purchased by commercial banks. As these liabilities were guaranteed by the state and as the interest rate was higher than that for non-government liabilities, it turned out that the government could easily absorb money from the rest of economy.

Money that was used in 1994 for speculations with hard currency also switched to the operation with government securities. In fact, after the government had accumulated enough hard currency reserves it announced that the exchange rate would be partially controlled and changes limited within rather narrow frontiers. The corridor for the exchange rate made savings and speculations with hard currency unprofitable, allowing the Russian government to expand the issue of government securities even more. On the other hand, however, government securities also absorbed money from the real sector, which had a negative impact on investment in fixed capital. The banks are still not interested in lending money for investment in fixed capital, as profits are higher and risks are lower in the case of investment in government bonds.

However, a feedback could be seen: the tight fiscal policy pursued in 1995 was followed by stable growth in tax and wage arrears, while the stock of inter-enterprise trade credit did not increase considerably. The stock of delayed tax payments to the budget reached nearly 54 trillion roubles on November 1st 1995, which is a bit less than one third of rouble M2, or one fifth of all tax revenues actually collected in the consolidated budget. Almost one half of the tax arrears stock consists of delayed VAT payments. On November 1st 1995 VAT arrears reached 26 trillion roubles, compared to 74.8 trillion roubles of actually collected VAT. The most rapid growth in tax arrears could be seen in the third and fourth quarter of the year, when the government expanded the issue of government bonds. During August-October the stock of tax arrears increased by 34 percent.

In turn, tax arrears may cause a further reduction in budgetary financing, or the necessity to issue more government bonds. This cannot, however, continue for a long time. The stock of arrears and the stock of government liabilities are already quite big compared to the money supply in the country. Once more, it should be emphasized, that the maturity of government liabilities lies between 3 and 6 months. Moreover, the stock of roubles, estimated at some 200 trillion roubles (or less than 43 billion US $) was rather small by the end of 1995, compared to the trade surplus for instance (some 20 billion US $ in 1995), that requires some amount of roubles for the exchange operations all the time. All this shows that the situation of the Russian economy remains rather unstable. The only reserve, that the government can now use is household money. The government has already issued government securities for the general public, which should be distributed through the Savings Bank.

4. Propensities for Economic Growth in Russia

According to official statistics, since the onset of transition the Russian economy has never experienced a deep fall in production. There are different points of view concerning the level of the output decline (see for instance ASLUND, 1995, or GAVRILENKOV and KOEN, 1994, where the authors argue against the official Goskomstat data). Finally, the Russian State Committee on Statistics (GOSKOMSTAT, 1995) revised the output data for 1992-1994, moving it quite close to Gavrilenkov and Koen's estimates.

Nevertheless, the data for 1995 are rather puzzling. A GDP fall of 4 percent in 1995 is unlikely to fit a 7 percent decline in retail sales and 16 percent decline in sales of paid services, which respectively caused some 9 percent of the decline in total household consumption. At the same time, according to Goskomstat, investment dropped by 14 percent. Even though the investment data does not include expenditures on capital repair, gaps between GDP and this data cannot be filled by a reported increase in net exports (in particular given the presence of decreasing government spending). Thus, the decline in real GDP in 1995 may have varied between 6 and 8 percent.

Industrial production decreased in 1995 by 3 percent while production of consumer goods dropped by 12 percent due to the shortage of domestic demand and high competition from imported goods. Export-oriented sectors (energy, metallurgy, timber and paper, some branches of chemistry) performed fairly well. However, their potential for growth is constrained by the rapid appreciation of the rouble. The agricultural sector also recorded a 8 percent fall in production.

There is a widely accepted point of view that Russia's potential for economic growth is very high. The abundance of natural resources and the quite educated labor force can in principle positively affect macroeconomic performance. However, in no way can Russia yet use this potential. What are the necessary conditions for sustainable economic growth in the country?

Insufficient investment is now considered as a main limiting factor for economic growth. The recession in the Russian Federation could be explained to a great extent by the elimination of production of non-competitive goods. It is hoped that new investment can replace the existing capital stock which is not able to produce competitive consumer goods (for export and domestic purposes). Thus, controlling inflation is aimed at providing stability for the financial system, so that it can act as an intermediary between savings and investment. The necessity to support private investment by partial government financing is also a declared priority of the most recent government economic program released in 1995. But, as already pointed out, this is in conflict with other government priorities including the sale of treasury bonds to domestic investors at very attractive rates. The Russian government intends to continue such practice in the future: the budget will pump the money that could be used for investment.

As was said, the tighter fiscal policy caused a fall in real incomes bringing down domestic demand to a low level. If domestic demand is low and saturated and if investment priorities hence are not clear, the uncertainty faced by investors is very high. Increasing social inequality before the elections, dramatic growth in the stock of wage delays also increases political risks for investors in Russia.

However, the main obstacle for investment is that in practice property rights are not well protected in the country. All exercises in macroeconomics are of little consequence without the establishment of an appropriate market-oriented legal system. Four years of reform, however, is a relatively short period to institutionalize property rights. Adjustments of this nature require multi-directional flows including privatization: reforms at the micro level hence are also necessary.

The lack of solvent demand for Russia's exports caused by the dissolution of the USSR should be considered as another constraint for economic growth in Russia. In mutual inter-republican trade Russia used to be the main exporter of raw materials to the republics, while it imported manufactured goods and agricultural products from the republics.

The Russian economy (as well as the economies of the other former Soviet republics) inherited price distortions from the planning system. In brief, energy and raw materials were cheap, while manufactured goods used to be too expensive. For instance valued in terms of oil Russian, chemicals, metals, cotton fabrics and many other commodities were several times (even as much as 10 times in some cases) more expensive than the same commodities on world markets (GAVRILENKOV, 1994). In a liberalized economy, the elimination of price distortions is an absolute and unconditional prerequisite.

After the liberalization of prices and the deregulation of foreign trade, the transformation of the inter-industrial price structure has been a major factor affecting macroeconomic performance in the former Soviet Union. In general it means that prices for Russia's exports to the republics increased (and should continue to increase in the future) more than prices for imports from the republics into Russia. Prices for many goods manufactured in Russia and in the CIS countries have already moved quite close to world market prices (and even exceeded them), while prices for raw materials and semi-products are still below world market prices. In such a situation the bulk of CIS exports to Russia is not competitive on the Russian market. Thus, a lack of inter-republican trade caused a decline in production in Russia. For instance, in 1989-90 Russia exported some 120-130 million tons of crude oil to the republics of the USSR. In 1994 crude oil exports to the former Soviet republics reached only 35 million tons. However, even in this case insufficient payment was received in return. Russia could in principle increase exports to CIS countries, but it does not make sense in such a situation.

There are no signs that the CIS market can develop rapidly in the near future. This means that CIS trade will not seriously stimulate economic growth in Russia. At any rate, the development and strengthening of domestic markets is a necessary condition for sustainable economic growth in such a large country as Russia with 148 millions people.

The other factor which can in principle stimulate economic growth is foreign trade with non-CIS countries. Partly this has already happened in 1995: the shortage of domestic demand has been compensated by external demand for some tradable Russian goods. Such industries as chemistry, cellulose and paper, metallurgy were able to increase production in 1995 due to an increase in exports. But this cannot last for a long time. Tight fiscal policy, resulting in rapid appreciation of the rouble in real terms, makes domestic production less competitive. Even the production of exported tradable goods (energy, raw materials and semi-products) currently has to make do without changes in technologies and efficiency gains in production. Investment is urgently needed.

Ongoing privatization should in principle stimulate economic growth in Russia. According to Goskomstat nearly 120,000 enterprises had been privatized by the end of the third quarter of 1995. A great number of newly established firms appeared in the country. Privatization has been most successful in trade. Now the bulk of retail sales is channeled through the private sector and competition in this sector is perhaps the strongest in Russia. Trade and some other kinds of services have been growing. But many former state enterprises in basic industries are not profitable.

Russian producers still have not changed their behavioral patterns, they are not thinking in terms of reducing cost and increasing efficiency. It still is usual practice to claim subsidized credits, increased protection from foreign competition through higher import duties, etc. At the same time equity markets, necessary for an efficient reallocation of property (especially in the case of industrial enterprises) have not yet developed.

Unemployment in Russia is still very low compared to the decline in output: 2 million officially registered unemployed for a country with a population of 148 million where output collapsed by more than one third during the last years is quite surprising.[2] Despite the ongoing marketization paternalistic expectations are very high in the country as a whole, being, however, very uneven across Russia. The gap between Moscow, St. Petersburg and some other big cities are far ahead in transforming the economy, and the gap between them and the Russian provinces is increasing rapidly. Many conservative-oriented local authorities have enough power to counteract the federal government. On the background of increasing social inequality, this may have a serious impact on the results of elections and the direction of reforms.

All the attempts to solve macroeconomic problems face serious difficulties: unsettled legislation, insufficient experience with implementing new laws, political instability in various regions hamper market transformation. It should also be said that Russian reformers reducing centralized investment in fixed capital have also forgotten about the necessity to invest in human capital. No market-oriented propaganda and very few educational programs have been launched in Russia and it takes time to change the mentality of the society. This is a crucial point for Russia, explaining why the country has not yet realized its potential for growth.

Wealth is concentrated more and more in some sectors of the economy, regions and social groups, but due to political uncertainty, an unsettled legal system and poor equity markets, that would allow a more efficient allocation of property, the start of economic growth in Russia may be delayed.

Endnotes

1 For instance the Gini coefficient in 1992 in the USA was 0.466, while in the other former socialist countries it was much lower (0.283 in Bulgaria, 0.251 in Romania, 0.240 in Poland).

2 Unemployment calculated in accordance with the ILO methodology is, however, much higher and is growing faster. It amounted to some 5.7 million people by the end of 1995.

References

ASLUND, A. (1995), *How Russia Became a Market Economy*, The Brookings Institution, Washington D.C.

FRIEDMAN, M. (1968), "The Role of Monetary Policy," *American Economic Review*, Vol. 58, 1-17, also reprinted in KORLIRAS, P. G. and THORN, R. S. (eds.) (1979), *Modern Macroeconomics*, 91-102.

GAVRILENKOV, E. (1994), "Macroeconomic Crisis and Price Distortions in Russia," *Review of Economies in Transition*, No. 3, Bank of Finland, 39-58.

GAVRILENKOV, E. and KOEN, V. (1994), "How Large Was the Output Collapse in Russia? Alternative Estimates and Welfare Implications," IMF Working Paper 94/154, International Monetary Fund, Washington D.C., December.

CENTRE FOR ECONOMIC ANALYSIS, *Russia: Economic Situation*, 1992, 1993 (No.1-4), 1994 (No.1-4), 1995 (No.1-2), Moscow.

GOSKOMSTAT, *Russian Statistical Yearbook*, 1994 and 1995, Goskomstat of the Russian Federation (in Russian), Moscow.

Comments on

Banking, Privatization and Economic Growth in Russia

Daniel Gros

This is an interesting paper that contains some essential points for any observer of the Russian economy. I very much agree with the warning of the author that one should not put too much faith in the official figures on budget deficits, growth rates, etc., that often dominate the public discussion. All one can hope for is a more qualitative picture.

This point is not new. Consider the following statement: "The economic system of Russia has undergone such rapid changes that it is impossible to obtain a precise and accurate account of it. (....) Almost everything one can say about the country is true and false at the same time." This is what Lord M. Keynes said in 1925, but it remains true even today.

I also agree with the emphasis the author puts on the energy sector. The performance of this sector is crucial for the entire Russian economy. This is a complex problem that can, however, be reduced to two issues: (i) energy prices need to be increased to world market levels and customers need to be forced to pay effectively for the energy they consume, (ii) more competition is required in the gas sector, which has so far been monopolized by Gazprom.

All in all I am tempted to conclude that Russia is continuing its 'Pas de deux between destabilization and reform' (as described in chapter 14 of GROS and STEINHERR, 1995).

But let me now turn to the main topic of this conference namely the banking system. Its poor state has often been described: there are too many banks and too many of them are just fronts for illegal interests. This is a fact of live. But is there anything the authorities could do to improve the situation?

How to reform the Russian banking system? Some observers favor the 'split-up' bank in order to guarantee the stability of the system. But while it appears to be a very attractive option in developed economies, it might not be useful in reforming economies, such as Russia. In particular, a well functioning capital market - not only for government securities but also for corporate issues - needs to exist to make the model work. Deposit banks would need liquid short-term government securities and liquid money market instruments to be able to manage their assets efficiently. Loan and investment banks would need certificates of deposit and long-term bond markets of sufficient liquidity to manage their liabilities.

Since all this does not exist I would submit for consideration a different route, namely to issue different classes of bank licenses as originally proposed by GROS and STEINHERR (1995). But the classes should be related to criteria directly measuring "quality" rather than an activity measures correlated with risk exposure. The three tiers proposed are:

- License A for top of the range banks as measured by their risk-weighted capital ratio and satisfaction of credit exposure norms.
- License B for banks satisfying a lower echelon of the same criteria. They would pay higher deposit insurance premiums and may be barred from participation in the payments system, or would be required to hold larger minimum reserves.
- License C for banks falling below the criteria set for License B. Deposits at such banks would not be insured, lender of last resort facilities would not be available and therefore participation in the payments system would not be possible. Debt of C banks would receive the same risk-weighting as non-banks.

This proposal has the disadvantage of not making asset allocation rules and deposit insurance superfluous and also requires acceptance of the universal bank structure. But some very clear advantages also emerge from this tiering of bank licenses which (by law) would need to be visibly exposed.

First, it would provide flexibility for the co-existence of differently structured and managed banks. Depositors could opt for riskier or safer deposits -

and be remunerated differently - according to their preferences or portfolio needs. Housewives and grandmothers that bring their savings to a bank with license C would know what risk they are taking for the high interest rates they are promised.

Second, the activity scope of banks would not be constrained by regulations. Of course, if a bank wishes to minimize risk it would, in fact, become a deposit bank. To operate like a universal bank with a substantial share of equity holdings of private corporations, and to enjoy Class A privileges would require a sound capital base. Perhaps no bank could achieve that in a hard-hit economy like Russia. Then, de facto, there would be a split between safe banks, equivalent essentially to deposit banks, and universal banks, corresponding to low-tier investment banks. But some banks in Russia have now such a strong capital base that they should be able to have a license A and still become universal banks.

Third, the moral hazard problem would be greatly reduced by forming more uniform classes. Tier A banks would attach importance to not losing their status and lower-tier banks would try to be upgraded. The risk of the lender of last resort is substantially reduced by not covering Class C banks and depositors would request a risk premium for uninsured deposits at lower-tier banks. Failure of a Class C bank would not generate a run on the overall banking system.

These practical advantages might turn out to be decisive: regulating the thousands of banks that exist in Russia with an understaffed and underpaid banking supervision authority is a nightmare. The proposal made here would reduce the need for supervision greatly because it would be large self-enforcing for the reasons mentioned above.

References

GROS, D. and STEINHERR, D. (1995), *Winds of Change: Economic Transition in Central and Eastern Europe*, Longman, London.

D. Historical Lessons of Foreign Banking in Eastern Europe The Case of Tsarist Russia

Peter Hertner

1. Foreign Banking in the 19th Century: Possible Choices and Real Development

Before talking of any lessons that could be provided by the historical evolution of foreign banking in eastern Europe we should consider the different options open to banking as it was getting more and more involved in financial activities abroad.

Looking at the period which covered the last third of the 19th century and ran up to World War I we can distinguish three possible fields where banks could become active abroad:

- the financing of foreign trade
- intermediation in the field of portfolio investment abroad
- a role as intermediaries for foreign direct investment.

These three different activities could have been performed exclusively from the home base, but they could also have been exercised with the help of agents or agencies established abroad. Alternatively a bank could take a participation in a foreign bank or establish a subsidiary abroad. Finally, there was the possibility of cooperation with foreign banks by, for instance, coming together in syndicates or in "Studiengesellschaften", as the German banks called those short-lived associations which were founded in order to explore the financial and technical viability of new products or processing methods. Thus banks just behaved like other firms which had to choose between three ways of economic coordination: "by *direction*, by *co-operation*, or through *market transactions*"(RICHARDSON, 1972, p. 890; italics as in original text).

Banks active abroad in these ways could belong to all possible types of banking from purely commercial banking to universal banking passing through various intermediate stages. But it seems quite obvious that commercial banks of the British type normally did not engage in the promotion of foreign direct investment whereas, on the other hand, the finance of foreign trade belonged to their normal outlets. There was no natural connection between the structure of home banks and their foreign off-spring: German banks active in Latin America since the 1880s were not at all universal banks as were their mother companies (HERTNER, 1990), and French banks in tsarist Russia were much more of the "universal" or "banque d'affaire" type than some of their Parisian founders like, for instance, the Société Générale (GIRAULT, 1973, p. 492 ff.; BONIN, 1994). The division of labor between the mother bank and its foreign subsidiaries depended in each individual case on the prevailing problems of information and control, on national differences in legislation and on the different efficiencies of national capital markets. A short look at a historical case study will show us under which conditions foreign banking could become an important factor in national economic development.

If any lessons can be drawn from these historical developments remains to be seen. We shall try to give some answers to this question at the end of this short essay.

2. Russia's Economic Development and its Foreign Debt between the 1860s and the First World War

Why do we propose the case of Russia between the 1860s and the First World War as a case study for the historical development of foreign banking? In the first place, because it was "the largest borrowing country of pre-war Europe," as Herbert Feis put it already in 1930 (FEIS, 1965, p. 210). Secondly, because it was neither a colony nor had it ever been part of an informal empire - it was quite on the contrary one of the great European powers despite its political, social and economic backwardness. This makes the Russian case much more comparable to recent developments in European or extra-European countries in case we want to draw any lessons from this historical example.

Pre-1914 Russia was quite peculiar compared to other European or extra-European countries of that period. From a military point of view it figured among the great powers at least since the early 18th century, but by 1914 it had also become one of the world's leading economic powers. It then "... ranked as the world's fourth- or fifth-largest industrial power behind the United States, the United Kingdom, France, Germany, and perhaps Austria-Hungary". There was, however, also "... the clear dichotomy between Russia's aggregate economic power, as dictated by the magnitude of the Russian empire, and its relative poverty on a per capita basis" (GREGORY, 1994, p. 17). In 1861, when serfdom was abolished, Russia had "a per capita income roughly half that of France and Germany, one-fifth that of the United Kingdom, and 15 percent that of the United States. By 1913 Russia's relative position had deteriorated because of rapid population growth and relatively slow output growth until the 1880s. Russia's 1913 per capita output was less than 40 percent that of France and Germany, still one fifth that of the United Kingdom, and one-tenth that of the United States". It was also "well below that of Spain, Italy, and Austria-Hungary" (IBIDEM, p. 21). There were other signs of its backwardness: In 1913, about three quarters of its labor force were engaged in agriculture. "Grain output per capita in Russia was roughly equal to that of Austria-Hungary in both 1861 and 1913; yet per capita output of industrial products in 1913 was typically half that of Austria-Hungary" (IBIDEM, p. 21f.). The growth of the railway network, on the other hand, can be regarded as "Russia's most impressive relative improvement between 1861 and 1913" (IBIDEM, p. 22): In 1860 its length was 1,626 km, in 1880 it had already increased to 22,865 km. In 1900 the entire network amounted to 53,234 km, and in 1913 it ended up with no less than 70,156 km (KAHAN, 1985, p. 551). On a per capita basis this was comparable to otherwise more advanced countries like Italy or Austria-Hungary.

From the 1880s, Russia's growth record became quite outstanding: between 1883/87 and 1909/13 total output in the Russian economy grew by 3.25 percent per annum (GREGORY, 1994, p. 24), and this was more than respectable if compared with a figure of 2.7 percent calculated by Maddison for output growth in the countries of western Europe and North America during the period 1870-1913 (MADDISON, 1964, p. 28). "In fact, Russian growth was equaled or surpassed by only the United States, Canada, Australia, and Sweden, and it equaled or exceeded the growth of the two most important "follower" countries (Japan and Italy) before World War I" (GREGORY, 1994, p. 25 f.).

A distinctive feature in the Russian economy was the important part government consumption had in the distribution of national income: in 1885/89 it amounted to 8.2 percent whereas in Japan its share was 7.7 percent and in Germany 6.8 percent. The other countries of western Europe and North America as well as Australia followed clearly behind. In 1909/13, government consumption in Russia was still leading with a share of 9.7 percent, followed by 8.8 percent in Japan and 8.4 in Germany. The Russian rate of domestic capital formation measured 8.2 percent in 1885/89 and was surpassed only by the corresponding German, U.S., and Australian rates. Twenty-five years later, in 1909/13, only Germany and the United States could boast higher rates than Russia, which ended up at 12.2 percent 1.4 percent of which had been added by net foreign investment (GREGORY, 1994, p. 33).

Annual foreign investment in the Russian economy was on average 43 million rubles for the period 1885-1897 and 191 million rubles for the period 1897-1913, which was more than four times as much. "As a ratio of national income, for the pre-gold-standard era, the ratio of foreign investment to national income was slightly over 0.5 percent (or 5.5 percent of net investment); for the gold-standard era, it was about 1.5 percent (11 percent of net investment)" (IBIDEM, p. 70f.). Since the middle of the 1880s, government borrowing had been used mainly to acquire gold and convertible currencies which, on average, made up about two thirds of the yearly sum borrowed abroad, whereas the rest went into railway construction and general public spending. These accumulated funds then enabled Sergei Witte, the legendary minister of finance from 1892 until 1903, to manage the transition of the country's currency to the gold standard in 1897 (CRISP, 1953; VON LAUE, 1963, p. 138ff.). Once it had been introduced the gold standard was meant to attract additional direct foreign investment by guaranteeing stability for its future profit transfers. Witte, for whom industrialization was an absolute priority, underlined the fundamental importance of attracting foreign direct investment in a memorandum sent to the Tsar at the beginning of 1899, where he stated "... that the influx of foreign capital is the chief means for Russia in her present economic condition to speed up the accumulation of native capital..." (VON LAUE, 1963, p. 181).

For a more precise idea of Russia's foreign debt, its size and its development over time, we should take note of the following facts: from 1884 until 1889, an average of 65 percent of the country's state debt had been placed abroad, and in 1914 this percentage amounted to 48.5 with the absolute figures greatly increased (NÖTZOLD, 1966, p. 173). According to other estimates, Russian public debt rose up to 8.6 billion roubles in July 1914. Of this sum 4.3 billion belonged to foreign creditors: 3 billion had been placed in France, 0.5 in Germany, 0.43 in the Netherlands and 0.2 billion roubles in Britain (SIDOROV, 1975, p. 270). Foreign investment in private Russian companies - most of it of a controlling nature and therefore direct investment - amounted to 48 percent of total nominal capital of all joint-stock companies at the beginning of 1914. This figure does not change very much even if we try to include all other types of private companies (BONWETSCH, 1974, p. 422). According to relatively recent estimates, the Russian share of the total stock of French foreign investment - portfolio and direct - reached 32 percent in 1913 (GIRAULT, 1973, p. 84f.). As to the German case, Russia's share amounted to about 13 percent of its investments abroad in 1914, but this according to quite old estimates (GIRAULT, 1973, p. 74) whereas in the early 1890s it might have been quite close to about 20 percent (MAI, 1976, p. 207).

Against this background, it becomes quite clear that the foreign banks operating from Berlin or Paris as well as the Russian banks controlled by foreign capital must have played a crucial role in promoting capital flows from western Europe into the tsarist Empire while at the same time carrying out the "ordinary business" of financing trade between Russia and its foreign partners.

3. Foreign Banks and Foreign Investment in Russia until the 1870s

Foreign investment on a larger scale did, however, not start in Russia until the early 1860s. Before the Crimean war, "foreign *commercial* finance - the financing of international trade - was of more value to Russia than direct investment in government loan and railways" (PLATT, 1984, p. 39). After the Crimean war, things changed only gradually: according to Bertrand Gille (quoted by PLATT, 1984, p. 40) still in 1861 "foreign capital formed less than 13.5 percent of total capital invested in Russia ..., rising to nearly 25 percent in 1889...". It is nevertheless quite surprising that the limited capital needs of Russia until the late 1860s were covered mainly by the Dutch who had been a great financial power in the 18th century. As a result of the decline of the Amsterdam capital market during the revolutionary wars and the Napoleonic period, Dutch capital played a much reduced international role thereafter (RILEY, 1980, p. 248f.), and its Russian engagement comes therefore quite unexpected. The Amsterdam banking house Hope & Co. was active in placing the Russian loan of 1820 as well as the loan of 1840 of which "Dutch investors again took the bulk" (PLATT, 1984, p.69). Hope had given an interest in the two silver ruble loans of 1831 and 1832 to Barings, the well-known London merchant bank, and in 1850 Barings, despite the lack of sympathy of the British public for tsarist Russia, launched a loan which was to contribute to the completion of the Moscow - St. Petersburg railway (IBIDEM,

p. 62f.). Furthermore, Hope and Barings launched yet another Anglo-Dutch loan in 1866 as well as a railway loan together with a French syndicate during the following year. Altogether there seems to be agreement that "the Dutch market retained its leadership in Russian finance into the late 1860s" when the onset of the Russian railway boom proved to go far beyond the limited capacities of the Amsterdam market (IBIDEM, p. 51f., 73).

These recurrent services delivered by foreign capital to the Russian state should, however, not tempt us into overestimating their importance. One should agree with D.C.M. Platt when he comes to the conclusion, that "Russia's needs for foreign finance were relatively slight before the railway boom of the late 1860s. Commercial credit may, in fact, have occupied a more important role than a conventionally recognizable investment by foreigners in Russian railways or Imperial loans" (IBIDEM, p. 73).

The railway boom of the late 1860s and early 1870s was conspicuous and changed the country's capital needs in a profound manner. Average annual railway construction had amounted to 443 km during the period 1861-65. It increased to 1,378 km in 1866-70 and to 1,660 km in 1871-75, a figure surpassed only during the second half of the 1890s (FALKUS, 1972, p. 55). One of the reasons for this sudden increase must be that the government had changed its policy towards railway construction: instead of building the lines itself, the government increasingly left the initiative to private groups and preferred to support them by guaranteeing their dividend and interest payments. Consequently, between 1866 and 1872, more than twenty new private railway companies were founded in Russia (MAI, 1970, p. 52). Until 1870, French capital was heavily engaged in these new ventures. But, once the Franco-Prussian war and its aftermath had temporarily closed the Paris market and reduced French lending capacity, it was Germany who became the principal supplier of capital to the Russian empire for the course of the following two decades (PLATT, 1984, p. 59f., 65).

German banks had, of course, not been totally inactive earlier. Mendelssohn & Co., one of the most important private banking houses in Berlin, had already launched two Russian loans in 1854 and 1855 when, during the Crimean war, London and Paris had remained practically closed to Russian capital needs whereas the Prussian capital offered at that time a sort of a neutral haven. Immediately after the war, Mendelssohn had launched another Russian loan, most of which was, however, subscribed in London (SCHAEFER, 1995, p. 218f.). From 1863, when the first Russian railway loan was introduced at the Berlin stock exchange, a growing number of German banks was engaged in launching Russian railway bonds and shares in Germany. Among them were Berlin-based private banking houses like Mendelssohn & Co., Warschauer & Co., and Bleichröder as well as joint-stock banks from Berlin - among them most noteworthy Disconto-Gesellschaft and Berliner Handels-Gesellschaft. Sal. Oppenheim of Cologne, the Darmstadt Bank für Handel und Industrie as well as the Frankfurt branch of the Rothschilds were also quite active in this field (MAI, 1970, p. 48ff.). Other banks in other German cities like Hamburg or Breslau followed. Thus, at the end of the 1860s, in Germany "here was a large network of banks which traded in Russian railway securities"(IBIDEM, p. 55).

4. Foreign Banking in Russia until the 1880s

The inflow of German capital during the 1860s and 1870s was closely connected with the various activities of German banks. They acted not only as mere intermediaries on the Berlin capital market, and through their agents in Russia itself, but also tried to get a firm hold of the Russian capital market by participating in newly founded credit institutions in St. Petersburg, Warsaw, Riga, and Helsinki. This type of direct investment became feasible only when, in the aftermath of the Crimean war, the Russian state decided to liquidate the monopoly of state banks and to found a state- owned commercial bank in 1860. From this point onwards private capital, from inside or outside of the country, could flow into the banking sector without risking direct intervention by the Russian state. There had been private banking houses before, founded in Russia by immigrants from Germany, but their founders had quickly acquired Russian nationality for tax reasons and therefore cannot be considered to be foreign investors (MAI, 1970, p. 64f.).

A first participation of foreign banking houses can be traced back to 1864, when the first private Russian joint-stock bank, the St. Petersburg Private Commercial Bank, was founded. 20 percent of its capital came from abroad, but a precise distribution of its origin and of its further development does not seem to be possible (IBIDEM, p. 68). The "Gründerjahre", as the highly speculative boom years around 1870 have been called, were not an exclusively central European phenomenon. And this may be illustrated by the fact that, between 1869 and 1873, 37 new joint-stock banks and 58 banks founded according to cooperative principles were created all over the Russian Empire (POHL, 1988, p. 13). There were two of the new joint-stock banks which were to become quite important and had foreign banks among their founders right from the beginning: the St. Petersburg Bank of Discount and the St. Petersburg International Commercial Bank, both of them created in 1869. In the case of the Bank of Discount three major German banks, Disconto-Gesellschaft, Bleichröder, and probably also Mendelssohn & Co. participated. Among the founders of St. Petersburg International Commercial Bank there were private banking houses from Hamburg and Frankfurt as well as from London and Amsterdam. The capital of this bank was increased considerably in 1872 with rather conspicuous participations of the Österreichische Credit-Anstalt of Vienna and of the Berlin Disconto-Gesellschaft who delegated each two representatives on its board. A considerable part of the new shares were then launched by Disconto-Gesellschaft on the Berlin stock exchange (MAI, 1970, p. 69f.). There were other joint-stock banks founded with foreign participation at Riga, Warsaw, and Helsinki during these years: The Riga Commercial Bank of 1872 saw, among others, the Berliner Handels-Gesellschaft and private banking houses from Hamburg, Berlin, and Königsberg among its founders The Warsaw Discount Bank was created in 1870/71 with the help of St. Petersburg and Warsaw merchant bankers as well as by the Schlesische Bankverein of Breslau and another Breslau private banking house. Several banks from Berlin were to be found among the founders of the Lodz Commercial Bank, opened in 1872. In Finland, then a Russian grand duchy, three banks from Denmark, Norway, and Sweden together with Erlanger & Söhne from Frankfurt, Norddeutsche Bank and Vereinsbank from Hamburg and the Berlin banking house Gebrüder Meyer founded, in 1872, the Nordic Joint-Stock Bank for Trade and Industry with headquarters in Helsinki (IBIDEM, p. 71f.).

The only French bank which became established formally in Russia during that period was Crédit Lyonnais, then the most important French deposit bank: In January 1878 an agency was inaugurated at St. Petersburg, but for the moment it had to bear the name of its manager Cellérier because the Russian authorities would not admit the name of the mother company. This refusal was finally withdrawn by Imperial order in August 1879 (BOUVIER, 1961, Vol. 2, p. 753ff.). Crédit Lyonnais was, in any case, the first foreign bank to be allowed to establish a proper branch office in the Russian Empire. Until then, foreign banks had just taken participations in newly founded or already existing Russian banks.

Two years later, in 1881, the Deutsche Bank and its ally, the Wiener Bankverein, took an important share in the capital increase of the Russian Bank for Foreign Trade, St. Petersburg, and controlled from now on - if we are to believe Joachim Mai - about 25 percent of the capital of this important Russian bank (MAI, 1970, p. 159f.). This seems to have been the last really important German investment in the Russian banking sector before 1914.

A few years later there was a fundamental change in Russo-German relations, and its most spectacular signal became Bismarck's famous *Lombardverbot* of 1887, when the chancellor interdicted to the Reichsbank to accept Russian securities as collateral. This, together with a guided press campaign against Russia's credit, "caused a panic among German holders of Russian bonds" and drove these securities to the French market (CRISP, 1976, p. 101). The *Lombardverbot* was, in a certain way, the prelude to the ensuing *renversement des alliances*, and as a consequence the French Republic relieved the German Empire as Russia's prinicipal ally and creditor.

5. Foreign Banking from the 1890s to the First World War

It is interesting so see that during the first two decades of the Franco-Russian *tête-à-tête* the Parisian banks did their growing business in Russia mostly with local agents who had access to the highest government and military circles instead of engaging themselves heavily in the Russian credit sector. There were, of course, exceptions: Crédit Lyonnais had, as already mentioned, started with its St. Petersburg agency. In 1891 and 1892 two other agencies were established in Moscow and Odessa.

Société Générale, another big French deposit bank, chose the other possible way by creating, in 1901, a subsidiary, the Northern Bank. By doing this, the French bank wanted, to some degree, get rid of at least part of its industrial Russian securities which became too visible on its balance sheets. Transferring them to its Russian subsidiary seemed to be an elegant solution. The Russian authorities on the other hand, who had to grant the concession for this joint-stock bank, might have seen there a better opportunity for placing their industrial securities on the French market (GIRAULT, 1973, p. 359ff.). Five years later, Banque de l'Union Parisienne (B.U.P.) and Banque de Paris et des Pays-Bas (Paribas), two typical French *banques d'affaires,* became partners in Northern Bank. It is difficult not to see this at least partially as a result of the economic crisis of 1901/02 and of the deep political crisis of 1905/06 which had hit quite badly the tsarist Empire and particularly its banks. By accepting new banking partners, Société Générale clearly demonstrated that it had learnt from these negative experiences and that it was trying to reduce its risks for the foreseeable future. As a matter of fact Northern Bank grew quite rapidly during the following years increasing its network of agencies all over the Empire from a number of 14 in 1904 to about 50 six years later (BONIN, 1994, p. 41). At the beginning of 1910 and according to the volume of its assets, Northern Bank occupied the eighth rank among the Russian joint-stock banks (GIRAULT, 1973, p. 495). Azov-Don Bank, which then held the fourth rank, profited from a substantial participation of Société Marseillaise de Crédit Industriel et Commercial in its capital increase of May 1906, and two years later a group of French banks, led by B.U.P., guaranteed another capital increase of Azov-Don (IBIDEM, p. 496). At the end of 1909, Crédit Mobilier Français, a *banque d'affaires* created a few years earlier which had, apart from its name, nothing to do with famous Crédit Mobilier gone bankrupt in 1866, took, together with private banking houses from London and Paris, an important participation in St. Petersburg Private Commerce Bank (IBIDEM, p. 504f.).

The deepest inroad made by French banking into the Russian credit sector came in 1910 when Paribas and Société Générale decided to merge Northern Bank and Russo-Chinese Bank, this latter one founded in 1895 to further Russian influence in the Far East, and especially in Manchuria, but recently quite in trouble because of mismanagement and Russia's defeat in the war of 1905 with Japan. This merger which created Russo-Asiatic Bank as it was then called, not least for political reasons, found the agreement of the Russian Ministry of Finance[1] and was approved by the Tsar in June 1910. It became at once the largest Russian joint-stock bank and acted as sort of a bridgehead of French capital in the Empire launching an important part of new Russian industrial securities, particularly those in which French capital was interested (GIRAULT, 1973, p. 499ff.). B.U.P. which, as we have seen, had acquired an interest in Northern Bank in 1906, did not participate in the foundation of Russo-Asiatic Bank. In 1910, when the latter one came into being, B.U.P. on the contrary took an important share in a Moscow credit institution, United Bank, which was itself the result of a merger organized two years earlier (IBIDEM, p. 506ff.).

One can find other French participations in the Russian credit sector, but they were of comparatively minor importance and cannot be illustrated here in detail. It should be mentioned, however, that by 1914 French capital controlled not only the biggest bank, the Russo-Asiatic, but that there were also important French shares in the capital of the third largest, the seventh, and the ninth largest Russian bank. The overwhelming part of these investments had been done since 1907. It was as if all of a sudden the French investors had detected the overall importance of banking for the stability of their industrial and commercial undertakings in the tsarist Empire. René Girault believes that, since French investors could no longer exercise enough control by their loan policy, they switched over to banking as an instrument of information and control (IBIDEM, p. 514).

Let us finally talk of two other problems connected with foreign banking in the Russian Empire: (1) Can the precise dimensions of the foreign share in Russian banking be fixed or do we have to rely on rather rough estimates ? and (2) What do we know on the activities of these foreign-controlled banks ?

6. Foreign Banking in Russia on the Eve of World War I: Quantitative and Qualitative Evidence

In 1922, P.V. Ol' published a book on "Foreign capital in Russia" which has rightly become of much use and which in 1983 finally came out in an English translation (OL', 1983). According to Ol' total French investment in the Russian credit sector (only joint-stock banks) was 113.3 million rubles in 1914. The French share of the capital of seven Russian banks, all of them quoted at the Paris stock exchange, amounted to 39 percent; apart from this, Ol' counted other less important French holdings in other Russian banks (IBIDEM, p. 38ff.). Ol's estimates have been criticized by economic historians like Carstensen or Crisp who think that they are generally too high and should be redone (quoted IBIDEM, p. XXVff.). But, as Ol's editors say quite convincingly, as long as a thorough revision of his data has not been undertaken, "Ol's data remain the most comprehensive and reliable set of estimates" (IBIDEM, p. XXVIII).

Ol' calculates furthermore that overall German investment in Russian joint-stock banks amounted to 84.7 million rubles. The German share in the eight banks which had been quoted at the Berlin stock exchange (not all of them identical with the ones quoted in Paris and mentioned above) amounted to 27 percent of their capital (IBIDEM, p. 100ff.). Again, there has been considerable criticism of these data: A well-renowned expert like Heinz Lemke insists that we do not know to what extent Deutsche Bank and/or Disconto-Gesellschaft owned shares of Russian Bank for Foreign Trade or St. Petersburg International Trade Bank. For decades, they certainly maintained close ties with either bank, but the shares which they presented at the annual meetings could also have been owned by their German customers, and their percentage was in any case much lower than Ol's estimates would allow (LEMKE, 1985, p. 199ff.). The only other foreign economy with an important stake in the Russian banking sector was the British one which came third with an investment estimated by Ol' at 25.7 million rubles (OL', 1983, p. 55).

What the banks based in Paris, Berlin or London did, can be more or less reconstructed: they financed trade with Russia for their native firms but also for Russian firms who wanted to export or import. Many of them also launched, as we have seen, Russian securities - state and private - on the international market. All these activities are by now rather well known.

What did those Russian banks do which had been founded by foreign capital or which had received foreign capital at a later stage? If we look at the entire branch of Russian joint-stock banking we can conclude with Olga Crisp that "from the 1860s until the 1890s the joint-stock banks mainly provided working capital by discounting bills of industrial firms and by advancing documentary credits for the importation from abroad of machinery, raw cotton, chemical products, etc. [...] From the 1890s onward, at first gradually, and then on an increasing scale, the joint stock banks added to their existing activities a new branch - namely, provision of fixed capital for the formation of new concerns or the redevelopment of old ones. In this way the largest joint stock commercial banks added investment banking, on an appreciable scale, to their ordinary deposit banking business" (CRISP, 1976, p. 141f.). St. Petersburg banks, working especially with investment goods producers, came increasingly close to the central European type of universal banking whereas joint-stock banks from Moscow, which had particularly close relationships with the textile industry, were more similar to the British type of commercial banking.

Neither the French nor the German banks which had acquired considerable stakes in a number of Russian joint-stock banks managed to control them completely even if they owned a clear majority of their capital (ANAN'ICH and BOVYKIN, p. 274f.; LEMKE, 1985, p. 199ff.)[2]. The reason might be found in the particular role of the Russian state which could, via the concession system, keep a continuous influence on the growth of joint-stock banking. Besides, the State Bank, since 1897 central bank of issue, maintained, together with the Treasury, substantial deposits in many joint-stock banks and could thus also exercise considerable influence on their behavior. All this meant that bank managers had to keep constantly an eye on the State's interests, and these did not necessarily coincide with the views of their foreign majority owners. Russia was not a dependent territory, which could eventually be looted, but "an independent sovereign nation", and therefore "economic gain depended on economic performance" (McKAY, 1970, p. 385).

7. Some Conclusions and Possible Lessons

It is certainly not easy to draw provisional conclusions from this single albeit very important case. One fact seems to come out quite clearly: portfolio investment in government securities could be managed from the home base via local agents (who, of course, needed to be well placed, not least politically). Direct investment, especially in those branches in perennial need of government support, could probably find a more solid and durable support if there were bankers on the spot who were able to control and monitor the individual situation in the interest of the foreign creditors. As direct investment of the "state support" - type increased capital participation in Russian banks became more and more important for foreign investors.

If we want to draw any lessons from this we must keep in mind that tsarist Russia, despite its autocratic regime and continuous revolutionary threats, was, already during the 1860s, considered to be a very solid debtor who never delayed any interest payments. The currency reform of 1897 with its transition to the gold standard created the monetary stability and the obvious links with the rest of the world that helped to attract foreign capital in a decisive manner. Comparatively still rather high real interest rates (TILLY, 1994, p. 211f.) combined with the gold standard's guarantees for profit transfer created the climate in which a steady inflow of foreign investment could - with the exception of a few crisis years - develop and even grow increasingly. If there was a recipe it must have been as simple as that: economic and political stability.

Endnotes

1 Société Générale, Historical Archives, Paris: Minutes of the Board of Directors (Conseil d'Administration), vol. 15, p. 271 (1/2/1910), p. 293 (22/2/1910), p. 346 (19/4/1910).

2 In the German case, clear proof of the feeling that there was not much of control over these banks must be seen in the fact that the foundation of new affiliates of German banks in Russia had been discussed several times by diplomats and bankers during the last years before the outbreak of World War I (LEMKE, 1885, p. 164 ff.).

References

ANAN'ICH, B. V. and BOVYKIN, V. I. (1991), "Foreign banks and foreign investment in Russia," in CAMERON, R. and BOVYKIN, V. I. (eds.), *International banking, 1870-1914*, Oxford University Press, New York, Oxford, 253-290.

BONIN, H. (1994), *La Société Générale en Russie*, Société Générale, Paris.

BONWETSCH, B. (1974), "Das ausländische Kapital in Rußland. Bemerkungen zum Forschungsstand," *Jahrbücher für Geschichte Osteuropas*, N.S. Vol. 22, 412-425.

BOUVIER, J. (1961), *Le Crédit Lyonnais de 1863 à 1882*, S.E.V.P.E.N., Paris.

CAMERON, R. and BOVYKIN, V. I. (eds.) (1991), *International banking, 1870-1914*, Oxford University Press, New York, Oxford.

CRISP, O. (1953), "Russian financial policy and the gold standard at the end of the nineteenth century," *Economic History Review*, 2nd Ser., Vol. 6, 156-172.

CRISP, O. (1976), *Studies in the Russian economy before 1914*, Macmillan, London.

FALKUS, M. E. (1972), *The industrialisation of Russia*, Macmillan, London.

FEIS, H. (1965), *Europe, the world's banker, 1870-1914* [1st ed. New Haven 1930], W.W. Norton, New York.

FISCHER, W. (ed.) (1985), *Handbuch der Europäischen Wirtschafts- und Sozialgeschichte*, Vol. 5, Klett-Cotta, Stuttgart.

GEYER, D. (ed.) (1975), *Wirtschaft und Gesellschaft im vorrevolutionären Rußland*, Kiepenheuer & Witsch, Cologne.

GIRAULT, R. (1973), *Emprunts russes et investissements français en Russie, 1887-1914*, A. Colin, Paris.

GOOD, D. F. (1994) (ed.), *Economic transformations in East and Central Europe. Legacies from the past and policies for the future*, Routledge, London, New York.

GREGORY, P. R. (1994), *Before command. An economic history of Russia from emancipation to the first five-year plan*, Princeton University Press, Princeton, N.J.

HERTNER, P. (1990), "German banks abroad before 1914," in JONES, G. (ed.), *Banks as multinationals*, Routledge, London, New York, 99-119.

JONES, G. (ed.) (1990), *Banks as multinationals*, Routledge, London, New York.

KAHAN, A. (1985), "Rußland und Kongreßpolen, 1860-1914," in FISCHER, W. (ed.), *Handbuch der Europäischen Wirtschafts- und Sozialgeschichte*, Vol. 5, Klett-Cotta, Stuttgart, 512-600.

VON LAUE, T. (1963), *Sergei Witte and the industrialization of Russia*, Columbia University Press, New York, London.

LEMKE, H. (1985), "Finanztransaktionen und Außenpolitik. Deutsche Banken und Rußland im Jahrzehnt vor dem Ersten Weltkrieg," Akademie der Wissenschaften der DDR, Zentralinstitut für Geschichte, Berlin (GDR).

MADDISON, A. (1964), *Economic growth in the West. Comparative experience in Europe and North America*, The Twentieth Century Fund, New York.

MAI, J. (1970), *Das deutsche Kapital in Rußland, 1850-1914*, VEB Deutscher Verlag der Wissenschaften, Berlin (GDR).

McKAY, J. P. (1970), *Pioneers for profit. Foreign entrepreneurship and Russian industrialization, 1885-1913*, University of Chicago Press, Chicago, London.

NÖTZOLD, J. (1966), *Wirtschaftspolitische Alternativen der Entwicklung Rußlands in der Ära Witte und Stolypin*, Duncker & Humblot, Berlin.

OL', P.V. (1983), *Foreign capital in Russia* [1st ed. Petrograd 1922], translated from the Russian with an introduction by G. Jones and G. Gerenstain, Garland Publishing, New York, London.

PLATT, D. C. M. (1984), *Foreign finance in continental Europe and the United States, 1815-1870. Quantities, origins, functions and distribution*, George Allen & Unwin, London.

POHL, M. (1988), *Geschäft und Politik. Deutsch-russisch/sowjetische Wirtschaftsbeziehungen 1850-1988*, v. Hase & Koehler, Mainz.

RICHARDSON, G. B. (1972), "The organisation of industry," *Economic Journal*, VOL. 82, 883-896.

RILEY, J. C. (1980), *International government finance and the Amsterdam capital market, 1740-1815*, Cambridge University Press, Cambridge.

SCHAEFER, K. C. (1995), *Deutsche Portfolioinvestitionen im Ausland 1870-1914*, LIT Verlag, Münster.

SIDOROV, A. L. (1975), "Zur Finanzlage Rußlands vor 1914: Staatshaushalt und Staatsschuld," in GEYER, D. (ed.), *Wirtschaft und Gesellschaft im vorrevolutionären Rußland*, Kiepenheuer & Witsch, Cologne, 252-276.

TILLY, R. (1994), "German banks and foreign investment in Central and Eastern Europe before 1939," in GOOD, D.F. (ed.) (1994), *Economic transformations in East and Central Europe*, Routledge, London, New York.

Comments on

Historical Lessons of Foreign Banking in Eastern Europe

The Case of Tsarist Russia

Hans Kernbauer

The role of banking in general and of foreign banking in particular in economic development is a topic which is of great importance not only for historians but for today's economic policy makers, too. ALEXANDER GERSCHENKRON's (1952) propositions about the respective role of banks and the state in fostering economic growth is still a useful hypothesis to start with. It has been demonstrated by the work of EDUARD MÄRZ (1968) in his history of the Austrian Creditanstalt how in the second half of the last century banks of the credit mobilier type were used in Austria on purpose to overcome the relative economic backwardness of the country. It is clear that a transformation of historical lessons into economic policy prescriptions for tomorrow is not possible. Nevertheless, an historical analysis can lead to insights about the causes and consequences of particular institutional settings in an historical context.

The topic of Hertner's paper points to an issue which is currently debated among economists under the heading: corporate governance. Corporate governance relates to the mechanism used by shareholders and creditors to control the management of large companies. In a stylized way, two main types of control mechanism exist (DITTUS, 1994): "One relies on widely dispersed share ownership, combined with highly liquid securities markets and a sophisticated market infrastructure. Share price movements and the potential threat of take-overs provide here the disciplinary forces for management. This type of control is widespread in the United States and the United Kingdom. The other model is characterized by concentrated share ownership. Shareholders with a substantial stake in a firm can reap a large enough portion of the fruits of effective monitoring to make such activity worthwhile. Large deviations by management from the path of maximizing the value of the firm can be detected by the shareholders, which can then induce the necessary corrections, including the replacement of management. In many countries this monitoring function is carried out partly by banks which hold the firms debt and have additional advantage of privileged access to information. Shareholder control with a large role for banks is predominant in continental Europe and Japan."

It is obvious that there does not exist a free choice for policy makers as to which of this stylized models of corporate governance they would like to introduce in a particular situation. Certain preconditions determined largely by the state of economic development have to be given if an economy is to rely on dispersed ownership for the managerial control of firms, e.g. liquid securities markets, company laws which induce firms to publish reliable information about the value of the firm, existence of a minimum amount of monetary wealth, confidence in the stability of the currency.

For banks to be able to perform the monitoring role of management they need inter alia an appropriate capital base and expertise in credit evaluation. In addition to these microeconomic necessities some macroeconomic preconditions must be met: In particular, the proper regulation and prudential supervision of banks has to exist in order to make sure that banks play the envisaged role in the long run.

The role of banks versus credit markets as outside control mechanism for firms can be discussed under the topic of intermediation between savings and investment, too. The Anglo-Saxon model evolved on the basis of a stock of money capital which had been accumulated through international trade in goods, commodities and precious metals. The continental model was somehow implanted in economies characterized by the dominance of agriculture and small firms producing for local markets. In addition, when analyzing the developments of capital markets one has to look at the structure of public finances in a particular country: By which means does the State fund its expenditures? Is an effective tax system in place, that is, a tax system that does not hamper economic growth but is able to generate the necessary revenues? What about the expenditures of the state? Do, in particular, military expenditures present a too heavy burden for the economy?

This and other factors seem to have influenced the type of intermediation, the importance of capital market versus banks in different countries.

With this theoretical framework in mind it is possible to summarize some highlights of foreign banking in central and eastern Europe in the 19th and early 20th century:

- Domestic banks were financing the needs of the aristocracy, the state and small firms, but not engaged in the funding of industrial ventures.
- Banks founded by foreign capital with the participation of locals, sometimes encouraged by economic policy considerations, acted along the credit mobilier type.
- As creditors and large shareholders banks controlled many industrial firms by taking seats in the boards of directors.
- The value of the industrial assets was assessed more by informed guesses of the members of the board of directors than by other information.
- The underdeveloped state of the capital market hindered banks from getting rid of their industrial shares except in short periods of speculative activities on the stock exchanges.
- Banking supervision did not exist until the interwar period. The controllers of industry were not controlled by a supervisory authority.
- When the domestic capital base of banks was eroded by the territorial break-up of the Habsburg monarchy banks became exposed to the vagaries of foreign money markets and were only able to attract short-term capital by paying a high premium.

- The collapse of the monarchy forced the banks to dispose of their most valuable assets abroad. This was the hour of local banks which took over the most profitable firms in their national territory.
- Some lessons can be drawn from the crises of continental banks in the 1920s and 30s:
  - (a) As there seems to be no alternative to the function of lender of last resort by the central bank and the taxpayer an appropriate legal framework and an effective prudential supervision must be institutionalized to prevent mismanagement and moral hazard at the same time.
  - (b) Long-term investments should be funded by domestic (long-term) savings. The dependence on short-term foreign capital puts the banking industry on a shaky basis.
  - (c) As the underdeveloped state of securities markets is a feature of the relative backwardness of economies banks will have to play an important role in financing industrial ventures. The improvement of the functioning of capital markets, which rests on the long-run stability of the monetary, economic and legal framework should nevertheless be supported by economic policy measures. Intermediation via capital markets leads in the end to deconcentration and a wider distribution of risks, thereby enhancing the stability of the financial, economic and political system of a country.

References

GERSCHENKRON, A. (1952), "Economic Backwardness in Historical Perspective," in HOSELITZ, B. F. (ed.), *The Progress of Underdeveloped Areas*, Chicago, 3 -29.

DITTUS, P. (1994), *Corporate Governance in Central Europe/The Role of Banks*, Bank for International Settlements.

MÄRZ, E. (1968), *Österreichische Industrie- und Bankpolitik in der Zeit Franz Joseph I. am Beispiel der k.k. priv. Österreichischen Credit-Anstalt für Handel und Gewerbe*, Wien 1968

E. Restructuring and Privatization of Polish Banks

Miroslaw Bojanczyk

1. Restructuring the Banking Sector

As a result of the macroeconomic changes under way since 1989 and the inability of banks and enterprises to function effectively in the new market environment, the Polish economy has been inflicted with a problem of bad debts. Polish enterprises were indebted to both their suppliers and banks. Bad loans constituted 20-30% of banks total loan portfolios.

The gravity of this situation has led the Polish government to take steps to resolve the problem: it was to this end that the Financial Restructuring of Banks and Enterprises Program was developed. The aim of this program was both to cure the problem of bad debts and to eradicate the main causes that lie behind it. As such, it goes beyond the simple removal of bad debts from bank portfolios. The Restructuring Program was primarily intended to achieve the following:

- to offer a second chance to those debtors that show some potential for future growth and are also capable of preparing a realistic business plan and a financial strategy;
- to eliminate those that are incapable of functioning efficiently in a new economic environment;
- to improve the health of the whole financial sector by substantially eliminating the problem of bad debts.

The Polish Restructuring Program focused at the very beginning on the nine state-owned commercial banks (SOCBs) which had been hived off from the National Bank of Poland in 1989. Later this program was extended to specialized banks such as PKO BP, BGZ S.A., PKO S.A. In 1991 the Government decided that these banks should be privatized and as a first step the banks were transformed into joint stock companies with the State Treasury as the sole shareholder.

The Program for Financial Restructuring of Enterprises and Banks (in the form of law) was prepared at the Ministry of Finance and came into force in February 1993. The main goal of this program was to raise the safety and stability of the banking sector by removing "bad loans" from the banks' balance sheets, injecting capital into selected state-owned banks, and restructuring the firms which were the banks' debtors.

1.1 Legal Solutions Applied under the Program

The seven SOCBs and the three other state-owned specialized banks have been recapitalized with 15-year redeemable treasury bonds worth **$1.9bn**. These bonds are denominated in Polish currency, with an interest rate based on the National Bank of Poland rediscount rate. As long as the SOBSs are not privatized the bonds are serviced and redeemed by the use of budgetary resources. After privatization both the interest payments on the bonds and their redemption will be financed by the Polish Bank Privatization Fund (PBPF), which currently amounts to $459mn. The PBPF is financed through grants and loans extended originally by the foreign governments to support the stabilization of the Polish Zloty. The financing of the remaining part of recapitalization bonds was put on the budget.

The restructuring strategy adopted in Poland was different to that usually applied in developed countries.

Some experts proposed a standard approach to the bank restructuring process, which can be described as a one-off solution that aims to increase bank assets by transferring their bad loans to a specially created loan recovery institution and replacing them with interest bearing treasury bonds. The Ministry of Finance rejected this approach because we did not believe that:

(1) a centralized, government planned institution can vigorously and effectively recover bad debts,

(2) an adequate incentive system could be designed that would ensure an active approach toward the indebted enterprises,

(3) the centralized solution addresses the causes of a problem, which we believed lay primarily in the lack of experience and expertise of the banks in handling credit activities in a market environment.

The method of restructuring adopted in Poland also intended to contribute to the growth of experience and expertise of the banks in conducting credit operation and resolving bad debts.

The improvement of the banking sector was to be achieved by increasing banks capital while at the same time reducing their financial commitment to creditunworthy borrowers.

The SOCBs included in the restructuring program were compelled to separate 'doubtful' and 'lost' credits which were in their credit portfolio at the and of 1991 and on the date of the Law's enactment. In the case of the state-owned specialized banks the first date was the end of 1992. The nominal value of these loans constituted the basis for calculating the amount of an additional capital required by the banks. The banks were recapitalized by using long-term treasury bonds. The capital injection was supposed to increase the capital solvency ratio of participating banks up to 12 percent.

The Act of Financial Restructuring of Enterprises and Banks imposed on the banks subject to recapitalization certain duties and limitation with respect to the loans removed from the portfolio during the audit for December 1991 (December 1992 in the case of specialized state-owned banks). The banks were obliged to complete the restructuring of separated loans by the deadline set down by the Minister of Finance under the authorization contained in the Act.

The Act of Financial Restructuring of Enterprises and Banks and changes to some other acts (Dz. U. No 18, Clause 82) came into life on the 18th of March

1993. Its basic goal was to supply such legal instruments as to allow the effective restructuring both of the enterprises having difficulties with servicing their debts and of the banks' loan portfolios.

In order to receive funds from the Ministry of Finance a bank, according to Art. 52 Subsection 2 of the Act on Financial Restructuring of Enterprises and Banks, is required to

(1) have an experienced firm of accountants perform an audit on its financial statements,

(2) separate the low quality loan portfolio from the other credits,

(3) establish a department to manage the low quality loan portfolio .

(4) prepare restructuring plans for each credit in the low quality loan portfolio.

Capitalized banks were no longer allowed to grant loans or guarantees to those debtors, whose debts were separated in accordance with Art. 52 Subsection 2 Clause 2, except in the case where the new funds are associated with the banking agreement or where the debtor is the State Agency for Agricultural Property.

In order to make the banks undertake special measures towards enterprises generating bad debts, the Ministry of Finance obliged the banks to sell unrepayable loans which were separated in accordance with Art. 52 Subsection 2 Clause 2 by 31 March 1994. This sales obligation did not apply to cases of:

- conciliation or court settlement with a debtor,
- debtor bankruptcy,
- debtor liquidation,
- regular repayment by the debtor for at least 3 months,
- debtors in the hands of the State Agency for Agriculture Property or State Farm Enterprises.

In the event that a bank fails to restructure the debt by any of the above mentioned methods or decides that none of the methods is feasible, the Act on Financial Restructuring obliges it to sell the loan in the open market before the established deadline.

The financial restructuring could be made only in those cases in which there existed a real possibility of survival in the new economic situation. The major restructuring instruments envisaged by the restructuring law were: writing off debts, rescheduling debt service obligation and debt-equity swaps.

The seven commercial banks and three specialized banks have been recapitalized through the use of 15-year redeemable bonds. The treasury bonds received by the banks amounted to PLN 4 billion (PLZ 40 trillion) in total or US$ 1.9 billion - taking into account the rate of exchange from the period of emission of treasury bonds.

The Bank Conciliation Agreement (BPU) led to a 38% - 70% reduction of debt and to an acceleration in the privatization of debtors, i.e. state-owned enterprises, given the use of debt-equity swaps.

1.2 Outcome of the Program

The recapitalized banks were forced to restructure their low quality credit portfolio (3 & 4 credit classification group) before the deadline established by the Ministry of Finance. In the course of the program the banks restructured 2.915 debts which amounted to PLN 4.7 billion total (PLZ 47 trillion), it equals about $ 2 billion.

Table E1 Instruments of Restructuring

Bank conciliation agreement	587 enterprises
Sales of debt	572 debtors
Liquidation	157 debtors
Bankruptcy	243 debtors

Although only recapitalized banks were forced to clean their credit portfolio, all banks could use the instruments introduced by the Act on Restructuring, i.e. the bank conciliation agreement.

2. Privatization of Polish Banks

The creation of new private banks is of major importance for the development of the banking system. Nevertheless, there can be no doubt that state banks continue to play a prime role within the Polish banking sector. Thus, measures resulting in a permanent change in the ownership structure of the entire system are crucial. One of the projects that may make a substantial contribution to Poland's financial sector efficiency is the program for privatizing the nine state banks popularly known as the "commercial" banks, all of which were established in February 1989 by hiving off local branches from the National Bank of Poland (NBP).

2.1 Current Status of the Polish Banking Sector

Ownership structure

- State-owned banks: PKO SA, PKO BP, BH, BGZ, BGK, PBR, BZ, PBK, PBG, BDK, PBKS.
- Former state-owned banks, now privatized, listed on the Warsaw Stock Exchange: BRE, WBK, BSK, BPH, BG.
- There are circa 80 private banks in Poland - 11 of which are listed on the Stock Exchange.
- Over 1620 cooperative banks.

Profitability of the industry

- Average return on total assets (1994) was more than 2%, compared to an European average of around 0.5%.

Major developments

- Changes in traditionally dominant market shares - demonopolization of the market: PKO SA and PKO BP in domestic savings, Bank Handlowy (BH) in foreign trade and BGZ in agriculture.
- Lower interest rates: the NBP refinancing credit reference rate has decreased by 39% points, from 72% in 1991 to 31% in 1994.
- Lower average spreads: falling from around 15% points in 1991 to around 6% points in 1994.

2.2 Overview of Polish Banking Sector Privatization

Framework notes

The privatization program of the nine commercial banks, developed by the Ministry of Finance, was approved by the Government Economic Committee on the 18th of March, 1991. The Government program of ownership reform within the banking sector envisages the gradual elimination of the Treasury dominant stake in all the banks concerned.

The program intends to:

- specify owners who have their own capital stake in the bank's activity;
- facilitate restructuring;
- facilitate the transfer of modern banking know-how and the entry of Polish banks in foreign markets (through the acquisition of shares by foreign investors);
- encourage a competitive banking environment;
- increase the flexibility of banking operations with supply adapting to changes in market demand;
- increase central government revenues from privatization.

It was assumed that after bank privatization the ownership structure of the 9 banks, taken as a whole, might be the following:

- Treasury - 30%
- domestic investors (both corporate and individual) - 40-50%
- bank employees - 10%
- foreign investors - 10 - 20%.

The intention to involve foreign banks as strategic investors stems from the need for capital support for the banks and for banking know-how. At the same time, any foreign partner would acquire broad access to the Polish market through the existing branch network of the privatized banks and their developed client relationships.

<u>The privatization cases</u>

- Privatization of the first bank: Bank Rozwoju Eksportu S.A. (BRE - the Export Development Bank) was completed in 1992, with the assistance of a syndicate led by the investment bankers N.M. Rothschilds & Sons, Ltd. This privatization was completed by distributing a majority of shares through a public offer. No strategic investor was appointed during that period. A few months ago Commerzbank bought a 21% stake in BRE.
- In the case of Wielkopolski Credit Bank (WBK) the role of strategic investor was played by the EBRD. Over 16% of shares of WBK are owned by Allied Irish Banks PLC.
- The case of Bank Slaski in Katowice (BSK): ING Bank bought a nearly 26% share with several obligations regarding investment in the Polish Bank as well as know-how transfer and joint ventures to be undertaken by the two partners.
- Privatization of BPH - market valuation approach: after the broadly discussed privatization scheme of BSK, the Ministry of Finance decided to change the approach. The offer came through a separate session of the Stock Exchange, where the investors' bids exceeded the minimum price set by the Ministry. Preparation for privatization was not associated with a search for foreign banks/strategic investors (as in the case of BSK). However, involvement of such

an investor should not be excluded at a later stage. At the moment the role of strategic investor is being played by the EBRD.

Upcoming privatizations

Due care has to be paid to the issue of marketability of the privatized banks. Major uncertainty arises around the potential market depth (the BPH offer exceeded $150 million). One has to bear in mind that there are 11 more banks already listed on the Polish Stock Exchange, some private banks want to be listed in the near future and the Polish government will privatize 5 large state-owned commercial banks (among these Powszechny Bank Kredytowy will be privatized in spring 1996).

In 1993 and 1994 40 trillion zl were disbursed in the form of long-term Treasury bonds for the recapitalization of the nine state-owned banks, PKO BP and the Bank for Food Economy (BGZ).

The cost of a bank recapitalization may be shared by the central government and the Polish Bank Privatization Fund (established in 1992 through the use of part of the Zloty Stabilization Fund, which was set up in 1990 by a number of developed countries to support the Polish currency). Under an agreement between the Polish government and the governments contributing to the Stabilization Fund, the Restructuring Bonds held by a particular bank will be serviced (both interest payments and redemption of principal) by the central government until the bank concerned is privatized.

The resources from the Bank Privatization Fund were made available under the condition that by January 1995 another bank was to be privatized - the one after Bank Slaski (BPH in Cracow) - and that the other six banks were to be privatized by the end of 1996. The Polish government is making efforts to fulfill this condition. It is expected that in the next couple of weeks the Polish government will accept the privatization and consolidation program submitted by the Ministry of Finance.

Table E2 Ownership Structure of Privatized Banks

Bank Name	Year of Privatization	Main Shareholders	%
Bank Rozwoju Eksportu	1992	Commerzbank	21.00
		Agencja Rozwoju Gospodarczego	9.31
		PPTFP PIONEER	7.90
Bank Wschodnio-Europejski	1993	PHZ Bartimpex	78.13
		State Treasury	10.31
Wielkopolski Bank Kredytowy	1993	Allied Irish Bank	36.26
		EBOR	23.90
		State Treasury	5.10
Bank Slaski	1993/94	ING BANK	54.08
		State Treasury	5.00
Bank Przemyslowo-Handlowy	1994/95	State Treasury	46.67
		EBOR	15.06
		ING BANK	5.31
Polski Bank Rozwoju	1995	State Treasury	62.48
		Agencja Rozwoju Przemyslu	16.28
		Citibank (Poland)	8.12
Bank Gdanski (stan na 1.02.1996)	1995	Skarb Panstwa	39.94
		BIG i podmioty zalezne	26.75
		The Bank of New York (Depository Bank - GDR)	25.14

Source: M. Bojanczyk.

Table E3 Number of Banks, December 1995

Groups of Banks	Number of Banks	Names of Key Players
Banks emerged from NBP	9+1	BSK, WBK, BPH, PBK, BG, PBI
Specialized banks	6	BH, PKO S.A., PKO BP, BGZ
Banks with majority share of Polish capital	44	BIG, BOS, BUDBANK
Banks with majority shares of foreign capital	18	CITI, ING, ABN AMRO, CHASE BANK (GE)
Banks in the process of organization	2	
Banks in the process of registration	2	
Other	7	
Total (without cooperatives)	**89**	
Co-operative banks	1500	

Table E4 Value of Treasury Bonds Earmarked for the Capital Injection to Banks

Bank	Value of treasury bonds received in 1993	Value of Treasury bonds received in 1994
Bank Depozytowo-Kredytowy S.A.	1,790,210	-
Bank Gdanski S.A.	1,609,590	-
Bank Przemyslowo-Handlowy S.A.	1,598,430	-
Bank Zachodni S.A.	1,445,060	-
Pomorski Bank Kredytowy S.A.	1,363,670	-
Powszechny Bank Gospodarczy S.A.	1,256,390	-
Powszechny Bank Kredytowy S.A.	1,936,650	-
Powszechna Kasa Oszczednosci BP	5,734,200	-
Bank Gospodarki Zywnosciowej S.A.	4,265,800	15,300,000
Bank Polska Kasa Opieki S.A.	-	3,700,000
Total	**21,000,000**	**19,000,000**
Total in USD	**$ 1.1 billion**	**$ 0.8 billion**

Table E5 Impact of the Capital Injection on the Cook Ratio

Bank	Before recapitalization		After recapitalization on 31.12.94.	
	Capital bn PLZ	Cook ratio %	Capital bn PLZ	Cook ratio %
Bank Depozytowo-Kredytowy S.A.	1,709	9.8	3,341.2	13.2
Bank Gdanski S.A.	1,135	14.7	3,430.0	35.9
Bank Przemyslowo-Handlowy S.A.	929	3.2	2,124.4	23.7
Bank Zachodni S.A.	1,394	5.8	4,145.5	21.5
Pomorski Bank Kredytowy S.A.	917	3.5	1,524.0	18.2
Powszechny Bank Gospodarczy S.A.	1,485	9.5	2,077.5	16.7
Powszechny Bank Kredytowy S.A.	1,327	12	2,516.0	18.9
Powszechna Kasa Oszczednosci BP	750	bd	8,506.7	9.3
Bank Polska Kasa Opieki S.A.	3,591.7	bd	6,210.0	16
Bank Gospodarki Zywnosciowej S.A.	bd	-75.3*	15,553.0	-29.61**

* 09.09.94 r.

** BGZ S.A. requires further engagement of the State Treasury in 1996.

Table E6 Information about the Bank Conciliation Agreement (BPU) as of 31 May 1995 (values in mn PLN)

Bank	Number of BPU	Value of debts at the day of signing BPU	Value of reduction of debts at BPU %	Debt into equity swap at BPU %	Number of creditors in BPU	Appeal against BPU in a court					
						Number			Value		
						A	B	C	A	B	C
BDK S.A. W LUBLINIE	26	153	50%	35%	7803	0	24	1	0	7.4	0.05
BG S.A. W GDANSKU	14	548	38%	43%	2797	0	56	1	0	57	2.8
PBG S.A. W LODZI	31	676	66%	27%	6550	0	22	0	0	23.9	0
BPH S.A.W KRAKOWIE	16	661	53%	19%	5722	0	5	2	0	2.3	0.5
PBK S.A. W WARSZAWIE	23	370	70%	0%	3756	0	10	0	0	12.8	0
PBKS S.A. W SZCZECINIE	20	275	51%	4%	3377	0	16	0	0	7.2	0
BZ S.A. WE WROCLAWIU	45	206	65%	6%	7937	0	31	2	0	7.5	0.08
TOTAL	**149**	**2736**			**30139**	**0**	**140**	**5**	**0**	**110.7**	**3.38**

A = acknowledged by court.
B = rejected by court.
C= others.

Source: Information from banks.

Table E7 The Effect on Banks of the Act on Financial Restructuring of Enterprises and Banks

		31. 05. 1994			30.09.1994			30. 06. 1995			As at 30. 06. 1995		
		Seven commercial banks		% Share in total	PKO BP		% Share in total	PKO S.A.		% Share in total	BGZ		% Share in total
		No.	Credit + interest in 000's		No.	Credit + interest in 000's		No.	Credit + interest in 000's		No.	Credit + interest in 000's	
Credit classification*	I	112	2,200		8	58		6	120		33	310	
	II	49	1,210		0	0		10	190		16	310	
	III	64	1,270		7	147		19	630		52	560	
	IV	429	9,800		279	2,856		393	8,080		1300	18,020	
Others		138	1,260			0			0			0	
TOTAL		**792**	15,750	**100.0**	**294**	**3,060**	**100.0**	**428**	9,010	**100.0**	**1401**	19,200	**100.0**
Conciliation or court settlement				**48.1**			**29.4**			**21.2**			**28.1**
not completed		32	250	**1.6**	17	740	**24.2**	72	1,540	**17.1**	132	3,390	**17.7**
completed		166	7,320	**46.5**	4	160	**5.2**	20	370	**4.1**	150	1,990	**10.4**
Sales of debt				**5.8**			**23.2**			**7.5**			**24.0**
not completed		47	560	**3.6**	49	230	**7.5**	5	130	**1.4**	45	630	**3.3**
completed		47	340	**2.2**	41	480	**15.7**	14	550	**6.1**	324	3,970	**20.7**
Liquidation				**2.6**			**2.0**			**5.0**			**4.4**
not completed		13	90	**0.6**	5	60	**2.0**	13	440	**4.9**	73	640	**3.3**
completed		31	320	**2.0**	0	0	**0.0**	1	10	**0.1**	21	220	**1.1**
Bankruptcy				**10.1**			**43.7**			**34.3**			**24.4**
not completed		1	10	**0.1**	153	1,100	**35.9**	98	2,890	**32.1**	217	4,150	**21.6**
completed		126	1,570	**10.0**	10	240	**7.8**	12	200	**2.2**	26	540	**2.8**
Loan recovery		201	1,720	**10.9**	11	20	**0.7**	13	80	**0.9**	54	230	**1.2**
cash													
shares		0	0	**0.0**	0	0	**0.0**	0	0	**0.0**	0	0	**0.0**
assets		2	50	**0.3**	0	0	**0.0**	2	10	**0.1**	0	0	**0.0**
Current servicing of the loan		109	3,450	**21.9**	0	0	**0.0**	1	0	**0.0**	19	100	**0.5**
Action not started		**17**	60	**0.4**	**4**	40	**1.3**	**178**	2,800	**31.1**	**340**	3,320	**17.3**
completed		**682**	14,780	**93.8**	**235**	2,140	**69.9**	**204**	5,090	**56.5**	**540**	9,150	**47.7**
not completed		**93**	910	**5.8**	**55**	880	**28.8**	**47**	1,120	**12.4**	**521**	6,720	**35.0**

Completed = completed under the terms of the Act.

Uncompleted = uncompleted under the terms of the Act.

*The table contains only separated portfolio credits (3 & 4 group; over 1 bn PLZ), during the execution of the Act some credits went good.

Table E8 Financial Results of the Banking Sector in 1994

Specification	Public Banks S.A.	Private banks: major domestic capital	Private banks: major foreign capital	Co-operative banks	"9" Banks	Four specia-lized banks	Banks quoted on the stock exchange
Share in total income of the banking sector (%)	58.4	13.4	2.6	10.70	26.8	31.6	10.5
Share in income expense of the banking sector (%)	60.1	16.2	2.2	16.4	24.5	33.4	9.6
Gross financial result as a share of gross profit of the banking sector (%)	47.9	-4.4	1.9	-25.3	40.9	20.4	16.3
Taxes and financial result expenses as a share of total financial result expenses (%)	19.6	6.0	2.0	1.5	13.9	8.6	6.5
Share in net profit of the banking sector (%)	552.5	-190.2	67.4	-500.6	519.6	216.2	189.9
Income expenses as a share of total income (%)	88.7	104.6	71.7	132.4	79.0	91.2	78.7
Gross profit index (%)	8.4	-13.4	25.9	-25.8	18.0	5.5	16.8
Profitability as for 1000 zl income in zl	69.1	-104.0	186.1	-341.9	142.0	49.9	132.1

Source: *Analizy*, No. 5 (28), May 1995, Foundation of Education and Scientific Research.

Figure E1 Bad Loans Compared to Total Loans for Selected Polish Banks on 31st December 1995 (in 000's PLN)

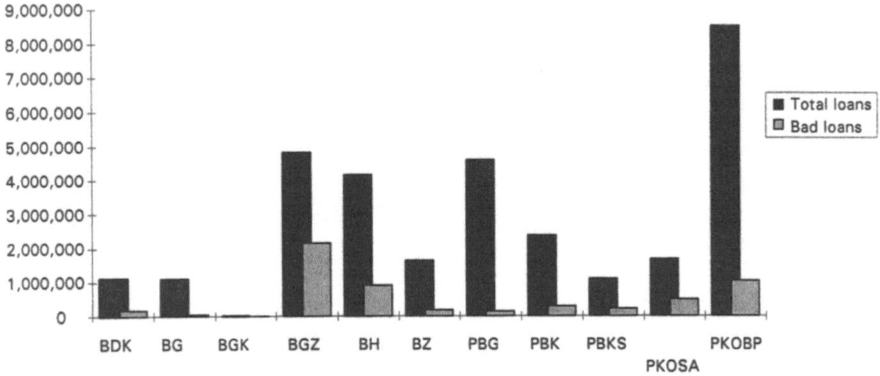

Table E9 Financial Results of Selected Banks, 31 Dec. 1995 (in 000's PLN)

Bank	Capital	Assets	Gross profit	Net profit	ROE	ROA	Solvency ratio	Current ratio
BDK	297,264	2,900,408	157,923	78,178	26%	3%	21%	0.71
BG	457,896	4,019,201	184,697	106,413	24%	3%	25%	0.71
BGK	45,300	251,524	6,782	5,798	13%	2%	71%	1.16
BGZ	1,602,862	12,596,424	361,964	361,964				0.42
BH	1,485,709	9,253,852	741,224	427,511	32%	5%	17%	1.04
BZ	353,939	3,836,152	194,087	107,344	30%	3%	16%	0.71
PBG	238,977	8,664,448	123,957	55,640	23%	1%	18%	0.67
PBK	547,546	7,446,566	264,801	174,890	33%	2%	21%	0.69
PBKS	256,503	3,188,376	117,994	44,215	17%	1%	17%	0.58
PKOSA	728,785	19,565,703	311,536	189,800	27%	1%	13%	0.71
PKOBP	1,051,593	28,212,398	475,871	313,317	30%	1%	9%	0.69
PBI S.A.	177,733	3,470,698	67,256	26,231	15%	1%	...	
PROSPER	15,000	230,803	-41,905	-41,905				
TOTAL	7,066,375	99,935,050	2,940,835	1,865,069	26%	2%	23%	0.74

F. High Public Debt: Consequences for Investment and Growth

Timothy Lane[1]

1. Introduction

The development of financial markets has widened the scope for governments to finance fiscal imbalances. In some cases, including some European countries, these imbalances have accumulated to create large public debts (Figure F1) - in some instances of such a magnitude to engender talk of unsustainability (CORSETTI and ROUBINI, 1991).[2] Concerns over the possible economic and financial consequences of these debts has been among the factors that have spurred governments, in Europe as elsewhere, to fiscal adjustment in recent years (LACHMAN, 1994). The possible disruptive consequences of the debts of countries in a common currency area have led to the incorporation of a maximum level of public debt as one of the Maastricht criteria for participation in Economic and Monetary Union (EMU). Financial markets have penalized high-debt countries in the form of real interest rate spreads *vis-à-vis* their more financially-sound neighbors (Figure F2).[3] And the magnitude of the public debt is routinely blamed for the sluggish development of private financial markets in some countries: in Italy, for instance, the conventional wisdom is that equities markets are stunted because they cannot withstand the competition from government bonds.

Notwithstanding the presumption that high public debt constitutes a drag on an economy, the experience suggests that the story is more complex. The growth record of high-debt European countries relative to their neighbors presents no clear pattern (Figure F3). Casual empiricism gives some support for the notion that public debt crowds out private investment, as several high-debt European countries have had a relatively low share of investment in GDP; others, however - notably Italy and

Greece - have devoted a reasonably large share of their GDP to investment (Figure F4). It is likely that there are other difference between these high-public-debt countries which compensate for the burden imposed by fiscal imbalances. This discussion suggests a need to re-examine the predictions of economic analysis for the consequences of high public debt, and interpret the experience in this light.

High public debt is certainly not a new phenomenon. For instance, during the 1920s several European countries had war-related debts amounting to well over 100 percent of their GDP (ALESINA, 1988; EICHENGREEN, 1990). Then, as now, governments adopted two main approaches to dealing with their debts: servicing them through higher taxes, with the attendant distortion to economic activity; or eroding them through inflation and currency depreciation, thus imposing other social costs. A third approach, adopted in some instances under extraordinary circumstances, involved extreme measures such as default, forced debt consolidation, or capital levies.

This paper seeks to put the costs of high public debt in perspective, focusing on its potential impact on investment and economic growth. It takes as its starting point a standard representative-agent framework in the neoclassical growth model. In this framework, Ricardian equivalence holds, implying that high public debt inhibits investment only to the extent that debt servicing is financed through future distortionary taxes. Moreover, in the neoclassical model the long-run growth rate is equal to an exogenous rate of technical change; thus in the steady state taxes can affect the capital stock and gross investment, but not the growth rate. Moreover, in this model, inflation enters only as a tax on bonds, fully compensated by the nominal interest rate, and thus has no long-run effect on the capital stock.

The remainder of the paper discusses the various qualifications and extensions of the basic model, drawing on relevant strands of the analytical and empirical literature. Section 3 discusses the implications of endogenous growth

Figure F1 Debt-to-GDP Ratios (in Percent)

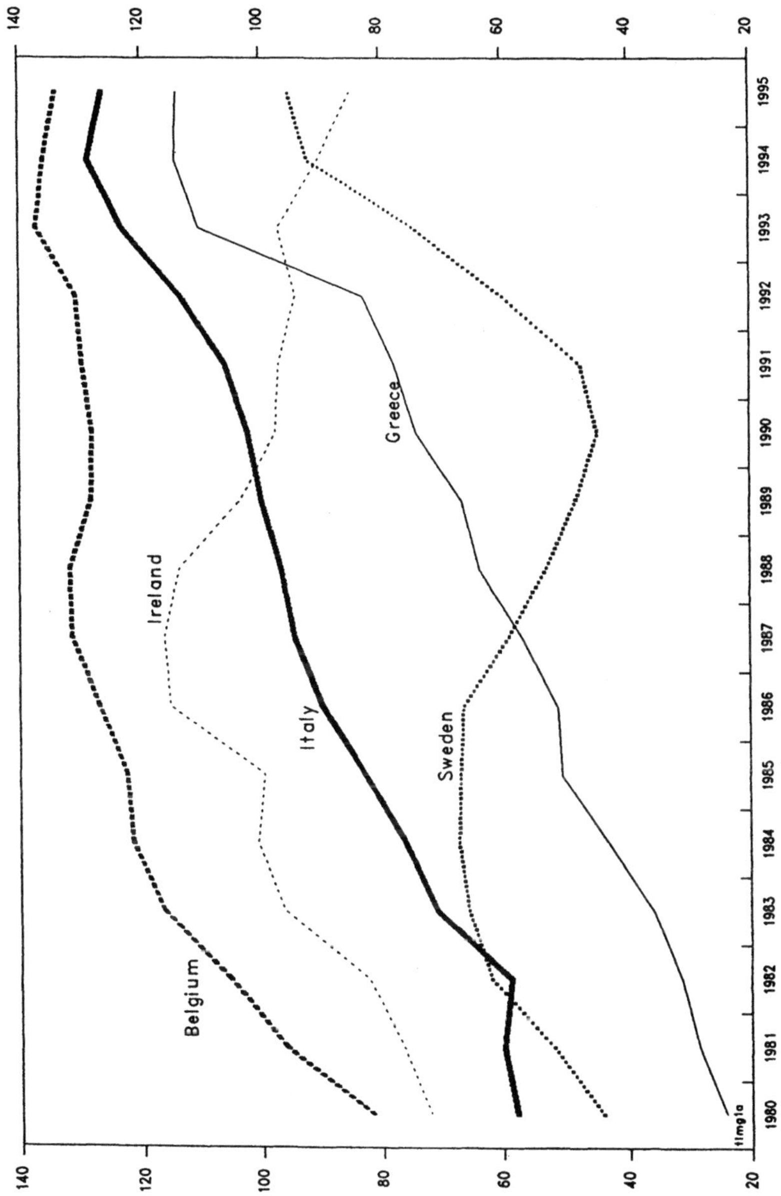

Source: International Monetary Fund, World Economic Outlook database.

Figure F2 Real Interest Rate Differentials (relative to Germany)

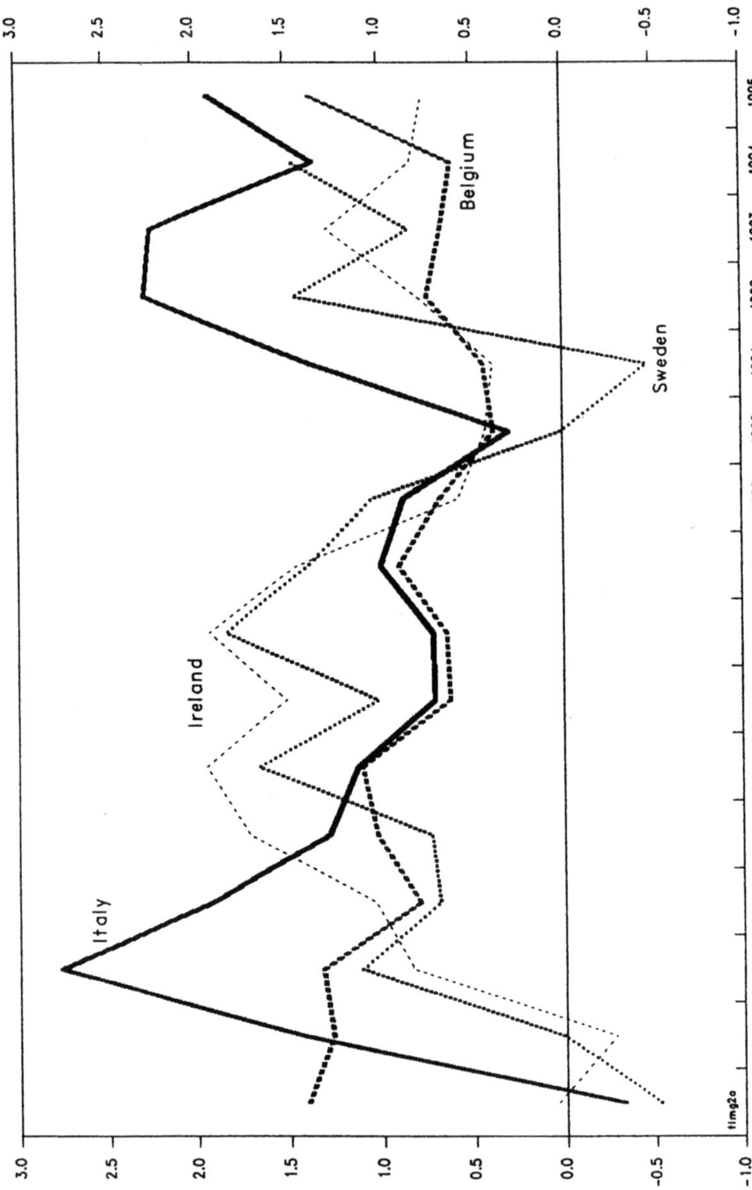

Source: International Monetary Fund, International Financial Statistics.

Figure F3 Real GDP Growth (in Percent)

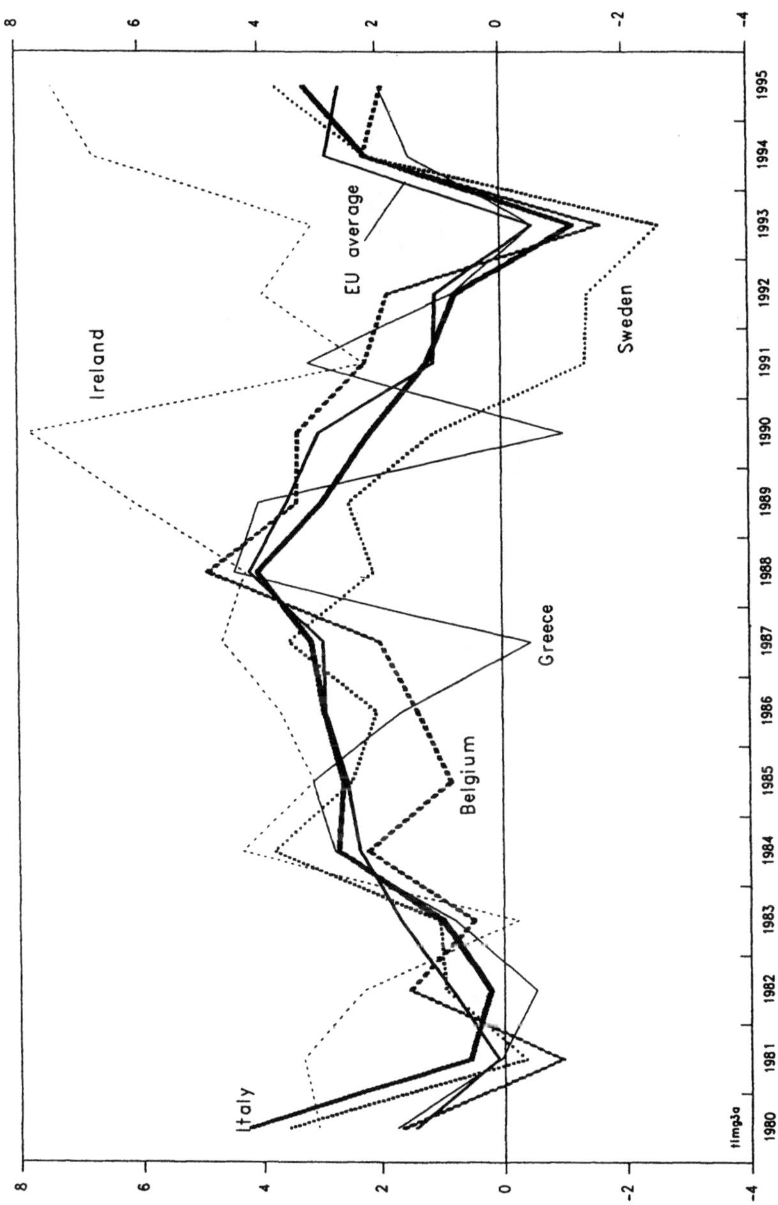

Source: International Monetary Fund, World Economic Outlook database.

Figure F4 Gross Fixed Capital Formation (in Percent of GDP)

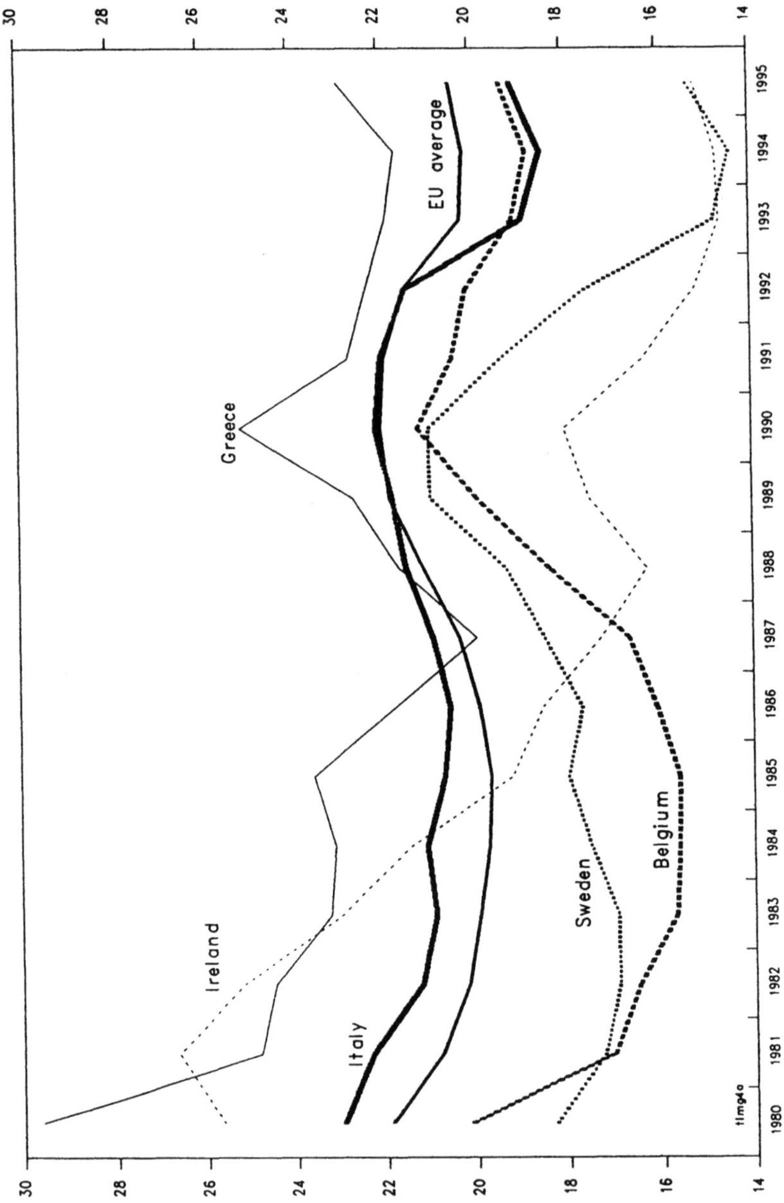

Source: International Monetary Fund, World Economic Outlook database.

models, and the influence of infrastructure accumulation on growth. Section 4 discusses the limitations of Ricardian equivalence, which are by the same token limitations of the neoclassical growth model. Section 5 briefly discusses the social costs of inflation, including the empirical evidence on the link between inflation and growth. Section 6 discusses empirical evidence bearing directly on the link between fiscal variables and growth. Section 7 discusses some approaches that treat government behavior as endogenous, including political economy models and models of regime switching. Section 8 presents some general conclusions.

2. A Simple Framework

The relationship between an indebted government and the household sector can be discussed in the context of a discrete-time representative-agent model. The government's budget constraint is

$$G_t - T_t + (1 + r_{t-1})B_{t-1} = B_t \tag{1}$$

where G_t is government expenditure, T_t tax revenue, r_{t-1} last period's interest rate, and B_t the stock of public debt. It is subject to the limiting condition that

$$\lim_{t \to \infty} \beta^t B_t = 0 \tag{2}$$

where β is a discount factor. Constraint (1) can be developed by specifying the types of taxation available:

$$T_t = T_t^L + \theta_t (Y_t - \delta K_t + r_{t-1} B_{t-1}) + \phi_t (1 + r_{t-1}) B_{t-1} \tag{3}$$

Here, T_t^L represents a lump-sum tax (or equivalently in this model, a pure tax on labor). In the second term of (3), θ_t represents a rate of income tax applying both to income from bonds and from real production Y_t, with an allowance for depreciation of private capital K_t at a rate δ. In the third term, ϕ_t may be interpreted as an inflation tax on nominal assets (bonds), whether anticipated or unanticipated. It is related to the inflation rate π_t as $\phi_t = \pi_t/(1 + \pi_t)$. For simplicity, we ignore money.

The tax on nominal assets ϕ_t also subsumes the possibility of debt repudiation (or variants such as forced consolidation), which, in a representative agent model with only one financial asset, enters in the same way.

The government's objective is to choose a sequence of taxes and spending, G_t, θ_t, and ϕ_t, subject to equations (1) to (3). Another issue is to specify what government spending is used for: one standard approach would be to assume that government spending enters the household's consumption function separably, although there is empirical evidence suggesting that it may be a complement or substitute for private consumption (ASCHAUER, 1985).

The presentation that follows is agnostic with regard to the government's behavior. An obvious approach would be to assume that the government maximizes social welfare, defined as the discounted utility of the representative agent, which here depends only on the time profile of public and private consumption. However, unless one admits the possibility that the government does not optimize social welfare, policy conclusions are foregone.

The household seeks to maximize its own utility. The household is assumed both to consume and to invest, in order to maximize

$$\max \sum_{t=0}^{\infty} \beta^t [U(C_t) + V(G_t)] \tag{4}$$

Its budget constraint is

$$C_t + K_{t+1} + B_t = (1-\theta_t)[F(K_t, L_t; K_t^G) - \delta K_t] - K_t + \frac{1+r_{t-1}}{1+\pi_t} B_{t-1} - T_t^L \tag{5}$$

with transversality condition

$$\lim_{t\to\infty} \beta^t B_t = 0 \tag{6}$$

The production function depends on labor L and capital K (which can be interpreted as including human as well as physical capital):

$$Y_t = F(K_t, L_t) \tag{7}$$

The household is assumed to supply inelastically the labor at its disposal, L_t, which grows over time as

$$L_t = (1+\gamma)L_{t-1} \tag{8}$$

Here, the parameter γ can be interpreted either as a rate of population growth or a rate of Harrod-neutral technical change. In this initial discussion, this parameter is treated as exogenous, thus ruling out the considerations of the endogenous growth literature; the latter will be discussed later in the paper.

In maximizing (4) subject to (5), (6), and (7), the household chooses time paths for consumption, investment, and bond holdings. This problem can be solved using standard dynamic programming methods by defining a value function $J(K_{t+1},B_t)$ as the maximized discounted value of utility beginning in period t+1. The first-order conditions give rise to familiar results:

$$\frac{U'(C_t)}{\beta U'(C_{t+1})} = (1-\theta_{t+1})\frac{1+r_t}{1+\pi_t} \tag{9}$$

where U' denotes dU/dC. That is, the marginal rate of substitution of present for future consumption equals the after-tax real interest rate.

Another familiar condition pertains to investment:

$$F_K(K_t, L_t) = \frac{1+r_t}{1+\pi_{t+1}} - (1-\delta) \tag{10}$$

where F_K denotes $\partial F/\partial K$. Neither the tax rate θ nor lump-sum taxes T^L enter equation (10) - thc familiar result that investment is unaffected by taxes to the extent that these apply evenly to income from bonds and capital.

Finally, the whole economy is faced with a resource constraint:

$$F(K_t, L_t) = C_t + (K_{t+1} - (1-\delta)K_t) + G_t \tag{11}$$

A key question is whether a rise in the deficit G-T will result in crowding out - necessitating a rise in interest rates to stimulate a rise in savings or fall in private investment to satisfy resource constraint (11). A related question is whether a larger inherited government debt has any real effects on resource allocation, either through larger interest payments or through other channels.

In the case in which all taxes are lump sum (or equivalently in this model, taxes on labor, T^L), the model displays Ricardian equivalence (BARRO, 1974): the consumption path chosen as in equation (9) is unaffected by changes in the intertemporal distribution of lump-sum taxes and transfers that leave their present value unchanged - as for instance a cut in taxes that results in a deficit to be financed through future taxes. Such a tax cut results in an equal increase in savings, with no effect on overall consumption or capital accumulation, or therefore growth.[4]

Conversely, taxation that is to fall on future investment income (from both bonds and capital) may discourage current savings and thus investment in both bonds and capital. This would imply that a larger outstanding stock of public debt, by necessitating a higher rate of future taxation to service it, may lead to an increase in current consumption at the expense of savings and investment. This effect may be partly or fully offset by a variation in the real interest rate.

This possibility can be explored in the context of the steady state. In the long run, the capital-labor ratio k stabilizes at a constant level; the capital stock and consumption grow at the rate of labor force cum technical change, γ. This also implies that the marginal rate of substitution $U'(C_t)/\beta U'(C_{t+1})$ is a constant. The steady-state after-tax real rate of interest, given by the right-hand side of equation (9), is thus invariant with respect to the income tax rate; a higher income tax rate is associated with a lower real interest rate.

The following results emerge. According to equation (10) it is the before-tax real interest rate that affects investment (given that the same tax rate applies to income from both capital and bonds). Therefore, higher anticipated future taxation results in a lower steady-state capital-labor ratio:

$$\frac{dk}{d\theta} = \frac{\dfrac{1+r}{1+\pi}}{(1-\theta)f''(k)} < 0 \tag{12}$$

and thus in lower steady-state output and consumption. (The steady-state growth rate is, of course, unaffected as this depends only on the rate of labor force growth cum technical change γ.) A lower steady-state capital labor ratio corresponds to lower investment and thus a lower rate of growth in the medium term, while the economy is converging toward the steady state.

The inflation tax has no such effect on the steady-state capital-labor ratio. A higher inflation rate π results in a proportionately higher interest rate r, with no effect on $(1 + r)/(1 + \pi)$. Thus, from equation (11) the steady-state capital stock is unaffected, and thus, so is the average rate of capital accumulation needed to reach the steady state.

This simplified model has been used first to illustrate that whether a high public debt affects investment and growth depends on how this debt is serviced:

1. If it is serviced through lump-sum taxation, it has no effect on the consumption path, and therefore *a fortiori* none on the steady state or on consumption dynamics. This is the pure Ricardian-equivalence case in which public debt is irrelevant.
2. If it is serviced through income taxation, including taxation of returns to investment, long-run growth is unaffected, but the long-run capital stock is lower, implying lower growth over the medium term.
3. If it gives rise to an inflation tax, there is no effect on the steady-state capital stock, and thus no effect on average investment over the medium term, although thc adjustment of the interest rate nullifies the net revuenues from the inflation tax. It is nonetheless possible that the inflation affects the transition path, depending on the dynamics of real interest rates and consumption; this in turn will depend more specifically on the form of utility and production functions.

This model is very simplified in several respects, but it provides a starting point for a discussion of several directions in which the basic framework could be modified. The discussion that follows will draw on the endogenous growth literature, the debate over Ricardian equivalence, and considerations related to the social costs of inflation. It will then consider the empirical evidence on the effects of fiscal policy on growth. Finally, it will consider alternative approaches to interpreting the behavior of governments.

3. Endogenous Growth and Infrastructure

In the neoclassical growth model just presented, the long-run growth rate is exogenous, and equal to the rate of labor force growth *cum* technical change. Endogenous growth models generate economic growth through other channels: through externalities from human capital or learning-by-doing (LUCAS, 1988); through constant returns to scale production of physical and human capital (REBELO, 1991); through the process of innovation (ROMER, 1990); or through the provision of public infrastructure (BARRO and SALA-I-MARTIN, 1992). Endogenous growth ›ly that public finance can influence the long-run growth rate through ›es for human capital accumulation or innovation, through the encouragement of innovation, or through the provision of public goods (XU, 1994). Such models are generally characterized by optimal taxation rules implying that tax rates should be smoothed over time. They tend to yield results that favor lower rates of taxation for physical and human capital, since these are the engines of growth.[5] Since a major impact of fiscal policy in such models is to influence the accumulation of human and physical capital, such models favor imposing a high tax burden in the short run in order to lower the tax burden later on (MILESI-FERRETTI and ROUBINI, 1994) - an example of the time inconsistency of optimal policy. This is a rationale for front-loaded fiscal adjustment to reduce the debt to a manageable level.

Figure F5 General Government Capital Expenditure (in Percent of GDP)

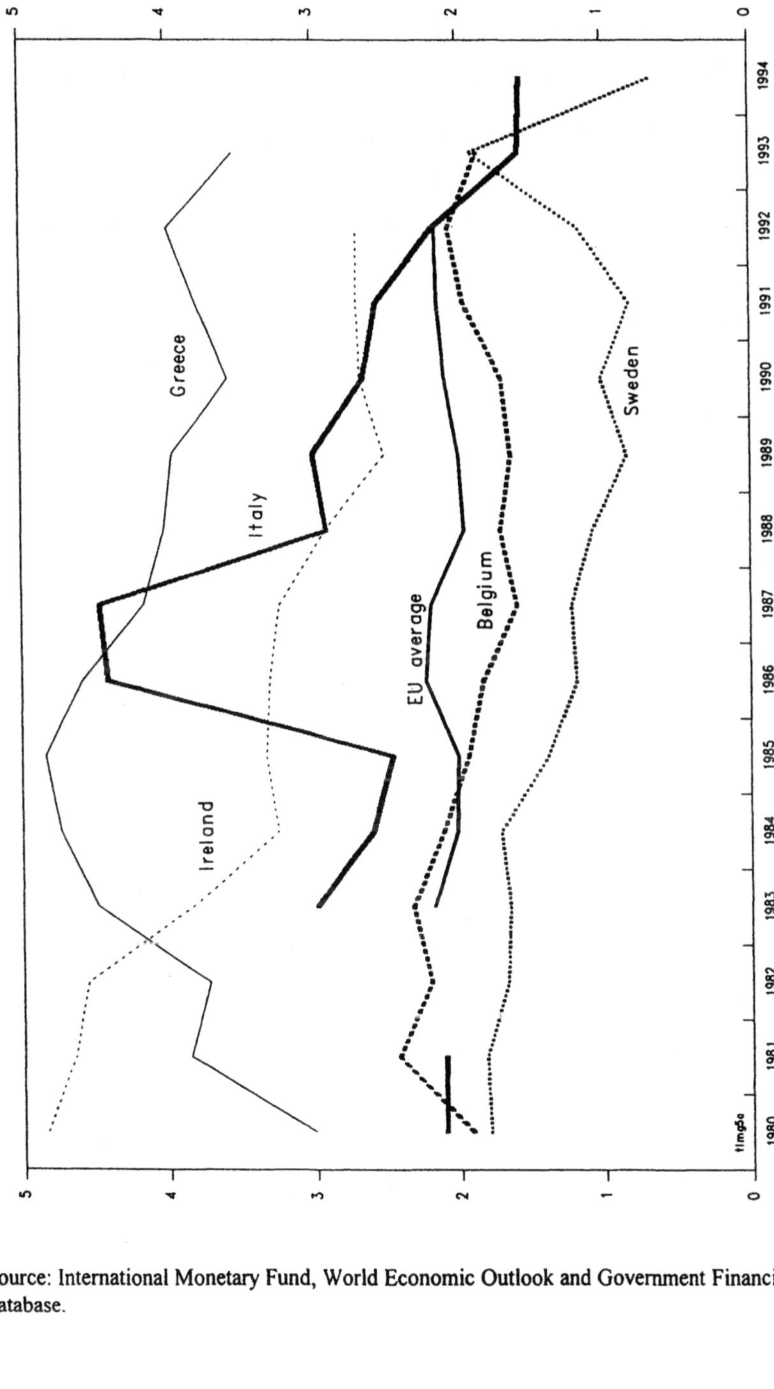

Source: International Monetary Fund, World Economic Outlook and Government Financial Statistics database.

The endogenous growth literature's treatment of public expenditure is suggestive. BARRO and SALA-I-MARTIN (1992) consider the implications of models in which public and private rates of return differ - as in the case in which human capital has externalities. In this framework, there is a rationale for tax policies that encourage investment expenditures and for the debt-financed provision of public goods; tax smoothing in this case implies that such expenditures be financed through debt serviced by an income tax, which in this model is in the nature of a user charge.[6]

There has as yet been relatively little exploration of the empirical relevance of this strand of the literature. Many of the high-debt European countries (with the exception of Sweden) have been characterized by relatively high levels of infrastructure investment (Figure F5). A cross-country study (CANNING et al., 1992) found evidence that specific types of infrastructure investment (telecommunications, electricity, and transportation) had positive effects on growth, but these results must be regarded as tentative. International comparisons are slippery in this area, though, since it is difficult to ascertain the efficiency of investment particularly for the provision of public goods.

4. Ricardian Equivalence

The neoclassical growth model is predicated on most of the same assumptions on which Ricardian equivalence is based - and Ricardian equivalence emerges as a special case of the model. Ricardian equivalence implies that a tax cut that raises the deficit would generate an equal increase in private savings, which would neutralize its effect on the economy. The effect of a rise in government spending would depend on the extent to which it is a complement or substitute for private spending.[7] BARRO's (1974) presentation of the Ricardian equivalence proposition provoked a prolonged debate over its relevance, with a large number of empirical studies seeking to test its relevance.[8] Some of the criticism of Ricardian equivalence has focused on the assumption of infinitely-lived consumers: Barro showed that the same implications would result in a world of families in which parents' savings decision is influenced by a bequest motive, precluding the possibility that government deficits now can truly shift a burden onto future generations. Critics pointed out various ways in which the family link between generations could be broken (TOBIN, 1980); one paper presented a *reductu ad absurdum* showing that if BARRO's argument is taken to its logical conclusion, it implies that all redistributive policies are neutral (BERNHEIM and BAGWELL, 1988). However, others have maintained that some of these criticisms, although valid, are beside the point, since in practice the majority of the burden of the public debt falls on the present generation (POTERBA and SUMMERS, 1987); the latter argument is probably, if anything, even more valid in high-public-debt countries.

Other studies suggested modifications to the standard model that would alter the influence of government deficits on private savings. One modification was to introduce liquidity constraints, such that households are unable to borrow against future income (DANIEL, 1993); in this case, government borrowing is a substitute for private borrowing which is limited by capital market imperfections. Others developed the argument that if lifetime income is uncertain, a tax cut that swells the deficit may still have positive real effects on private spending (BARSKY, MANKIW and ZELDES, 1986; FELDSTEIN, 1988).

Two decades of empirical work on Ricardian equivalence have failed to lead to conclusive results. Most empirical studies have examined U.S. data but the international experience offers no clearer picture: while some high-debt countries (Belgium, Italy, and Greece) have had relatively high private savings rates which would mitigate the effects of the deficit, this is by no means a universal pattern (Figure F6).

Figure F6 Private Savings (in Percent of Personal Disposable Income)

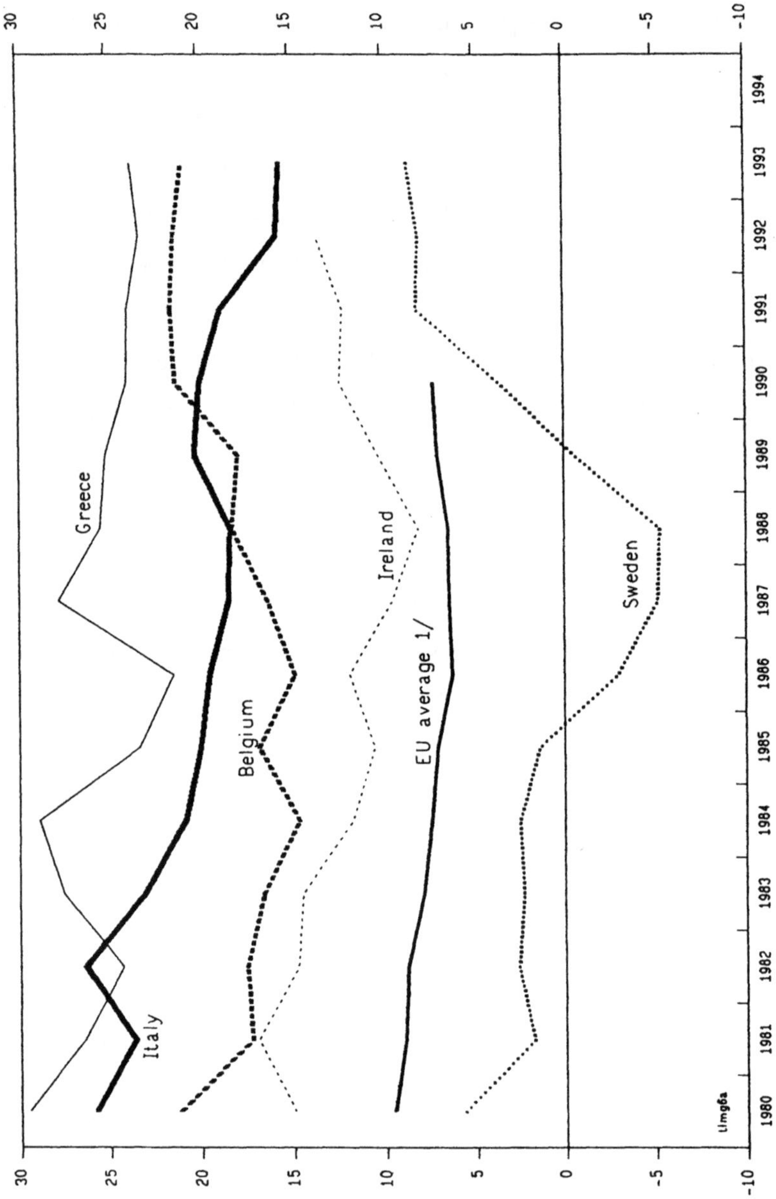

1/ Except Luxembourg.
Source: OECD Economic Outlook database.

Figure F7 Current Account Balance (in Percent of GDP)

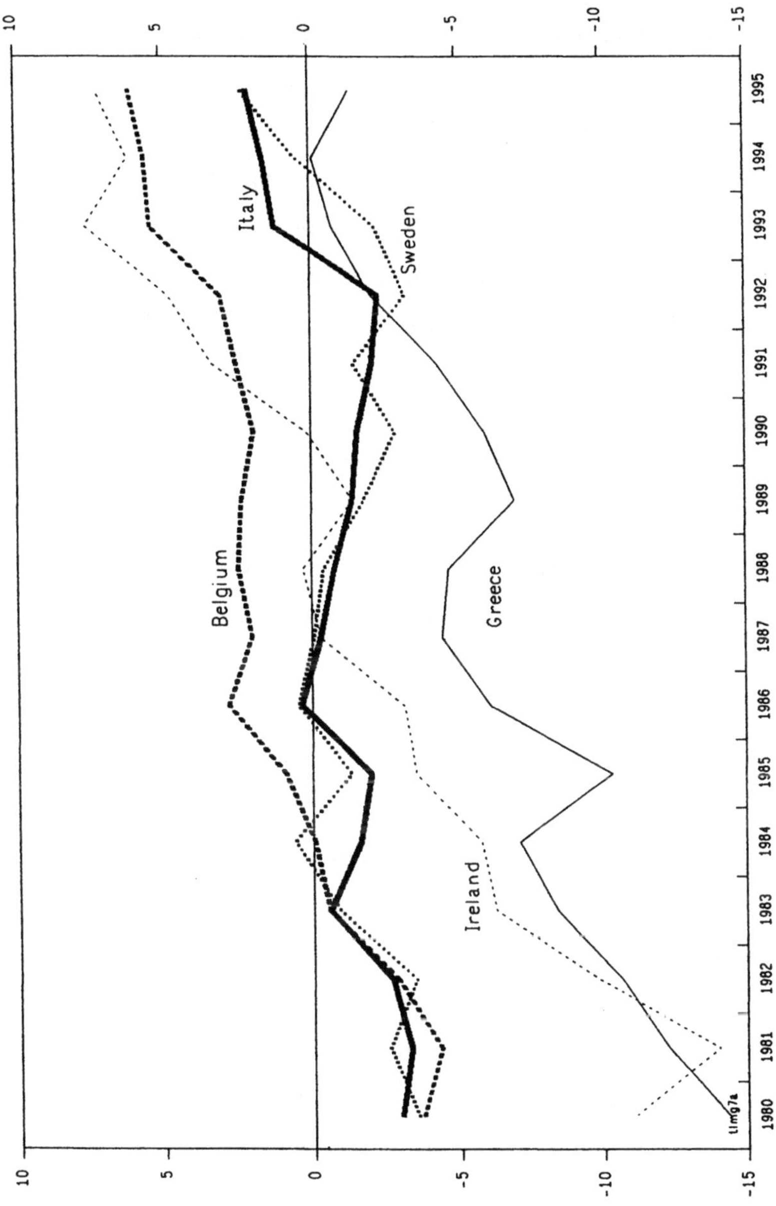

Source: International Monetary Fund, World Economic Outlook database.

In an open economy, the aggregate of public and private savings decisions are reflected in the current account, it is useful to consider the current-account-balances of high-debt countries; these produce no obvious pattern, though (Figure F7). In the case of Greece, fiscal deficits and the accumulation of public debt had a clear link with current account deficits and the accumulation of external debt (ALOGOSKOUFIS and CHRISTODOULAKIS, 1990), a current account imbalance that has been diminishing over the past several years. In Italy, in contrast, immoderate government deficits have been associated with moderate external current account deficits which have recently given rise to surpluses, whittling away what is already a rather moderate level of external indebtedness.

One line of empirical research has linked the assessment of Ricardian equivalence with a more general analysis of the effects of government spending on household spending behavior. KORMENDI (1983) found some empirical support for an extension of the principle of Ricardian equivalence, a "consolidated approach" in which households take account of government consumption and investment in their own consumption and investment decisions.[9] ASCHAUER (1985) employed a similar approach in an explicit optimizing framework, finding support for Ricardian equivalence, and also finding public consumption to be a substitute for private consumption. LEONARDO and RAZIN (1988) estimated an Euler-equation model that also permitted them to test the relevance of finite lifetime and liquidity constraints; they found, using Israeli data, that the use of an infinite-lifespan model and the absence of liquidity constraints could not be rejected by the data, but their results contained other anomalies that bring them into question. NICOLETTI (1991) found a negative effect of deficits on consumption in Italy and Belgium, an effect that became stronger as these countries' debts reached the point at which the debt dynamics threatened to become unsustainable.

Further indications can be gleaned from the experience of countries that have undertaken major fiscal consolidations and nevertheless experienced growth of private expenditures. Two such instances are the cases of Denmark (beginning in

1982) and Ireland (beginning in 1987): GIAVAZZI and PAGANO (1990b) suggest that their experience provides support for the view that the fiscal consolidation had a positive effect on private consumption expenditure through expectations of lower future taxation, with positive overall short-term effects on growth.

If Ricardian equivalence fails to hold, for any of the reasons advanced in the literature, this would imply that government spending could exert a net positive effect on current-period resources, driving up interest rates and thus crowding out private investment expenditure.

5. Costs of Inflation

Another feature of the basic neoclassical model is that it was assumed that there were no costs to inflation, either with regard to its rate or to uncertainty surrounding that rate. In this framework, inflation was non-distortionary as it had no impact on the long-run capital-labor ratio - although it was also of no help in paying off the public debt, since the interest rate rose to reflect the higher inflation rate. This result was in part because the model abstracted from the use of money as a medium of exchange, thus omitting the costs associated with inflation as a tax on money. One can also envisage more pervasive effects of inflation on money as a unit of account and medium of exchange - for instance, as ragged inflation, with asynchronous changes in prices, increases the uncertainty of relative prices and effects capricious income redistribution (LEIJONHUFVUD, 1977). DE GREGORIO (1993) analyzes an endogenous growth model in which inflation affects the productivity of investment, and thus the incentive to invest; in this framework, inflation impairs long-run growth. He finds empirical support for this model using data for Latin American countries.

In general, it has been difficult to trace the effects of inflation on economic growth empirically. One exception is a multi-country cross-sectional study by FISCHER (1993), which decomposed long-period growth into labor, capital and productivity components: inflation had significant negative effects on both capital accumulation and productivity (but not on the labor force). KORMENDI and MEGUIRE (1985) also found a negative effect of inflation on growth. Many other studies found little or no effect, however. The failure of these studies to find a significant effect is attributed by SAHEL (1995) to possible non-linearity in the relationship: he estimated a relationship between inflation and growth for a large panel of countries, and found a structural break - concluding that inflation rates over 8 percent have a significantly more deleterious effect on growth than more moderate inflation.

6. Empirical Evidence on Fiscal Policy and Growth

A large number of empirical studies have directly addressed the issue of whether fiscal policy - measured in terms of taxation, expenditures, the deficit, or some other measure - has a positive, negative or zero effect on growth. Most studies have found a negative effect on growth from the size of government - measured in terms of the ratio of either expenditures or taxation to GDP (e.g. FISCHER, 1993; LANDAU, 1983); RAM (1986) is one of the few studies with contrary results. However, LEVINE and RENELT (1992) question the robustness of regressions with growth rates as the dependent variable: they cite 40 studies of this kind, and find that virtually all the results established in the literature - including those relating growth to deficits and inflation - are very fragile. In particular, the choice of additional variables to include in regression equations can have an enormous effect on coefficient estimates. This casts doubts on empirical results of this nature, and calls for a search for more robust methods of analysis.

7. Political Economy and Regime Switching

Many models of public finance assume either an optimizing government or one whose behavior is taken as exogenous. Two strands of recent literature have attempted to model the behavior of the government in other ways. Proponents of the political economy approach have argued that one can make better sense of the accumulation of debt by treating the government as subject to political influences that may lead to non-optimal behavior.[10] For instance, in the context of a voting model, the formation of electoral coalitions may lead to cycling among alternative distributions of the tax burden, or may lead to randomness. The resulting variations in and uncertainty about tax rates may create a disincentive for capital formation. A large public debt amplifies the vulnerability of interest rates to political events which may affect the probability of a change in fiscal regime. Moreover, there are indications that some political structures are more vulnerable to deficits than others; in this regard, ROUBINI and SACHS (1989) and ROUBINI (1991) have presented empirical evidence on the political and economic determinants of budget deficits.

Even if the government behaves optimally to maximize the utility of the public, it may try to surprise the public - since in principle, a surprise tax has no distortionary effects. Optimal government policy would therefore entail surprise inflation and high taxation of capital this period and monetary and fiscal probity forever after. The literature on dynamic inconsistency (CALVO, 1978) recognizes this, but concludes that the public will come to expect a certain magnitude of surprise - so that it is no surprise at all. This analysis determines the share of the public debt that will be monetized. The expectation that some of a large public debt will inevitably be monetized also underlies the case of "unpleasant monetarist arithmetic" (SARGENT and WALLACE, 1985), in which a tightening of monetary policy now results in such a large worsening of the debt dynamics that the net effect is inflationary. In this case, the existence of the debt spells monetization, sooner or later, and higher inflation is accordingly built into expectations.

Large public debts may in some instances give rise to the perception that debt repudiation, forced consolidation, or a capital levy are real possibilities. The costs of the occurrence of these events are unfathomable, but there are also costs if such events are viewed as possible but, in the event, never occur.[11] A threatened but unrealized default involves a deadweight loss, as it is a tax that has a distortionary effect without yielding revenues for the government.[12]

A less extreme example of the possibility that events could trigger monetization of the debt is a confidence crisis, which could force a change in monetary policy regime in the presence of a high public debt (see GIAVAZZI and PAGANO, 1990b). In this setting, public debt constitutes a source of vulnerability for monetary policy; the perception of the markets is that in case of a confidence crisis the government would be reluctant to raise interest rates but would instead be inclined to accept a change in monetary policy that would result in an immediate depreciation of the currency. The prospect that this might occur could in turn result in higher interest rate premia, reflecting the possibility of a sharp depreciation of the currency.

It is also possible that, under some circumstances, governments would respond to market forces to head off unsustainable situations: as debts reach excessive levels, markets begin to attach higher risk premia to lending rates, spurring the government to adjust. The effective working of market discipline depends, however, on several conditions that may or not be met (LANE, 1993): markets must be open, with adequate information available, there must be no prospect of bailout of an indebted government, and the government must respond rationally to market signals (or be forced to adjust when lending is cut off). While market discipline may play a significant role in keeping excessive deficits in check, it cannot be relied upon to ensure sound fiscal policies.

8. Conclusion

This paper has sought to illustrate the different levels on which high public debt may influence investment and growth. The starting point was a simple neoclassical model in which, despite Ricardian equivalence, public debt and deficits can affect capital accumulation by necessitating distortionary taxation. In endogenous growth models, taxation may affect the incentives to accumulate human capital, and this may affect the long-run growth rate. On the other hand, debt accumulated to permit the development of infrastructure or to provide investment incentives may, in principle, generate externalities that can encourage growth - although in practice, targeting these measures is fraught with difficulties. On the other hand, high public debt may lead to inflation, which in turn may create inefficiencies that reduce the incentives for capital accumulation. Finally, the paper touched on political economy considerations that make the means of servicing the debt unpredictable; such considerations may lead to risk premia that discourage capital accumulation.

In conclusion, the links between public debt, investment and growth are much more complex and subtle than is captured by simple crowding-out models. This suggests that high public debt may have much more pervasive effects on growth than is readily apparent.

Endnotes

1 The author thanks Stanley Black and other conference participants for helpful comments. Research assistance from Patricia Gillett-Lorusso is also appreciated. The author is solely responsible for any errors. Views expressed are the author's and do not represent the official view of the International Monetary Fund.

2 Countries included in Figure F1 are the five most heavily-indebted European Union (EU) countries.

3 In Figure F2 long-term interest-rate differentials vis-à-vis Germany are adjusted for the consumer price inflation differential.

4 In this case, as in CHAMLEY (1986), zero taxation of capital goods is optimal; the existence of distortionary taxation must depend on the absence of lump-sum taxation or non-optimal government behavior.

[5] DEVEREUX and LOVE (1994) find in a two-sector endogenous growth model, however, that wage taxation has a greater effect on long-run growth than capital taxation, with the latter affecting mainly the accumulation of capital during the transition.

[6] BARRO (1990) develops an optimal growth model in which government consumption expenditures lower growth and savings rates; in this model, government investment initially raises growth and savings rates and subsequently lowers them.

[7] FELDSTEIN (1982) argued that increased government spending might have a negative effect on consumption expenditure for a different reason, independent of Ricardian equivalence: by signalling to consumers that government spending would be permanently higher, implying higher taxes in the future.

[8] For surveys see e.g. BERNHEIM (1987), LEIDERMAN and BLEJER (1988).

[9] See, however, the extensions by BARTH et al. (1986), and criticisms of the approach by FELDSTEIN and ELMENDORF (1990), MODIGLIANI and STERLING (1990), and the reply by KORMENDI and MEGUIRE (1990).

[10] This approach is taken in various papers collected in GIAVAZZI and SPAVENTA (1988). See also the review by ROUBINI (1989).

[11] EICHENGREEN (1990) discusses the historical example of public discussions of a capital levy in France in the late 1920s.

[12] However, this effect has been relatively small for high-debt European countries, as reflected in same-currency risk premia which, in the case of Italy, have tended to be of the order of 25-50 basis points.

References

ALESINA, A. (1988), "The End of Large Public Debts," in GIAVAZZI, F. and SPAVENTA, L. (eds.), *High Public Debt: The Italian Experience*, Cambridge University Press, Cambridge.

ALOGOSKOUFIS, G. S. and CHRISTODOULAKIS, N. (1990), "Fiscal Deficits, Seignorage, and External Debt: The Case of Greece," Centre for Economic Policy Research Discussion Paper No. 468, London.

ASCHAUER, D. A. (1985), "Fiscal Policy and Aggregate Demand," *American Economic Review*, Vol. 75, 117-127.

BARRO, R. J. (1974), "Are Government Bonds Net Wealth?" *Journal of Political Economy*, Vol. 82, 1095-1117.

BARRO, R. J. (1990), "Government Spending in a Simple Model of Endogenous Growth," *Journal of Political Economy*, Vol. 98, S103-S125.

BARRO, R. J. and SALA-I-MARTIN, X. (1992), "Public Finance in Models of Economic Growth," *Review of Economic Studies*, Vol. 59, 645-661.

BARSKY, R. B., MANKIW, N. G. and ZELDES, S. P. (1986), "Ricardian Consumers with Keynesian Propensities," *American Economic Review*, Vol. 76, 676-691.

BARTH, J. R., IDEN, G. and RUSSEK, F. S. (1986), "Government Debt, Government Spending, and Private Sector Behavior," *American Economic Review*, Vol. 76, 1158-1165.

BERNHEIM, B. D. (1987), "Ricardian Equivalence: An Evaluation of Theory and Evidence," in FISCHER, S. (ed.), *NBER Macroeconomics Annual*, MIT Press, Cambridge MA, 263-304.

BERNHEIM, B. D. and BAGWELL, K. (1988), "Is Everything Neutral?" *Journal of Political Economy*, Vol. 96, 308-338.

CALVO, G. (1978), "On the Time Consistency of Optimal Policy in a Monetary Economy," *Econometrica*, Vol. 46, 1411-1428.

CANNING, D., FAY, M. and PERROTTI, R. (1992), "Infrastructure and Growth," *Rivista di Politica Economica*, Vol. 82, 113-147.

CHAMLEY, C. (1986), "Optimal Taxation of Capital Income in General Equilibrium with Infinite Lives," *Econometrica*, Vol. 54, 607-622.

CORSETTI, G. and ROUBINI, N. (1991), "Fiscal Deficits, Public Debt, and Government Solvency: Evidence from OECD Countries," *Journal of the Japanese and International Economies*, Vol. 5, 354-380.

DANIEL, B. C. (1993), "Tax Timing and Liquidity Constraints: A Heterogeneous-Agent Model," *Journal of Money, Credit and Banking*, Vol. 25, 176-196.

DE GREGORIO, J. (1993), "Inflation, Taxation, and Long-Run Growth," *Journal of Monetary Economics*, Vol. 31, 271-298.

DEVEREUX, M. B. and LOVE, D. R. F. (1994), "The Effects of Factor Taxation in a Two-Sector Model of Endogenous Growth," *Canadian Journal of Economics*, Vol. 27, 509-536.

EICHENGREEN, B. (1990), "The Capital Levy in Theory and Practice," in DORNBUSCH, R. and DRAGHI, M. (eds.), *Public Debt Management in Theory and History*, Cambridge University Press, Cambridge.

FELDSTEIN, M. (1982), "Government Deficits and Aggregate Demand," *Journal of Monetary Economics*, Vol. 9, 1-20.

FELDSTEIN, M. (1988), "The Effects of Fiscal Policies When Incomes are Uncertain: A Contradiction to Ricardian Equivalence," *American Economic Review*, Vol. 78, 14-23.

FELDSTEIN, M. and ELMENDORF, D. W. (1990), "Government Debt, Government Spending, and Private Sector Behavior Revisited," *American Economic Review*, Vol. 80, 589-599.

FISCHER, S. (1993), "The Role of Macroeconomic Factors in Growth," *Journal of Monetary Economics*, Vol. 32, 485-512.

GIAVAZZI, F. and PAGANO, M. (1990a), "Confidence Crises and Public Debt Management," in DORNBUSCH, R. and DRAGHI, M. (eds.), *Public Debt Management in Theory and History*, Cambridge University Press, Cambridge.

GIAVAZZI, F. and PAGANO, M. (1990b), "Can Severe Fiscal Contractions Be Expansionary? Tales of Two Small European Countries," in

BLANCHARD, O. J., FISCHER, S. (eds.), *NBER Macroeconomics Annual*, MIT Press, Cambridge MA.

GIAVAZZI, F. and SPAVENTA, L. (eds.) (1988), *High Public Debt: The Italian Experience*, Cambridge University Press, Cambridge.

KORMENDI, R. C. (1983), "Government Debt, Government Spending, and Private Sector Behavior," *American Economic Review*, Vol. 73, 994-1010.

KORMENDI, R. C. and MEGUIRE, P. G. (1985), "Macroeconomic Determinants of Growth: Cross-Country Evidence," *Journal of Monetary Economics*, Vol. 16, 141-163.

KORMENDI, R. and MEGUIRE, P. G. (1990), "Government Debt, Government Spending, and Private Sector Behavior: Reply," *American Economic Review*, Vol. 80, 604-617.

LACHMAN, D. (1994), "Budget Deficits and Public Debt in Sweden: The Case for Fiscal Consolidation," *IMF Staff Papers*, Vol. 41, 502-516.

LANDAU, D. (1983), "Government Expenditure and Economic Growth: A Cross-Country Study," *Southern Economic Journal*, Vol. 44, 783-792.

LANE, T. D. (1993), "Market Discipline," *IMF Staff Papers*, Vol. 40, 53-88.

LEIDERMAN, L. and BLEJER, M. I. (1988), "Modelling and Testing Ricardian Equivalence: A Survey," *IMF Staff Papers*, Vol. 35, 1-35.

LEIJONHUFVUD, A. (1977), "Costs and Consequences of Inflation," in HARCOURT, H. (ed.), *Microeconomic Foundations of Macroeconomics*, Westview Press, Boulder CO.

LEONARDO, L. and RAZIN, A. (1988), "Testing Ricardian Neutrality with an Intertemporal Stochastic Model," *Journal of Money, Credit and Banking*, Vol. 20, 1-21.

LEVINE, R. and RENELT, D. (1992), "A Sensitivity Analysis of Cross-Country Growth Regressions," *American Economic Review*, Vol. 82, 942-963.

LUCAS, R. E., Jr. (1988), "On the Mechanics of Economic Development," *Journal of Monetary Economics*, Vol. 22, 3-42.

MILESI-FERRETTI, G. and ROUBINI, N. (1994), "Taxation and Endogenous Growth in Open Economies," IMF Working Paper WP/94/77.

MODIGLIANI, F. and STERLING, A. G. (1990), "Government Debt, Government Spending, and Private Sector Behavior," *American Economic Review*, Vol. 80, 600-603.

NICOLETTI, G. (1991), "Consommation Privée et Endettement Public en Italie et en Belgique: Existe-t-il une Relation Stable?" *Observations et Diagnostics Economiques*, Vol. 37, 79-121.

POTERBA, J. M. and SUMMERS, L. H. (1987), "Finite Lifetimes and the Effects of Budget Deficits on National Savings," *Journal of Monetary Economics*, Vol. 20, 369-391.

RAM, R. (1986), "Government Size and Economic Growth: A New Framework and Some Evidence from Cross-Section and Time Series Data," *American Economic Review*, Vol. 76, 191-203.

REBELO, S. (1991), "Long-Run Policy Analysis and Long-Run Growth," *Journal of Political Economy*, Vol. 99, 500-521.

ROMER, P. (1990), "Endogenous Technological Change," *Journal of Political Economy*, Vol. 98, S71-S102.

ROUBINI, N. (1989), "High Public Debt: The Italian Experience. A Review Essay," *Journal of Monetary Economics*, Vol. 24, 471-478.

ROUBINI, N. (1991), "Political and Economic Determinants of Budget Deficits in the Industrial Democracies," *Journal of International Money and Finance*, Vol. 10, 549-572.

ROUBINI, N. and SACHS, J. D. (1989), "Political and Economic Determinants of Budget Deficits in the Industrial Democracies," *European Economic Review*, Vol. 33, 903-933.

SAHEL, M. (1995), "Nonlinear Effects of Inflation on Economic Growth," IMF Working Paper WP/95/56.

SARGENT, T. J. and WALLACE, N. (1981), "Some Unpleasant Monetarist Arithmetic," *Federal Reserve Bank of Minneapolis Quarterly Review*, Vol. 9, 19-31.

TOBIN, J. (1980), "Government Deficits and Capital Accumulation," in *Asset Accumulation and Economic Activity: Reflections on Contemporary Macroeconomic Theory*, University of Chicago Press, Chicago, 49-72.

XU, B. (1994), "Tax Policy Implications in Endogenous Growth Models," IMF Working Paper WP/94/38.

Comments on
High Public Debt: Consequences for Investment and Growth

Stanley W. Black

1. Introduction

Timothy Lane's paper provides an effective survey of the literature on the effects of public debt on investment and economic growth. In his initial discussion of the problem, Lane points out that western European data do not show that high debt levels are correlated with low growth, although there is some correlation with low investment levels. The potential responses to excessively high debt levels include raising taxes, inflating away the debt, and repudiation.

Turning to theoretical analysis, Lane develops a simple infinite horizon neoclassical framework to illustrate several propositions. If lump-sum taxes were available in this model, Ricardian equivalence would prevail and private saving would offset public dis-saving. In the presence of distortionary taxation, higher debt implies higher future taxes and encourages current consumption. In the steady state, the after-tax real interest rate must equal the intertemporal marginal rate of substitution, thus higher debt raises the before-tax real rate of interest and reduces the equilibrium capital stock. The rate of growth, however, is unaffected.

Endogenous growth models involving externalities, human capital, innovation, or public infrastructure allow the growth rate to vary with investment. Thus raising taxes now to lower future taxes and debt burdens can raise investment and growth.

A number of factors besides distortionary taxes can lead debt to reduce national saving. Finite horizons raise the private discount rate relative to the public discount rate and imply that public debt issuance will reduce saving. Liquidity constraints can be eased by public borrowing, reducing national saving. In the political economy approach, the public debt becomes an instrument manipulated by governments to influence voters or successor governments.

2. High Public Debt in the European Union

Let me turn from the literature to contemporary issues, in the European Union, central and eastern Europe, Japan, and the United States. The Maastricht Treaty's provisions on European Monetary Union defined what is meant by "high" debt levels in the EU as exceeding 60 percent of GDP, with deficits exceeding 3 percent of GDP. This formula assumes nominal GDP growth of 5 percent. Several questions have been raised about the adequacy of the definition (BUITER et al., 1993). It depends on what is included in the public sector, particularly how pensions are funded. Assets are ignored, as are the implications of selling them. Finally, one wonders how flexible these rules will be when faced with temporary spending needs, such as natural disasters or recession.

On the other hand, one might use the capital budgeting approach enshrined in the German constitution to justify the 3 percent rule if one believed that the normal need for government capital spending were 3 percent of GDP. Even that approach leaves open the question of whether education spending should be regarded as investment or consumption. However, it must be admitted by an American that these rules dominate the simplistic notion of a balanced budget or the elaborate mechanisms of the Gramm-Rudman-Hollings procedures.

Is there an intergenerational transfer due to high current borrowing? This depends on the absence of Ricardian equivalence, which is widely disbelieved by policymakers. While the empirical evidence on the question is mixed, it does appear that unfunded government social insurance schemes have had the effect of lowering private saving. This suggests strongly that there is an intergenerational transfer occurring, which is being paid by increasing taxes on younger generations. As a larger share of the population ages into retirement, this burden is expected to increase sharply by 2020. The absence of funding mechanisms implies a failure to build up the capital stock in anticipation of the needs to produce more in the future.

While the Maastricht rules have a formal logic to them, the underlying reasoning for their existence is less clear. The rules are not necessary unless one does not believe in the credibility of the Maastricht rule forbidding the European Central Bank to bail out insolvent governments. This rule uses the market to enforce fiscal prudence, requiring each government to rely on its own revenue sources. However, if one doubts the ECB's credibility, the rules make more sense. A second argument for the fiscal rules is to eliminate from the ECB weak governments that might be tempted to press for inflationary policies. However, as noted by GROS (1995), the fiscal rules apply only ex ante and not after EMU occurs. In that sense, the rules are neither necessary nor sufficient to guarantee that EMU is not inflationary.

GROS (1995) and DE GRAUWE (1995) have proposed that the fiscal rules be used ex post to discipline weak governments by preventing their governors from voting in the ECB Council. This is part of a package to reassure the Germans that EMU will not be inflationary. German Finance Minister Waigel's proposal for a "stability pact" with fines against violators of the fiscal rules can be seen in the same light.

There are suggestions that such reassurance is needed, as some German investors appear unwilling to buy DM bonds with maturities above the year 2000. Others are moving funds to Switzerland to avoid holding assets whose future currency denomination is unclear. While Germans are used to the asymmetric European Monetary System with the Bundesbank at the center, they appear less pleased with the idea of a symmetric European Monetary Union, even if the headquarters is to be located in Frankfurt.

"High debt" is a euphemism for insufficient monetary and fiscal rectitude. Achieving the Maastricht targets has been likened by JEFFREY FRANKEL (in

BUITER, et al., 1993) to a mythological "quest", as in Jason's search for the Golden Fleece. If the quest is successful, then the Bundesbank will yield its daughter, the deutschemark, however reluctantly. Of course the Bundestag must also declare that it is in Germany's national interest. And France must be one of the successful claimants, which seems to be questionable at best since the election of Chirac.

3. Central and Eastern Europe

Our recent study of the financial problems of the central and eastern European countries (BLACK and MOERSCH, 1996) concluded that the primary source of finance for their restructuring and economic growth must come from domestic savings. Among the limiting factors on the domestic supply of savings are real interest rates, real wage rates (which affect retained earnings of firms), and the problems of financial intermediaries. Bad debts to banks must be resolved in order to permit banks to perform their credit allocation functions properly.

The diversion of savings into public sector budget deficits is a major drain on domestic savings. Countries where these deficits are at high levels include most of the countries of the former Soviet Union and Poland, Hungary, Romania, and Bulgaria. In many cases state-owned enterprises remain an important factor in these deficits. In Bulgaria and Hungary, debt levels remain relatively high, while Poland's has been reduced by a Paris Club restructuring.

4. Japan

The bursting of the "bubble" economy left many Japanese firms, banks, and individuals with excessive debt levels relative to the values of the underlying assets. Price deflation has been exacerbating the problem. The government and monetary authority are actively using the tools of monetary and fiscal policy, along with restructuring of financial institutions, to help the country out of its financial collapse.

5. United States

After the budget agreement of 1993, the US debt/GDP ratio stopped rising, but is expected to rise again in the future as underlying structural deficit problems re-emerge. A long-term solution requires dealing with the financing of health care for the poor and the elderly and the looming problem that pay-as-you-go social security cannot keep up with the increasing proportion of retired people in the population. But there is little reason for draconian measures in the short run. Ideological battles over the size and role of the government in the economy dominate this debate.

References

BLACK, S. W. and MOERSCH, M (1996), "Investment and Its Financing in Central and Eastern European Countries," in BLACK, S. W. (ed.), *Europe's Economy Looks East*, Cambridge University Press, New York, forthcoming.

BUITER, W., CORSETTI, G. and ROUBINI, N. (1993), "Excessive Deficits: Sense and Nonsense in the Treaty of Maastricht," with discussion by Rafael Repullo and Jeffrey Frankel, *Economic Policy*, No. 16, 57-100.

DE GRAUWE, P. (1995), "Monetary Union and Convergence Economics," presented at the Tenth Annual Congress of the European Economic Association, Prague, Sept. 1-4, 1995.

GROS, D. (1995), "Towards a Credible Excessive Deficits Procedure," CEPS Working Document No. 95, Centre for European Policy Studies, Brussels.

Part II

International Capital Flows and Growth

G. Banking, Foreign Investment, Endogenous Growth and Systemic Transformation

Jozef M. van Brabant

1. Introduction

From the very first signs of the major changes afoot in the eastern part of Europe,[1] it has been clear that restructuring the postcommunist economies in transition (PETs) would require, among others, the identification of a new, modernizing growth path through massive purposeful resource mobilization. At the transition's inception, many observers posited that, with proper domestic policies, the bulk of these resources would initially originate from abroad, though public funds would in some cases be needed to lubricate these transfers. Only by erecting quickly an open foreign-exchange and trading regime, it was widely argued, could the core expectations regarding the principal purposes of the transition be met: catching up in a comparatively brief period of time with levels of living, productivity, technological sophistication, and international integration through intra-industry trade and finance characteristic of the advanced countries, chiefly in western Europe. After all, society-wide structural transformation[2] policies in PETs should be buttressing a more efficient mode of production *and* regaining a sustainable, high pace of growth, precisely to permit catching up.

This paper argues for viewing foreign, including direct (FDI), investment (FI) with a greater degree of apprehension than most observers have displayed to date. To dispel the impression that such skepticism implies fundamental opposition to FI, after a brief *tour d'horizon* on recent developments in PETs and the setbacks with the earlier anticipated transformation path, I look at the need to view the desirable expansion of PETs in a more encompassing framework than the transformation agenda now widely adopted. Next I specify a few key features of FI. Then I try to explain why the PET leadership and many assistance providers should not have been so disappointed about the comparatively weak flows to the PETs; this may even be a blessing in disguise! Even at that level, a number of adverse side effects have already emerged, which I illustrate next. After a brief review of how FI has figured in some of the more recent modernization strategies, notably in the successful newly industrializing economies (NIEs) of east and south Asia, I specify how more active policy measures could be taken in the PETs to 'guide' FI into a constructive, more symbiotic relationship with the coveted new growth trajectory, precisely to firm up the latter's robustness and sustainability through cumulative causation. This may be even more critical for financial services than for manufacturing or mining investment, as I argue before concluding.

2. The Holy Trinity and Successful Transformation

It is a paradox of sorts that the well-known homilies of the so-called Washington consensus - stabilization, liberalization, and privatization - of transformation policies in PETs have for some time now seemed to ignore the transformation's primary motivation: regaining sustainable growth at a fairly elevated pace. Since this could not be achieved overnight, from the outset there has been an acute need to maintain minimal socio-political consensus on forceful transformation, in spite of its unavoidable hardships. Likewise, the duration of this transition was bound to depend to a large extent on erecting the institutions of the market necessary to reap the benefits of the Washington consensus on the 'holy trinity'. Robust financial institutions and effective prudential regulations play a paramount role here. Downplaying the latter two building blocks of comprehensive and coherent transformation policies is not very helpful if policy makers want to maintain policy credibility, not just policies that are credible, but also that can be implemented and sustained in a credible manner (UNECE, 1993, p. 7), given the need to maintain the domestic consensus as well as to marshal support from abroad. This naturally depends on the prevailing disarray, the acceptable adjustment burden, and the successes attained while advancing with substantive transition. Otherwise transformation will fail to germinate.

Even more surprising, at least to this observer, has been the way in which success with transformation policies has recently been adjudicated. Thus a marked reduction in inflation (but still well at double-digit level), elimination of the shortage economy, a movement towards more general access to foreign exchange, a reduction in budget and current-account imbalances, a rise in exports, and so on have all, individually or in some combination, been viewed as marking successful transition. Never mind that in many PETs the 'fundamentals' for a sustainable growth strategy are still woefully inadequate, in spite of some important improvements booked in some PETs in the past year or so:

- Inflation is still double-digit or worse in all too many PETs.
- Budget imbalances in many PETs are still sizable, largely for lack of an adequate tax base and effective collection policies, while entitlement expenditures and debt-service obligations are generally rising. Their financing through recourse to financial markets has been difficult, because the latter, when they exist at all, are still primitive or incomplete.
- Current-account imbalances in several PETs continue to be large and the prospects of closing the external accounts on a predictable basis through sustainable long-term capital inflows related to real investments are not particularly good, even in countries with positive current accounts.
- Export gains are being booked for products, mainly from state-owned enterprises (SOEs), in which most PETs do not have a long-term comparative advantage or with which they cannot hope to merge themselves into the virtuous network of rapidly expanding intra-industry trade. Genuine structural change is taking place rather slowly, if at all.

- Measured as well as real levels of unemployment are substantial, leading to large economic, political, psychological, and social costs.
- Gains in income and welfare for broad layers of the population are meager at best. For many the transformation has meant a marked deterioration in levels of living, especially if such worsening social ills as sharply reduced social security, marked income and wealth dispersion, falling health standards, and rising organized crime are factored into the success equation.
- Not enough domestic savings is being channeled into productive investments, in part because of poor intermediation but also because of substantial uncertainty, which translates into high-risk perception for which appropriate premia are levied. These deter long-term productive investment.

Many other less bright features of the transition could be cited. Without denigrating the genuine achievements since 1989, I contend that viewing the realities of the transformation in a highly partial perspective (emphasizing price stabilization, limited convertibility, budget balance, external balance, removal of the shortage economy, and so on) and with a terminology (such as on stabilization, convertibility, privatization, and balance) whose meaning is being deliberately obfuscated is not helpful. True, a pep talk may impart positive psychological incentives. Yet I honestly feel that one should not deviate from the mainstream view that successful transformation over the medium run - gradually, but steadily, catching up with more advanced countries in western Europe - should be defined in terms of indicators of positive growth and its sustainability over the longer run, while generating rising living standards over a protracted period of time.

Given the losses sustained in recent years, growth in and of itself is not a good success indicator; but I certainly do not want to denigrate the unquestionable achievements that have recently been booked in some PETs. The pace of growth has to be strong, bolstered notably by capital formation in activities that signal decisive structural change and shore up prospects for sustained expansion. Elsewhere (BRABANT, 1995a) I have made a case for viewing the resumption of strong growth, at moderate levels of inflation and based largely on solid investment financed mostly from domestic savings in activities that somehow are considered 'modernizing,' while far from a perfect criterion, certainly as a more useful success indicator.[3]

I advocate this more comprehensive stance because the holy trinity's realism depends on the assumption that policy makers and their advisers, as well as assistance providers, must quickly put in place the framework that unfetters economic agents, thus enabling them to exploit prevailing comparative advantages: chiefly low labor costs but in some countries also cheap raw materials. This is presumed to lead to "high-quality growth", whatever this overused IMF slogan may concretely mean, in purely hortatory fashion, for there is neither much theoretical nor empirical evidence to buttress the proposition that growth will necessarily emerge. Neoclassical economics has next to nothing to say about other than equilibrium growth (NELSON, 1995, pp. 67ff.). Neither has the libertarian approach, as demonstrated in a great number of countries since the 1970s (BRESSER PEREIRA, MARAVALL, and PRZEWORSKI, 1993), though it may have contributed to stabilizing economies, empowering economic agents, and freeing up the environment from regulations. Liberalization has certainly not imparted a major new impetus to productivity growth, enabled developing countries as a whole to catch up with the industrialized countries, or expeditiously restored growth in PETs.

A wholly different twist on the transformation agenda has been infused by those who contend that liberalization (and implicitly libertarianism) is not only needed for its own sake, but also to whittle the overbearing role of the State under communism essentially to that of night watchman, with perhaps some modification for the social safety net. It is also justified to utilize the opportunities provided by the "extraordinary politics" offered as a result of the transition's eruption to destroy explicitly the venal elements of the State, thus permitting better-motivated policy makers to embark on the construction of democracy and a market economy.[4]

3. Towards Modernization and FI

Defining a new growth strategy in PETs with massive resource mobilization is justified for at least two reasons. One is the need to come to grips with the capital losses, physical and human, sustained as a result of the *de facto* collapse of many structures built during communist rule to prevent living standards from crashing and perhaps remaining stuck for years at a low equilibrium. Very substantial fresh funds will also be required to start off along the new growth trajectory and build upon this momentum through cumulative causation. Such resource mobilization, the transitology literature emphasizes, should primarily originate from private sources abroad, possibly initially paced by official transfers.

FDI in greenfield operations, for joint ventures, and through privatization in particular was expected to provide modern managerial expertise and corporate-governance structures, fresh financial resources and access to modern technology, an impetus to bolster exports and marketing skills, and inhouse training to hone the human capital inherited from communism to the requirements of a new, dynamic growth strategy. Responding to the multiple needs in this fashion, it was thought in an almost dirigistic manner reminiscent of communist administration, would short-circuit the "learning process" on whose basis sustained economic growth could be predicated. FI therefore deserved all kinds of privileges in terms of import-duty rebates, tax holidays, favorable investment regulations, labor rules, and so on. These expectations were based on two erroneous assumptions. One was that liberated financial markets are efficient, the other that the PETs can offer foreign 'excess savers' better conditions than other locations. I revisit these issues in Section 4.

Rather than carefully examining the foundations of cumulative causation along a new growth dynamic, many observers of the East's scene have advocated the holy trinity as a necessary and almost sufficient condition for regaining "high-quality growth" in which massive FI, largely from the private sector, is expected to make a major difference in the 'quality' of that growth path (KRUGMAN, 1995). I have railed elsewhere against the simplistic assumptions required to make this proposition into more than a conjurer's trick (BRABANT, 1995a). Growth is not likely to appear automatically. Neither will massive FI flow into the PETs simply because a modicum of the holy trinity can be achieved. Rather, financial resources will have to be mobilized purposefully and primarily in the domestic economy to reach a 'good modernization path', one based on steady productivity gains. Swift and efficient financial intermediation, at least at the most elementary level through commercial banks, will therefore play a critical role in encouraging domestic investment and repatriation of flight capital once other stability conditions reduce the prevailing degree of uncertainty in these economies. Given the exceedingly weak banking infrastructure in PETs, largely inherited from the communist era (BRABANT, 1994a, b, d), can we expect more from FI flows into the financial sector?

From the beginning of the debate on mobilizing resources as a quasi precondition for adhering to the transition's economic agenda, it has been surprising to me that so many commentators have taken for granted that the PETs would offer massive opportunities for FI, particularly FDI.[5] Not only has it been an act of faith that ample inflows would be forthcoming. Also little concern has been expressed about the ability of the PETs to absorb such volumes productively to benefit the mutation towards a new growth trajectory (see Section 4).

In some contrast to the stress on attracting FI and progressing rapidly with the holy trinity, most commentators underemphasized the need to make headway with the financial infrastructure in PETs (PORTES, 1994, pp. 1187-8). Whereas much attention was devoted to the speedy establishment of stock and bond markets, for example, the urgency of transforming the existing banking sector, including putting in place adequate prudential regulations and effective surveillance, tended to be relegated to the later stages of sequential transformation. This was particularly the case for restructuring domestic banking: coming to grips with bad debt, recapitalizing banks, and effectively transferring technical knowledge so that these organs could discharge banking functions in a professional manner through learning or the infusion of the requisite human capital from abroad.

The central importance of lowering costs, in order to enhance market transactions and hence engineer a turnaround in the PETs, should be clear. In the absence of institutions that will expedite reciprocal payments in an efficient manner, collect 'excess savings'[6] at minimal cost (including risk), grant loans to 'excess investors' on the basis of a thorough assessment of creditworthiness, and market new financial instruments (including those that in time are bound to justify the establishment of other capital-market components), the transformation process could only be hamstrung. Whereas the first two tasks could conceivably be enacted swiftly through resolute government intervention, although in practice it is difficult to envisage a one-off credible cleaning up of bank portfolios, learning even the rudiments of the banking profession could never occur spontaneously or quickly (BRABANT, 1994a, b). Could this process have been short-circuited through foreign assistance? I examine this question in Section 9.

Contrary to the optimistic scenario on massive FI, the attracted volumes have lagged far behind expectations. Their pace has been slowing down recently in several PETs. FI has entered the PETs with motivations that have little to do with the desire of policy makers to raise efficiency and accelerate moving towards a new, durable growth path.[7] It has not brought in the latest technology. It has been concentrated geographically and sectorally. Many actual and potential investors have been disappointed with the results recorded to date, and the labor force has on the whole not been very pleased about new job creation or the lagging gains in remuneration for those able to hold on to their position.

This result could have been anticipated. Although our general knowledge about the precise determinants of FI is not very deep or reliable (MARKOWSKI and JACKSON, 1994; UNCTAD 1993), there is evidence that a country's size, its expected pace of growth with its likely variability, and prevailing imbalances (in external payments, in exchange rates, in domestic budget finances, and in consumption) relevant to the determination of foreign-exchange risk are in general the major determinants of FI inflows. For smaller and less developed countries, in addition the level and stability of the exchange rate, external indebtedness, and the degree of openness also have a bearing on the volume and kind of FI flows. Of particular importance for productive investment, then, are two critical factors: the expected rate of return on such investments and the variability or risk associated with this expectation. On both counts, the PETs do not appear to be very attractive sites for FDI for some time to come. Expected rates of return would depend on the progress with structural transformation, including regaining positive growth. Risk abatement would in addition be a function of the restoration of economic, political, and social confidence in these countries. Substantial progress with stabilization and the establishment of the 'institutions' of a viable market economy, in addition to liberalization and privatization, are critical.

Seen against this backdrop, as well as the experiences with administrative planning, one may well ask whether it is possible for the PETs to be successful in their transformation and attain acceptable rates of growth if current transformation precepts continue to be adhered to. Against the holy trinity's expectation of automatic resource mobilization for growth, I like to stress the proposition that current signs of an economic upturn must not be confounded with the success criterion specified earlier. It is inherently difficult to envisage how PETs could catch up with living standards, productivity, and technology in western Europe when the growth strategy is focused on conquering external markets or attracting FI essentially on the basis of cheap labor or, in some PETs, cheap natural resources. It should furthermore be noted that FI is often lured into these countries through preferences that are not securely tied to technology or training commitments (FLEMMING, 1993, p. 198) as anchors for further economic expansion paced by productivity gains.

When growth is being in part accounted for by FDI utilizing cheap labor, one should be cautious about assertions to the effect that the first harbingers of a sustainable catch-up recovery and growth dynamic have been sighted. Without having put in place the foundations for a sustainable rise in factor productivity and ensuring that FI gets fully integrated into this strategy, sustainable growth paced by cheap labor or natural resources is unlikely to materialize. To try and do so with FDI is likely to lead in time, as wages move up (WADE, 1995), to "little but abandoned factories and unemployed low-skilled labour" (KREGEL, 1994, p. 37). This reality of history is indeed the heart of the proposition that I should like to buttress in what follows.

4. Towards Endogenous Growth

Unlike the agenda set by the holy trinity, real success with transformation appears to be predicated on the identification and application of an endogenous growth strategy, one that will be sustainable over the long haul through productivity gains and yield equitable growth at a level permitting catch-up with the more advanced countries, financed primarily from domestically raised resources. How this can best be done, relying on the experience of western European latecomers and selected NIEs, I cannot, of course, set forth in just a few paragraphs (see BRABANT, 1993a, pp. 171ff.; 1995b). Nonetheless, I hope that a sketch of the major reference points in this deliberately modest endeavor to pull together disparate strands of thought will elicit more cogent reflections on transformation tasks by pondering the core questions of why economic development differs among nations and whether anything could be undertaken to reverse recent trends.

There are alternative visions of how economies in equilibrium function, such as the neoclassical agenda, or how the entrepreneurial spirit can be mustered to roam freely, as in the Austrian agenda, which is free of social conflicts (BRABANT, 1993a, pp. 172-81; SAWYER, 1992). More illuminating approaches to economic development can be identified from the way in which countries have succeeded or failed to impart a positive impetus to their modernization. Each involves a particular view of how markets work, of the relevant objectives of economic policy, of the nature of economic interdependence, and of available governance capabilities. The salient stylized facts can usefully be posited around such concepts as learning, uncertainty, integration, and globalization. These and other features call for greater harmonization of forces in society that exhibit central features of what is largely immanent, hence endogenous, in the development process.

After the many mistakes made with development policies in recent decades in particular, there can be little doubt about the imperfections of markets and the danger of gross government errors. Sustainable development requires broader guidance mechanisms and incentives than either the market or the State's central plan can impel upon individual agents. At the same time, market institutions need to be created, maintained, and upgraded, including through proper governance. Spontaneous market forces, even if not imperfect, are not likely to take care of these tasks. Rather they tend to accentuate imperfections, as between goods and factor markets, if no other caretaker will redress the situation. Under certain conditions, this may be the government or non-state governance structures whose results are neither adjudicated in the market according to profit realized nor validated through the coercive powers vested in the State.

A crucial role may accrue to government also in helping to identify, and at times foster, the foundations of a growth path that is sustainable in a longer perspective precisely because catching up with more advanced countries requires jumping hurdles that, given the uncertainty and scale of the required commitment, private initiative is likely to eschew. That is to say, the essence of the modernization approach revolves around policy intentions on how best to nurse along other than steady-state growth, or dynamic economic efficiency, through an industrial strategy targeted at the production process itself rather than solely through policy instruments. Forging the actual production process over time by acting upon 'investment' in the broad sense - that is building capabilities in structures, machinery, people, organizations, and so on - is at the heart of endogenizing growth.

But it can only be a means towards strengthening other critical determinants of obtaining steady gains in factor productivity.

The key recognition is that firms are not simple production functions, as in neoclassical economics. Neither are they simple exploiters of opportunities stemming from asymmetric information, as in the Austrian approach. Rather, they pursue organizational cohesion and profit through commitment, worker participation, and cooperation, if only because considerable information and knowledge reside with individual or groups of workers, who are not generally owners. They will utilize this human capital fruitfully, thereby enhancing efficiency, only within the right institutional setting. For this an appropriate macroeconomic framework is essential; indeed, it may be a prerequisite for success. But the full array of microeconomic considerations deserves to be heeded as well.

In short, the functioning of organizations depends on internal processes. They codetermine political, social, and cultural aspects of resource allocation under strategic management. Furthermore, such behavior at the firm level brings economic agents into conflict through rivalry, which may threaten profit and survival. At that point, firms will seek to merge or foster agreements for networking - the equivalent of developing trust, which is vital to intra-firm management - and blending it with market incentives (CHANDLER, 1977; KAY 1992; PORTER, 1990). Indeed, endogenous growth does not obviate the need for competition and rivalry. Rather, by promoting competition it reduces the resources 'wasted' such as through excessive advertising, product differentiation, change generated by the competitive process, idling workers and production capacity, or regional disparities. There is hence a built-in tendency pushing towards monopoly and concentration of profitable activities because of cumulative causation.

An integral component of this approach is the realization that substantial parts of coordination, competition, and cooperation as the essence of good economic governance (BRABANT, 1995b) are achieved *within* firms and households or groups whose decisions are not directly validated in the market place.

When appropriate, planning will be undertaken to mold market relations and the development process more generally. This occurs through a complementary relationship among market (and plan), firms, and government, but this time with the State responding to the private sector's expressed need for greater governance. In addition to assuming antitrust stances, the State must play a pro-active, developmental role. The latter involves the positive promotion of industrial expansion through targeting or strategic industrial policy (DIETRICH, 1992), with state agencies taking on an entrepreneurial role directly or indirectly. This creates opportunities for private firms that would otherwise not have materialized. But it also calls for exercising caution in creating SOEs and in ensuring that, if deemed necessary, these firms be subject as much as possible to market discipline, at least for factor inputs. Also, managerial criteria should be devised by which this outcome can be ensured, especially in emerging democracies bent on quickly eradicating the vested interests of the old regimes.

Such a type of industrial policy in the PET's context should, then, have a dual target. One is to recognize that much of the inherited economic structure is unlikely to be competitive, yet substantial components thereof cannot be abandoned overnight without entailing chaotic, dysfunctional social and political upheavals. Rather than allowing these sores to fester on their own, usually supported by one type of subsidy or another, there is a need to disengage those obsolete structures in an orderly fashion. The other task is to bolster creative activity to identify a new growth trajectory and indeed to stay on it for a protracted period of time. That too requires management. With incipient markets at best, both policies require the full use and deliberate shaping of market competition, cooperation, and coordination - the core ingredients of good economic governance - such as is possible under the disequilibrium conditions typical of transformation policies.

The bearing of all this on financial markets, including FI, should be clear. With the massive destruction of existing capital and the sizable need for new capital formation, financial actors should have a role, at least in relative terms, that transcends beyond their normal function in a regular market setting. However, financial markets even in mature economies exhibit a wide range of market failures due, among others, to asymmetric information and reputation problems. Given that markets in PETs are far from mature, pervaded as they are with adverse legacies, failures in capital markets are bound to be even larger than in normal economies. Mobilizing, then, the resources that are available in favor of the identified growth strategy will require an element of scale and risk that FI, just like domestic private savings, on its own strengths is likely to eschew. That is not to say that FI should be precluded from financial sectors. But policy makers may well become quickly disappointed by banking literally on FI to rescue financial sectors or, even if FI enters in sizable volume, that it will come in support of the dual task of managing destruction of the obsolete capital stock and mobilizing new investment funds for technological change, innovation, and productivity gains.

5. Expectations and Realities about FI Inflows

The theory of international capital movements is not well developed. Capital mobility tends to be treated as an extrapolation of conventional open macroeconomics. This takes it for granted that external financial liberalization is desirable because it enhances efficiency in resource allocation. The benefits are expected to exceed significantly the loss of policy autonomy - the ability of governments to achieve national objectives by using the policy instruments at their disposal. It is generally recognized that this proposition holds only if other imbalances in the economy, such as budget deficits, external imbalances, and imperfections in goods and factor markets, are eliminated. Since these obstacles cannot be overcome overnight, sequencing in external liberalization is required. Although there is no uniform view, most observers argue that domestic financial markets and the current account should be liberalized before the capital account and, with greater controversy, that fiscal balance and monetary stability should be attained before any liberalization.

This position raises three broad questions: the nature of the benefits claimed from domestic and external liberalization, when is a resolution of domestic problems sufficient, and when can one best proceed with domestic financial liberalization under imbalances (AKYÜZ, 1993c, pp. 144-8) as a precondition for activating the next sequence of the reform, notably external liberalization? It may be useful to bear in mind that this policy stance can logically be disaggregated into: (1) the ability of residents to borrow freely in international markets and non-residents to lend freely in domestic markets for other reasons than financing trade, (2) allowing residents to transfer capital and hold financial assets abroad and non-residents to issue liabilities in domestic financial markets, and (3) allowing debtor-creditor relations among residents in foreign currencies. To the extent that (1) is motivated more than (2)-(3) by the desire of firms to finance investments in productive capacity, FDI is more desirable than other types of FI flows.

The benefits claimed for external financial liberalization are similar to those expected from domestic liberalization. They derive from the belief that the internationalization of finance, like domestic liberalization, allows savings to be pooled and allocated globally through capital movements across countries in response to opportunities for productive investments. By thus equalizing rates of return on investment, adjusted for risk differentials, global resource allocation improves. In capital-short countries, like the PETs, capital inflows will lower domestic real interest rates, bringing them closer to the world level as relative capital scarcity is reduced. Likewise in the case of domestic liberalization: by removing restraints on interest rates or credit allocation, the real rate of interest moves up, thereby motivating economic agents to save and producers to export.

I have used the word 'belief' in the above summary without intending to cast aspersions. Yet, the theoretical position taken rests on the assumptions and features of the model posited; in the case of external liberalization, views about how the global economy operates that are hardly realistic.[8] In fact, judging by the degree to which differences in the rates of return on capital have been reduced, even in major industrial countries, capital movements as such do not improve the international allocation of savings; nor has the link between saving and investment in individual countries been markedly loosened (AKYÜZ, 1993a, pp. 51-2). Reality is therefore at odds with the theory. Why is this so?

Obviously the assumption that capital movements occur in search of real returns on investment does not hold, as most capital movements tend to be propelled by portfolio decision makers in search of short-term capital gains rather than by real investment opportunities and long-term risk and asset values (AKYÜZ, 1993b, c). These more speculative types of capital movement exert pressures on exchange and interest rates as well as on asset prices that have little to do with the underlying fundamentals. In other words, financial openness as defined may create economy-wide problems regardless of the order of liberalization and the sequential removal of distortions. The exposure to short-term, speculative portfolio decisions for countries that are not in fundamental equilibrium is much greater and riskier. The very nature of the instability provides opportunities for quick windfall profits on short-term capital movements. Yet the ability of policy makers in PETs to influence the size and direction of such flows through monetary policy is more limited than is true for mature economies. Those limitations reside in the limited ability to restore balance and engineer the domestic liberalization that provides sufficient protection against speculative FI entering and leaving in response to external liberalization. For as long as this condition is not met, should FI be allowed to enter at all and, if so, under what kind of a regime? In other words, what network of controls can conceivably be put in place to ensure that long-term FI in production is encouraged while holding speculative FI at bay?

The issue of financial liberalization is directly related to the way in which policy makers hope to integrate the economy internationally through trade and foreign-exchange reforms. Successful export performance requires close interaction of resident banks with world financial markets, if only to provide trade-related credit and facilitate international payments. The ability to borrow in international capital markets allows diversification in corporate finance, while FI in capital markets can help broaden the domestic equity base of firms and reduce domestic leverage. Also, foreign banks can deliver greater competition in the provisioning of banking services, thus reducing transaction costs of finance.

Yet, while all this *could* be useful, I contend that the focus of capital-market policies in PETs at the early stages of their transformation, if governance capabilities are available, should primarily be on the orderly scrapping of obsolete human and physical capital, on the encouragement of rapid technological upgrading and modernization, and on securing the conditions for moving towards and maintaining considerable stability not only in economic, but also in political and social affairs. Under those conditions, domestic and external finance should serve the modernization objectives rather than the other way around. It is these justifications of economic policy that provide the logic for intervention and control over financial activities. At the same time, they buttress the rationale for reforming the State. They also help to rationalize intervention modalities and justifications by upgrading governance capabilities, including through foreign assistance, as an alternative to simply abdicating economic policy to the spurious 'free-market benefits'.

The strong complementary nature of technological development, investment, and training emphasizes the need to coordinate policy on a broad front rather than to allow each to proceed in isolation. The main reason is that technologies are not identical or characterized by relatively stable production functions across industry and countries. Indeed, they are not off-the-shelf, procurable at comparatively low cost through capital imports or FDI. Neither can they be rapidly assimilated and diffused throughout the economy. There is at least a need for complementary investments and institutional change to ensure an appropriately skilled and adaptable labor force (LANDES, 1990), given particular demands of technological development (BARRO, 1991). Active education and training through public and private initiatives have been required to import, to adapt, to identify, and to overcome design and development problems in harnessing available technologies for particular socio-economic conditions. This has involved formal and firm-specific training, in-house R&D, and purposeful accumulation of tacit industrial knowledge in such areas as production, quality control, and marketing. All have been decisive in ensuring competitiveness. These considerations apply at least equally when the expanding role of foreign firms is incorporated into the analysis. Although they provide an essential conduit of technology in the global economy, and often a package of skills and opportunities, there are no automatic durable benefits from FDI by firms whose global strategies can readily diverge from perceived national requirements.

Recent research in the area of technical change offers support for such measures by recognizing that technological knowledge is not a readily transferable public good fully embodied in mobile physical capital. Rather, considerable time and effort are required to obtain, assimilate, use, and improve technological knowledge with a view towards enhancing productivity and upgrading industrial activity (PACK and WESTPHAL, 1986). Moreover, much technological dynamism derives from gradual and incremental improvements to existing products and processes, rather than from radical breakthroughs that dramatically enhance performance. Together these two features draw attention to the need to gradually acquire and build upon appropriate capabilities and the importance of a learning culture to the process of continual technological development, both through formal educational channels and R&D activity organized at an industry or national level, and through hands-on learning, disciplined search and experimentation routines, and creative partnerships among designers, engineers, entrepreneurs, and managers in firms.

In any case, the unquestionable benefits of trade liberalization even with functioning markets can no longer be assumed to hold in situations with imperfect competition, externalities, economies of scale, and economics of learning in all of its dimensions (BOLTHO and HOLTHAM, 1992). Under those circumstances time is required to build up capacities for strategic exports supportive of modernization. Modernizing economies must break into the system of economic exchange at a point other than comparative advantage in low-cost labor or in natural resources. They need capabilities to improve marketing, access better technology, or improve organization singly or in combination. If only for these reasons, unbridled entry of FI or offshore facilitation is rarely a panacea. Either may interfere with sustaining the modernization path; it may even entail severe problems, such as when wage pressures take off with modernization.

6. Some Illustrative Negative Aspects of FI

I do not want to bias the case for or against FI in assisting the PETs in their efforts to regain sustainable growth, and ultimately lift welfare. The earlier assumption that massive FDI flows would enter the PETs, predicated on an abundance of cheap skilled labor, proximity to vibrant western markets, the potential for substantial growth of internal demand, and liberal commercial legislation, has not generally been validated. In fact, there has recently been a slowdown in FDI inflows, perhaps owing to the fact that the 'crown jewels' of privatization have already been picked off; that strategic investment positions have been taken, without really resulting in benefits in terms of capital, market access, technology, management, marketing, and so on; and that the rather slow pace of recovery in the PETs is not encouraging follow-on investment, even if committed, precisely because of the pervasive uncertainties prevailing in many PETs. With growth now on the way in several PETs, this sentiment may be changing for the better. But there can be no guarantee that once buoyancy regained it will be sustained for a protracted period of time if merger into the European economy is based on prevailing demand and supply. The business cycle is bound to reduce the chances of sustainable growth in PETs.

I deem it useful to draw attention to a number of adverse impacts of FI experienced in some of the PETs, largely because these countries are not (yet) equipped to manage such inflows in harmony with the envisaged growth trajectory, or the one yet to be elaborated, and that foreign investors are frequently motivated by strategic behavior and rent seeking.

- FDI has been heavily concentrated not only geographically, moving into the countries with generally a more liberal regime and more stable socioeconomic and political conditions. Also sectorally foreign firms have grabbed in particular those with a relatively high potential for rent seeking, owing to monopolistic positions and special arrangements with host governments, such as on customs duties, tax regimes, and cofinancing.
- Particularly in the automobile sectors, a number of countries, including Hungary and Poland, have felt compelled to offer substantial import protection, either through high import duties (as in Poland) or through confining import quotas (as in Hungary), thereby strengthening the monopolistic position - hence 'rents' - of the foreign investor in comparatively small markets.
- Strict monetary policy has been the adage that central banks in PETs are expected to observe, though some have paid more lip service than dues to this maxim. Nonetheless, with rather rudimentary financial markets in place, short-term speculative FI inflows in particular are undermining the capacity of central-banking authorities to keep money supply in line with anti-inflationary stances. Sterilizing FI that cannot be productively invested in a non-inflationary manner has its limits, given the narrow arsenal of monetary policy instruments in even the more advanced PETs. In most, such as recently in Russia, this inflow is being monetized as a result of the central bank's effort to hold down the appreciation of the exchange rate by issuing domestic currency, which fuels inflation if not held in wealth portfolios.
- Domestic banks in PETs in the aggregate have been sitting on sizable local-currency deposits that should be mobilized for onward lending to domestic

users. Because of FI inflows, both direct borrowing by companies abroad and by banks for onlending to domestic corporate borrowers, in combination with the deterioration in bank assets, the larger domestic banks are being further squeezed into insolvency. In a number of cases, these funds from abroad can be provided with a competitive edge because foreign lending is not fully subject to domestic fiscal rules precisely because of loopholes favoring FI inflow.

- Speculative capital inflows are to some extent related to the still shaky foundations of the banking sector in the PETs. The many new private banks, though small in terms of banking assets and liabilities, are as a rule undercapitalized and poorly equipped to manage risk. They are thus contributing to double jeopardy because of the limited room for assimilating the art and skills of risk assessment, which is one essential function of the banking business (in addition to ensuring effective and expeditious clearing of payments, the promotion and marketing of new financial instruments, and the collection of savings not used in one sector, usually households) in its incipient phases (BRABANT, 1994a, b, d).
- Because monetary policy in many PETs has remained stringent with high domestic interest rates and in many cases exchange rates continue to be undervalued, once these countries regain a modicum of confidence in international credit markets, speculative funds are likely to enter for two reasons. One is that foreign lenders are eager to expand their business, and indeed to carve out market share, at attractive interest rates in foreign currency, thus avoiding any foreign-exchange risk. Domestic borrowers with some positive credit rating can attract foreign-currency loans from abroad at interest rates that are considerably below domestic ones (say, a LIBOR plus of just over 7 percent as compared to domestic rates of over 11 percent in the Czech Republic in early 1995) and, furthermore, in the expectation that the exchange rate under pressure will be revalued, thus lowering their domestic borrowing costs. And this pressure derives precisely from FI inflow, not trade performance.

- In many PETs, wages are still derisory. Even if adjusted for productivity differentials, they are but a fraction of wage costs in many other countries. Foreign firms are therefore likely to offer rather generous wages as compared to prevailing norms. When labor markets are managed with rather low short-term unemployment, the wage stance adopted by FDI in particular may begin to exert pressure on local wages before such raises can be justified by real, sustainable productivity gains. To the extent that wages are sticky downward, this may complicate policy making particularly if the incipient signs of economic growth are not really the harbingers of the sustainable path that PETs need to catch up with, say, western Europe.
- Particularly in the successor States of the Soviet Union, FDI inflows have been heavily concentrated in mining and raw materials. To the degree that information is available at all, one must doubt that these investment projects, if indeed started up, are knitting forward and backward linkages through which technology, know-how, management abilities, corporate-governance structures, and marketing skills will be transferred. Very few countries have modernized on the basis of natural-resource development. There is no reason to believe that the selected successor States will fare much better.
- Countries that have adopted a fixed exchange rate, notably in the form of a currency board (BRABANT, 1995c), have encountered problems in working off pressures stemming from FI inflows because adjustment will now have to be engineered via wages and prices, which may be sticky downward, and interest rates, which cannot diverge too much from those in the markets of the vehicle currency to which the rate is pegged.

I am singling out these features of FI implications that have recently come to the fore in some or all PETs not because I oppose FI. Rather, I want to underline the limits of FI as a basic source for financing modernization and draw attention to the fact that policy makers in PETs ought to place greater emphasis on policies designed to mobilize domestic savings, including resources parked abroad, for modernizing investment projects.

7. Economic Development and FI

Why some nations are richer than others, why growth rates differ among nations, and why integration benefits some countries and hurts others have been among the bread-and-butter questions for development economics for well over two centuries. Whatever the paradigms advocated or the policies tried out, 'learning' in all of its dimensions - to learn, to choose, to import, to do, and so on - remains *the* most critical variable in bringing about structural change and economic transformation. 'Learning capabilities' cannot be delivered flexibly, that is in an adaptive mode as experience is gained, either in a highly liberal environment or through centralized economic policy. Rather, the features of a well-functioning market economy geared towards international competitiveness (not necessarily an extremely open trade regime) should be fully exploited so that markets become more and more integrated, are created where absent, and are complemented when feasible and justifiable through measures that seek to emulate as closely as possible market-based incentive criteria.

Rather than depend principally on improving markets and exploiting (static) comparative advantages, a modernization strategy in all but 'starter industrializers' aims to remove inherited economic differences. It does so through the mastery, and frequently the adaptation, of unfamiliar and often complicated technologies. It achieves this also through the complementary development of a diverse array of individual and collective skills. All this can be provided within a reasonable time frame only by deliberately interfering with the established, largely short-termist criteria for decision making. This agenda includes positive action on the part of the State. But it also presupposes a degree of economic governance (BRABANT,

1993a, b, c; 1995b) that transcends what the State itself can engineer to bolster the pace of economic development through various kinds of 'planning.'

There are good reasons to argue that latecomers, precisely because they are latecomers, confront opportunities, such as from available technology, that should facilitate their catching up. At the same time, latecomers must confront challenges that differ distinctly from those that the pioneers faced. Indeed, catching up is a far more complex assignment than simply acquiring the technology of successful economies. Such borrowing requires, what MOSES ABRAMOVITZ (1986) calls, "social capability," or an aptitude to acquire technical competence through education and training, historical conditioning, and the existence of the appropriate political, commercial, industrial, and financial institutions. In other words, lagging behind may be an advantage when a country possesses in a non-trivial way the capability to assimilate, modify, adapt, maintain, and repair such technology (ROSENBERG, 1988). This can be ensured only once certain conditions are met (NELSON, 1995). Of vital importance is an adequate infrastructure of competent skills, which are partly acquired through education. But also organizational capabilities, such as 'the institutions of the market', including foreign competition and flexible exit and entry, must realistically be available. The economy must furthermore possess institutions that permit firms to function in all but the most elementary, slowly and autonomously maturing, environment in which the industrialization process first got under way.

Aside from the challenge to acquire such a 'social capability', latecomers as a rule face a degree of uncertainty that differs from the risks that the pioneers earlier successfully tackled. Not only is it larger, also the nature of risk differs. For one thing, imitating early starters places latecomers at the mercy of the former's competitive prowess and organization. Furthermore, imitating and adapting may have to be initiated at a scale - hence a demand for risk capital - that well exceeds the risk and lumpiness of investments earlier confronted by the 'leading' developers. Indeed, the history of capitalism is replete with examples that demonstrate the progressive introduction of a large number of institutional provisions to facilitate resource mobilization for innovation by reducing or replacing limitations on risk. Of essential importance, then, is the conversion of the capital proprietor's long-term risk into an investor's short-term risk. In some cases this may justify the socialization of risk through a pro-growth stance of an activist state.

This suggests that industrialization involves the conscious direction and management of comparatively large-scale capital flows to activities that embody considerable growth potential, judging from the prevailing development gap relative to more mature economies, but whose profitability is by no means guaranteed. That is to say, industrialization as a rule involves catching up with leader countries as the driving force of modern, successful economic development over the longer haul. Setbacks and errors are bound to occur. If converted into useful lessons, they should not inhibit progressing in accordance with the development trajectory's ultimate dynamism.

The experience with economic development during the last century readily suggests that harnessing an industrial strategy for sustained economic development is not easy. A successful early developer quickly confronts would-be emulators with the choice of exploiting comparative advantage or taking a leap forward by catching up. This development path was without a doubt facilitated by the availability of stable market institutions, secure property rights, and considerable factor mobility. In several cases this included FI inflows but not, as a rule, free capital mobility. Moreover, most governments had small budgets that were roughly in balance, public ownership remained on a limited scale but SOEs were erected when deemed necessary, and domestic economic management aimed at maintaining price and exchange-rate stability, helped in some cases by an agreed global monetary regime. But mobilizing adequate capital for investment was contingent on the comprehensive development of an own financial infrastructure.

When all is said and done, closing the development gap was anything but a natural process in nearly all successful economies. It certainly was not accomplished by fostering exports of low-wage goods produced with the simplest technologies in an open economic environment. Nearly all successful industrializers, the main exceptions being first starters (such as the United Kingdom) or resource-rich countries with a large, almost self-sufficient market (such as the United States), relied on considerable tariff and other forms of protection against foreign competition, notably the pioneers, for the implementation of their industrial ambitions. In addition to discriminatory trade policy, core industrialization consisted of a far richer palette of innovation, imitation, and learning mechanisms to enhance industrial capabilities as well as to forge considerable institutional innovation. Most striking was the enhanced role for the State to coerce, cajole, and coordinate the human, technological, and financial efforts required, notably in molding the structure and scope of private investment.

Of course, far more than the State was at work. As the sophistication and scale of technologies expanded, the pressures to ensure profitable exploitation led to more hierarchical firms in which these production decisions could be coordinated. Furthermore, closer links were knit with independent sources of finance, both private and public, and large distribution networks were organized. These firms often sought to create and protect a technological edge through their own R&D, including design capacities. Moreover, they were quick to use their lead in all these areas to expand production abroad. Subsequent development suggests an ongoing process of convergence in the economic performance of these core economies with increasing industrial sophistication buttressed by rapidly growing intra-industry trade. The latter has constituted the cornerstone of the fast postwar expansion of trade among developed countries and was one crucial precondition for the 'golden age' of capitalism (MARGLIN and SCHOR, 1990).

The development experience of industrially mature countries suggests that, while inherent scale and resource advantages can in part account for differences in performance, explicit policy choices have been equally important in creating and maintaining a certain industrial structure. Latecomers were aware that this could hardly be accomplished by exploiting given comparative advantages. Virtually all sought deliberate import substitution, domestic resource mobilization, and domestic investment guidance. These unbalanced growth strategies introduced their own innovative features in response to the pressures for sustaining change under prevailing realities such as primary factor resources, access to foreign capital, the risk of making large and lumpy investment decisions, the transformation of inherited external ties, and the shortage of domestic entrepreneurs.

8. The Experience of South and East Asia and the PETs

Lessons from the experience of late industrializers, notably in continental Europe, can be enhanced by looking at the more recent successful modernization in Asian NIEs. I can only cite seven features that I have found the most illuminating in explaining their success (BRABANT, 1993a, pp. 207ff.), other than presumed 'unique' features of time, history, and place.[9] First, these countries have had a strong involvement of the non-market sector in managing economic change. In some cases, this included intrusive centralized administrative, business, financial, and political powers. In others, it called for temporarily decentralizing the responsibility of governing economic change in favor of non-market actors that do not formally form part of government. A number of these non-market actors have had to be nurtured along in the process of governing the developmental state.

Second, successful government involvement in economic affairs was monitored largely by criteria that, in one way or another, referred to validation of the favored activities or firms relative to world markets and indeed through active international competition; but not necessarily through free-trade channels. The favored activities were as a rule selected on the basis of some variant of revealed comparative *dis*advantage (that is underrepresentation of the product relative to some comparator country or the world as a whole) for products with an apparently high income elasticity, a potential for substantial gains in factor productivity, and embodying technological modernization whose forward and backward linkages could be turned into an advantage. Also, these benefits were in general granted for a fixed period of time at the end of which the activity was expected to become sufficiently profitable to withstand international competition on its own. If not, the benefits could be withdrawn in a credible manner.

Third, a comparatively small amount of public money was devoted to industrial policy proper. But government involvement proceeded principally through other channels. Yet, whatever the funds appropriated, they were spent preferably to gear symbiotic pro-growth decisions of the private sector. Targeted assistance is therefore desirable within the context of good economic governance, that is, the coordination of the activities of diverse economic actors, and fostering cooperation and competition among them in the market environment, while making full use of non-market institutions. Where the latter did not exist, their emergence was encouraged by government or created under its auspices, but divested as circumstances permitted.

Fourth, government's involvement in industrial policy was delivered through, on the whole, a competent, devoted, rewarded, and respected civil service; but it was not omniscient; as far as corruption is concerned, neither was it simon-pure. Such coordination could be sustained only through a high degree of cooperation within the various branches of the civil service. Its robustness derived also from explicit policies to cultivate highly trained professionals and attract them to the public sector. Moreover, the core task of designing the development strategy was by and large entrusted to a small group of competent civil servants enjoying considerable discretion in designing, implementing, monitoring, assessing, and fine-tuning the development strategy and in orchestrating the coordination, cooperation, and competition characteristic of good governance.

Fifth, the role of government in managing structural change was a function of the degree to which actions could be taken that did not backfire. In a fully open environment it is much more difficult to promulgate autonomous policies than when government can marshal commercial and fiscal policies, and mobilize an independent credit policy for fostering industrial change and modernization. The developmental state therefore embraced commercial, financial, and technology policies that enabled the implementation and refinement of the core industrial policy. Most NIEs had anything but free capital or trade markets. Rather they selectively liberated the trade and exchange regimes with considerable management and change over a fairly protracted period of time. Nor did this shift occur smoothly in the sense that its actions and existence could be justified at all times until discontinued even when strategic-trade decisions in retrospect seemed sensible.

Sixth, it is foolhardy to hold the government's involvement in economic affairs under all circumstances to much more demanding success criteria than those applicable to the private sector. This is all the more so since government comanagement of industrial change involves socializing part of the risk that would otherwise have discouraged private enterprise from starting up such a new and risky endeavor or from transforming its inherited facilities into precisely such a risky enterprise.

Finally, an industrial policy should preferably be grafted onto the targeted supply of public goods, notably education and basic infrastructure; onto the consensus on socioeconomic change; and onto its largely economic rewards, sociopolitical stability, and security. In this context education in all of its formal and informal dimensions deserves special emphasis primarily because generating human capital to manage the process of technological change is a much more complex task than, say, putting in place physical infrastructure.

Successful modernization, and sustaining it by coordinating dynamic competition, implies more than augmenting the physical capacity of industry or orchestrating a temporary rise in output. Rather, its critical determinants are continual improvement of productivity and competitiveness through a variety of mechanisms affecting costs, product choice and quality, productive capacity, skill diversification, and other components. But this array cannot usefully be reduced to the ability to discipline the private sector by judicious use of carrot-and-stick mechanisms, particularly when the latter are by and large equated with pecuniary rewards and punishments. To diminish the successes achieved by recalling the failures of some of the industrial-policy measures without being quite selective is not very helpful. Without denigrating that success is premised on the dynamic and static efficiency of the individual firm, industrial dynamism is also predicated on the formation of extensive linkages among firms within a particular industry, across industrial boundaries, and between industrial and other activities. Coordinating all this means that institutional innovation forms an integral part of successful modernization.

9. Managing FI and Financial Restructuring - Lessons for PETs

By being cautious about the benefits of FI, I do not, of course, wish to intimate that net FI inflows will *not* bolster demand and change the supply in PETs. It may even impart an impetus to economic recovery and growth for a while, particularly if complementary activities are embraced. However, unbridled inflow of FI is not necessarily a blessing in economies that seek not only to come to grips with massive destruction of capital assets, human as well as physical, but also to bolster creativity through modernization that can yield sustainable growth paced by steady gains in factor productivity. How can this be related to the repair exercise required in the financial sectors of the PETs?

Also in this sector the PETs must eventually face up to the double task of coming to grips with the weaknesses of the existing banking infrastructure and of laying the foundations for an intermediating sector that fulfills reasonably efficiently the basic functions of banking. As regards the whittling down of existing banking operations, four tasks are at hand: coming to grips with bad bank debt, recapitalizing banks, privatizing state-owned banks, and creating the incentives for the banking sector to learn financial intermediation. The latter requires as a minimum the four tasks that I have earlier stressed: an effective payment system, collection of savings, evaluation of creditworthiness, and marketing new financial instruments.

Where could FI come into the picture in the repair exercise? Frankly, I see little room for FI to help with the bad-debt problem. That fundamental problem stems from the fact that bank assets no longer belong fully to the nominal owner - the State - but have been captured by management in place or key bank customers - the large SOEs (BRABANT, 1994a, b, d). The bank's liabilities, however, are being shunned by the new *de facto* owners, and the State cannot completely rid itself of its responsibilities with respect to bank depositors. As a result, the facile prescription of effectuating a simple washout of bad assets against bad liabilities in the state sector is possible only on paper. Similarly, writing assets down to market values in a situation where there are no reliable markets for financial assets is a useless policy prescription. Coming to grips with bad debt is likely to have fiscal consequences to the extent that the State gets involved in the repair exercise as it must, unless it is prepared to incur the wrath of depositors, hence the electorate. As the recent experiences in the East have amply illustrated, this is messy political economy. I see little benefit in attracting FI into this sector, except in launching an effort to overcome the problem in a holistic manner, including divestment.

As concerns bank recapitalization, however, an infusion of FI into existing banks could clearly be welcome. One may well ask, however, why an expatriate bank would wish to appropriate a share of the existing state banks, whose assets are partly captured by management in place or other owners, except to reap rents. Again, recapitalization at the time of divestment, if handled properly, constitutes an exception. But otherwise I see little merit in attracting FI into the recapitalization of banks at least until the bank's asset portfolio has been cleaned up. Experience has amply demonstrated that this is not an easy exercise.

Learning the banking profession is a different matter. Clearly, FI brought in by the foreign-banking sector can usher into the PETs much more advanced banking technology and links with expatriate financial circuits than the banks in place could accomplish autonomously, given their fifty years plus experience with largely financial bookkeeping. Techniques of creating and marketing new financial instruments and evaluating credit risk can also be passed on. However, it is doubtful that foreign bankers have better knowledge of the specific local conditions of these economies in wholesale restructuring. Perhaps a joint effort to address the real grass-roots problems could be considered a promising way to usher FI into the financial sectors.

Better risk management and intermediation at an affordable transaction cost will have to be learned, largely the hard way. Though foreign banks may offer useful experience, their ignorance of local conditions and of the extraordinary circumstances of the transition guarantees that commercially-motivated bank behavior will, in fact, emerge only through experience and only over a fairly protracted period of time. Training and transfer of banking technology may bolster experience and shorten the learning period. But it cannot close the gap overnight.

Finally, divestment is part and parcel of the banking repair exercise throughout the PETs. Some countries have sold off part of state-owned banks to foreigners, possibly in conjunction with a multilateral financial institution. I am not sure whether this should be treated as an exception proving the rule or as a signal of what could have been accomplished much earlier in the transition had divestment of the banking sector been given a higher priority and attitudes towards divestment of banks been less cautious (BRABANT, 1992; WELFENS, 1993).

Also on the other task facing PET leaders - identifying a modernization path - I remain rather skeptical about the major contribution that FI could make. Technical assistance in organizing effective payment systems, in streamlining the collection of savings, in learning the techniques of risk evaluation, and in commercializing new financial instruments for wealth portfolios is one thing. Expecting FI to enter the PETs and mobilize its resources to accomplish these tasks with a view to lubricating investment flows to underpin the modernization strategy is a rather fanciful proposition. There is undoubtedly considerable need to put in place, including by the governance structures, measures that enhance market conformity, that complement markets, and that integrate markets in order to help the private sector. These are especially important to make room for the new small and medium-size firms (SMEs) that, in my view, will be the real carriers of change in the PETs. All these circumstances may confront foreign investors with steep hurdles.

From what I have been able to observe, aside from rent seeking, foreign banks have low interest in performing banking operations, other than those required for facilitating foreign investment and ordinary foreign trade, during the initial phase of the transformation. Activities referring to collecting deposits and allocating loans tend to be restrained, owing in part to the substantial risk aversion associated with the pervasive uncertainty in these countries and the banks' unfamiliarity with doing business there. It is therefore doubtful that new viable financial institutions from foreign capital to serve domestic needs will emerge quickly; I have argued elsewhere that the impetus to domestic resource mobilization for creating viable new financial institutions is also highly limited (BRABANT, 1994a, b).

For all practical purposes, then, the initial impetus to financial-sector reform will have to take the form of recapitalization of existing banks, chiefly from the public purse. Those resources could conceivably be used to establish new state-financed or cofinanced institutions, but that would not be desirable unless one were to advocate a dual-track commercial-banking system, presumably because government in effect cannot adequately monitor existing financial institutions, but it might be able to hold new ones to more rigorous surveillance rules. This too is easier said than done.

10. Conclusions

I have argued essentially six theses in this paper.

- There is a need to redirect the focus of attention on transformation agendas and economic performance of PETs to the economic goals that were at the origin of the political shifts in the East in the late 1980s.
- Economic modernization to catch up with advanced countries requires a degree of resource mobilization to jump catch-up hurdles that is unlikely to be forthcoming by adhering to the holy trinity of stabilization, liberalization, and privatization. FI under the circumstances will either seek rents or exploit low labor costs. When either or both disappear, FI will move elsewhere.
- Liberalization should be pursued with some orderly sequencing, particularly when governance capabilities are available or can be acquired fairly soon. Though the preferred phasing depends on concrete circumstances of time and place, as a rule external financial liberalization will be appropriate towards the end of the sequenced transformation strategy.
- True, complementing this through good economic governance, the erection of the still missing or limping institutions of the market, and establishing and maintaining the sociopolitical consensus may require capabilities at the level of central government that, at least for now, are lacking. But every effort should be made to acquire them soonest, including by mobilizing foreign assistance.
- Modernization in PETs will by and large have to rely on domestic resources. Mobilization of domestic savings remains a critical variable in financing the catch-up process.
- Finally, if carefully nurtured and blended with the modernization strategy, particularly the kind that derives from longer-term commitments to production, technology transfer, and human training, FI could play a complementary role, certainly once the catch-up strategy takes hold and expectations that economic agents are progressing along a new, sustainable growth path solidify. FI in

domestic banking, particularly the financial intermediation required to service the needs of the developmental state and new SMEs in PETs will remain limited for some time to come, save for speculative capital flows. But those should best be avoided during the early stages of the transformation. FDI and trade financing are areas in which expatriate banks and capital can and should play a more than trivial role in the reconstruction of PETs.

Endnotes

1 Comprising the former European planned economies, including Yugoslavia, Czechoslovakia and the USSR as well as their successor States. This area is also denoted as East with a capital *E*.

2 Inasmuch as 'transformation policies' suggests incisiveness of action over a fairly protracted period of time, I much prefer this to 'transition policies.' In what follows, I use the latter notion for the generic events in the East since 1989 and the former to designate policies purposefully directed at steering expeditiously, and with some determination, towards market-based decision making in a pluralistic political setting (see BRABANT, 1993c, 1994c, 1995b).

3 Ideally I would like this to be complemented with two other variables: the progress achieved with the movement towards a stable, functioning democracy, which calls for erecting the institutions of civil society (GELLNER, 1994, IGNATIEFF, 1995), and a fair division of the benefits of growth so that egregious income and wealth dispersions will not in due course undermine the other success indicators.

4 The argument of those espousing this thesis is admittedly more complex than I have paraphrased it here. For an extreme view on the issue, see the recent writings of ANDERS ÅSLUND (for example, 1993). Note that this assumes not only that there are presently no governance capabilities in the PETs but that good governance capabilities will spontaneously emerge from the transformation processes put in train as a result of 'shock therapy' - a misnomer of sorts (BRABANT, 1995b) as if the market, let alone an incipient one, were capable of creating the institutions and governance mechanisms that define a functioning market (MURRELL, 1995)!

5 The literature on FI, particularly FDI, into PETs is by now vast. The conventional arguments are available in WELFENS (1992, 1993, 1994).

6 I am not referring to aggregate investment because the internalized transformation of savings into investments is subject to other transaction costs than the mediated one (AKYÜZ, 1993a).

7 Without imposing guidelines on capital inflows, congruence of domestic and foreign interests is fortuitous as FI enters for its own reasons, motivated largely by cheap labor.

8 A similar sequence of objections can be formulated with respect to domestic liberalization under conditions of disequilibrium. The main point is that the rise in the real interest rate raises the cost of debt. This can be offset easier by oligopolistic firms in the nontraded sector by raising prices than by firms engaged in stiff foreign competition; the latter can mainly agitate on real wages, lest their ability to preserve real profit, hence retention for investment purposes, be undermined (AKYÜZ, 1993c, pp. 146-8).

9 The literature on the NIEs, both for and against the opening hypothesis, is vast. I base my conclusions on the faction that has delved with some intensity into the domestic circumstances of

policy formulation and implementation. For a selection of the main indicators and conclusions, see AKYÜZ (1993a), AMSDEN (1989, 1992, 1993), BRUTON (1992), CASTELLS (1992), CHANG (1994), LALL (1994), NOBLE (1989), RODRIK (1995), SAMUELS (1990), SINGH (1994, 1995), WADE (1988, 1990, 1995).

References

ABRAMOVITZ, M. (1986), "Catching up, forging ahead, and falling behind," *Journal of Economic History*, No. 2, 385-406.

AKYÜZ, Y. (1993a), "Financial liberalization: the key issues," in AKYÜZ, Y. And HELD, G. (eds.), *Finance and the real economy - issues and case studies in developing countries*, ESCAP, UNCTAD, and WIDER, Santiago, 19-68.

AKYÜZ, Y. (1993b), "On financial openness in developing countries," in *International monetary and financial issues for the 1990s, volume II*, United Nations publication, sales no. UNCTAD/GID/G24/2, New York, 111-24.

AKYÜZ, Y. (1993c), "Does financial liberalization improve trade performance?" in AGOSIN, M. R. And TUSSIE, D. (Eds.), *Trade and growth - new dilemmas in trade policy*, St. Martin's Press, New York, 142-64.

AMSDEN, A. H. (1989), *Asia's next giant: South Korea and late industrialization*, Oxford University Press, New York and Oxford.

AMSDEN, A. H. (1992), "A theory of government intervention in late industrialization," in PUTTERMAN, L. and RUESCHENMEYER, D. (Eds.), *State and market in development - synergy or rivalry?*, Lynne Rienner, Boulder, CO and London, 53-84.

AMSDEN, A. H. (1993), "East Asian financial markets: why so much (and fairly effective) government intervention?" in AKYÜZ, Y. and HELD, G. (eds.), *Finance and the real economy - issues and case studies in developing countries*, ESCAP, UNCTAD, and WIDER, Santiago, 69-101.

ÅSLUND, A. (1993), "The nature of the transformation crisis in the former Soviet countries," in SIEBERT, H. (ed.), *Overcoming the transformation crisis - lessons for the successor States of the Soviet Union*, JCB Mohr (Paul L. Siebeck), Tübingen, 39-56.

BARRO, R. J. (1991), "Economic growth in a cross-section of countries," *Quarterly Journal of Economics*, No. 2, 407-43.

BOLTHO, A. and HOLTHAM, G. (1992), "The assessment: new approaches to economic growth," *Oxford Review of Economic Policy*, No. 4, 1-14.

BRABANT, J. M. van, (1992), *Privatizing Eastern Europe - the role of markets and ownership in the transition*, Kluwer Academic Publishers, Dordrecht, Boston, MA, and London.

BRABANT, J. M. van (1993a), *Industrial policy in Eastern Europe - governing the transition*, Kluwer Academic Publishers, Dordrecht, Boston, MA, London.

BRABANT, J. M. van (1993b), "Governance, the state, and industrial policy in Eastern Europe," paper prepared for the Third American-Polish Round Table, Charleston, SC, 15-16 September.

BRABANT, J. M. van (1993c), "Lessons from the wholesale transformations in the East," *Comparative Economic Studies*, No. 4, 73-102.

BRABANT, J. M. van (1994a), "Towards rational banking in transition economies," paper prepared for the Third Freiberg Symposium on Economics 'The Emergence and Evolution of Markets', Freiberg, Germany, 1-3 September.

BRABANT, J. M. van (1994b), "Money as an essential vehicle for rational financial intermediation," paper presented at the conference on 'Social and Economic Problems of Ukraine as Transitional Society at the Break of Millennium', organized by the University of Kiev, Ukraine, 1-4 December.

BRABANT, J. M. Van (1994c), "Privatization, industrial policy and governing the transitions," *MOCT-MOST*, No. 1, 63-85.

BRABANT, J. M. van (1994d), "Transforming the bank and enterprise balance sheets in Eastern Europe," *MOCT-MOST*, No. 3, 7-36.

BRABANT, J. M. van (1995a), "Microeconomics, endogenous growth, and systemic transformation," paper presented at the Fourth Freiberg Symposium on 'Microeconomics of Transition and Growth', Freiberg, Germany, 28-30 August.

BRABANT, J. M. van (1995b), "Governance, evolution, and the transformation of Eastern Europe," in POZNANSKI, K. (ed.), *The transformation of Eastern Europe and evolutionary economics*, Westview Press, Boulder, CO and London, 157-82.

BRABANT, J. M. van (1995c), "Transformation, endogenous growth, and currency boards for the new East," paper presented at the conference 'Macroeconomics of Recovery in East-Central Europe', Budapest, Hungary, 19-21 June.

BRESSER PEREIRA, L. C., MARAVALL, J. M. and PRZEWORSKI, A. (1993), *Economic reforms in new democracies - a social-democratic approach*, Cambridge University Press, Cambridge and New York.

BRUTON, H. J. (1992), "International aspects of the role of government in economic development," in PUTTERMAN, L. and RUESCHEMEYER, D. (ed.), *State and market in development - synergy or rivalry?*, Lynne Rienner, Boulder, CO and London, 101-30.

CASTELLS, M. (1992), "Four Asian tigers with a dragon head - a comparative analysis of the state, economy, and society in the Asian Pacific rim," in APPELBAUM, R. P. and HENDERSON, J. (eds.), *States and development in the Asian Pacific rim*, SAGE publications, Newbury Park, CA, London and New Delhi, 33-70.

CHANDLER, A. D., Jr. (1977), *The visible hand: the managerial revolution in American business*, Harvard University Press, Cambridge, MA.

CHANG, H.-J. (1994), *The political economy of industrial policy*, St. Martin's Press, New York.

DIETRICH, M. (1992), "The foundations of industrial policy," in COWLING, K. and SUGDEN, R. (eds.), *Current issues in industrial economic strategy*, Manchester University Press, Manchester and New York, 16-32.

FLEMMING, J. S. (1993), "The role of external assistance in overcoming the transformation crisis," in SIEBERT, H. (ed.), *Overcoming the transformation crisis - lessons for the successor States of the Soviet Union*, JCB Mohr (Paul L. Siebeck), Tübingen, 197-204.

GELLNER, E. (1994), *Conditions of liberty: civil society and its rivals*, Penguin, London.

IGNATIEFF, M. (1995), "On civil society - why Eastern Europe's revolutions could succeed," *Foreign Affairs*, No. 2, 128-36.

KAY, J. (1992), *Foundations of corporate success: how business strategies add value*, Oxford University Press, Oxford.

KREGEL, J. (1994), "Capital flows: globalization of production and financing development," *UNCTAD Review 1994*, United Nations publication, sales no. E.94.II.D.19, New York, 23-38.

KRUGMAN, P. (1995), "Dutch tulips and emerging markets," *Foreign Affairs*, No. 4, 28-46.

LALL, S. (1994), "Industrial policy: the role of government in promoting industrial and technological development," *UNCTAD Review 1994*, 65-89.

LANDES, D. (1990), "Why are we so rich and they so poor?" *American Economic Review*, No. 2, 1-13.

MARGLIN, S. A. and SCHOR, J. B. (eds.) (1990), *The golden age of capitalism: reinterpreting the postwar experience*, Clarendon Press, Oxford.

MARKOWSKI, S. and JACKSON, S. (1994), "The attractiveness of Poland to direct foreign investors," *Communist Economies and Economic Transformation*, No. 4, 515-35.

MURRELL, P. (1995), "The transition according to Cambridge, Mass.," *Journal of Economic Literature*, No. 1, 164-78.

NELSON, R. R. (1995), "Recent evolutionary theorizing about economic change," *Journal of Economic Literature*, No. 1, 40-90.

NOBLE, G. W. (1989), "The Japanese industrial policy debate," in HAGGARD, S. and MOON, C. (eds.), *Pacific dynamics: the international politics of industrial change*, Westview Press, Boulder, CO, and Center for International Studies, Inha University, Inchon, 53-95.

PACK, H. and WESTPHAL, L. E. (1986), "Industrial strategy and technological change - theory versus reality," *Journal of Development Economics*, No. 1, 87-128.

PORTER, M. E. (1990), *The competitive advantage of nations*, The Free Press, New York.

PORTES, R. (1994), "Transformation traps," *Economic Journal*, No. 3, 1178-89.

RODRIK, D. (1995), "Getting interventions right: how South Korea and Taiwan grew rich," *Economic Policy*, No. 20, 69-111.

ROSENBERG, N. (1988), "Technical change under capitalism and socialism," Mimeo, Stanford University, Stanford, CA, January.

SAMUELS, R. J. (1990), "The business of the Japanese state," in CHICK, M. (ed.), *Governments, industries and markets - aspects of government-industry relations in the UK, Japan, West Germany and the USA since 1945*, Edward Elgar, Aldershot and Brookfield, VT, 36-60.

SAWYER, M. (1992), "On the theory of industrial policy," in COWLING, K. and SUGDEN, R. (eds.), *Current issues in industrial economic strategy*, Manchester University Press, Manchester and New York, 3-15.

SINGH, A. (1994), "Growing independently of the world economy: Asian economic development since 1980," *UNCTAD Review 1994*, United Nations publications, sales no. E.94.II.D.19, 91-105.

SINGH, A. (1995), "How did east Asia grow so fast? - slow progress towards an analytical consensus," UNCTAD Discussion Papers, No. 97, February, Geneva.

UNCTAD (1993), *Explaining and forecasting regional flows of foreign direct investment*, United Nations publication, sales no. ST/CTC/SER.A/26, New York.

UNECE (1993), *Economic survey of Europe in 1992-1993*, United Nations publication, sales no. E.93.II.E.1, New York.

WADE, R. (1988), "The role of government in overcoming market failure: Taiwan, Republic of Korea and Japan," in HUGHES, H. (ed.), *Achieving industrialization in East Asia*, Cambridge University Press, Cambridge and New York, 129-62.

WADE, R. (1990), *Governing the market - economic theory and the role of government in East Asian industrialization*, Princeton University Press, Princeton, NJ.

WADE, R. (1995), "The east Asian miracle: why the controversy continues," in *International monetary and financial issues for the 1990s, volume V*, United Nations publication, sales no. E.95.II.D.3, New York, 65-79.

WELFENS, P. J. J. (1992), "Foreign investment in the East European transition," *Management International Review - Journal of International Business*, No. 3, 199-218.

WELFENS, P. J. J. (1993), "The growth of the private sector: privatization and foreign direct investment in Eastern Europe," in SIEBERT, H. (ed.), *Overcoming the transformation crisis - lessons for the successor States of the Soviet Union*, JCB Mohr (Paul L. Siebeck), Tübingen, 119-66.

WELFENS, P. J. J. (1994), "Privatization and foreign direct investment in the East European transformation: theory, options and strategies," in CSABA, L. (ed.), *Privatization, liberalization an destruction - recreating the market in Central and Eastern Europe*, Dartmouth, Aldershot, 35-68.

Comments on
Banking, Foreign Investment, Endogenous Growth and Systemic Transformation

Volker Clausen

As the title of the paper "Banking, Foreign Investment, Endogenous Growth and Systemic Transformation" already indicates, Mr. van Brabant covers a wide range of topics making it impossible for me to comment on the wealth of issues raised in the paper. So let me consider just a few aspects which I deem important about this contribution. First, I would like to discuss a few theoretical issues. This is then followed by comments on practical or policy issues.

1. Theoretical Issues

"Cumulative Causation" is a frequently used term in the paper and serves as a basis for policy prescriptions, for example, for industrial policy. This concept is not sufficiently defined in the paper. Does it mean that sectors reinforce each other in their economic activity? In this respect the paper by SCITOVSKY (1954) represents a valuable guide. Scitovsky distinguishes very clearly between pecuniary and non-pecuniary externalities and contrasts their importance from a static as well as from a dynamic (or growth) perspective. Furthermore, it is necessary to specify to which extent increasing returns to scale matter in the process of cumulative causation. It is certainly implausible that the overall economy exhibits increasing returns to scale. If so, what will happen if sectors with increasing returns to scale and constant returns to scale co-exist and this in the tradeable as well as in the non-tradeable sector? Which conclusions can be drawn for industrial policy? MATSUYAMA (1995) provides a record to date. This literature is still in its beginnings but will certainly influence our thinking on industrial policy and government intervention.

Second, the author claims that financing domestic investment by domestic savings is more attractive than external finance. With respect to the theoretical basis for this claim, it would be interesting to see how external finance can be viewed as a transfer problem and how this affects terms of trade, international competitiveness, and welfare in the economy. Say the government finances investment in basic infrastructure by a loan denominated in foreign currency. Interest payments in foreign currency will have to be due in future periods. Both types of transactions tend to lead to a depreciation of the domestic currency. In contrast, the case of domestic financing in the domestic bond market tends to raise domestic interest rates attracting foreign capital and leading to an appreciation. Clearly, both types of financing have different implications. It seems worthwhile to have a closer look at these issues in a suitably specified model. The contributions by KEYNES (1929) and OHLIN (1929) on the impact of German reparations on the terms of trade labeled the Keynes-Ohlin-controversy may provide some guidance.

On the issue of domestic versus external finance I was surprised not to meet the contribution of MCKINNON (1973). He argues in his book *Money and Capital in Economic Development* that distortions and inefficiencies in domestic financial markets are a very important obstacle to economic growth. Liberalization of financial markets and incentives to save may suffice to finance domestic investment. Reliance on foreign capital will therefore be reduced or even completely eliminated.

2. Policy Issues

Mr. van Brabant argues mostly qualitatively and does not present any quantitative relationships. He argues that domestic investment will have to be financed by domestic savings. I agree with that. Since FELDSTEIN and HORIOKA (1980) and numerous follow-up papers we know that this is an empirical regularity. The question is what will be the size of capital accumulation or investment ratios necessary to achieve the desired growth rate. Since the size of foreign capital inflows is expected to be small we can immediately infer the amount of savings in the economy to be generated. By comparison with the actual (private and public) savings we may get a better picture on whether it can be assumed that domestic savings are sufficient in volume to make an elevated and sustained growth path realistic. In short, I would have liked to see more information on the quantitative relationships as well as some back-of-the-envelope calculations.

The second policy issue concerns the role of foreign investment in the banking sector. Mr. van Brabant identifies a number of weaknesses in the existing banking infrastructure - the bad debt problem, bank recapitalization, learning the banking profession, divestment - and furthermore he defines numerous tasks to improve financial intermediation - effective payment systems, collection of savings, evaluation of creditworthiness of the demand for loans, and marketing new financial instruments. Overall, Mr. van Brabant sees only a relatively limited role for foreign investment and he strongly favors state-financed or co-financed banks.

I do not share this view. Growth does not only depend on the volume but also on the efficiency of investment. I believe that a private banking sector carefully monitoring the creditors and the profitability of projects will be a very important condition for the efficient allocation of savings and strong and sustainable growth. Improving the conditions for international lending and especially for domestic lending will be an important exercise. This leads me to my final comment. The paper does not mention a substantial role for international organizations in financial sector reform in post-communist countries in transition. Is it the lack of space in your paper, a lack of confidence or do you believe that international organizations like the IMF, the World Bank (IFC) or the EBRD have nothing to offer?

References

FELDSTEIN, M. and HORIOKA, C. (1980), "Domestic Saving and International Capital Flows," *Economic Journal*, Vol. 90, 314-329.

KEYNES, J. M. (1929), "The German Transfer Problem," *Economic Journal*, Vol. 39, 1-7.

MATSUYAMA, K. (1995), "Complementarities and Cumulative Processes in Models of Monopolistic Competition," *Journal of Economic Literature*, Vol. 33, 701-729.

MCKINNON, R. I. (1973), *Money and Capital in Economic Development*, The Brookings Institution, Washington, D.C.

OHLIN, B. (1929), "Transfer Difficulties, Real and Imagined," *Economic Journal*, Vol. 39, 172-178.

SCITOVSKY, T. (1954), "Two Concepts of External Economies," *Journal of Political Economy*, Vol. 62, 143-151.

H. Capital Flows in Eastern Europe: Some Lessons from the Emerging Markets in Latin America and Asia

*Elmar B. Koch**

1. Introduction

Given the scale of the transformation of the economies in eastern Europe, it is perhaps not surprising that the revival of capital flows into that region has occurred somewhat later than that of flows into Asia and Latin America. Although events are still unfolding at the time of writing, it may be useful to take a look at emerging capital flow trends in central Europe[1] in the light of the experiences in Latin America and Asia. Section 1 briefly reviews recent developments in global capital flows. Section 2 looks at the size of the capital flows for the three regions under review. Section 3 juxtaposes in a highly stylized way some factors which influence the capital flow experiences in Latin America, Asia and central Europe. A more detailed analysis of the composition and nature of the capital flows in the three groups of countries is contained in Section 4. Three important policy-related issues are then addressed in Section 5: the effect of inflows on monetary policy (including the issue of sterilization); whether inflows reflect excessive domestic consumption rather than investment (including the relationship with fiscal policy); and, finally, how far foreign direct investment has been export-oriented. Some conclusions follow in Section 6.

1.1 The Integration of World Financial Markets

The last decade has seen an explosion in the volume of capital movements.[2] The main general contributory factors to this development have been the removal of exchange controls in all major industrial countries and in many emerging market economies, domestic financial liberalization and rapid advances in financial technology. These general developments have been helped and accelerated by financial market developments themselves, the evolution of derivative instruments to facilitate new forms of hedging and position-taking, the boom in securitization through an increase in the share of financial liabilities and assets that are readily tradable, and greater institutionalization of investment activity, as restrictions on financial institutions' investment abroad have been eased.[3] A distinguishing feature of recent trends is the increased significance of portfolio capital movements - as opposed to bank or official lending, which predominated in the 1970s and 1980s. Unlike bank or official lending, such flows are not closely linked to particular end-users or particular investments.

There has been a sharp rise in the proportion of financial assets held by non-residents. Such holdings are, in general, very sensitive to shifts of sentiment in international financial markets. Unrealistic exchange rates or inadequate economic policies have become more subject to the sanction of capital markets. A large amount of funds can now easily be moved into individual countries - and out again just as easily. This increased volatility of capital flows, and their potential reversibility, has become a key concern of policy-makers everywhere.

2. Capital Inflows to Central Europe

Capital flows into central Europe did not rise strongly until 1993. During the two-year period 1993-94, the inflow of capital to the eastern European countries amounted to $26bn.[4] Of this total, more than one-third accrued to Hungary and roughly the same amount to Poland and the Czech Republic together.[5] This represented about 8½% of total inflows to the three regions shown.[6]

Inflows to central Europe reached about 7% of GDP in 1993 and stayed high, at nearly 5% of GDP, in 1994. This is well above the rates seen in Asia in recent years and close to the peak values of almost 5% reached in Latin America in 1992 and 1993.[7] Asia has seen a steady growth of capital inflows, which have hovered around 3% of GDP during the last two years. In terms of exports, however, the average capital inflow of around 14% for the central European countries over the period 1990-94 is closer to the Asian experience.

Yet what has happened to these inflows in general terms? Have they been absorbed by the official foreign exchange reserves? All three country groups saw their reserve position strengthen during the period 1990-94 (Table H1).

Table H1 Capital Flows and Reserves

	1975-82 annual average	1983-90 annual average	1990	1991	1992	1993	1994	Cumu-lative 1990-94
	in billions of US dollars							
	Net capital flows (inflows = +)							
Eastern Europe[1]	..	..	2.2	5.4	3.2	13.7	11.9	36.3
Czech Republic	..	..	-0.2	-0.3	0.2	2.6	2.1	4.4
Hungary	..	..	-0.8	2.4	0.4	6.0	3.3	11.4
Poland	..	..	1.7	0.5	0.9	2.1	2.7	7.9
Latin America[2]	20.4	4.6	10.9	29.2	52.8	57.6	31.1	181.7
Asia[3]	8.3	7.6	8.3	30.1	43.1	44.1	49.2	174.8
	Net change in reserves (increase = +)							
Eastern Europe[1]	..	..	-0.1	3.7	2.0	5.5	7.6	18.7
Czech Republic	..	..	-0.5	0.8	-0.1	3.0	2.4	5.5
Hungary	..	..	-0.6	2.7	0.8	2.6	-0.6	4.8
Poland	..	..	2.4	-0.8	0.6	-0.2	1.7	3.7
Latin America[2]	0.9	1.3	12.4	16.4	24.4	19.7	-7.6[4]	65.3
Asia[3]	3.4	16.4	19.8	34.6	45.9	33.1	45.8	179.3
Memorandum items: Total developing countries								
Net capital inflows	*22.4*	*37.5*	*36.1*	*156.4*	*145.3*	*151.2*	*129.8*	*618.7*
Net increase in reserves	*9.4*	*15.4*	*32.6*	*70.5*	*68.9*	*66.0*	*52.8*	*291.1*

[1] Bulgaria, the Czech Republic, Hungary, Poland, Romania, the Slovak Republic and Slovenia. [2] Argentina, Brazil, Chile, Colombia, Mexico and Venezuela. [3] China, India, Indonesia, Korea, Malaysia, Singapore, Taiwan and Thailand. [4] The drop in Mexico's reserves was $17.7bn.

Source: National sources.

The Latin American countries absorbed only about one-third of their inflows (a $65bn increase in reserves, with a $182bn capital inflow) and the proportion going into the reserves fell during the early 1990s. The rate of absorption was much higher for Asia. In the central European countries, around one-half was taken into the reserves. The change in central European official reserves grew from small amounts in 1990 to a cumulative $14bn by 1994.[8] By end-1994, the cumulative change in reserves was broadly similar in the three countries concerned.[9] However, individual country experience varied widely. The Czech Republic channeled all inflows into reserves. Indeed, inflows have grown more rapidly than in the other two countries since the separation from the Slovak Republic in January 1993. Poland took nearly half of its inflows into reserves. The increase was smallest in Hungary, where reserves actually fell in 1994.

Table H2 Capital Flows

	1990	1991	1992	1993	1994	Average 1990-94
	as a percentage of GDP					
Central Europe[1]	0.5	2.0	1.0	6.9	4.7	**3.2**
Czech Republic	-0.7	-1.3	0.8	8.3	5.8	2.9
Hungary	-2.5	7.3	1.2	15.7	8.0	6.2
Poland	2.7	0.7	1.1	2.5	2.9	2.0
Latin America[2]	1.2	3.0	4.9	4.8	2.3	**3.2**
Asia[2]	0.8	2.6	3.3	3.0	3.1	**2.7**
	as a percentage of exports					
Central Europe[1]	2.2	8.6	4.6	30.1	19.2	13.8
Czech Republic	-2.5	-4.0	2.6	19.7	14.5	8.2
Hungary	-8.3	23.0	4.1	67.9	30.6	22.6
Poland	56.7	4.1	6.3	15.5	25.2	11.6
Latin America[2]	10.5	28.7	49.4	51.2	24.0	32.8
Asia[2]	2.7	8.5	11.0	10.1	9.0	8.3

[1] The Czech Republic, Hungary and Poland. [2] See Table H1 for a list of countries.

Source: National sources.

3. Stylized Macroeconomic Features Influencing Capital Flow Experiences in Latin America, Asia and Central Europe

Some comparisons of broad macroeconomic indicators for Asia, Latin America and central Europe are shown in Table H3. Sound macroeconomic performance will underpin consistent and substantial capital flows. One major component of good macroeconomic performance is the recipient country's domestic growth.

At 8%, GDP growth in Asia was more than two and a half times as high as in Latin America during 1990-94. Moreover, gross national saving and investment ratios (of around 34% each) were much higher in Asia than in Latin America (19 and 21% respectively). The high export ratios and strong export growth in Asia also suggest a better capacity to service any future external liabilities arising from capital inflows.

Table H3 Selected Macroeconomic Indicators

	Central Europe[1]			Latin America	Asia
	1990-92	1993	1994	1990-94	1990-94
GDP growth (in %)	-5.8	1.9	4.0	2.8	7.8
Gross national savings (as % of GDP)	29.8	24.5	21.9	18.8	33.6
Gross domestic investment (as % of GDP)	23.3	19.5	15.6	20.6	34.0
Government consumption (as % of GDP)	19.3	20.0	17.3	11.6	9.4
Budget deficits (as % of GDP)	-2.8	-2.6	-2.7	-0.0	-2.1
Total exports[2] (as % of GDP)	25.3	27.5	28.7	11.3	28.6
External debt/export[2] ratio	251.0	228.0	184.0	272.0	147.0
Monthly inflation (in %)	4.4	2.5	2.0	11.4	0.8
Monthly inflation variance	2.3[3]	1.4[3]	0.7	57.4	0.2
REER[4] appreciation (cumulative, in %)	24.1	5.8	0	15.7	-4.6

[1] The Czech Republic, Hungary and Poland (weighted by the 1990 purchasing power parity (PPP) valuation of country GDPs). [2] Export earnings (goods, services and income). [3] Excluding the initial months of price liberalization. [4] For Latin America and Asia, in terms of consumer prices; for central Europe, consumer prices and wholesale prices are given equal weight.

Source: National sources.

The divergence in inflation performance - very marked in the 1980s, when inflation was far higher in Latin America than in Asia - has persisted but is now somewhat smaller. The fairly good inflation performance in Asia also helped to keep real effective exchange rate appreciation in check or low, while in Latin America anti-inflation policies using exchange-rate-based nominal anchors contributed to a sizeable real appreciation.[10] GDP growth and saving/investment ratios in central Europe have all been closer to those of Latin America than those of Asia. Thus, both Latin America and central Europe share the low investment/low growth characteristics.

Domestic savings are the major source of future investments. Saving rates in central Europe were high before transition, largely because limited consumption opportunities led to forced saving.[11] The low saving rates seen more recently may owe something to high and variable inflation rates in the past, as well as to weak financial intermediation.[12] These low saving rates have gone hand in hand with low investment rates, which stood at around 20%, close to the levels seen in Latin America during the last few years. In fact, since 1989, capital investment in almost all countries in central and eastern Europe has fallen by more than GDP, only to rise somewhat in 1994 in the countries most advanced in the transition process. The lack of investment funds,[13] reflecting low levels of saving, is probably the most serious constraint on growth in central Europe in the medium-term perspective.[14] Finally, government consumption is proportionately higher in central Europe than in either Latin America or Asia.

Central European economies appear to be more open and more reliant on foreign trade than Latin America, and nearly match the high export/GDP ratio of Asia. Debt/export ratios for central Europe fall between those in Latin America and those in Asia. Another important similarity is that both Latin America and central Europe recorded substantial real effective exchange rate appreciation during the period up to 1993.

Table H4 Central Europe: Inflation and Real Effective Exchange Rates

	Consumer price inflation (in %)				Real effective exchange rate appreciation (cumulative, in %)			
	Monthly rate		Monthly variance		CP	WP	CP	WP
	1991-94	1994	1991 9	1994	1991-94[1]		1994-95[2]	
Czech Republic	2.5	0.8	0.2	0.3	11.8	5.0	6.0	1.2
Hungary	3.0	1.8	1.8	0.4	22.5	-0.1	-5.4	-9.1
Poland	6.5	2.5	4.1	0.9	18.1	3.2	2.6	-8.3

Note: CP = consumer prices; WP = wholesale prices (industrial producer prices).
[1] For Hungary and Poland, starting in March 1991; for the Czech Republic, starting in February 1993.
[2] To June 1995.

Source: National sources.

In 1994-95, however, the real effective exchange rate for central Europe as a whole depreciated. Hungary's real effective exchange rate depreciated substantially during 1994-95, while the real effective exchange rate of the Czech koruna appreciated somewhat, reflecting to some extent the pressure on that currency. The evidence for Poland is less clear (see Table H4). While the real effective exchange rate based on consumer prices shows a small appreciation, the indicator based on wholesale prices exhibits a fairly substantial depreciation. The large discrepancies in the real effective exchange rates based on consumer and wholesale prices are remarkable and are attributable to a relatively faster rise in service prices, as the backlog of demand was particularly large in this area and this sector continues to grow faster than others.

The evolution of the real effective exchange rate over time, however, does not indicate whether or not the real exchange rate of a country is under or overvalued. In this context, it was a well-established strategy at the beginning of the transformation process to devalue by a large margin in order to provide the tradable goods sector of the economy with the necessary room for maneuver. Since then, the real effective exchange rates in all three countries have been appreciating, eroding this room for maneuver. By 1994, it appeared that the Czech koruna was, indeed, still substantially undervalued in relation to its estimated "correct" real exchange rate level. Evidence for the other two countries appears to be less firm, indicating that perhaps the Hungarian forint may be slightly overvalued, while the Polish zloty may be slightly undervalued.

The implications for capital flows appear to be that they are more likely to be sustainable in the case of the Czech Republic.

Returning to Asia and Latin America, another factual difference between these two regions concerns the volatility of the return on financial assets. Asia may look back on a history of fairly stable implied returns of the order of 8-10% during the 1980s and 1990s, more or less in line with growth performance during most of this period. Latin American countries, in contrast, experienced depressed returns in the 1980s, followed by extremely high returns during the 1991-93 period and a sharp drop in 1994. Of course, this volatility reflects to some extent the risks involved in these flows. The experience has, to say the least, been less positive for the stock exchanges in central Europe. The large see-saw movements on the Warsaw Stock Exchange bear ample witness to this.[15]

As far as fiscal balances are concerned, the average for the central European countries hides important differences. While the Czech Republic had a central government budget surplus amounting to 1% of GDP in 1994, the Hungarian budget deficit has been deteriorating during the last few years, to stand at 7½% of GDP in 1994 (Table H5).

Table H5 Central Europe: Selected Macroeconomic Indicators

	GDP growth			Budget balance*			Exports*		
	1990-92	1993	1994	1990-92	1993	1994	1990-92	1993	1994
Czech Republic	-6.9	-0.9	2.6	-0.8	0.1	1.0	31.0	47.5	47.0
Hungary	-5.8	-0.8	2.0	-3.9	-5.6	-7.5	35.2	30.6	28.3
Poland	-5.4	3.8	5.1	-2.8	-2.8	-2.7	20.0	18.6	21.5

* In percentages of GDP.

Source: National sources.

While the fiscal deterioration in Hungary owes something to the initial drop in output and the associated rise in unemployment at the beginning of transition, the Government also experienced difficulties in decisively reducing its role in resource allocation and streamlining social programs. Whereas subsidies were lowered during this period, transfers increased. The Government's interest payments were also a drag, as they increased from 2.3% of GDP in 1989 to 6.8% in 1994. Austerity measures were introduced in March 1995, and included a sharp 9% forint devaluation, an 8% import surcharge and cuts in welfare spending (in particular by placing a cap on the rise in public sector wages. However, the final judgment on whether they had a salutary impact on budget balances is still outstanding, owing to parliamentary opposition to some of these measures.[16]

4. Composition of Capital Flows

Past experience may not be a good basis for predicting future events, in particular in the area of capital flows. In any case, if any lessons are to be drawn from the capital flow history in Asia and Latin America, a closer look must be taken at the individual components of capital flows and how they might differ between these country groups (Table H6).[17]

For a recipient country, it may be most important whether inflows are of a debt or non-debt-creating nature.[18] Furthermore, it is important to know whether or not any inflows are easily reversible in particular, if they can be withdrawn at short notice. It would, for example, be quite useful to have a maturity profile for all debt-creating flows.[19] One aspect of the statistical nature of some of these inflows has been that the differentiation between short-term and long-term instruments, which was a standard feature of balance-of-payments presentation in many major industrialized countries in the 1980s, has fallen more and more into discredit. At that time it was realized that, for example, a three-month eurocredit can be as long-term as a five-year bond issue, while a Treasury bond with a 30-year maturity can easily be more liquid than a time deposit at a commercial bank.[20]

One standard classification has been the distinction between foreign direct investment (FDI) and portfolio investment (P). FDI flows[21] are thought to be determined more by long-term fundamental economic considerations and are not easily reversible, whereas portfolio flows are more oriented towards shorter-term rates of return and, thus, are potentially more volatile, that is, they are more easily reversible.

Table H6 Composition and Nature of Capital Flows

	Central Europe	Asia	Latin America
Sterilization	Approx. 1/2 sterilized (but large country differences)	Approx. 2/3 sterilized; little difficulty in sterilization	Approx. 1/3 sterilized; difficulty in sterilization
Direct investment (FDI)/portfolio mix	Small portfolio flows	2/3 FDI flows	2/3 portfolio flows
Investment/consumption	FDI inflows have tended to increase consumption (initially)	FDI inflows have tended to increase investment	FDI inflows have tended to increase consumption
Nature of FDI flows	Privatization; some greenfield operations, but only in Hungary	More in the form of greenfield operations and joint ventures	Major privatization and debt/equity swaps
Return on financial investment	Very volatile equity markets; returns dependent on holding period	Higher in past on average and less volatile	Lower in past on average and more volatile

In fact, one of the hallmarks of the difference between capital flows has been the dominance of direct investment flows to Asia, while the reverse has been true for Latin America, rendering Latin American countries in general more vulnerable than Asia to swings in foreign investor sentiment.[22]

Table H7 Foreign Direct Investment (FDI) and Portfolio Investment (P)

	1990	1991	1992	1993	1994	Cumulative 1990-94
	FDI as a percentage of FDI plus P					
Central Europe	..	..	..	57	48	66
Latin America	25	30	23	17	57*	28
Asia	85	81	79	65	72	73

* Due to a sharp drop of P from $68bn in 1993 to $17bn in 1994.

Source: National sources.

Whereas about two-thirds of the flows to Asia have been FDI flows (and only one-third portfolio flows), the reverse is true for Latin America. This difference is probably due in part to the better long-term prospects in Asia, as explained above, and more prudent financial policies. It also appears that, in a number of Asian countries, controls on both inward portfolio investment and domestic financial markets have been kept tighter, while there has been less tight control of portfolio inflows into Latin America. The prospects for short-term gains from portfolio investment looked relatively more promising in Latin America during the 1991-93 period, as it re-emerged from the 1980s depression, than in Asia, in which foreign investment was already occurring. Another factor was high nominal interest rates, combined with the policy of adjusting the exchange rate only partially for inflation: this meant that domestic interest rates, when converted into dollars, were extremely high.

About 65% of the cumulative capital inflows to central Europe during 1990-94 were in the form of direct investment.[23] The remaining 35% covers flows of quite diverse characteristics. About three-quarters of non-direct investment flows were accounted for by *Hungary* during 1993 and 1994. These flows were mainly attributable to the large borrowing program of the National Bank of Hungary, which took the form of international bond issues (Table H8).[24] This program reflected increasing budgetary and external deficits. The fiscal deficit widened to 6-7% of

GDP in 1992 and 1993 and 7½% in 1994, while the debt/export ratio (at 250%) was the highest in central Europe.

A large proportion of what is recorded as short-term capital inflows to *Poland* apparently reflects unrecorded export earnings: the foreign exchange inflows are deposited at exchange offices located near border posts. This interpretation is also supported by the large discrepancy between customs and balance-of-payments data. Foreign participation in the Warsaw Stock Exchange is still quite limited. Some of the flows to the *Czech Republic* are in the form of government bonds but the bulk of the inflows is attributable to the private sector.[25]

Table H8 Central Europe: Net Bond Issues

	1992	1993	1994	1995, H1	*Memorandum item: Debt/export earnings in 1994*
	in billions of US dollars				*in %*
Central Europe	0.8	4.3	2.7	1.0	
Czech and Slovak Republics	0.0	0.6	0.3	0.1	*60.0*
Hungary	0.8	3.7	2.4	0.6	*250.0*
Poland	0.0	0.0	0.0	0.3	*210.0*

Source: National sources.

If these features are borne in mind, it appears, indeed, that only about 10% of the capital inflows into central Europe (some flows to the Czech Republic and small amounts of equity inflows) during the 1990-94 period may be considered as easily reversible "hot" flows. For this reason, it is instructive to examine the Czech experience in more detail, as it raises a number of important issues of domestic monetary policy management.

5. Some Key Policy Issues

5.1 Inflows and Monetary Policy: A Case Study of the Czech Republic

The capital inflows episode has been particularly important and has probably raised the most concerns in the Czech Republic. A closer look at that country's capital account confirms the significance of portfolio flows during 1993-95, which coincided with fairly consistent FDI inflows. However, other long-term capital, which usually accounts for one-quarter of inflows, was essentially in the form of corporate borrowing and appears to have contributed to strong inflows in 1995. Moreover, 1995 seems to have yielded a new development: short-term capital flows - which are apparently due in the main to enterprise and bank borrowing abroad - predominated in the first quarter.

Table H9 Czech Republic: Capital Accounts

	1992	1993	1994	1995 Q1
	in millions of US dollars			
Foreign direct investment	980	520	840	110
Portfolio investment	-25	1,060	820	85
Other long-term capital	320	530	500	505
Short-term capital	-1,280	535	-50	1,170
Total	0.0	2,650	2,110	1,870

Source: National sources.

The capital flow experience of the Czech Republic since mid-1993 appears to display the typical symptoms associated with rapid capital inflows: strong reserve growth, providing a cushion against adverse capital movements; a further real appreciation of the koruna, albeit very modest in scale, as the 1991-92 period had seen a much faster real appreciation; higher-than-projected money growth, which could put at risk the move towards a low-inflation path; and a significant pick-up in imports, leading to a weakening current account position.

How has the Czech National Bank (CNB) reacted? In general, countries are not prepared to adopt a laissez-faire stance and simply allow, for example, the nominal exchange rate to drift upwards as a result of large capital inflows. The response to capital inflows will depend on the monetary policy/exchange rate policy framework in place when such flows occur. In the Czech Republic, a nominal anchor, the exchange rate, was chosen to provide a framework for the development of stable expectations.[26] When confronted with such flows, countries invariably tend to err on the side of caution, that is, the initial reaction is to sterilize these flows - if it is not certain whether they are permanent or temporary in nature - in order to minimize their impact on the anchor. This essentially reflects the policy stance of the CNB. Open market operations involving CNB bills, T-bills and National Property Fund (NPF) bills were used to sterilize excess liquidity, with most of them winding up in banks' portfolios. The transfer to the CNB of some NPF deposits held by commercial banks and the decline in government indebtedness to the CNB, both in 1994, can also be included among the further sterilization measures.[27] Furthermore, the short-term capital inflows were partially eliminated, as installments had to be paid for exceeding the marginal credit in the clearing account with the Slovak Republic.[28] In addition to using open market operations and administrative measures, the CNB also mopped up some liquidity by raising reserve requirements in August 1994 and June 1995. The Czech Republic partially liberalized capital outflows in October 1995 - the first country in central Europe to do so - and this may also be interpreted as a typical response to soften the impact on the exchange rate of rapid capital inflows.

These policy measures raise a number of questions for the CNB. When should it seek to limit mounting reserves, for example, by allowing a nominal appreciation? Should the CNB continue its policy of sterilized intervention, or should some non-sterilized intervention be allowed, permitting the money supply to expand at a faster rate?

Allowing a nominal appreciation of the currency could serve to reduce short-term inflows, but perhaps at the risk of causing overvaluation in real terms. Much depends on the prospects for real productivity growth: if productivity rises strongly, then anti-inflation policy would be better served by taking the associated real wage increase in nominal appreciation rather than in higher nominal wages.

Opinions in the literature seem to be divided on the desirable rate of monetary expansion. While CALVO et al. (1995) attribute enterprise borrowing abroad to a "genuine shortage of credit" in the economy, leading to the policy recommendation of monetary loosening and perhaps non-sterilization of some of the inflows, the IMF in its report on the Czech Republic (1995), considers the inflows simply as substitution of foreign credit for domestic credit and the role of banks in this process as crucial and does not interpret this as an increase in money demand, thereby implying with the implication that continued sterilization may perhaps be called for.

The substitution of foreign credit for domestic credit has supposedly occurred because there is a maturity mismatch between credit demanded and credit supplied: demand for bank credit by enterprises is concentrated at the longer end of the maturity spectrum. Long-term domestic bank lending (over four years) as a share of total lending dropped by more than 4 percentage points in 1993, but appears subsequently to stabilized at around 30%. In addition, more than 75% of new loans are currently short-term, lending further support to the argument that banks are keen to reduce the risk in the maturity mismatch originating from short-term deposits and long-term lending. Banks' unwillingness to transform maturities may also owe something to the fact that in the past they were being overburdened with long-term credit which was both low-yielding and non-performing. The latter argument also explains to some extent the still-high margins between banks' borrowing and lending, which have not yet moved substantially below 6% but which, nevertheless, have come down from a level of 7% at the end of 1992 to stand at 5.8% in March 1995.[29] Taken by themselves, high domestic interest margins may by themselves be a factor encouraging borrowing from abroad, especially in cases where the domestic "real" interest rate for borrowed funds is high.[30] Another explanatory factor appears to be the relative movement between the domestic and the "foreign" interest rate on bank credits.[31] If we were to proxy[32] the latter rate by the German bank credit rate, this would show that domestic borrowers may have substituted foreign for domestic credits as the rate on domestic credits came down by 1% from end-1992 to March 1995, while the German rate came down substantially faster, namely by 2½% during this period.

Table H10 Czech Republic: Financial and External Indicators

	1991	1992	1993	1994	1995
Koruna/$ exchange rate	29.5	28.3	29.2	28.8	26.0(7)
Consumer price inflation (in %)	56.7	11.1	20.9	10.0	9.7(7)
Official reserves ($bn)	0.8	0.8	3.8	6.1	9.8(7)
Broad money (change in %)	26.7	23.0	20.2	22.1	17.1(6)
Real broad money (change in %)	-19.1	10.7	-0.6	11.0	6.4(6)
Imports (in $) (change in %)	..	46.5	24.0	14.5	28.0(5)
Current balance ($bn)	1.1	-0.3	0.4	0.3	-0.7*
<u>Banks</u>					
Loan/deposit ratio	..	1.002	0.983	0.977	1.003*
Margin between lending and borrowing (in %)	..	6.34	7.06	6.05	5.81*
Term structure:					
- deposits					
up to 1 year	..	71.9	72.1	72.0	70.8*
1-4 years	..	20.5	21.0	22.6	23.6*
over 4 years	..	7.6	6.9	5.4	5.6*
- loans					
up to 1 year	..	38.3	41.2	40.7	40.0*
1-4 years	..	27.3	28.8	30.1	30.5*
over 4 years	..	34.4	30.0	29.2	29.5*
- new loans					
up to 1 year	..	..	73.2	73.1	77.7*
1-4 years	..	..	18.7	16.9	15.0*
over 4 years	..	..	8.1	10.0	7.3*

* First quarter.

Source: National sources.

Examination of the data does not confirm a general credit crunch as neither the nominal nor the real interest rates have moved up, but have in fact moved down. The banks' behavior reflects a degree of understandable adjustment in their maturity transformation role, but there seems to be little indication of their squeezing out long-term borrowers. As the loan/deposit ratio has remained more or less unchanged, there is no general indication that banks have been reluctant to extend credit.[33] It appears that the prime mover may have been simply the relatively lower borrowing costs abroad in the context of a stable or even slightly appreciating currency. A subsidiary factor, however, might be that the reluctance of local banks to grant anything but short-term loans may have led some enterprises to borrow from banks abroad.

5.2 Saving, Investment and Deficits

Table H3 shows that investment, which tends to be much more import-intensive than the other demand components, has accounted for a far larger and more buoyant share of GDP in Asia than in Latin America.

Heavy imports of capital goods in Asia have not only increased the productive potential but probably also attenuated upward pressure on the exchange rate.[34] The central European countries, however, have experienced a falling investment/GDP ratio. The larger current account deficits in these countries thus mainly reflected increases in (private) consumption rather than investment.[35]

As in Latin America, there was a backlog of unsatisfied demand for private consumer goods in central Europe after the initial liberalization in 1990-91, and the share of consumption in GDP moved up rapidly. Household consumption dominated this process. By 1992-93, the share of total consumption in GDP had reached over 85% in Poland and Hungary, and more than 75% in the Czech Republic. Preliminary data for 1994 - at least for the three countries in this sample -

suggest that there has not been much change since then, except for some marginal reversal in Poland.

Table H11 Gross Fixed Investment (GFI) and Foreign Direct Investment (FDI)

	1990	1991	1992	1993	1994
	in percentages				
Central Europe					
FDI/GFI	1.3	7.3	10.2	9.9	6.8
Czech Republic					
GFI/GDP	26.3	23.1	28.5	26.6	26.7
GFI growth	-2.1	-17.7	9.0	-7.7	4.4
Hungary					
GFI/GDP	19.2	20.7	19.7	18.7	19.7
GFI growth	-7.0	-10.4	-2.7	1.7	11.5
Poland					
GFI/GDP	21.0	19.5	16.8	16.0	15.5
GFI growth	-10.6	-4.4	2.3	3.0	7.0
Latin America					
FDI/GFI	3.4	5.7	5.5	5.6	8.4
Asia					
FDI/GFI	4.5	4.7	6.4	7.2	7.9

Source: National sources.

One possible interpretation is that the current capital inflows are financing a permanently higher level of consumption and that, by 1994, a certain equilibrium level had been reached, that is the initial buying spree had run its course. Yet there has not been any rebound in savings, and consumption levels, while not increasing, have remained rather high - at least by the standards of countries with major development potential.

At times, parallels are drawn with the experience in Latin America and Asia in this regard. Capital inflows have been employed more wisely in Asia, as they have been used to support high rates of investment. For Latin America, on the other hand, the evidence indicates that the increase in inflows coincided to some extent with falling average investment and rising consumption.[36] In central Europe, the consumption boom clearly occurred before the more substantial flows to this region and is thus to be associated more with the general liberalization tendencies of that period, namely trade liberalization and concomitant import growth. Yet it could be argued that capital inflows allowed the high rates of consumption attained during the boom to be prolonged.

Table H12 Central Europe: Consumption in the Private and Public Sectors

	1990	1991	1992	1993	1994
	as a percentage of GDP				
Total consumption	68	83	85	87	83
Household consumption	50	63	65	67	66
Czech Republic	50	45	52	56	58
Hungary	62	70	73	74	74
Poland	46	69	67	69	67
Public consumption	18	20	20	14	12
Czech Republic	20	19	23	23	22
Hungary	11	11	12	14	12
Poland	19	23	22	20	17

Source: National sources.

It appears, therefore, that the behavior of the central European countries is tending towards "Latin American behavior" that is, greater consumption. However, there has been marked diversity across countries. Hungary, for example, seems to be "overconsuming", as its consumption share reached 86% of GDP by 1994, compared with 73% in 1990.[37]

5.3 Direct Investment: Export-Oriented?

Direct investment is often regarded as a form of investment which leaves the recipient country less exposed to swings in foreign investor sentiment. It allows the recipient country to share the risks of investment with the investor: the "servicing" of direct investment liabilities depends on the generation of profits and does not create a fixed burden in the same way as bank or bond debt. From an external point of view, this self-stabilizing feature of direct investment is reinforced when direct investment is export-oriented.

Figure H1 reproduces a graph originally designed to show that direct investment has been much more export-intensive in Asia (i.e. the regression line shown in the figure is flatter) than in Latin America. Observations for the three central European countries have been superimposed on this figure.

Figure H1

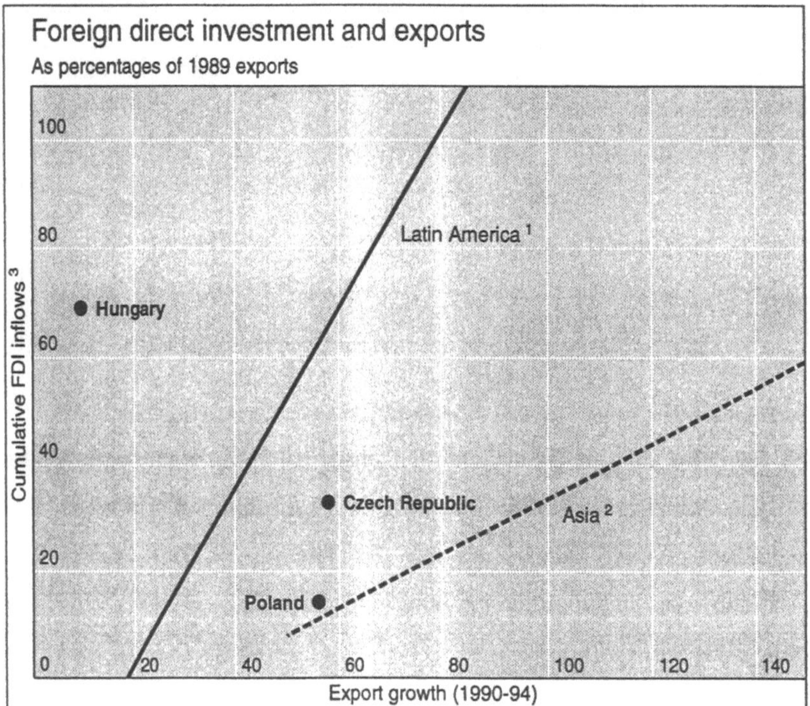

[1] Argentina, Brazil, Chile, Colombia, Ecuador, Mexico, Peru and Venezuela. [2] China, Hong Kong, India, Indonesia, Korea, Malaysia, Philippines, Singapore, Taiwan and Thailand. [3] For central Europe, 1990-94; otherwise, 1989-92.

The difference in export orientation suggested by this graph is supported by surveys conducted in Latin America and Asia on the behavior of foreign companies in these areas, which show that relatively more is exported by foreign companies in Asia than by those in Latin America.[38] On this score, Hungary clearly shows the least export-oriented performance of the three central European countries, and of all countries contained in the graph, as high FDI inflows contrast with the lowest export growth. The Polish experience is close to the Asian regression line; data for Poland are comparable to those for Korea, India and Taiwan. In fact, export performance may have been even stronger if exports have been under-recorded, as suggested earlier. The Czech Republic's performance ranks between that of Colombia and Chile (Latin American countries), on the one hand, and of the Philippines and Indonesia (Asian countries), on the other.[39]

Perhaps more importantly, the nature of FDI has differed between Latin America and Asia: in Latin America it has mainly taken the form of debt/equity swaps and privatization, which do not necessarily generate additional capital formation. In Asia, by contrast, FDI has mostly been in the form of acquisitions or the setting-up of new enterprises. Data on central Europe seem to indicate that greenfield investments have had a relatively insignificant share of FDI inflows in Poland and the Czech Republic, whereas they may have amounted to as much as one-third in Hungary.[40]

While this dichotomy is relevant it may, however, be worth bearing in mind that the second-round effects of these investments may be poorly captured by the statistical classification, for the purchase of a run-down factory by a non-resident (privatization) may lead to further substantial investments.

6. Conclusion

Central Europe has experienced a dramatic capital account turnround since the beginning of transition, as capital outflows have given way to large capital inflows, which, during 1993 and 1994, were greater when scaled by GDP than those experienced in Latin America and Asia. The capital flow experience of the three regions displays certain similarities, but also important differences. Central Europe has attracted about 2% of world capital inflows since transition started. International capital has flowed unevenly into eastern Europe, being attracted to those countries most advanced in the transition process, that is, the central European economies. This phenomenon, namely that only a certain number of countries in a particular region attract capital inflows, is also not unknown in Latin America and Asia.[41]

The integration of "world" capital markets will in future also encompass the emerging markets in central (and eventually also eastern) Europe, as portfolio inflows - which have so far been fairly small - will continue to increase and are potentially a more volatile element of capital flows. How far these capital inflows (and also outflows) should be permitted ought to be the subject of a serious policy discussion in the countries concerned. A stable macroeconomic environment is probably one condition for maintaining sustainable capital inflows.

In Asia the build-up of credibility due to solid financial institutions and markets and good macroeconomic performance, has rendered the countries of the region less vulnerable to any harmful capital flow shocks than Latin American countries. In fact, the Asian economies appear to have had much less difficulty in sterilizing capital inflows than those in Latin America.

While FDI inflows to eastern Europe have occurred since the beginning of transition, portfolio inflows are a more recent phenomenon (1993-95). Only the countries most advanced in the transformation process have been able to attract such flows and they have also been the first ones to register small amounts of FDI outflows (the Czech Republic, Hungary and Poland). The fairly successful transition experienced by the Czech Republic, and in particular its stable nominal exchange rate, have recently led to short-term capital inflows, and the case study has demonstrated that the way in which these inflows have been handled by the CNB corresponds in many respects to the standard policy response of neutralizing the effects with a mix of policy measures, which is no different from policy responses in other "industrialized" developing economies. In Poland, despite the boom and bust periods of the Warsaw Stock Exchange, there has recently been a resumption - albeit limited - of foreign participation in this market, against the background of a relatively favorable macroeconomic outlook, the resolution of the external debt problem and a fairly positive risk assessment of Poland's recent borrowings on capital markets. The composition of capital flows may thus shift more to portfolio investment during the coming years.

The capital flows into eastern European countries since 1990 have not left these countries vulnerable to any sudden withdrawals, as they have been predominantly in the form of FDI. In the cases of Poland and the Czech Republic, these flows have been fairly export-intensive, with positive effects on the current account balance in the longer run. By contrast, inflows to Hungary do not appear to have been export-intensive. The nature (privatization) and fairly modest size of these flows have not, however, had a noticeable impact on depressed fixed investment activity. Nor does privatization necessarily generate any additional investment.

The consumption/investment counterpart of the inflows does give grounds for concern. Consumption picked up rapidly at the beginning of transition. Although this phenomenon can be interpreted as a normal reaction to the forced saving during the "pre-transition" period, high levels of consumption have persisted. In Hungary, current consumption levels are now extremely high. A particularly worrying aspect of this is Hungary's high budget deficit (around 7½% of GDP in 1994), while the final judgment on the austerity measures introduced in March 1995 is still outstanding.

Investment ratios appear to be too low to sustain rapid growth. They are similar to those found in Latin America but substantially below ratios in Asia. It appears that domestic savings are the essential ingredient any substantial and sustained increase in investment.

Although this paper has attempted to present certain common elements in the capital flow experiences of the transition economies, it has become clear that individual country experiences differ markedly. Nevertheless, there are lessons to be learnt from the experiences of Latin America and Asia, and these two regions provide convenient benchmarks with which to begin the analysis of capital flows to central Europe.

Endnotes

* A major debt of gratitude is owed to Philip Turner, who made a host of helpful comments. I would also like to thank Angelika Donaubauer, Ib Madsen and Hugo Schaffner for efficient statistical assistance.

1 This paper defines "eastern Europe" as comprising Bulgaria, the Czech Republic, Hungary, Poland, Romania, the Slovak Republic and Slovenia; "central Europe" encompasses only the Czech Republic (or the former Czechoslovakia), Hungary and Poland. These definitions have been chosen for presentation purposes only.

2 One possible measure of this is cross-border transactions in bonds and equities (gross purchases and sales). See BANK FOR INTERNATIONAL SETTLEMENTS (1992), p. 193.

3 For a more detailed analysis of these individual factors, see CROCKETT (1994) and BANK FOR INTERNATIONAL SETTLEMENTS (1993), pp. 147-148.

4 CALVO et al. (1994, pp. 2 et seq.) also review the period leading up to the watershed years 1990-91. They show that for the period 1987-91 capital outflows for the region as a whole (Bulgaria, Czechoslovakia, Hungary, Poland and Romania) amounted to \$24bn, financed by a reduction in reserves.

5 This implies that capital inflows have been unevenly distributed in the region and justifies to some extent the focus in this paper on the three central European countries: the Czech Republic; Hungary; and Poland.

6 Capital flows into these groups of countries account for about 20% of global flows, with the countries in central Europe receiving nearly 2% of "world" capital inflows during this period.

7 Inflows into Mexico decreased by about \$20½bn from 1993 to 1994, while the decrease for all other Latin American countries was \$3½bn.

8 The definition of official reserves varies: for the Czech Republic, they comprise convertible foreign exchange and SDRs; for Hungary, non-gold reserves in convertible currencies (excluding SDRs and IMF reserve position); for Poland, gold, convertible foreign exchange and IMF reserve position (excluding SDR holdings).

9 The developments in 1995 confirm those in 1993-94. Official reserve accumulation accelerated in the Czech Republic (\$9.8bn at end-July) and Poland (\$11.0bn at end-July), while Hungarian reserves stagnated (\$7.5bn at end-June).

10 See BANK FOR INTERNATIONAL SETTLEMENTS (1994), p. 154.

[11] IMF (1995, pp. 68-69): "There is little doubt that aggregate savings in these countries are much lower than they were before transition".

[12] "Weak" intermediation refers to a whole gamut of problems, ranging from, inter alia, inadequate financial instruments to large gaps between lending and borrowing rates. Admittedly, by increasing uncertainty about the future, high and variable inflation may promote precautionary saving. On the other hand, by heightening the uncertainty about the effective rate of return on saving, variable inflation may directly discourage saving. This latter effect may have prevailed in central European countries with extremely high and variable inflation rates.

[13] The investment ratios look much more dismal when all central and eastern European countries are included. For example, the saving ratio for Russia was reckoned to be close to 10% in 1994 (see UN, 1995).

[14] The UN (1995, May, p. 89) agrees, arguing that "the lack of investment funds, reflecting low savings levels, modest levels of foreign investment and official assistance, high interest rates and inefficient financial intermediation, is probably one of the most binding constraints on growth in transition economies in the medium-term perspective".

[15] The volatility of the emerging stock markets does not necessarily deter for foreign capital from flowing into these markets. One argument follows the familiar portfolio line that the low correlation of these markets with financial markets in industrial countries provides significant scope for diversification (see IMF, 1994, p. 70). In addition, the macroeconomic literature tends at times to ignore the potential for gain in falling stock markets.

[16] The IMF (1995) considers these measures to be "important steps" and adds (p. 55): "Further measures will nevertheless be needed, including a broadening of the income tax base, a reduction of the burden of the pension system, and an acceleration of privatization".

[17] There is a long history of looking at and interpreting individual capital flow items from the balance of payments. Recently, CLAESSENS et al. (1993) pointed out that there is sufficient substitution between and interaction among the various flows to make an analysis of the time series of one flow possibly misleading. They also find little evidence that the composition of flows is of use in forecasting the overall levels of flows, suggesting that the overall capital account is independent of the type of flow. The upshot of these results is that the distinction between "hot" and "cool" flows based on balance-of-payments labels is questioned and that "the preoccupation with analyzing the time-series properties of short-term (portfolio) flows is overdone. The root cause of volatility is more likely changes in institutional structure than an inherent property of a certain type of flow, and adverse effects of sudden, large movements in a particular type of flow are likely a result of distortions in the domestic economy".

[18] Neither official flows nor banking flows are considered in the following. Moreover, the whole question of arrears, financing by non-payment, is left out.

[19] The World Bank's "World Debt Tables" provide some insight.

[20] CLAESSENS et al. (1993) warn against evaluating capital flows according to their label (for example, the instrument traded or the transactor recorded in the balance-of-payments statistics).

[21] FDI data in eastern Europe are based on balance-of-payments concepts and currently do not capture any retained earnings. However, this latter component of FDI will become more important with the passage of time. INOTAI and MARER (1993) classify profit repatriation on past direct investment as still "insignificant" in the case of Hungary. Another methodological question concerns direct investment outflows: several eastern European countries publish only net direct investment data. As direct investment abroad by these countries has, until now, been very small, net direct investment has, therefore, at times been equated with FDI inflows. For example, the volume of Czech direct investment abroad has not yet been particularly noteworthy. Its value in 1994 amounted to $21m (see CZECH NATIONAL BANK 1995, p. 30).

[22] See TURNER (1995), p. 18.

[23] Cumulative FDI flows for all central and eastern European countries during 1990-94 amounted to about 2½% of global FDI flows. About one-third of these flows was invested in Hungary, while another third may be attributed to Poland, the Czech Republic and Russia together. Hungary emerges as the largest recipient when these flows are scaled against GDP or per capita.

[24] The Hungarian balance-of-payments statistics do not include a category for "portfolio" flows. The classification in Table H6 follows the IMF/IFS taxonomy. (The IMF identifies these flows as "nie" = not included elsewhere.) Less than one-quarter appears to be in the form of flows into the equity markets.

[25] The portfolio flows into the Czech Republic include the central bank bond issues of 1993 and the City of Prague eurobond issues ($250million) of 1994.

[26] The Czech koruna is currently pegged to a currency basket consisting of US dollars (35%) and Deutsche Mark (65%). The daily rate may deviate by 0.5% from the value calculated by the CNB.

[27] See CNB (1995b), p. 19.

[28] See CNB (1995b), p. 12.

[29] It is also argued that these high margins continue to reflect inefficiencies in the intermediation process itself.

[30] With inflation running at around 10% since the beginning of 1994 and the nominal interest rate on loans at about 13%, and moving recently towards 12.5%, the implied "real" interest rate does not seem to be excessive.

[31] CALVO et al. (1995) arrive at a different conclusion, as they compare the relative development in the CNB and T-bill markets.

[32] Obviously this is a very crude proxy as foreign interest costs are difficult to pinpoint, since they vary according to lender, loan maturity, currency denomination and the risk assessment of the borrower.

[33] On this point, see CALVO et al. (1995).

[34] See WELFENS (1994).

[35] See CALVO et al. (1995).

[36] See TURNER (1995, pp. 14 ff.).

[37] Clearly this argument simplifies the process as, for example, a lot will depend on the "efficiency" of investment. TURNER (1995) proxies efficiency by looking at the reciprocal of ICOR (incremental capital output ratio of gross investment to GDP divided by the average rate of real growth for the period), which is twice as high in Asia as in Latin America for the 1984-93 period.

[38] BANK FOR INTERNATIONAL SETTLEMENTS (1995, p. 68): "While US firms in Asia export more than one-half of their output, those in Latin America export only about one-quarter of their production. [...] Chinese statistics [...] suggest that the exports of foreign-funded enterprises [...] have accounted for an average of about 60% of the increase in China's exports during the 1990s, with this percentage rising in the last few years."

[39] The Czech National Bank notes that even though inflows were "directed towards large enterprises and joint ventures their share of exports has not as yet been substantial" (CZECH NATIONAL BANK (1995), p. 28).

[40] INOTAI (1995) states that "greenfield investments have been spreading in most of the central European countries; if you look at Hungary, more than one-third of total investment has been

greenfield, which is about 3 billion dollars". It should be noted that Inotai's data for Hungary refer to the CSO data, which differ from the BOP data of the National Bank of Hungary (HNB). The HNB statistics cover only cash payments by foreigners, while the CSO data also cover payment in kind (e.g. machinery). This methodological difference means that by end-1994 the FDI stock was about $8½bn (CSO) or $7½ bn (BOP).

[41] See FERNANDEZ-ARIAS and MONTIEL (1995).

References

BANK FOR INTERNATIONAL SETTLEMENTS (1993), *63rd Annual Report, 1992-1993.*

BANK FOR INTERNATIONAL SETTLEMENTS (1994), *64th Annual Report, 1993-1994.*

BANK FOR INTERNATIONAL SETTLEMENTS (1995), *65th Annual Report, 1994-1995.*

CALVO, G. A., SAHAY, R. and VEGH, C. A (1995), "Capital flows in central and eastern Europe: Evidence and policy options," IMF Working Paper No. 57, May.

CHRISTENSEN, B. V. (1994), "The Russian Federation in Transition: External Developments," IMF Occasional Paper No. III.

CLAESSENS, S. and GOOPTU, S. (eds.) (1993), "Portfolio investment in developing countries," World Bank Discussion Paper No. 228.

CLAESSENS, S., DOOLEY, M. P. and WARNER, A. (1993), "Portfolio capital flows, hot or cool," in CLAESSENS, S. and GOOPTU, S. (eds.).

CORBO, V. and HERNANDEZ, L. (1993), "Macroeconomic adjustment to capital inflows: Rationale and some recent experience," in CLAESSENS, S. and GOOPTU, S. (eds.).

CORBO, V. and HERNANDEZ, L. (1994), "Macroeconomic adjustment to capital inflows: Latin America Style vs. East Asian Style," World Bank Policy Research Working Paper No. 1377, November.

CROCKETT, A. (1994), "Monetary policy implications of increased capital flows, in changing capital markets: implications for monetary policy," Federal Reserve Bank of Kansas City, August 1993.

CZECH NATIONAL BANK (1995a), *Annual Report 1994.*

CZECH NATIONAL BANK (1995b), *Report on the monetary development in the Czech Republic*, first quarter.

DITTUS, P. (1994), "Capital flows and monetary policy in central Europe," Mimeo, Bank for International Settlements.

FERNANDEZ-ARIAS, E. and MONTIEL, P.J. (1995), "The surge in capital inflows to developing countries," World Bank Policy Research Working Paper No. 1473, June.

GULATI, S. (1988), "Capital flight: causes, consequences and cures," *Journal of International Affairs*, Vol. 42, No.1, 165-185.

IMF (1995), *World Economic Outlook*, May.

IMF (1994), *World Economic Outlook*, October.

IMF (1995), *Czech Republic, Economic Reviews*, April.

INOTAI, A. and MARER, P. (1993), "Foreign investment in Hungary," Joint Hungarian Blue Ribbon Commission, December.

INOTAI, A. (1995), "Five years of reform in countries in transition: assessment and prospects," Round-table discussion, UN Economic Commission for Europe, June.

PODKAMINER, L. (1995), "Accelerated growth in central and eastern Europe, slower decline in Russia and Ukraine," Research Report, The Vienna Institute for Comparative Economic Studies, July.

REISEN, H. (1993), "South-east Asia and the impossible trinity," *International Economic Insights*, May/June, 21-23.

TURNER, P. (1995), "Capital flows in Latin America: A new phase," BIS Economic Papers, Bank for International Settlements, May.

UN (1995), *Economic Survey of Europe in 1994-1995*, Economic Commission for Europe, March (prepublication version; final version, May 1995).

WELFENS, P. J. J. (1994), "Foreign Direct Investment and Privatization," in SCHIPKE and TAYLOR (eds.), *The Economics of Transformation*, Springer Verlag.

WILLIAMSON, J. (1993), "Issues posed by portfolio investment in developing countries," in CLAESSENS, S. and GOOPTU, S. (eds.).

WORLD BANK (1995), *Global Economic Prospects and the Developing Countries*, April.

Comments on

Capital Flows in Eastern Europe: Some Lessons from the Emerging Markets in Latin America and Asia

Albert Schweinberger

This paper pursues several aims:

(1) A comparative study of capital flows in the three regions of the world: eastern Europe, Latin America and Asia.

(2) An explanation of the size and the composition of capital inflows to the three regions on the basis of stylized macroeconomic features of the three regions.

(3) An evaluation of the capital flows into eastern Europe in terms of reversibility or volatility (decomposition into direct foreign investment and portfolio investment).

(4) A case study of the Czech Republic focusing mainly on the policy response of the Czech National Bank to capital inflows.

(5) A study of the effects of foreign direct investment in the three regions, especially on export performance.

Let me say right at the outset that this is a very interesting paper. It raises a vast range of important issues and provides impressive empirical support for its conclusions (in terms of many tables of data).

It would be impossible for this reviewer to address even very briefly all the issues. Therefore what follows is a highly selective review.

Considering the title of the paper, there is one key question which we should ask ourselves: can eastern Europe draw any lessons from the experience in Asia and Latin America?

Granted Asia and Latin America represent benchmark cases, one may still doubt that eastern Europe can indeed learn something from the experiences of these other two regions. Eastern Europe is arguably undergoing a process of political, social and economic transformation which is unprecedented in history. It may be objected that the People's Republic of China is also engaged in such a comprehensive process of reforms. However, in the paper the comparison is between Asia and eastern Europe.

In my view the author correctly emphasizes the importance of the domestic savings ratio in determining (via investment) the growth rate of an economy. Savings ratios are much higher in Asia than in eastern Europe, not only because of pent up consumption needs in eastern Europe in the pre-reform period but also for other much more fundamental reasons. Asians generally have much longer time horizons, low rates of time preference reflected in dynastic thinking and a tradition of self-reliance. The latter is the very antithesis of the welfare state mentality, which apparently is widespread not only in eastern but also western Europe.

It is generally agreed that the reforms in eastern Europe can only be successful if the economies manage to "escape history". But precisely when there is a considerable lack of information and a general feeling of uncertainty historical standards reassert their role. The matter can be put very simply. In Asia many time-honored traditions and institutions encourage economic progress at least in the sense of achieving a stable growth path. Historical experiences have exactly the opposite effect in eastern Europe.

By the standards of Walrasian or Arrow-Debreu general equilibrium theory all countries are ridden with distortions, but the distortions in eastern Europe are certainly very different from the distortions in Asia or Latin America. Again this has to do with the special starting point for the reforms in eastern Europe.

To evaluate the role of capital flows in eastern Europe and their effect on economic performance, it seems crucial to take into account the special kinds of distortions which exist in eastern Europe. It cannot be denied that macroeconomic stability must be a key target of economic policy in eastern Europe. This follows immediately from the fact that macroeconomic stability logically precedes many other reforms. In this regard the paper makes several interesting contributions, see for example the case study of the Czech Republic. On the other hand we know from theory and experience that we should not ignore the interdependence between macroeconomic stability and microeconomic reform, as for example reflected in the target of structural change (which seems of overwhelming importance in many countries in eastern Europe).

A number of key questions are implicit in the paper. One of them concerns the role of capital flows in the reform process in eastern Europe. The author correctly disaggregates capital flows into several categories, such as direct foreign investment and portfolio investment. A major concern of the author seems to be that if a country relies too much on capital inflows of a certain kind it may become vulnerable to changes in foreign investors' sentiment. The author is, of course, right. There is ample evidence that capital flows may be destabilizing and the cause of significant problems in a number of countries. On the other hand, it should not be forgotten that portfolio investment and direct foreign investment are often complementary as in the case of multinational firms and that the volatility of certain kinds of capital flows may only be the triggering effect for instability, the underlying cause being the lack of discipline of governments or bad policies in general. In fact it could be argued that foreign capital flows have a beneficial side effect on policy making because they impose discipline on governments.

Furthermore, we should not jump to conclusions and forget other benefits of foreign capital flows. An obvious but often neglected aspect in this context is that in eastern Europe capital and financial markets are generally much less developed than in western Europe or do not exist at all. Capital flows may therefore yield gains in excess of the traditional trade gains resulting from price differences. It seems very probable that many agents in eastern Europe are rationed in one way or another because of the lack of such markets.

The practical problem is, of course, to identify (ex ante) capital flows which are destabilizing (because of their easy reversibility and therefore volatility). In this context it is interesting to observe that in a distortion-free small open economy foreign investment which is sensitive to price changes may be preferable to fixed foreign investment, because in the latter case the value of income of domestic factor owners can be shown not to be maximized by free trade in goods (at world market prices). On the other hand, if foreign investment is price or rate of return sensitive, the value of income of domestic factor owners is maximized. This result has to be qualified in certain distorted economies (see NEARY and RUANE, 1988; SCHWEINBERGER, 1989).

This brings me to my final point. Under which conditions are foreign capital inflows desirable? This is undoubtedly an extremely complex question. It is impossible to do justice to it in a few lines, especially with regard to eastern Europe (mainly because of the many distortions that exist there as a legacy of former regimes). At the macroeconomic level it seems important to note that if savings ratios are likely to remain low in the future, see especially Hungary, it would appear important to make use of foreign capital to raise investment which is crucial to achieve a higher growth rate. The latter is certainly widely accepted as a policy target in many countries of eastern Europe.

What about the structural effects of foreign direct investment in eastern Europe? These may or may not be favorable. If foreign investment is taking place in a highly protected sector, foreign investment will, *ceteris paribus*, bring about a fall in the value of output at international prices. This is because the sector absorbs too many resources (see again SCHWEINBERGER, 1989). What is of great relevance in this context is the existence of an inefficient state sector. The most productive workers may move from the state sector to the sector where the foreign investment occurred. This will create additional losses (see MURPHY et al., 1992). The author has shown that in some countries foreign investment has led to an increase in exports, in others this effect is much less evident. This is an interesting empirical fact but it does not allow us to draw definite conclusions with regard to the desirability of foreign investment. The efficiency of the export sector may have improved at the expense of other sectors (particularly the state sector). Moreover, since many sectors in eastern Europe are far from perfectly competitive, there is no guarantee that as a result of foreign investment the output of the more competitive sector will in fact rise.

There is yet another effect of capital flows in eastern Europe which may be of considerable practical relevance. As is well known a number of exports of eastern European countries face import restrictions in western Europe. It can be shown that under certain circumstances western European ownership of factors in eastern Europe should lead to a reduction in import taxes in western Europe for goods produced in eastern Europe (see SCHWEINBERGER and VOSGERAU, 1995).

Up to this point we considered only standard second best effects on the allocation of resources of foreign investment. It has often been argued that the dynamic effects - such as various spillover effects, learning and above all the acquisition of foreign technology and hence improvement of quality standards of goods at low cost in the form of technology transfers - more than offset possible losses for other reasons. Unfortunately, in this regard the empirical evidence in eastern Europe is very sparse. To draw more definite conclusions regarding the effects and desirability of capital flows in eastern Europe a much more disaggregated analysis is undoubtedly called for.

References

MURPHY, K., SCHLEIFER, A. and VISHNY, R. W. (1992), "The Transition to a Market Economy: Pitfalls of Partial Reform," *Quarterly Journal of Economics*, Vol. 107, 887-906.

NEARY, J. P. and RUANE, F. (1988), "International Capital Mobility, Shadow Prices and the Cost of Protection," *International Economic Review*, Vol. 29, 571-585.

SCHWEINBERGER, A. G. (1989), "Foreign Capital Flows, Tariffs, and Welfare: A Global Analysis," *Canadian Journal of Economics*, Vol. 22, 310-327.

SCHWEINBERGER, A. G. and VOSGERAU, H.-J. (1995), "Foreign Factor Ownership and Optimal Tariffs," *Review of International Economics*, forthcoming.

I. Catching Up of Economies in Transformation

Thomas Gries and Stefan Jungblut[1]

1. Introduction

The breakdown of the economies in eastern Europe is probably one of the most important economic events of this century. Providing an idea of the potential time path of transformation economies and the consequences of different policy strategies is a major challenge for economic theory. This is especially true since comparable events are hard to find in economic history.[2] There seems to be a broad consensus among economists concerning the important elements of the transformation process. These aspects include institutional reforms, price liberalization, privatization of state-owned enterprises, the creation of financial systems and capital markets, trade liberalization, and the reorganization of labor markets.[3] Another aspect is the problem of timing and sequencing of policies in the initial period of transformation.[4] Given this variety of issues research about the transformation is often restricted to be partial in nature. Therefore a comprehensive as well as long run theory of transformation seems not to be at hand.

Recently growth theory has provided some interesting new insights into dynamic macroeconomics, which can be used in the theory of transformation as well.[5] The main innovation of the 'new growth theory' is the introduction of mechanisms allowing for endogenous technical progress and knowledge accumulation. Traditional as well as new growth theory focuses on the existence and stability of steady state equilibrium attainable in the long run. However, since the process of convergence clearly takes time[6] it is also important to analyze the adjustment towards the steady state. This is especially true for transformation economies. The model presented in Section 2 intends to combine some elements of new growth theory with non-steady-state transitional dynamics. Instead of focusing on special issues (like those mentioned above) that are important in the very first period of transformation, the model is designed to derive an explicit time path of an upgrading country in transition. The convergence towards the leading market economies is linked with a process of technological catch up and knowledge accumulation. Technological progress however does not occur without costs. Upgrading is the result of resources devoted to imitation, research, and development activities. The dynamics of upgrading as well as factors determining the final steady state position are presented in Section 3. Furthermore, for a better understanding of the transformation process, it is important not only to look at aggregate transitional dynamics, but also to understand the dynamics of structural changes and the process of sectoral adjustment and reallocation. Therefore the structural adjustment associated with upgrading and the implications for labor reallocation is analyzed in Section 4. In Section 5 unemployment during different transition phases is described in more detail and Section 6 will summarize the basic findings.

2. A Model of an Economy in Transformation

As discussed in the previous section the following model does not focus on special issues of transformation processes which are important in the very first period of transformation. Issues of privatization, institutional problems, etc. are not explicitly modeled. The model tries to focus on the time path after these very first problems of transformation have been solved. We try to give an idea of what is happening during the catch up process with the leading industrialized market economies.[7]

The transformation economy under consideration is a small open economy. The economy is characterized by a technological gap relative to the industrialized market economies and consists of three sectors: a modern industrial sector, a traditional sector, and a research sector. Production in the modern sector uses unskilled and skilled labor - labeled human capital - on the basis of Cobb Douglas technology:

$$X = g(T) H_X^{\alpha} L_X^{1-\alpha}, \tag{1}$$

where X is the output of the modern sector, H_X and L_X are the amount of human capital and labor, respectively, used in the modern sector, and $g(T)$ is a productivity index depending on the stock of knowledge of the economy.

The traditional sector uses only labor as a factor of production:

$$N = h(T) L_N, \tag{2}$$

where N is the output and L_N the amount of labor used in the traditional sector. $h(T)$ is the productivity index in the old sector.

The third branch, the research sector, provides additional technological knowledge, which can be used to increase the productivity in the modern and traditional sector. Knowledge is not continuous. New knowledge is introduced into production, if a new machine with a distinct new technique is installed. Obviously it is not possible to change the manufacturing process continuously. We, therefore, assume that the actual stock of knowledge $\tilde{T}$ follows a Poisson process with discrete technological jumps. Since the intensity rate ρ of the Poisson process characterizes the process, we have to discuss its determinants.

The small backward country does not create any real new knowledge, but acquires new technologies by imitating foreign designs. So the intensity rate of the stochastic process describes the characteristics of an imitating process. The imitation process consists of three elements:

- Trade and imports enable the country to acquire modern technologies incorporated in imported goods.
- The technological properties and secrets embodied in the imported goods have to be discovered. Thus the country has to use up resources for imitation activities.

- The rate of increase of the domestic stock of technological knowledge depends positively on the technological gap between the backward country and the industrialized world. [8]

Human capital is the only factor used in the research or imitating sector. The research sector is, therefore, the most human capital intensive sector, followed by the modern industrial sector and the traditional labor intensive sector. Let H_T be the amount of human capital used for research, *Im* the imports, and *V* the stock of knowledge of the industrialized world.

As the intensity rate ρ depends on these three factors, we may write:[9]

$$\rho = H_T Im(1 - T / V). \tag{3}$$

The expectation of the actual technology $\tilde{T}$ is labeled *T*. We get $T(t)=E(\tilde{T}(t))=\rho t$, which follows from the characteristics of the Poisson process. So an increase in the expected domestic technological knowledge can be written as

$$\dot{T} = \frac{\partial E\tilde{T}(t)}{\partial t} = H_T Im(1 - T / V). \tag{4}$$

The amount of resources devoted to the research sector is politically determined and a constant fraction of GNP. Using the expectation to approximate the technological knowledge this can be written as

$$p_T \dot{T} = \gamma(X + pN + p_T \dot{T}), \tag{5}$$

where p_T is the relative price of copied technologies and p the relative price of traditional products, both in terms of the industrial product. Due to the small country assumption the relative price p is taken as given. Further, the endowments of labor and human capital are constant over time:

$$\begin{aligned} H_X + H_T &= H, \\ L_X + L_N &= L. \end{aligned} \tag{6}$$

In order to determine the amount of imports the demand side has to be considered. For simplicity we assume a Cobb Douglas type utility function: $U = C_X{}^{\delta} C_N{}^{1-\delta}$, where C_X and C_N are the consumption amounts of industrial and traditional products. Without international borrowing or lending the consumption budget constraint of the economy is given by: $C_X + C_N = X + pN$. From the households' optimization problem we obtain the demand for industrial products:

$$C_X = \delta(X + pN). \tag{7}$$

Because of the backwardness of the small country we assume that the country has a comparative advantage in producing traditional goods. Thus the amount of imports may be written as:

$$Im = C_X - X = \delta pN - (1-\delta)X. \tag{8}$$

In what follows we will only consider the case in which the economy is not specialized in the production of one good only.

Efficient resource allocation requires equal values of marginal productivity of labor between the industrial and the traditional sector and equal values of marginal productivity of human capital between the industrial and the research sector:

$$\begin{aligned} &(1-\alpha)g(T){H_X}^{\alpha}{L_X}^{-\alpha} = ph(T), \\ &\alpha g(T){H_X}^{\alpha-1}{L_X}^{(1-\alpha)} = p_T Im(1 - T/V). \end{aligned} \tag{9}$$

With equations (1) to (6), (8) and (9) the optimal employment of labor and human capital in the different sectors may be obtained as:

$$\begin{aligned} L_X &= (1\ \ \alpha)^{1/\alpha}(1-\gamma)p^{-1/\alpha}\lambda^{-1/\alpha}H - \gamma\frac{1-\alpha}{\alpha}L, \\ L_N &= -(1-\alpha)^{1/\alpha}(1-\gamma)p^{-1/\alpha}\lambda^{-1/\alpha}H + \frac{\alpha+\gamma(1-\alpha)}{\alpha}L, \\ H_X &= (1-\gamma)H - \frac{\gamma}{\alpha}(1-\alpha)^{-(1-\alpha)/\alpha}p^{1/\alpha}\lambda^{1/\alpha}L, \\ H_T &= \gamma H + \frac{\gamma}{\alpha}(1-\alpha)^{-(1-\alpha)/\alpha}p^{1/\alpha}\lambda^{1/\alpha}L, \end{aligned} \tag{10}$$

where the structural term $\lambda(T) = h(T)/g(T)$ is the ratio of the productivity measures in the traditional and industrial sector. Since we only consider the case in which the economy is diversified, L_X, L_N, H_X and H_T are all positive.[10]

3. Dynamics of the Transition Process

Considering equations (1) to (4) and (10), the following differential equation can be derived:

$$\begin{aligned}\dot{T} =& h(T)(\gamma H + \frac{\gamma}{\alpha}(1-\alpha)^{-(1-\alpha)/\alpha} p^{1/\alpha}\lambda^{1/\alpha} L) \\ &\left\{\delta p\left(\frac{\alpha+\gamma(1-\alpha)}{\alpha} L - (1-\alpha)^{1/\alpha}(1-\gamma)p^{-1/\alpha}\lambda^{-1/\alpha} H\right)\right. \\ &-\frac{(1-\delta)}{\lambda}((1-\gamma)H - \frac{\gamma}{\alpha}(1-\alpha)^{-(1-\alpha)/\alpha} p^{1/\alpha}\lambda^{1/\alpha} L)^{\alpha} \times \\ &\left.((1-\alpha)^{1/\alpha}(1-\gamma)p^{-1/\alpha}\lambda^{-1/\alpha} H - \gamma\frac{1-\alpha}{\alpha} L)^{1-\alpha}\right\}(1-\frac{T}{V}).\end{aligned} \tag{11}$$

Now assume that $g(T)$ and $h(T)$ are linear functions of T like $g = \mu T$ and $h = \nu T$ such that $\lambda = \bar{\lambda}$ is constant (symmetric sectoral diffusion of technologies). Then (11) may be written as:

$$\dot{T} = \psi T(1 - T/V) \text{ with } \psi = \nu\varphi \text{ and}$$

$$\begin{aligned}\varphi =& \left(\gamma H + \frac{\gamma}{\alpha}(1-\alpha)^{-(1-\alpha)/\alpha} p^{1/\alpha}\bar{\lambda}^{1/\alpha} L\right) \\ &\left\{\delta p\left(\frac{\alpha+\gamma(1-\alpha)}{\alpha} L - (1-\alpha)^{1/\alpha}(1-\gamma)p^{-1/\alpha}\bar{\lambda}^{-1/\alpha} H\right)\right. \\ &-\frac{(1-\delta)}{\lambda}\left((1-\gamma)H - \frac{\gamma}{\alpha}(1-\alpha)^{-(1-\alpha)/\alpha} p^{1/\alpha}\bar{\lambda}^{1/\alpha} L\right)^{\alpha} \times \\ &\left.\left((1-\alpha)^{1/\alpha}(1-\gamma)p^{-1/\alpha}\bar{\lambda}^{-1/\alpha} H - \gamma\frac{1-\alpha}{\alpha} L\right)^{1-\alpha}\right\}.\end{aligned} \tag{12}$$

For this special case the development of $w = T/V$, *i.e.* the relative position of technological capabilities of the small backward country relative to the industrialized neighborhood is given by:

$$\dot{w} = \psi w(1-w) - \frac{\dot{V}}{V}w. \tag{13}$$

As the development of technological knowledge of the industrialized neighborhood V for the small country is given by the rate n, we obtain the following logistic equation:

$$\dot{w} = \omega^I(w) = (\psi - n)w - \psi w^2. \tag{14}$$

In the more simple one-sector case discussed in GRIES and WIGGER (1993) a logistic equation similar to (14) is derived. Thus only a brief discussion will be given here. If w_0 is the initial value of w, the explicit solution of (14) is:

$$w = \frac{\psi - n}{\psi + \left(\frac{\psi - n}{w_0} - \psi\right)e^{-(\psi - n)t}}. \tag{15}$$

Figure I1 Dynamics of Upgrading

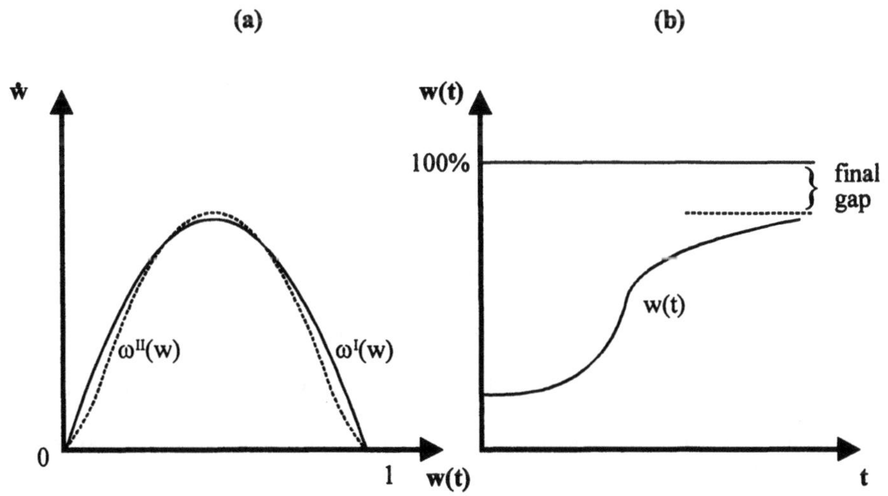

For $\psi \leq n$, w converges to zero, *i.e.* the country cannot close the technological gap at all. A process of divergence starts. For $\psi > n$, w increases and a process of upgrading will begin. But the process of convergence will not lead to a position of full catching up. Even in the long run a final gap $1 - n/\psi$ will remain. A full closure of the gap requires the switching from imitation to innovation.[11]

4. Structural Problems in Transition Economies

Studying the structural problems during transition, we can suppose that the sectoral diffusion of technology is not symmetric. Therefore the parameters μ and ν (indicating the conversion of general technical capabilities T into sectoral productivity) and the structural term $\lambda(w)$ are not constant. The sectoral technological diffusion is assumed to follow a logistic function depending on the relative state of technological knowledge w. Presumably during a first phase of the transition process, an upgrading country more easily adopts technologies related to the traditional sector, before being able to broadly introduce modern technologies in the modern sector as well. As a result of non-symmetric diffusion this process is reversed in a second phase of transition. During this phase, productivity growth is larger in the modern sector than in the traditional sector. Therefore, for asymmetric logistic diffusion processes of technologies the structural function $\lambda = \lambda(w)$ is unimodal (see Figure I2a):[12]

$$\lambda'(w) \begin{cases} >0 \text{ if } w \text{ is relatively small } (\textit{phase I}), \\ <0 \text{ if } w \text{ is relatively large } (\textit{phase II}). \end{cases}$$

In contrast to the previous section, ψ is now given by $\psi = \nu(w)\varphi(\lambda(w))$.[13] Since ψ is difficult to handle, we simplify the algebra by defining a general function $\psi = \psi(w)$. As $\varphi(\lambda)$ is monotone and $\lambda(w)$ is unimodal, $\psi(w)$ is likely to be unimodal[14] as well. A simple approximation of an unimodal function with the required properties can be picked as: $\psi(w) = w(1+w) + \overline{\psi}$ $[\overline{\psi} = \text{const.} > 0]$. This simple approximation covers all important qualitative properties and is easy to handle. Now we are able to investigate the dynamics of the transition process including structural adjustment:

$$\dot{w} = \psi(w)w - nw - \psi(w)w^2. \tag{16}$$

With the above approximation of $\psi(w)$ we obtain:

$$\dot{w} = \omega^{II}(w) = w^4 - 2w^3 + (1-\overline{\psi})w^2 + (\overline{\psi} - n)w. \tag{17}$$

Even if this differential equation cannot be solved explicitly, the properties of the adjustment path can be investigated. Analyzing the properties of $\omega^{II}(w)$ in the relevant region $0 \le w \le 1$, we obtain the plot given in Figure I1a.[15] A differential equation of this shape implies a stable steady state at $\tilde{w}$ and a path of upgrading as plotted in Figure I1b. This path shows a similar shape as the path obtained under symmetric sectoral diffusion of technologies and considered in Section 3. Therefore, the introduction of structural asymmetries does not essentially change the aggregate s shaped pattern of upgrading. The structural adjustment processes on the other hand are important. Since production and factor allocation in every period directly depend on the country's relative position (w), the transition process generates the pressure for structural adjustments.[16] For the two phases of structural diffusion introduced above [*phase I*: $\lambda' > 0$; *phase II*: $\lambda' < 0$] Table I1 gives the adjustment reactions in every period.

Table I1 Allocation Effects in Different Transition Periods

	Phase I: $\lambda' > 0$	*Phase II*: $\lambda' < 0$
dL_X	(–)	(+)
dH_X	(–)	(+)
dL_N	(+)	(–)
dH_T	(+)	(–)

This result of a permanent structural adjustment process implies some interesting interpretations. The permanent factor reallocation is due to some simple mechanisms similar to the effects identified by the Rybczinsky theorem.

For constant international prices productivity in the traditional sector will increase relatively in *phase I* ($\lambda' > 0$). This effect will generate additional comparative advantages, expand factor absorption in the traditional sector, shift labor from the modern sector to the traditional sector ($dL_x < 0$, $dL_N > 0$) and lead to lay offs of human capital in the modern sector ($dH_X < 0$). Simultaneously, the shift of human capital to the imitating sector ($dH_T > 0$) and the additional comparative advantages in the traditional sector will raise the imitation rate. As a result the parameter ψ will increase, thereby accelerating the process of technological upgrading.

Phase II is generally characterized by reverse reactions with important implications for the transition process. The relative productivity gain in the modern sector will reduce comparative advantages and relatively cut back the speed of imitation, which is governed by trade opportunities. An additional shift of human capital from the imitation to the modern sector will accelerate this effect. As a result, ψ will decline and the upgrading process will slow down. The structural reallocation process will turn in favor of the modern sector, as might be generally expected for upgrading countries.

These findings can be summarized by two major conclusions: 1. A transition process generates permanent requirements of structural adjustment. Efficient upgrading may in a first phase turn towards the traditional sector, reinforce comparative advantages, strengthen trade positions and improve technological capabilities. In a second phase the structural adjustment reverts towards an increasing weight of the modern sector as generally expected for a process of catching up. 2. The speed of transition may be overestimated in the first phase. In the second phase, decreasing trade advantages and reallocation of human capital from the imitation sector to the modern sector will slow down the process of upgrading.

Figure I2 Allocation Effects in Different Transition Periods

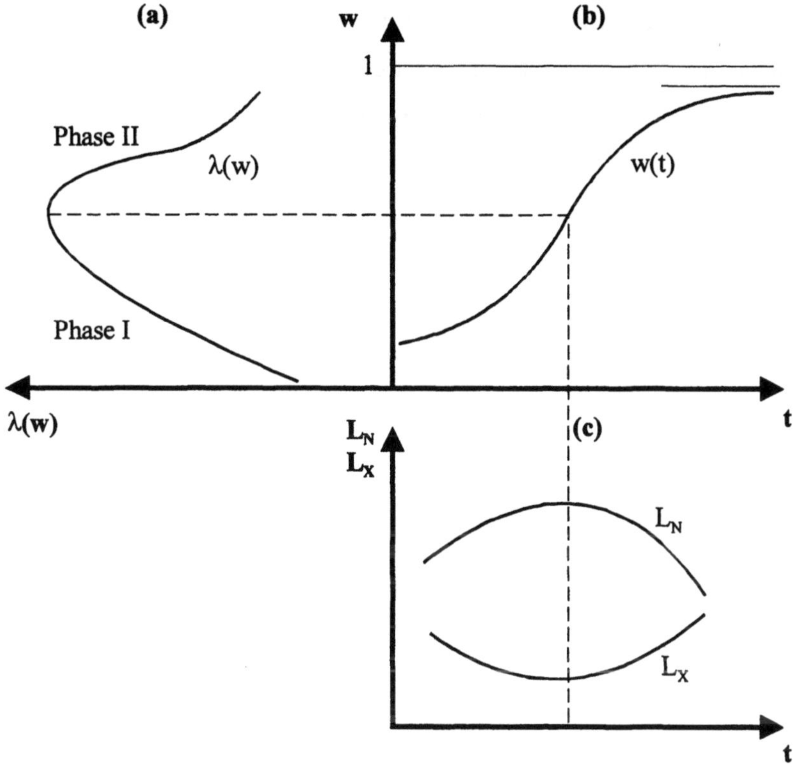

5. The Employment Problem

A characteristic problem for economies in transformation is the employment problem. Due to the move towards efficient production, firms have to lay off workers, replacing the previously hidden unemployment with open unemployment. A second reason for the sudden and tremendous rise in unemployment at the beginning of the transformation process is a dramatic change in the production structure of these economies. Therefore, with respect to the unemployment problem of transformation economies, the full employment model described above does not fit the stylized facts of transformation very well.

Nevertheless, the model does have some implications for the employment situation in these economies during the process of catching up. As discussed above the model does not analyze the very first moment of transformation with specific political and institutional problems, but focuses on the time path over several years or even decades. For this path of transformation at least one aspect of unemployment can be identified.

Figure I3 Unemployment Problem

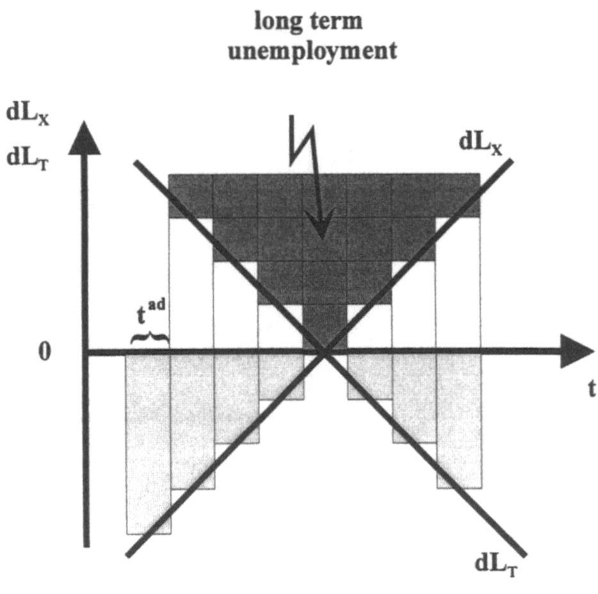

In the previous chapter the process of catching up was accompanied by a permanent process of structural change. In a first phase resources moved to the traditional sector and thereafter they were shifted back to the modern sector. This structural adjustment problem is likely to be an employment problem as well. In the perfect world of the model the reallocation process works perfectly: $dL_X = -dL_N$ and

$dH_X = -dH_T$ with $H_X + H_T = H$ and $L_X + L_T = L$. Suppose reallocation of resources takes time, so that the search and reeducation process necessary to move resources from one sector to the other takes time t^{ad}. For a linear approximation[17] of the reallocation process, the perfect reallocation curves are drawn as dL_X and dL_T in Figure I3. In discrete time periods the bars represent the number of laid off or newly employed workers. As can be seen, in the first period of structural changes the economy accumulates unemployment: The modern sector reduces employment and the traditional sector cannot start to employ additional workers due to the introduced friction in terms of reallocation time. In the second period most of the workers unemployed in the first period are reemployed, but additional workers are laid off (gray columns). While the sum of unemployed people does not change (sum of the gray columns and the dark squares), there is a group of workers, which is unemployed for at least two periods (dark squares). By considering the next period we can see that this group of long term unemployed workers expands over time.

From Figure I3 we can derive two results with regard to the problem of unemployment during the process of transformation:

(i) The unemployment problem will be a permanent problem: The view that the economy will turn back to full employment rapidly after the original distortions is too optimistic. After having solved the original transformation problems a long period of painful adjustment in terms of unemployment will take place. In this respect the transformation economies will follow the industrialized market economies which previously were on a similar path.

(ii) The problem of long term unemployment: Long term unemployment is not constant, but changes over time. The following happens close to the structural switching point: Moving towards the structural switching point will increase long term unemployment. Having passed this point long term unemployment will decrease again.

6. Summary

Many aspects of the transformation problem are discussed in the recent literature. In the center of this discussion are problems like institutional reforms, privatization, price liberalization, etc. While these aspects are extremely important in the first period of transformation, other problems become important thereafter. What are the factors driving the transition process when the economies start to move on a track of upgrading towards the leading market economies? This question was considered in this paper. We investigated the time path of the adjustment process of economies in transition. Three results are important: 1. The original stock of human capital will determine the speed of catching up as well as the level of the potential final position of upgrading. 2. During the process of catching up the economies will face permanent pressure to adjust structurally. Resources will have to shift permanently from one sector to the other. 3. Given the distortions at the beginning of the transformation process, the view that a fast return to full employment will occur is too optimistic. The permanent structural change will cause permanent unemployment, if some frictions in the reallocation process are present.

Endnotes

1 For important comments and many helpful discussions we are grateful to H. Meyer.

2 This does of course not mean, that economic history does not provide any guidelines to many of the problems concerned. See for example SIEBERT, SCHMIEDING and NUNNENKAMP (1992); NELSON (1993); AHRENS (1994).

3 See for example SCHIPKE and TAYLOR (1994); BLANCHARD, FROOT and SACHS (1994), Vol. 2, and ARNOLD (1994) among others.

4 See RYBCZYNSKI (1991); NEWBERY (1992); GENBERG (1992); PORTES (1993) and FUNKE (1993).

5 These may be associated with ROMER (1986, 1990); LUCAS (1988); BARRO (1990); and GROSSMAN and HELPMAN (1991) among others. For a critical survey see GRIES, WIGGER and HENTSCHEL (1994).

6 Empirical evidence suggests that the time needed to close *half* of the gap between actual and steady state values may very well be up to four decades; see BARRO and SALA-I-MARTIN (1994, Ch. 11, 12).

7 Basic elements of the model are taken from GRIES and JUNGBLUT (1995).

[8] This in fact is the well known Veblen Gerschenkron Hypothesis which states that at the outset of a catching up process simple technologies will be copied, which can be easily imitated, while later on more sophisticated technologies have to be discovered.

[9] See GRIES and WIGGER (1993) for further remarks on this functional form.

[10] This may be warranted by suitable choice of the exogenous variables p, L and H.

[11] A full discussion of the parameters determining the final gap and the speed of the adjustment process is given in GRIES and WIGGER (1993).

[12] For a proof see GRIES and JUNGBLUT (1995).

[13] The proof for $\frac{\partial \varphi}{\partial \lambda} > 0$ can be found in GRIES and JUNGBLUT (1995).

[14] $\left(\frac{d\psi}{dw}\right) = \underbrace{v'\varphi}_{+} + v\underbrace{\frac{\partial \varphi}{\partial \lambda}}_{+}\underbrace{\frac{\partial \varphi}{\partial w}}_{+,-}$: $\psi(w)$ can be monotone as well as unimodal. As the second case is more interesting, we choose the unimodal shape.

[15] Since in the region $0 \leq w \leq 1$ the function $\omega^{II}(w)$ has no or two points of inflection and $\omega'(0) > 0, \omega'(1) < 0$, the shape of $\omega^{II}(w)$ can be drawn as done in Figure I1a.

[16] he reactions of the relevant variables in every period of the processes is given in GRIES and JUNGBLUT (1995).

[17] This linear approximation will be close to the structural switching point.

References

AHRENS, J. (1994), "The Transition to a Market Economy: Are there Useful Lessons from History?" in SCHIPKE, A. and TAYLOR, A. M. (eds.), *The Economics of Transformation: Theory and Practice in the New Market Economies*, Springer, Heidelberg, 17-46.

ARNOLD, M. (1994), *Reform und Transformation von Wirtschaftssystemen am Beispiel der ehemaligen Sowietunion*, Europäische Hochschulschriften, Reihe V, Vol. 1579, Peter Lang, Frankfurt/Main.

ATKINSON, A. B. and MICKLEWRIGHT, J. (1992), *Economic transformation in Eastern Europe and the distribution of income*, Cambridge University Press, Cambridge.

BARRO, R. J. (1990), "Government Spending in a Simple Model of Endogenous Growth," *Journal of Political Economy*, Vol. 98, 5, part II, S103-S125.

BARRO, R. J. and SALA-I-MARTIN, X. (1995), *Economic Growth*, McGraw-Hill, New York.

BLANCHARD, O. J., FROOT, K. A. and SACHS, J. D. (eds.) (1994), *The Transition in Eastern Europe, Vol. 1: Country Studies, Vol. 2: Restructuring*, University of Chicago Press, Chicago/London.

EBERWEIN, W.-D., ed. (1992), *Transformation Processes in Eastern Europe: Perspectives from the Modelling Laboratory*, Peter Lang, Frankfurt/Main.

FUNKE, N. (1993), "Timing and Sequencing of Reforms: Competing Views and the Role of Credibility," *KYKLOS*, Vol. 46, 337-362.

GENBERG, H. (1992), "Transition Processes in Eastern Europe: The Sequencing of Reforms," in EBERWEIN, W.-D. (ed.), *Transformation Processes in Eastern Europe: Perspectives from the Modelling Laboratory*, Peter Lang, Frankfurt/Main, 63-94.

GRIES, T. and JUNGBLUT, S. (1995), "Catching-up and Structural Adjustment," International Economics," Working Papers, 9502, University of Paderborn, forthcoming.

GRIES, T. and WIGGER, B. (1993), "The Dynamics of Upgrading or How to Catch-Up: Imitation and Growth of Newly Industrializing Countries," *Economica Internazionale*, Vol. 46, 4, 3-13.

GRIES, T., WIGGER, B. and HENTSCHEL, C. (1994), "Endogenous Growth and R&D Models: A Critical Appraisal of Recent Developments," *Jahrbücher für Nationalökonomie und Statistik*, Vol. 213, 1, 64-84.

GROSSMAN, G. M. and HELPMAN, E. (1991), *Innovation and Growth in the Global Economy*, MIT Press, Cambridge MA.

LUCAS, R. E. Jr. (1988), "On the Mechanics of Development Planning," *Journal of Monetary Economics*, Vol. 22, 1, 3-42.

NELSON, J. M. (1993), "The Politics of Economic Transformation: Is Third World Experience Relevant in Eastern Europe?" *World Politics*, Vol. 45, 433-463.

NEWBERY, D. M. (1992), "Sequencing the Transition," in SIEBERT, H. (ed.), *The Transformation of Socialist Economies*, Symposium 1991, J.C.B. Mohr, Tübingen, 161-199.

PORTES, R. (ed.) (1993), *Economic Transformation in Central Europe: A Progress Report*, Centre for Economic Policy Research, London, and European Commission, Luxembourg.

PORTES, R. (1994), "Transformation Traps," *Economic Journal*, Vol. 104, 1178-1189.

ROMER, P. M. (1986), "Increasing Returns an Long-Run Growth," *Journal of Political Economy*, Vol. 94, 5, 1002-1037.

ROMER, P. M. (1990), "Endogenous Technological Change," *Journal of Political Economy*, Vol. 98, 5, part II, S71-S102.

RYBCZYNSKI, T. M. (1991), "The Sequencing of Reform: Microeconomics of Transition in Eastern Europe," *Oxford Review of Economic Policy*, Vol. 7, 26-34.

SCHMIEDING, H. (1992), *Lending Stability to Europe's Emerging Market Economies: On the Potential Importance of the EC and the ECU for Central and Eastern Europe*, Kieler Studien 251, J. C. B. Mohr, Tübingen.

SCHIPKE, A. and TAYLOR, A. M. (eds.) (1994), *The Economics of Transformation: Theory and Practice in the New Market Economies*, Springer, Heidelberg.

SIEBERT, H., ed. (1992), *The Transformation of Socialist Economies*, Symposium 1991, J.C.B. Mohr, Tübingen.

SIEBERT, H., SCHMIEDING, H. and NUNNENKAMP, P. (1992), "The Transformation of a Socialist Economy: Lessons of German Unification," in WINCKLER, G. (ed.), *Central and Eastern Europe: Roads to Growth*, International Monetary Fund, Washington D.C., and Austrian National Bank.

WINCKLER, G. (ed.) (1992), *Central and Eastern Europe: Roads to Growth*, International Monetary Fund, Washington D.C., and Austrian National Bank.

Comments on

Catching Up of Economies in Transformation

Georg Erber

The paper originally presented at the conference has been heavily revised. Therefore a large part of my original criticism directed at other parts of the paper no longer applies to the paper appearing in this volume. By restricting the paper to the more mathematical analytical part discussed below the better part of the original paper was kept and the weaker parts left out. The revision has, therefore, led to a substantial improvement by reducing the paper's previous heterogeneity. The question still remaining is whether the model presented addresses the central issue of transformation economies or just constitutes a specific diffusion model with some interesting characteristics.

Let us now turn to the actual model presented in the revised version of the paper. The model distinguishes between three production sectors, a traditional, a modern industrial and a research sector. The production technologies assumed are at best simple Cobb-Douglas production functions for two types of labor inputs, i.e. skilled and unskilled labor. The rate of technological progress, which is assumed to be Harrod-neutral for these two factor inputs, is endogenized by equation (4). A certain fixed amount of human capital is applied in the research sector and determines the rate of technological progress. The three sector model is solved under two different types of assumptions concerning the diffusion process of technologies. The diffusion model utilized is a logistic function of the convergence to the efficiency boundary of the leading economy. A symmetric diffusion across the traditional and the modern industrial sector is compared with an asymmetric diffusion between the traditional and the modern industrial sector. Even in the quite simple setting of their model an explicit solution of the model could not be derived.

They, therefore, had to solve it numerically by assuming certain parameter values which seemed reasonable to them. For the symmetric diffusion model, they find that the gap between the leading economy and the follower cannot be closed, if the follower does not switch from imitating to innovating behavior. For the asymmetric diffusion process, they observe that structural change between the allocation of labor inputs becomes a necessary requirement of the catch-up process. One should, however, keep in mind that they rule out the accumulation of skilled labor, i.e. human capital, and a decrease in the amount of unskilled labor - see equation (6). Their results should, therefore, be considered with some reservation, because the accumulation of human capital and the reallocation of different types of human capital are separated and only the reallocation process is considered. In the real world both processes take place simultaneously in a catch-up process. In the asymmetric case considered in the paper, the authors find that two phases exist. In the first phase, the gap with respect to the traditional sector is closed, and in the second, the gap in the modern industrial sector follows. This leads to a non-logistic pattern for the catch-up process for the whole economy. If the whole economy is considered, the speed of the catch-up process is more rapid at first, while later it is slower than in a logistic catch-up process.

Taking up my initial criticism at the conference, that the authors' model does not address the issue of unemployment which is a central problem for all transformation economies, the authors now concede that long-term unemployment will arise if structural adjustment takes time especially in the labor market. However, the model discussed by the two authors has no analytical means to address the question of how long-term structural unemployment might be lowered substantially besides the general implication that the greater the labor market flexibility the lower will be long-term unemployment. But this is just the message any neoclassical model would tell us when dealing with labor market problems. Therefore, for the actual debate on transformation economies and the problem with long-term structural unemployment little can be learnt from the authors' analysis.

J. Savings, Credit Markets and Economic Growth in Europe

Holger C. Wolf[1]

1. Introduction

Two scenarios dominate the discussion about the future of eastern Europe. In the first, the combination of good fundamentals and proximity to the EU generates ASEAN-style tigers rapidly catching up with western Europe. In the second, the combination of inherited burdens and populist policies generates Latin-style inward looking economies turning eastern Europe into the perennial poor cousin.

Which scenario will play out depends ultimately on the volume and quality of investment: while there is room for improving efficiency, in the longer run growth will have to come from factor accumulation. The investment volume required for rapid catch-up has been the subject of a lively debate. Results vary quite significantly, largely reflecting different assumptions on how much "free" growth is attainable through better allocation of existing productive resources (BLACK and MOERSCH, 1995). A conservative estimate puts the minimum investment to GDP ratio for catch-up by 2010 at 30 percent, close to the average of the ASEAN economies.

A much less analyzed question is whether even the conservative end of this range of estimates is consistent with the likely evolution of savings (BORENSZTEIN and MONTIEL, 1991). In a world with perfectly integrated capital markets, the answer would be yes: provided investment projects in eastern Europe are attractive on a risk-return basis, the small absolute amount of required savings[2] should be readily fundable out of world savings. In practice, an extensive literature tracing back to Adam Smith has argued that de facto national savings and investment rates are highly correlated (FELDSTEIN and HORIOKA, 1980), or put differently, that the size of net foreign savings is quite limited relative to national investment and may, furthermore, partly act as a substitute rather than as a complement to national savings (OBSTFELD, 1995, WHITE, 1992).

Table J1 Stock and Flow of FDI

	FDI/I	I/Y
Asia	15.4	27.6
Latin America	11.6	16.5
Africa	10.5	19.6
Western Europe	5.6	20.2
North America	1.2	13.2

Source: United Nations (1994).

There is little reason to believe that eastern Europe will be an exception to the Feldstein-Horioka constraint on attainable foreign finance: at the top of the recent surge of inflows, the capital account balance of eastern and central Europe amounted to some US$ 14 bn, less than six percent of the envisaged annual investment, with foreign direct investment accounting for US$ 8 bn in 1994. Table J1 suggests that there may, in a good case scenario, be room for further growth in FDI (WELFENS, 1992), yet it is highly unlikely that FDI - or overall capital inflows - will in the end account for more than a fairly small fraction of the investment required for rapid catch-up.

The Feldstein-Horioka puzzle is the subject of a separate lively literature which is beyond the scope of the paper. Here we simply invoke Ockham's razor and assert that the sustainable inflow of foreign savings will not exceed Edward's constant of 3 percent of GDP.[3] In consequence, rapid convergence will only be achieved if national savings rates in the high twenties can be attained, levels that are not unprecedented but that certainly are at the higher end of the historically observed range (MADDISON, 1992).

How likely are such savings rates? We begin by drawing on both consumption theory and cross-country empirical results to conjecture about the likely future evolution of household savings. Our main conclusions can be summarized briefly: in the short run, household savings will be predominantly driven by demographics and income, both will exert a downward pressure on savings. In the medium run, evidence in favor of a causation from income growth to savings suggests that if a growth pick-up occurs, the low growth-low savings trap may give way to a high growth-high savings outcome. Alas, empirical evidence on the relative importance of income versus demographics puts a damper on this scenario: the graying of eastern Europe requires very substantial increases in income per capita growth simply to maintain an unchanged savings rate. On net, cross-country evidence suggests small and declining household savings rates in the transition economies for the medium run.

The pessimistic outlook for household savings - which are fairly invariant to policy at least in the short run - implies that the rapid convergence scenario has to rely on substantial public and corporate savings, with strong associated implications for policy. In an complete markets/full information setting, considering corporate and public savings as independent contributors to national savings would of course be inappropriate: households are the claimant to corporate savings and bear the liability for the present discounted value of the stream of government expenditures. Increases in corporate and public savings hence will be reflected in equal decreases in household savings, with zero net effect on national savings. In practice, ample empirical evidence suggests that households, for a variety of reasons, do not "pierce the corporate veil" nor act as pure Ricardians vis-à-vis the public sector. Given the imperfect offset and the outlook for household savings, substantial increases in corporate and public savings thus become a *sine qua non* if the ambitious investment objectives are to be attained. Put differently, a significant fiscal tightening (in practice a substantial tightening of the social net), a determined redistribution of income from labor to capital and - related - measures to support productive investment are pre-conditions for a rapid convergence scenario.

Of course, the required sizeable increase in corporate and public savings, while necessary, is not a sufficient condition for attaining the growth objectives: allocative efficiency provides the second supporting rod for rapid investment-led growth. Indeed, the history of the transition economies themselves in the 1980s, with investment ratios above 30 percent but near zero growth, provides the clearest warning sign against exclusive focus on aggregate savings and investment. We thus turn to allocative efficiency in the second part of the paper.

Again, our main conclusions can be summarized briefly: to a first approximation, the starting conditions in the transition economies suggest that external finance - either debt or equity - is unlikely to play a major role except for a core group of blue chip companies. In consequence, there are significant doubts whether public savings - even if attained - can be efficiently channeled to investment projects through intermediation of the private banking sector. As history provides little basis for attaching much confidence to the efficiency characteristics of direct state loans, public sector savings are thus unlikely to contribute much to efficient project finance. In the end, it is the old fail-safe of investment finance, retained earnings, which will have to initially carry the bulk of the load.

2. The Setting

Table J2 provides some background on the evolution of key aggregates in the first stages of the transition process. Government consumption is seen to have mostly increased. The increase exceeded the increase in revenues: by 1993 the public sector imposed a drain on national savings in all central European economies with the exception of the Czech Republic. Foreign savings, with the exception of Bulgaria, have increased to quite significant levels. This might seem to clash with our earlier assumption of quite limited inflows, yet it stands to reason that a significant fraction of these inflows reflect the one time stock adjustment of portfolios in response to the first time availability of east European assets, thus the sustainable capital account balance is likely to be significantly smaller. Net direct investment remains negligible for most transition economies. Even in Hungary and the Czech Republic, accounting for the lion's share of FDI, inflows do not much exceed 5 percent of GDP, a sixth of the minimum investment ratio required for rapid catch-up.

Table J2 The Setting

	Bulgaria	Czech Republic	Hungary	Poland	Romania	Slovakia
	Government Consumption (% of GDP)					
1987-91	16.6	21.3	11.0	14.2	NA	21.3
1992-93	15.8	15.5	12.8	22.8	NA	26.2
	Fiscal Balance (% of GDP)					
1993	-18.5	0.5	-6.9	-2.9	-0.1	-7.5
	Capital Account (% of GDP)					
1987-91	-4.0	-0.5	2.1	-5.2	-2.0	-0.5
1992-93	-8.5	4.5	9.3	1.1	6.8	1.3
	Net Direct Investment (% of GDP)					
1987-91	0.2	0.5	1.3	0.0	0.0	0.5
1992-93	0.5	2.7	5.6	0.5	0.3	-0.6
	Private Consumption					
1987-91	54.2	44.3	62.6	56.0	NA	44.3
1992-93	73.1	54.1	70.7	62.2	NA	55.6
	Private Savings Rate					
1989	29.2	—	29.9	24.2	21.2	—
1991	33.1	39.8	23.1	18.1	22.1	32.3
Latest	18.8	22.2	21.9	17.2	23.4	32.5
	Total Consumption					
1987-91	70.8	65.6	73.6	70.1	69.1	65.6
1992-93	88.8	73.1	83.5	85.0	76.8	81.7
	Gross Capital Formation (% of GDP)					
1987-91	31.5	27.9	25.3	27.5	29.2	27.9
1992-93	17.8	20.5	21.1	15.8	29.6	24.7

Source: CALVO et al. (1995); BLACK and MOERSCH (1995)

The share of private consumption in GDP - typically a quite steady figure- has increased dramatically since the beginning of the transition process. The decline in national savings dominated the rise in foreign savings, in consequent, investment ratios have fallen quite significantly and remain below the conservative estimate of the minimal levels required for rapid catch-up.[4] The overall picture is thus one of an externally financed consumption boom with declining national savings and investment - the Latin model. Put differently, in eastern Europe, as in Latin

America, but notably in contrast to Asia, foreign savings appear to serve as a substitute rather than as an addition to national savings, with obvious negative implications for the attainable growth rate.

3. Savings: Quantitative Aspects

The stylized facts presented above do not bode well for the high investment scenario underlying the early convergence theme. Yet not too much weight should be placed on the figures, for two reasons. First, the statistics for the transition economies, while improving, remain subject to quite broad confidence intervals. Second, current figures are likely to be significantly influenced by the dramatic economic and institutional change still unfolding and may hence be misleading as gauges of savings rates once the initial turmoil has subsided.

In the absence of reliable guides for the transition economies themselves, we turn in the following sections to the existing theoretical and empirical body of knowledge about savings rates to gauge the likely evolution of savings rates. We split the discussion by savings type, beginning with household savings before turning, much more briefly, to corporate and public savings.[5]

3.1 Household Savings

It is useful to structure the discussion around the standard individual consumption model.[6] The individual maximizes the present discounted utility derived from consuming private (c) and public (g) goods

$$U = \int_0^\infty E[U(c_t, g_t)]e^{-\delta t}dt \tag{1}$$

Subject to the intertemporal budget constraint:

$$\int_0^\infty c_t e^{-rt}dt \leq W = \int_0^\infty y_t(1-\tau_t)e^{-rt}dt \tag{2}$$

where δ and r denote the discount and interest rate, W denotes wealth and τ is the tax rate. Savings are given by

$$S_t = [y_t(1-\tau_t) - c_t] \tag{3}$$

and are subject on the downside to an exogenous borrowing constraint which may or may not bind:

$$-k \leq S_t \leq y_t(1-\tau_t) \tag{4}$$

3.1.1 Income Growth

If the absence of binding borrowing constraints, the optimal solution to the maximization problem is obtained by equating the ratio of marginal utilities to the discount rate - consumption is smoothed over time (CAMPBELL and MANKIW, 1990, 1991; ZELDES, 1989). The pattern of income evolution in the transition consistent with rapid catch-up assumes the form of a J-curve: an initial decline, as existing inefficient production structures are dismantled, and a sustained rapid recovery as new efficient structures emerge. Faced with this expected income path, the consumer - in the absence of borrowing constraints - will respond by reducing current savings, both to buffer against the temporary decline in income at the front end of the adjustment and to anticipate some of the expected future income gains. In combination, the consumption smoothing incentive thus suggests a quite severe decline in savings in the initial phase of the transition. The introduction of borrowing constraints, strongly supported by the empirical evidence (HAYASHI, 1985; HONOHAN, 1995; HAQUE and MONTIEL, 1989; ROSSI, 1988; CAMPBELL and MANKIW, 1990; Journal of Economic Perspectives, 1995, inter alia), does not alter the picture, though the decline in savings will now no longer suffice to fully buffer the temporary decline and to anticipate the future increase in expected income.

Both cross section and time series evidence strongly suggests a positive correlation between income growth and savings rates (BOSWORTH, 1993; CAMPBELL and

DEATON, 1989; DEATON 1990, 1995; EDWARDS, 1995; JAPELLI and PAGANO, 1994; MODIGLIANI, 1986, inter alia).[7] This raises the important issue of causality between income growth and savings. From a policy perspective, the issue is crucial: if savings are the driving force, policies to augment savings carry growth benefits, if not, policies are best directed at influencing investment and growth, leaving savings to adjust passively. The available evidence (BOSWORTH, 1993; CARROLL and WEIL, 1993; IMF, 1995) suggests that savings strongly respond to both current and lagged income growth, but that the reverse link is considerably weaker. If true, this implies that the positive relation between savings and growth rates observed in Asia - and often used to justify savings promoting policies - is largely the outcome of a fortuitous circle: high growth, once jump-started, generates the expansion of savings financing the investment which sustains the initial growth spurt. Applied to eastern Europe, the causality structure suggests that improving fundamentals rather than attempting to work on incentives provides the most promising route towards high savings.

3.1.2 Income Uncertainty

If the utility function is convex, a mean preserving spread of the distribution of future income reduces current consumption, resulting in precautionary savings (CABALLERO, 1990). To the degree that the collapse of the socialist system was unexpected, the move from a cradle to grave social security system with job tenure to the rough and tumble world of an emerging market economy dramatically increases income volatility in the transition economy and thus raises precautionary savings.

There are however a number of reasons to doubt that an increase in precautionary savings will play a major role in driving household savings. First, for standard parameters precautionary savings are likely to be quite small (AIYAGARI, 1994; GUISO, JAPELLI and TERLIZZESE, 1992). Second, uncertainty about future income levels has arguably already reached its peak: as the new legal, institutional and economic framework stabilizes, probability distributions of future income levels should narrow. Finally, the gradual re-establishment of functioning social insurance against health and - to a lesser extent - unemployment risk reduces the individual cost of adverse shocks.

3.1.3 Returns

The effect of a change in the rate of return on savings is ambiguous, determined by the relative importance of the substitution and wealth effect on the one hand and the income effect on the other. The empirical evidence on the interest elasticity is quite mixed.[8] With few exceptions the estimated elasticities with respect to aggregate savings of either sign are, however, quite small, suggesting that any net effect is minor. In contrast, estimated return elasticities for savings in particular asset classes tend to be higher, suggesting that households respond to changing returns by altering the allocation of a fairly invariant total volume of savings between alternative outlets, including domestic and foreign financial as well as real assets. Rising real rates of return in eastern Europe thus stand to have a minor first order impact, though, to the degree that savers switch from the currently preferred saving instruments - real and foreign financial assets - to savings in domestic financial instruments, a second order effect through growth is likely.

The evidence is consistent both with a low underlying intertemporal elasticity of consumption, and with borrowing constraints preventing utility increasing substitution.[9] In either case, the low interest sensitivity implies, as an important corollary, that, besides changes in equilibrium pre-tax returns, any government policies based on affecting marginal after-tax returns are also likely to have only a limited impact on savings rates (BOSKIN, 1978; BOVENBERG, 1989).[10]

3.1.4 Pension Systems

The availability of public pensions reduces private savings by eliminating one of the motives for precautionary savings against unexpected long life, and by reducing the need for accumulating private retirement savings (FELDSTEIN, 1980, 1994). A partial offset is however present to the extent that - as the evidence suggests - the availability of public pensions tends to reduce the retirement age and thus requires higher savings rates during the worklife. On net, the available evidence suggests that the former factors dominate, in consequence, the comprehensive public savings system in most transition economies (HOLZMANN, 1994) depresses household savings compared to economies with less generous systems.[11] As the transition pension systems operate on a pay-as-you-go basis, there is no public sector offset to the private sector decline, hence the qualitative results extend to national savings.

Looking forward, the effect of pension systems on savings depend on two factors. First, to the degree that the currently existing schemes are perceived as being unsustainable (AHMAD et al., 1994), the private savings reduction will be muted. Second, a shift from a defined benefits to a defined contribution system stands -judging from the preliminary evidence from Chile - to raise savings both directly and indirectly by conditionalizing households retirement income on economic performance, thus buttressing the political stability necessary for investment, and by reducing the incentive to work in the informal sector (CORSETTI and SCHMIDT-HEBBEL, 1991; DIAMOND and VALDES-PRIETO, 1994).

3.1.5 Wealth

Wealth provides a buffer to smooth consumption and hence, *ceteris paribus*, reduces the need for savings out of current income, a prediction born out by most empirical studies (BOSWORTH, 1993). The wealth-savings link may play an important role in the transition economies in two respects. First, the initial post-revolution inflation boomlet observed in most transition economies has dramatically reduced the real value of savings which were - lacking alternatives - mostly held in cash and non-indexed deposits. While the combination of stabilization and financial broadening had - with few exceptions - sharply reduced the inflation tax on wealth by 1995, the one time reduction in 1989-92 will continue to exert a positive influence on savings until previous wealth levels are reached, though the propensity to hold these savings in nominal domestic assets has likely declined.

The second - and offsetting - important factor is privatization. Apart from a few cases, variants of the Czech voucher scheme have been the model of choice, with an entailed transfer of wealth from the public to the private sector. In principle, the transfer of wealth corresponds to an equal increase in the future taxes and - in Ricardian terms - thus does not lead to an increase in private sector net wealth (BARRO, 1974). In practice, as we will argue below, the available evidence strongly suggests offsets far below unity, with an implied negative effect on savings.

3.1.6 Financial Reform

Financial liberalization in the transition economies will have substantial effects both on the rates of return on alternative assets and on the availability of assets. As argued above, the evidence on the interest rate elasticity of savings is mixed and suggests that changes in returns will predominantly affect the allocation rather than the volume of savings (CAPRIO, 1995; CAPRIO and LEVINE, 1994; FRIES and LANE, 1994). The likely shift from foreign to domestic and from real to nominal assets will, however, have substantial positive effects on allocative efficiency and will, thus, indirectly influence savings positively over time by raising growth.

Improvements in the availability of financial instruments may, in contrast, have a first order effect. Of particular importance in this respect is the development of consumer credit and of mortgage markets. Ample empirical evidence suggests that both the absence of mortgage and the absence of consumer credit markets significantly enhances private savings by requiring individuals to save prior to "big ticket" purchases.[12] Thus, as JAPPELLI and PAGANO (1991) note, while financial reform reducing credit barriers to firms, by increasing allocative efficiency, raises growth and hence indirectly savings over the longer term, financial reform reducing borrowing constraints to households has the opposite effect. On net, financial liberalization thus stands to reduce savings in the short run, with a possible longer term indirect offset through higher growth (MCKINNON, 1973; SHAW, 1973; KING and LEVINE, 1993, 1994). As MUELLBAUER (1994) notes, the negative effect is further aggravated by transitional dynamics as households revise precautionary balances accumulated under the expectations of continuing borrowing constraints and move towards their new less constrained optimal consumption paths.

3.1.7 Aggregation

The aggregate household savings rate, as the weighted average of individual savings, depends on the composition of the population, in particular on the income, wealth and age distribution. Beginning with the former, savings propensities are often argued to increase in income, generating a positive relation between savings and income inequality. However, the link is neither unambiguous on theoretical grounds nor particularly evident in empirical work (BLINDER, 1975; GERSOVITZ, 1988). While the transition economies will undergo a substantial widening of the income distribution, concentrated on a flattening of the upper tail, there is thus little grounds to expect major effects of income distribution changes on savings rates.

In contrast, demographic trends are likely to exert a first order influence. The typical hump shaped lifetime income profile implies that consumers not subject to borrowing constraints will dissave in their early and late years while saving in their middle years. The ratio of the population in the dissaving to the saving age-groups thus has, *ceteris paribus*, a major impact on aggregate savings (AUERBACH and KOTLIKOFF, 1992). Much of eastern Europe - with the exception of some FSU republics - shares with the OECD the feature of a rapidly increasing population of, likely dissaving, retirees relative to the working population (HELLER, 1989). Table J3 reports dependency ratios for a sample of transition economies. Reflecting the earlier retirement age, the active population was defined as comprising the ages 15 to 55, the "young" and "old" measures are the ratios of individuals below 15 and above 55 to the population in the middle group.

Table J3 Population Trends I

Country	Young		Old	
	1995	2025	1995	1025
Albania	0.56	0.39	0.20	0.39
Czech Republic	0.34	0.35	0.32	0.51
Estonia	0.40	0.38	0.34	0.48
Poland	0.42	0.38	0.30	0.45
Russia	0.40	0.37	0.32	0.50

Source: World Bank.

The longer term demographic trend towards higher dependency rates - aggravated by the above noted trend to earlier retirement - will exert downward pressure on savings. The virtually unanimous conclusion of the empirical evidence (LEFF, 1969; GRAHAM, 1987; MASSON and TRYON, 1990) furthermore suggests that the demographic trend is quantitatively, together with income growth, the most important driving force behind household savings, suggesting a significant negative influence.

3.1.8 Household Savings: Conclusion

The likely evolution of household savings rates in the transition economies is the joint outcome of a multitude of factors. By using empirical evidence from other economies, a reasonable case can, however, be made that many of these - including income uncertainty, changes in asset returns and income distribution - are likely to be second order effects. First order effects are likely to be limited to two key variables - the growth rate of income and the demographic trend - with the possible reduction of borrowing constraints in the wake of financial liberalization a potential third important factor.

The demographic trend is - despite substantial changes in fertility and mortality rates in the last few years - largely given and suggests, much as in the OECD, a trend decline in savings, as does financial liberalization. In like vein, the strong positive correlation between savings and income growth rates coupled with the steep decline in (at least measured) income in most transition economies implies that income developments have also exerted a strong downward influence on household savings in the initial transition phase. The income effect, in particular, likely explains a major portion of the observed jump increase in the personal consumption propensity illustrated above. Looking forward, a substantial rise in the household savings rate can only be expected as a consequence of rapid income growth offsetting the negative influences of demographics and receding borrowing constraints.

The prospects for such a recovery are, however, rather slim. Rapid savings increases following income growth in the Asian miracle economies came at a time when dependency ratios were low (FARUQEE and HUSAIN, 1995). In contrast, the transition economies have to achieve substantial income growth simply to offset the negative effects of demographics on savings. Plugging demographic data for the transition economies into the "baseline" cross country regressions estimated by EDWARDS (1995), for example, suggest that just to offset the impact of a graying population over the next decades requires an increase in per capita income growth ranging between five percent in Albania and almost eleven percent in the Czech Republic. The figures are, needless to say, subject to wide confidence intervals, in particular, an increase in the retirement age from 55 to 65 will reduce the necessary income growth. But they suggest, nevertheless, that based on other countries experiences a substantial increase in household savings appears unlikely. More likely, in fact, is a further decline in household savings rates to the low teens.

3.2 Corporate and Public Savings

If a high investment high growth scenario is to be achieved, the transition economies will thus have to look towards corporate and public savings as a source of finance. In a frictionless economy, this would of course be an impossibility: households are the claimants to corporate earnings and finance government expenditures, implying that any change in corporate earnings or the fiscal balance will simply lead to an equal opposite change in household savings, leaving national savings unchanged. In practice, Ricardian equivalence fails to hold and households apparently fail to "pierce the corporate veil". We discuss both sources of savings in turn.

3.2.1 Corporate Savings

A broad range of studies suggests that households do not treat a dollar of corporate earnings as equivalent to a dollar of household savings, for a variety of reasons including most importantly borrowing constraints, aggregation effects and tax considerations (BAYOUMI et al., 1995). Thus, FELDSTEIN (1973) finds the propensity to consume out of retained earnings to be 0.5, compared with a propensity to consume out of disposable income of 0.75, suggesting that a one dollar shift from dividends to retained earnings increases total private savings by 25 cents. Similar and often even higher net effects have been found by a range of other authors, including FELDSTEIN and FANE (1973), SMITH (1989), BHATIA (1979), VON FURSTENBERG (1981), POTERBA (1987) and MUSGRAVE and MUSGRAVE (1984), leading the latter authors to conclude in their textbook that "the savings impact of the corporate tax dollar is ... substantially above that of most other taxes" (1984, p. 662).

3.2.2 Public Savings

In an undistorted perfect foresight world with linked generations, changes in public sector savings do not affect national savings but are offset by opposing changes in private savings reflecting the change in expected net tax liabilities (BARRO, 1974). The result is, however, highly sensitive to rather strict assumptions and has generally been found to fail in empirical tests (GRAMLICH, 1989; HAQUE and MONTIEL, 1989; BERNHEIM, 1987; CORBO and SCHMIDT-HEBBEL, 1991)[13] with the main culprit, again, thought to be borrowing constraints faced by individuals. Empirical estimates of the offset coefficient (the decline in private savings associated with a one dollar increase in public sector savings) vary somewhat but tend to cluster in the 0.4 to 0.6 range (BERNHEIM, 1987; EDWARDS, 1995; BOSWORTH, 1993, inter alia). As CORBO and SCHMIDT-HEBBEL (1991) point out, in the presence of borrowing constraints the offset coefficient is however likely to differ for equal changes in public savings brought about by expenditure cuts versus tax increases. Consistent with this argument, they find an offset coefficient of 0.16-0.50 for expenditure cuts, but 0.48-0.65 for tax increases.[14]

3.2.3 Non-Household Savings: Conclusion

The evidence strongly suggests that raising corporate and public sector savings are effective means to raise the national savings rate. Furthermore, the fact that the successful east Asian economies are clear outliers in this respect, with public and corporate savings not only absolutely larger but also accounting for a larger share of total savings compared to less rapidly growing economies (EDWARDS, 1995), is quite suggestive.

There are two concerns, however. The first, to which we return below, is the relative efficiency of use of public versus private sector savings. The second is the realism of a substantial shift in eastern Europe. Substantial shifts in private sector savings from households to the corporate sector may encounter political resistance: in Russia, to quote just one example, a full two thirds of survey respondents now assert that the move to private property rights has not benefited them, a number that has sharply increased over the last years and bodes ill for the prospects of further supply side reform. Raising public sector savings through expenditure cuts may also be quite difficult at a time when decaying infrastructure and the social cost of transition impose sizeable demands on the budget. Finally, the scope for revenue increases appears curtailed by the ongoing tendency of economic activity to migrate towards the informal sector - latest estimates put the size of the informal sector in Ukraine at close to half of the official sector.

4. Savings: Allocative Aspects

Attaining a level of national savings commensurate with the investment target is a necessary condition for rapid growth in the transition economies. Yet raising the volume of savings is only part of the answer. After all, the failure of the socialist economies partly reflected the inability to deliver growth despite savings and investment ratios of almost Asian magnitudes. The second necessary condition, to which we now turn, is the efficiency of savings allocation.

Investment finance can be achieved internally - through retained earnings - or externally via debt or equity issue or bank loans. The financial systems inherited by the transition economies were singularly ill equipped to deal efficiently with external financing (CAPRIO, 1995; CAPRIO and LEVINE, 1994; FRIES and LANE, 1994). Financial arrangements followed the plan, banks did not conduct risk-return calculations, nor did they need to: bankruptcy risk was non-existent. In consequence, none of the mechanism of dealing with risk - from the existence of a uniformly applied accounting system suitable for risk assessment to the existence of insurance markets - were in place when the planning system crumbled.

Since then, substantial progress has been made, small equity markets are active in many transition economies - indeed, several transition economy country funds trade on international exchanges - markets for government paper have developed and commercial banks have sprung into existence. The financial widening is likely to continue, indeed, there are strong indications that it will accelerate as feedback effects between asset markets and new financial institutions emerge. And yet, as we argue below, the ongoing financial growth conceals structural weaknesses which will, for some time to come, sharply curtail the role of external finance for investment financing.

4.1 Bank Loans

The ability of banks to extend credit is and will likely remain sharply limited by four factors: a lack of collateral, the scarcity of qualified loan officers to supervise non-collateralized loans, the lending constraints imposed by existing bad debts and the difficulty to collect on bad loans. The continuing lack of well developed real estate property rights and markets is of particular importance in the first respect, as it sharply reduces the scope for the most common instance of collateralized loans. The issue of bad loans and the associated incentive distortions is itself the subject of an extended literature going beyond the scope of this paper, what matters for the current purpose is that the incentive to continue rollover and new lending to troubled customers - partly due to cross ownership, partly due to expectations of an eventual government bailout and partly to avoid triggering supervisory consequences - sharply limits the availability of fresh loans to new enterprises. The relative importance of these problems differs sharply across the transition economies: the Visegrad group is gradually approaching western standards though it is still suffering from human capital shortage and implementation flaws (GRAY, 1993) while some of the FSU republics, including the Ukraine, have not significantly budged from the starting points.

To some degree, the opening of the domestic banking system to foreign competition eases these constraints (BAKKER, 1993). However, while a number of countries have gone a considerable distance towards allowing foreign bank involvement, with few exceptions the customer base of these banks tends to be focused on the local blue chip companies, thus providing little relief for start-ups and the currently underdeveloped but crucial mid-size firms.

Table J4 Development of Banking System

	C-S	Hun.	Pol.	Bul.	Rom.	Rus.
Pre-transition						
State Commercial Banks	2	3	9	59	4	5
State Forex Banks	3	1	3	1	1	1
State Savings Banks	2	1	1	1	1	1
Other State Banks	1	10	3	8	1	3
Latest						
Private Banks	43	32	72	7	9	2200
- with foreign stake	18	18	7	3	5	NA
Private Banks Assets/Total	57	25	11	NA	20	NA

Source: CAPRIO (1995, p. 261).

While these shortcomings are - with the exception of human capital shortages - in principle capable of rapid improvement, bank lending in the transition economies also suffers from a more fundamental problem: compared to most economies, the distribution of future payoffs - even in the presence of perfect accounting standards - is significantly more dispersed than in established market economies, not least because the institutional system itself is evolving. In consequence, risk adjusted lending rates, in particular for long term projects, are sharply above levels observed elsewhere, leading both to high profitability thresholds for externally financeable investment projects and, maybe more importantly, to a continuing credit crunch (CALVO and CORICELLI, 1994).

In conjunction, the combination of institutional obstacles and information problems suggest that bank finance will largely flow to the more established and large enterprises with track records and to easily monitorable projects, suggesting that small, new and risky ventures will have difficulty obtaining loans. There is also, as MCKINNON (1991) among others has argued, a not insubstantial probability that the distorted incentives, in particular of formerly state owned banks with substantial bad loan exposure, coupled with the human capital shortages in the bank supervision, will continue to create significant and costly problems in the banking system, with Hungary being a prime example. While one may not agreed with McKinnon's almost rejection of bank lending in the early transition, there is clearly a case for recognizing that significant lending activity beyond the behemoths is technically unlikely, and that rapid growth of credit extended by undercapitalized and undersupervised banks carries substantial systemic risks and may thus not be desirable in any case.[15]

4.2 Equity

Equity markets have played a significant role in the financial transition, to the point that a number of east European closed end funds are now trading on western exchanges. The prominence of these markets however obfuscates an important stock-flow distinction: the existing active equity markets predominantly trade equities created during the one-time transfer of enterprises from the public to the private sector. What remains to be seen is whether these markets are capable of absorbing additional share issues in a sustainable manner and, more importantly, whether successful new offerings are limited to blue chips or whether a vibrant secondary issue market can arise to fulfill part of the venture capital role. The answer to these questions lies largely in the overall development of the financial markets: the creation of private pension funds, sound insurance companies and mutual funds, coupled with accounting standards will have important feedback effects on the vibrancy and absorptive capacity of the equity markets (CAPRIO and LEVINE, 1994, inter alia). But, as argued above, with the possible exception of the Visegrad economies, it is unlikely that these conditions are fulfilled before the turn of the century.

4.3 Sources of Financing: Conclusion

There is ample reason to believe that - conditional on property rights and supervision etc. being implemented - strong feedback links between pension plans, mutual funds, equity and debt markets will generate quite wide and deep financial markets within the next decade. Indeed, a gradual assumption by banks and other intermediaries of a more important role in channeling resources to investment projects is - if history is a guide - a necessary condition for sustained growth (MCKINNON, 1973; SHAW, 1973; FRY, 1988; GELB, 1989; CALOMIRIS and KHAN, 1991). Until now, however, and for the medium term future, the role of financial intermediaries - be it banks or mutual funds - in the allocation of new funds has and will remain limited. In consequence, it is doubtful whether public sector savings can be efficiently channeled to investment projects through the banking system. As there is little reason for optimism regarding the efficiency of direct state loans, this implies that from an efficiency point of view, the importance of retained earnings is further enhanced. Of course, exclusive reliance on retained earnings does not resolve the problem of providing venture capital, yet given the distortions in the financial system, the preferential allocation of investment funds to profitable enterprises implied by a reliance on retained earnings seems to provide at least a satisfactory solution to the allocative efficiency problem.

5. Conclusion

Is the eastern Europe of the year 2010 more likely to resemble the Asia or the Latin America of the present? While every country will go its own way, the evidence to date suggests that the more pessimistic Latin scenario is more likely: while in Asia, capital inflows complemented already high domestic savings, generating investment ratios in the thirty percent range and growth rates doubling per capita income every decade, capital inflows to eastern Europe - just as to Latin America - substitute for already more modest domestic savings, leading to consumption booms with declining investment rates.

Looking forward, the prospects for a significant increase in investment are also quite dim, a reflection of low and declining savings rates. Households savings, while likely to be stimulated by resumed income growth as the transition economies pass the nadir of the adjustment J-curve, are subject to significant downward pressure from demographic developments and financial liberalization. Public sector savings in most transition economies remain negative as governments grapple with the dual challenge of updating infrastructure while buffering the social aspects of transition in an environment of declining revenues. Finally, political backlash in many of the transition economies limits the scope for determined supply side reforms that would stimulate corporate savings. The latter are likely to prove crucial: as a combination of inherited bad debt, incentive problems, human capital constraints and lacking collateral inhibits external finance for all but a core group of enterprises, the old standby, retained earnings, will have to be the main source of investment finance for the next few years.

The overall rather gray outlook, however, hides some bright spots: five years after the collapse of the socialist regimes, substantial differentiation between the transition economies has emerged. A core group of determined reformers, notably the Czech Republic, has made great strides both in institutional reform and in achieving substantial public savings and may well live up to the rosy initial expectations. For the great majority of sluggish adjusters, the prospects for a high savings-high investment growth scenario appear however dim.

Endnotes

1 I thank Desmond McCarthy, Heinrich Matthes and participants at the *Banking, International Capital Flows and Growth in Europe* conference in Potsdam, October 13-14, 1995 for helpful comments.

2 A recent WORLD BANK (1995) study puts the required amount at 250 bn US$ annually for the next decade.

3 To the extent that the transition economies will have an above normal stock of expatriate workers, the figure may transitionally be higher, however, the available evidence on international migration suggests that if growth takes off, these workers will return.

4 There is however an argument to be made that the decline is mitigated by an increase in the quality of investment projects undertaken.

5 For comprehensive general surveys on savings behavior, see AGHLEVI et al. (1990), BAYOUMI et al. (1995), DEATON (1990, 1995), DOSHI (1994), GERVOSITZ (1988), HONOHAN (1995), KOTLIKOFF (1989), SCHMIDT-HEBBEL et al. (1992, 1994).

6 See e.g. EDWARDS (1995).

7 In the presence of changes in trend income growth, such as arguably took place around 1973, the positive correlation is hard to reconcile with the unconstrained optimization model. Borrowing constraints provide a possible explanation.

8 See BLINDER (1975), BOSKIN (1978), EDWARDS (1995), EVANS (1983), GIOVANNINI (1983), HONOHAN (1994), HOWREY and HYMANS (1978), MAKIN and COUCH (1989), OGAKI, OSTRY and REINHART (1994), SUMMERS (1981, 1985), TULLIO and CONTESSO (1986) inter alia.

9 OGAKI, OSTRY and REINHART (1995) present evidence that the elasticity increases in income, as does, in consequence, the responsiveness of savings to the rate of return.

10 Again we focus on the first order effect. The evidence for an effect of tax policy on investment is stronger, there thus may again be a second order effect on savings through higher growth.

11 The observed relaxation of qualification standards, in particular in Poland., may furthermore exert a downward pressure.

12 For the case of mortgages, JAPELLI and PAGANO (1994) estimate in cross-section that a 15 percent reduction in the ratio of required down payment to price reduces the national savings rate

by a quite sizeable 2.6 percent. MILES (1992) and BAYOUMI (1993) likewise find substantial negative effects of financial liberalization, specifically, housing finance.

[13] Though see also SEATER (1993).

[14] Thus a one dollar increase in public savings due to an expenditure cut (a revenue increase) will raise national savings by 0.50-0.84 $ (by 0.35-0.52 $).

[15] This is not to argue against a long term role of bank finance, nor against the various innovative steps suggested to create sound banks in transition environment, such as LONG and TALLEY's (1994) International Standards Bank proposal and similar plans to avoid the "heads I win, tails the government loses" incentive faced by zero or negative net worth banks.

References

AGHLEVLI, B., BOUGHTON, J., MONTIEL, P., VILLANUEVA, D. and WOGLOM, G. (1990), "The Role of National Saving in the World Economy," IMF Occasional Paper No. 67.

AHMAD, E., LUGARESI, S., MOURMOURAS, A. and SCHNEIDER, J.-L. (1994), "Pensions, Price Shocks, and Macroeconomic Stability in Transition Economies: Illustrations from Belarus," IMF Working Papers No. 94/52.

AIYAGARI, S. (1994), "Uninsured Idiosyncratic Risk and Aggregate Saving," *Quarterly Journal of Economics*, Vol. 109, 659-684.

AUERBACH, A. and KOTLIKOFF, L. (1992), "The Impact of the Demographic Transition on Capital Formation," in KOSKELA, E. and PAUNIO, J. (eds.), *Savings Behavior,* Blackwell Publishers, Oxford.

BAKKER, M. (1993), "Twinning as a Tool for Institutional Development of Banks," Mimeo, World Bank.

BARRO, R. (1974), "Are Government Bonds Net Wealth?," *Journal of Political Economy*, Vol. 81, 1095-1117.

BAYOUMI, T. (1993), "Financial Deregulation and Household Saving," *Economic Journal*, Vol. 103, 1432-1443.

BAYOUMI, T., MASSON, P. and SAMIEI, H. (1995), "International Evidence on the Determinants of Private Saving," IMF Working Paper No. 95/51.

BERNHEIM, D. (1987), "Ricardian Equivalence: An Evaluation of Theory and Evidence," in FISCHER, S. (ed.), *NBER Macroeconomics Annual*, MIT Press, Cambridge, Mass.

BHATIA, K. (1979), "Corporate Taxation, Retained Earnings, and Capital Formation," *Journal of Public Economics*, Vol. 11, No. 1, 123-34.

BLACK, S. W. and MOERSCH, M. (1995), "Investment and its financing during the transition in central and eastern Europe," Conference Paper.

BLINDER, A. (1975), "Distribution Effects and the Aggregate Consumption Function," *Journal of Political Economy*, Vol. 83, No. 3, 447-475.

BORENSZTEIN, E. and MONTIEL, P. (1991), "Savings, Investment and Growth in Eastern Europe," IMF Working Paper No. 91/61.

BOSWORTH, B. (1993), *Savings and Investment in the Open Economy*, Brookings, Washington D.C.

BOSKIN, M. (1978), "Taxation, Savings and the Rate of Interest," *Journal of Political Economy,* Vol. 86, Supplement.

BOVENBERG, L. (1989), "Tax Policy and National Saving in the United States," *National Tax Journal*, Vol. 42, June, 123-38.

CABALLERO, R. (1990), "Consumption Puzzles and Precautionary Savings," *Journal of Monetary Economics*, Vol. 25.

CALOMIRIS, C. and KHAN, C. (1991), "The Role of Demandable Debt in Structuring Optimal Banking Arrangements," *American Economic Review*, Vol. 81, No. 3, 497-513.

CALVO, G. and CORICELLI, F. (1994), "Credit Market Imperfections and Output Response in Previously Centrally Planned Economies," in CAPRIO et al., *Building Sound Finance in Emerging Market Economies*, IMF-World Bank, Washington D.C.

CALVO, G., SAHAY, R. and VEGH, C. (1995), "Capital Flows in Central and Eastern Europe," IMF Working Paper No. 57/95.

CAMPBELL, J. and DEATON, A. (1989), "Why is Consumption so Smooth?" *Review of Economic Studies*, Vol. 56, 357-74.

CAMPBELL, J. and MANKIW, G. (1990), "Permanent income, current income and consumption," *Journal of Business and Economic Statistics*, Vol. 8, 265-79.

CAMPBELL, J. and MANKIW, G. (1991), "The Response of Consumption to Income: A Cross-Country Investigation," *European Economic Review*, Vol. 35, 723-57.

CAPRIO, G. (1995), "The role of financial intermediaries in transitional economies," *Carnegie-Rochester Conference Series on Public Policy*, Vol. 42, 257-302.

CAPRIO, G. and LEVINE, R. (1994), "Reforming Finance in Transitional Socialist Economies," *World Bank Research Observer*, Vol. 1, No. 9, 1-26.

CARROLL, C. and SUMMERS, L. (1987), "Why Have Private Savings Rates in the United States and Canada Diverged?" *Journal of Monetary Economics*, Vol. 20, September, 247-79.

CARROLL, C. and SUMMERS, L. (1991), "Consumption Growth Parallels Income Growth," in BERNHEIM, D. and SHOVEN, J. (eds.), *National Saving and Economic Performance*, NBER, Chicago.

CARROLL, C. and WEIL, D. (1993), "Savings and Growth: A Reinterpretation," NBER Working Paper No. 4470.

CHO, Y.-L. and KHATKHATE, D. (1989), "Lessons of Financial Liberalization in Asia," World Bank Discussion Paper No. 50.

COLLINS, S. (1991), "Saving Behavior in Ten Developing Countries," in BERNHEIM, D. and SHOVEN, J. (eds.), *National Saving and Economic Performance*, NBER, Chicago.

CONWAY, P. (1995), "Saving In Transition Economies," Mimeo, World Bank.

CORBO, V. and SCHMIDT-HEBBEL, K. (1991), "Public Policies and Saving in Developing Countries," *Journal of Development Economics*, Vol. 36, 1.

CORSETTI, C. and SCHMIDT-HEBBEL (1995), "Pension Reform and Growth," Mimeo, World Bank.

CUKIERMAN, A., EDWARDS, S. and TABELLINI, G. (1992), "Seignorage, Political Instability and Inflation," *American Economic Review*, Vol. 72, June.

DEATON, A. (1990), "Savings in Developing Countries," *World Bank Economic Review*.

DEATON, A. (1995), "Growth and Savings: What do we know, and what might we learn?" Mimeo, Princeton University.

DELONG, B. and SUMMERS, L. (1991), "Equipment Investment and Economic Growth," *Quarterly Journal of Economics*, Vol. 106, August.

DIAMOND, P. and VALDES-PRIETO, S. (1994), "Social Security Reform," in BOSWORTH, B. et al. (eds.), *The Chilean Economy*, Brookings, Washington D.C.

DOSHI, K. (1994), "Determinants of the Saving Rate: An International Comparison," *Contemporary Economic Policy*, Vol. 12, January, 37-47.

EDWARDS, S. (1995), "Why Are Latin America's Savings Rates So Low?" Mimeo, World Bank.

EVANS, O. (1983), "Tax Policy, the Interest Elasticity of Saving, and Capital Accumulation," *American Economic Review*, Vol. 73, No. 3, 398-410.

FARUQEE, H. and HUSAIN, A. (1995), "Saving Trends in Southeast Asia," IMF Working Paper No. 95/39.

FELDSTEIN, M. (1973), "Tax Incentives, Corporate Saving, and Capital Accumulation in the United States," *Journal of Public Economics*, Vol. 2, No. 2, 159-171.

FELDSTEIN, M. (1980), "International Differences in Social Security and Saving," *Journal of Public Economics*, Vol. 12.

FELDSTEIN, M. (1994), "Fiscal Policy, Capital Formation and Capitalism," NBER Working Paper No. 4885.

FELDSTEIN, M. and HORIOKA, C. (1980), "Domestic Saving and International Capital Flows," *Economic Journal*, Vol. 90, June.

FELDSTEIN, M. and FANE, G. (1973), "Taxes, Corporate Dividend Policy and Personal Savings," *Review of Economics and Statistics*, Vol. 55, No. 4, 399-412.

FRIES, S. M. and LANE, T. (1994), "Transforming the Financial Structure in Emerging Market Economies," in CAPRIO et al., *Building Sound Finance in Emerging Market Economies*, IMF-World Bank, Washington D.C.

FRY, M. (1988), *Money, Interest and Banking in Economic Development*, Johns Hopkins University Press, Baltimore.

GELB, A. (1989), "Financial Policies, Growth and Efficiency," Policy Research Working Paper No. 202, World Bank, Washington, D.C.

GERSOVITZ, M. (1988), "Saving and Development," in CHENERY, H. and SRINIVASAN, T. (eds.), *Handbook of Development Economics*, North Holland, Amsterdam.

GIOVANNINI, A. (1983), "The Interest Elasticity of Savings in Developing Countries: The Existing Evidence," *World Development*, Vol. 11, July.

GRAHAM, E. (1995), "Foreign Direct Investment in the World Economy," IMF Working Paper No. 95/59.

GRAHAM, J. (1987), "International Differences in Saving Rates and the Life Cycle Hypothesis," *European Economic Review,* Vol. 31, 1509-29.

GRAMLICH, E. (1989), "Budget Deficits and National Saving: Are Politicians Exogenous?" *Journal of Economic Perspectives*, Vol. 3, No. 2, 23-36.

GRAY, C. (1993), "Debt Collection and Bankruptcy in Hungary," Mimeo, World Bank, Washington, D.C.

GUISO, L., JAPPELLI, T. and TERLIZZESE, T. (1992), "Earnings Uncertainty and Precautionary Savings," CEPR Discussion Paper No. 699.

HAQUE, N. and MONTIEL, P. (1989), "Consumption in Developing Countries," *Review of Economics and Statistics*, Vol. 121, No. 3, 408-15.

HAYASHI, F. (1985), "The effect of liquidity effects on consumption," *Quarterly Journal of Economics*, Vol. 100, 183-206.

HELLER, P. (1989), "Aging, Savings, and Pensions in the Group of Seven Countries," IMF Working Paper No. 89/13.

HOLZMANN, R. (1994), "Funded and private pensions for Eastern European countries in transition?" *Analisis Economico*, Vol. 9, No. 1, 183-210.

HONOHAN, P. (1995), "The Impact of Financial and Fiscal Policies on Saving," Mimeo, ESRI.

HOWREY, P. and HYMANS, S. (1978), "The Measurement and Determination of Loanable Funds," *Brookings Papers on Economic Activity*, No. 3, 655-685.

IMF (1994), "Eastern Europe - Factors Underlying the Weakening Performance of Tax Revenues," IMF Working Paper No. 94/104.

IMF (1995), *World Economic Outlook*, May.

JAPPELLI, T. and PAGANO, M. (1991), "Saving, Growth and Liquidity Constraints," CEPR Discussion Paper, December.

JAPELLI, T. and PAGANO, M. (1994), "Saving, Growth, and Liquidity Constraints," *Quarterly Journal of Economics*, Vol. 109, February.

JOURNAL OF ECONOMIC PERSPECTIVES (1995), "Symposium: Consumption Smoothing in Developing Countries," Vol. 9, No. 3, Summer, 81-128.

KING, R. and LEVINE, R. (1993), "Finance and Growth: Schumpeter Might Be Right," World Bank Policy Research Working Paper No. 1083.

KING, R. and LEVINE, R. (1994), "Capital Fundamentalism, Economic Development, and Economic Growth," World Bank Policy Research Working Paper No. 1285, April.

KOSKELA, E. and PAUNIO, J. (eds.) (1992), *Savings Behavior*, Blackwell Publishers, Oxford.

KOTLIKOFF, L. (1989), *What determines savings?*, MIT Press, Cambridge, Mass.

LEFF, N. (1969), "Dependency rates and savings rates," *American Economic Review*, Vol. 59, No. 5, 886-96.

LEVY, J. and OSTRY, J. D. (1994), "Household Saving in France," IMF Working Paper No. 94/136.

LONG, M. and TALLEY, S. (1994), "Strengthening the Russian Banking System," in CAPRIO et al., *Building Sound Finance in Emerging Market Economies*, IMF-World Bank, Washington, D.C.

MADDISON, A. (1992), "A Long-Run Perspective on Savings," in KOSKELA, E. and PAUNIO, J. (eds.), *Savings Behavior*, Blackwell Publishers, Oxford.

MAKIN, J. and COUCH, K. (1989), "Saving, Pension Contributions, and the Real Interest Rate," *Review of Economics and Statistics,* Vol. 121, No. 3, 401-7.

MASSON, P. and TYRON, R. (1990), "Macroeconomic Effects of Projected population Aging in Industrial Countries," *IMF Staff Papers*, Vol. 37, 453-85.

MCKINNON, R. (1973), *Money and Capital in Economic Development*, Brookings, Washington, D.C.

MCKINNON, R. (1991), *The Order of Economic Liberalization: Financial Control in the Transition to a Market Economy*, Johns Hopkins University Press, Baltimore.

MILES, D. (1992), "Housing Markets, Consumption and Financial Liberalization in the Major Economies," *European Economic Review*, Vol. 36, 1093-1135.

MODIGLIANI, F. (1986), "Life Cycle, Individual Thrift and the Wealth of Nations," *American Economic Review*, Vol. 76, June, 297-313.

MUELLBAUER, J. (1994), "The Assessment: Consumer Expenditure," *Oxford Review of Economic Policy*, Vol. 10, 1-39.

MUSGRAVE, P. and MUSGRAVE, R. (1984), *Public Finance in Theory and Practice*, McGraw-Hill, New York.

OBSTFELD, M. (1995), "Effects of Foreign Resource Inflows on Savings," Mimeo, UC Berkeley.

OGAKI, M., OSTRY, J. and REINHART, C. (1994), "Saving Behavior in Low- and Middle-Income Developing Countries: A Comparison," IMF Working Paper No. 95/3.

POTERBA, J. (1987), "Tax Policy and Corporate Savings," *Brookings Papers on Economic Activity*, No. 2, 455-515.

ROSSI, N. (1988), "Government Spending, the Real Interest Rate, and the Behavior of Liquidity Constrained Consumers in Developing Countries," IMF Staff Papers; Vol. 35, 104-40.

SCHMIDT-HEBBEL, K., WEBB, S. and CORSETTI, G. (1992), "Household Savings in Developing Countries," *World Bank Economic Review*, Vol. 6, September.

SCHMIDT-HEBBEL, K., SERVEN, L. and SOLIMANO, A. (1994), "Savings and Investment," Mimeo, World Bank, Washington, D.C.

SEATER, J. (1993), "Ricardian Equivalence," *Journal of Economic Literature*, Vol. 31, 142-190.

SHAW, E. (1973), *Financial Deepening in Economic Development*, Oxford University Press, New York.

SMITH, R. (1989), "Factors Affecting Saving, Policy Tools, and Tax Reform," IMF Working Paper No. 89/47.

SUMMERS, L. (1981), "Capital Taxation and Accumulation in a Life Cycle Growth Model," *American Economic Review*, Vol. 71, No. 4, 533-544.

SUMMERS, L. (1985), "Issues in national savings policy," NBER Working Paper No. 1710.

TULLIO, G. and CONTESSO, F. (1986), "Do After-Tax Interest Rates Affect Private Consumption and Savings?" Economic Papers; Commission of the EC, No. 51.

VON FURSTENBERG, G. (1981), "Saving,"in AARON, H. and PECHMAN, J. (eds.), *How Taxes Affect Economic Behavior*, Brookings, Washington, D.C.

WEIL, D. (1991), "What Determines Savings?" *Journal of Monetary Economics*.

WEIL, P. (1995), "Prudence, Heterogeneity and Borrowing Constraints," Mimeo.

WELFENS, P. J. J. (1992), "Foreign Investment in the East European Transition," *Management International Review*.

WHITE, H. (1992), "The macroeconomic impact of development aid," *Journal of Development Studies*, Vol. 28, 163-240.

WORLD BANK (1995), "Global Capital Supply and Demand," Mimeo, Washington, D.C.

ZELDES, S. (1989), "Consumption and Liquidity Constraints: An Empirical Investigation," *Journal of Political Economy*, Vol. 97, April.

Comments on
Savings, Credit Markets and Economic Growth in Europe

Heinrich Matthes

1. Introduction

I very much liked reading through the interesting paper by Mr. Wolf. I share most of his findings and agree with his principal conclusions. The paper has one important limitation. It was written under the assumption that more priority should be given to increasing aggregate saving to match aggregate "target" investment rather than to look at the microeconomic issue, that means, matching particular investment projects with funds.

However, I think that especially the experience with the transition process in east Germany and in central and eastern Europe has shown how important it is to get the institutions right and to get structural adjustment on track.

Indeed, under the socialist system, the countries of central and eastern Europe and the former Soviet Union displayed very high saving and investment ratios by international standards. We all know about the poor results of these high ratios. This shows that not the amount of savings and investment is crucial for economic success, but the quality of the projects the available savings are invested in. Consequently, at least in nuances, I disagree with the author on this issue.

2. Saving/Investment Trends since the Beginning of the Transformation Process

Since beginning pro-market reforms, practically all transition countries have suffered a sharp decline in their savings ratio.

The decline in investment/GDP ratios is explained by the reduction in corporate investment and, to a lesser extent, public investment. The usual negative impact of recession on enterprise investment has been augmented by the negative implications of transition itself, that means

- increased economic and political uncertainty,
- "pre-privatization agony", and
- the absence of well-functioning domestic financial markets.

3. The Allocation of Savings - Evidence

Unfortunately, reduced savings were often not channeled into projects which yielded the highest expected rate of return. In a large number of countries the pool of scarce private savings has been mostly absorbed by the state. The remaining part has often been channeled by the weak, non-competitive and largely state-owned banking system to loss-making enterprises and sectors, perpetuating the "soft-budget constraint" for these enterprises.

Consequently, I agree with the author when he assumes that the future recovery of investment ratios in transition countries is likely to be mostly financed by an increase in domestic saving, particularly corporate saving. This is also what the latest Commission macroeconomic forecasts for the associated countries and the latest projections contained in the IMF World Economic Outlook imply. Moreover, it is consistent with the fact that the recent recovery of corporate investment in the most advanced central European countries has been largely self-financed through an improvement in enterprise profitability.

The reason for the dominance of self-financing of enterprise investment is the limited access to external financing:

- foreign banks concentrate their activities on blue chips and the public sector (for example municipalities);

- domestic banks provide little ***long-term*** investment capital, since they lack human resources to evaluate investment projects, are still to a large extent under-capitalized, and they still subsidize loss-making enterprises through the roll-over of non-performing loans;
- domestic banks provide little investment capital at ***attractive terms*** as they still need a large lending-deposit spread to improve their balance sheets.

3.1 Improving the Allocation of Funds - Policy Recommendations

Which measures could be taken to improve the working of the financial sectors in these countries, and to provide enterprises with long-term capital at more favorable terms? There exist several possibilities. I would like to stress the following:

- Commercial banks have to be re-capitalized and their balance sheets have to be strengthened. This holds especially for those banks which have taken over the old claims against loss-making conglomerates. These banks still suffer from a high portion of non-performing loans which burden their capacity to provide capital for attractive investment projects.
- Competition in the domestic banking sector has to be increased. So far, most countries still have a banking sector which is characterized by regional or sectoral monopolies, mirroring the former structure under central planning. Regional saving banks are still dominating the market for private households savings, offering low interest rates to depositors, while sectoral investment banks are dealing with lending to "their" sector.
- Risk-assessment capacities in the banking sector will have to be substantially increased. This requires training efforts on a large scale, to be supported by international institutions.

4. Increasing Aggregate Saving

The author has focused in his discussion on the likely evolution of savings in eastern Europe on private households' savings. In principle, I agree with his findings. However, I would have appreciated a more profound discussion of the likely evolution of corporate savings since in the short and medium term the development of corporate savings will determine whether eastern Europe embarks on a success-story scenario or not.

Nevertheless, it is important to stabilize private households' savings which have eroded over recent years for different reasons (transition, access to western goods, shrinking real incomes, high or even hyperinflation in some countries).

How could domestic savings be increased in the short and medium term? The author rightly states that it is difficult to increase private households' savings by well targeted microeconomic instruments. I agree! I think: even more important than specific microeconomic instruments are macroeconomic policies that are set right.

Transition economies should pursue policies conducive to a stable macroeconomic framework and sustainable growth. In other words: 'stable money and sound finances' is what is required most in these countries. Increasing public savings is the safest and most direct way in which the authorities in these countries can have a positive impact on aggregate savings.

5. Which Scenario for Eastern Europe: Latin America or Asia?

The author's study is centered around the question in how far "the eastern Europe of 2010 will resemble Latin America or Asia". Will these countries see a "high growth - high saving" scenario, that means an Asian scenario, or will they suffer from a "low growth - low saving" scenario, that means the Latin American scenario?

However, the questions about Latin American versus Asian scenarios may be somewhat misleading and eastern Europe may follow its own path for the following reasons:

- Both Latin America and Asia were cases where rural economies had to be transformed into industrialized countries. The eastern European transformation process is about modernizing and restructuring industrialized countries with declining industries.
- Both Latin America and Asia had to build their infrastructure for an industrialized economy from scratch. In eastern Europe the capital stock is indeed in a bad shape, but it still serves as a basis on which one can expand.
- Asia, but especially Latin America were peripheral regions, their major markets located in North America and in Europe. However, for eastern Europe the main market, which is furthermore an open one, is directly in front of its main entrance.
- In both Asia and Latin America income distribution is characterized by the fact that large parts of the population still live at the subsistence level. Although the people of eastern Europe accept and already have accepted a considerable redistribution of income from labor to capital they will not follow the Asian path.
- For several decades Asia has run an extremely protectionist trade policy. Central and eastern European countries, namely the countries associated with the European Union, have substantially opened their domestic markets in response to the opening of the European Union's market. This market opening will not and should not be reversed. It will be beneficial for both sides.

In consequence, I am more optimistic than the author regarding the prospects for these countries' recovery process. But it will probably take decades before we will see a substantial **real** convergence with western Europe.

K. US Multinationals and Europe: An Update

Edward M. Graham

1. Introduction

Direct investment by US-based firms, once highly controversial in Europe, has become all but a non-issue. Long gone are the days of the late 1960s and early 1970s when "le défi americain" could dominate parlor talk in Europe. However, US direct investment in Europe has not gone away. Indeed, what has come to be termed the "globalization" of industry - largely the international spread of the operations of business firms into a multiplicity of nations via foreign direct investment (FDI) - has if anything accelerated since the middle 1980s. Indeed, FDI has been expanding at rates well above growth rates of either world output or world trade for about ten years now (United Nations 1991 and 1996). And, although not as dominant as a source (home) nation of FDI as thirty years earlier, a substantial portion of the world's direct investment is still carried out by US-based firms.

And, a very sizable fraction of this investment still takes place in Europe. Indeed, in very recent years, the percentage of US direct investment going into Europe has actually increased. Tables J1 and J2 tell an interesting story in this regard. At the end of 1991, just under 47% of the worldwide stock of US direct investment abroad was in Europe (Table K1). Of this, 40.3% was in the European Union, where the United Kingdom alone accounted for almost 16% of the worldwide stock. These shares are considerably in excess of Europe's, the EU's, or the UK's share of world income.

Table K1 US Direct Investment Position in Europe and the World (year end, 1991 and 1994)

Amounts in $US billions

	1991 amount	1991 per cent	1994 amount	1994 per cent
European Union	202.9	40.3	251.1	41.0
UK	79.8	15.9	102.4	16.7
Germany	32.4	6.4	39.9	6.5
France	21.6	4.3	27.9	4.6
Netherlands	20.3	4.0	24.2	4.0
Italy	15.1	3.0	15.0	2.5
Other Europe	32.7	6.5	49.0	8.0
Switzerland	25.7	5.1	34.5	5.6
Total Europe	235.2	46.7	300.2	49.0
Total World	502.6	100.0	612.1	100.0

Source: US Department of Commerce, Bureau of Economic Analysis, "U.S. Direct Investment Abroad: Detail for Historical-Cost Position and Related Capital and Income Flows, 1994", *Survey of Current Business*, August 1995.

Table K2 US New Equity Capital Ouflows (Direct Investment Abroad Account) for Europe and the World, 1992 - 1994

Amounts in $US billions

	amount	per cent
European Union	30.78	63.3
UK	11.19	23.0
Germany	4.07	8.4
France	6.56	13.5
Netherlands	NA	NA
Italy	2.24	4.6
Other Europe	2.17	4.5
Switzerland	0.39	0.8
Total Europe	32.95	67.8
Total World	48.61	100.0

Source: Same as for Table K1.

Given the sluggish economic performance of Europe contrasted with the performance of certain other nations, in particular the high growth nations of East Asia, one might have expected the European, EU, and UK shares of the stock of US direct investment abroad (USDIA) to have declined during the 1990s, but in fact this has not been the case.[1] Rather, at the end of 1994, the European share of the stock of USDIA had actually risen to 49%, the EU share to 41%, and the UK share to almost 17%. Indeed, with the exception of Italy (whose share indeed did fall) and the Netherlands (whose share remained about constant), the share of the stock of USDIA in all of the largest European nations rose between the end of 1991 and the end of 1994.

These increases in the share of stock of US direct investment abroad imply, of course, that Europe received even a larger share of flows of this investment during the early 1990s. The overall European share of US direct investment flows was 59.4% for the three years 1992, 1993, and 1994. The shares for the European Union and the United Kingdom were 44.0% and 20.6% respectively. (These last figures are not shown in the tables.)

Because direct investment figures include retained earnings, these rises in shares of flows might have been occasioned by exceptional earnings by European affiliates of US firms rather than by flows of new equity capital. However, this was not the case. New equity capital outflows by US firms on direct investment abroad account, consisting mostly of new direct investments, were even more concentrated in Europe during the early 1990s than were stocks or total flows of direct investment. Indeed, during the years 1992-1994, Europe received a staggering 67.8% of these flows, with the EU receiving 63.3%, the UK alone 23%, and France 13.5% (Table K2).

It has been noted elsewhere (e.g., GRAHAM, 1995) that direct investment flows to a nation or region do not correspond exactly to contributions to capital formation by US-based multinational firms. A better measure of the latter is capital expenditures by majority owned affiliates of US firms in the nation or region. With respect to these expenditures, they also were heavily concentrated in Europe during the 1990s, but the dominance of Europe by this measure was somewhat less pronounced than by the flow of total direct investment or new equity measures. In 1993, this share was 51.4%, down from a recent high of 57.1% in 1992. Table K3 summarizes the relevant figures.

Majority-owned affiliates of US firms in Europe seem to contribute about 3% of gross fixed capital formation in Europe (Table K4).[2] This figure is down from about 5% during the early 1980s. It is difficult to interpret exactly what this drop might imply.

Table K3 Capital Expenditures by Majority-Owned Affiliates of US Firms, 1991-94

Amounts of expenditures are in $US billions

	1991	1992	1993	1994
Total Worldwide	62.9	63.2	64.2	69.1
Europe	35.6	36.1	33.0	34.3
Europe as a percent of Total	56.6	57.1	51.4	49.6

Source: Bureau of Economic Analysis, US Commerce Department.

Table K4 Capital Expenditures by Majority-Owned Affiliates of US Companies in Europe (gross amounts, $ billions, and as percent of gross fixed capital formation) 1991-93

	1991	1992	1993
1. capital expenditures in Europe of Affiliates of US Firms	36.1	33.0	34.3
2. gross fixed capital formation in Europe	1,264.	1,243.5	1,182.7
1. as a percent of 2.	2.86	2.65	2.90

Sources: Capital expenditures of affiliates of US firms, from US Commerce Department, Bureau of Economic Analysis, *Survey of Current Business*, September 1994; fixed capital formation from Organisation for Economic Cooperation and Development, *Main Economic Indicators*, March 1995, national accounts tables.

2. Possible Reasons for US Direct Investment in Europe

These figures all would suggest that US direct investment in Europe as a proportion of total US direct investment worldwide is out of line with the relative importance of Europe in the world economy. It is particularly striking that recent US investment in Europe - whether measured by financial flows (new equity on direct investment account) or by actual contributions to fixed capital formation (capital expenditures by majority owned affiliates of US firms) are out of proportion to Europe's size in the world economy as well as to the potential contribution of Europe to world economic growth during the coming years. The issue addressed by this short essay is, why might be this so? Several possible reasons are offered as hypothesis, but no definitive answer can be given as to which, if any, of the hypotheses is correct. These hypotheses include:

A. Fear of US firms that European protectionism will increase in the future, and that this protectionism will be directed towards the United States.

This hypothesis would have made more sense during the late 1980s, when the "Europe 1992" program was being formulated. During this earlier time, much the same thing could have been said about US direct investment as has already been said about it during the early 1990s, notably that it was disproportionately directed towards Europe. During the formative years of Europe 1992, there were at least some reasonable grounds for fear that Europe might turn sharply protectionist. At least some of the framers of the 1992 program, including Jacques Delors, then President of the European Union, made public statements that had protectionist overtones. Thus, although the almost three hundred draft directives that constituted the action plan for 1992 were not in themselves protectionist, a protectionist "fortress Europe" was a concept that the US business press nonetheless took seriously.

In the end, of course, 1992 did not take a protectionist turn. Rather, following implementation of the reforms of Europe 1992 and the Maastricht Treaty, the renamed European Union was generally more open and more liberal with respect to trade than it had been during the previous decade. Indeed, during the next year, the European Union helped to bring to a conclusion the mostly liberalizing reforms of the Uruguay Round of multilateral trade negotiations. Also, the European Union at the time of this writing is pushing for the new World Trade Organization (WTO), at its ministerial meeting to be held in Singapore in December 1996, to begin work in new liberalizing directions (such as trade and competition policy). "Fortress Europe" seems to have passed into oblivion sometime in the early part of this decade.

It is possible that US direct investment in Europe during the 1990s has, however, to date reflected decisions made at an earlier time when "fortress Europe" was still a plausible possibility. After all, direct investment undertakings generally require long lead times from inception to execution (at least two to three years), and investments made in 1994 might be the result of decisions made in 1991 or even earlier. If this is so, then the disproportionately large direct investments of US firms in Europe of the early 1990s could reflect earlier fears of European protectionism that now are passé.

If this is so, one likely consequence is that the proportion of US direct investment flowing to Europe will undergo sharp curtailment in the very near future. Also, again assuming that recent US direct investment in Europe has been motivated by fears of protectionism, one characteristic of this investment would be that US exports will be displaced by local production. This author has presented empirical evidence elsewhere (GRAHAM, 1996) that, worldwide, US direct investment and US exports are in net complements rather than substitutes.[3] This in fact seems especially so for US direct investment in Europe. If recent US direct investment in Europe is primarily a reaction against potential European protectionism, this complementarity would thus be expected to weaken.

Table K5 US Exports and Imports Associated with Majority-Owned Foreign Affiliates of US Firms

Manufacturing sector only, 1993 ($US billions)

	US Exports Shipped to Affiliates by US Parent Firms	US Imports Shipped by Affiliates to all customers	US Imports Shipped by Affiliates to US Parent Firms
Total	66.55	87.00	77.39
Europe	17.36	12.76	11.62
(% of Total)	(26.1)	(14.7)	(15.0)
Canada	27.66	42.22	36.19
(% of Total)	(41.6)	(48.5)	(46.8)
Latin America	12.73	13.85	13.49
(% of Total)	(19.1)	(15.9)	(17.4)
Asia/Pacific	8.58	17.76	15.69
(% of Total)	(12.9)	(20.4)	(20.3)

Table K6 US Exports and Imports Associated with Majority-Owned Foreign Affiliates of US Firms, Less Canada and Mexico

Manufacturing sector only, 1993 ($US billions)

	US Exports Shipped to Affiliates by US Parent Firms	US Imports Shipped by Affiliates to all customers	US Imports Shipped by Affiliates to US Parent Firms
Total	29.11	33.33	29.87
Europe	17.36	12.76	11.62
(% of Total)	(59.6)	(38.3)	(38.9)
Latin America	2.96	2.42	2.16
(% of Total)	(10.2)	(7.3)	(7.2)
Asia/Pacific	8.58	17.76	15.69
(% of Total)	(29.5)	(53.3)	(52.5)

Source: (both tables) US Commerce Department, Bureau of Economic Analysis, *US Direct Investment Abroad: Operations of US Parent Companies and their Foreign Affiliates* (prelim. 1993 estimates)

We might note that, relative to the size of US direct investment in Europe, US trade generated by affiliates of US firms in Europe is low (see Table K5). For the manufacturing sector, only about 26% of all US exports to all majority owned foreign affiliates of US firms is to their European affiliates, while these European affiliates generate only about 15% of US imports, whether to parent firms or to all customers. However, these figures are heavily affected by cross-border trade between US parent firms and their affiliates in both Canada and Mexico, which in turn is governed by proximity effects. Taking this trade out of the total brings the European figures into line with the overall stock of US direct investment in Europe with respect to exports (Table K6). With this adjustment, almost 60% of US exports to all majority owned foreign affiliates is to European affiliates. However, the figures for US imports generated by these European affiliates remain low in proportion to the stock of US direct investment in Europe. Exactly why this is so is not clear. Perhaps what the figures in Tables J5 and J6 reveal is weak European comparative advantage in manufactured goods relative to the Asia/Pacific countries, whose trade shares by this measure are far higher than their investment shares. With respect to the predictions offered above, of course only time will tell.

B. US firms are very risk averse, and they see investment in the rapidly growing nations of East Asia as being very risky and prefer to place their resources instead into "safe" Europe.

This is an alternative hypothesis to the one posed immediately above: that is, the previous hypothesis could be restated that US firms have invested massively in Europe because they perceived that it was risky to their business <u>not</u> to do so, whereas the current hypothesis is that US firms do not invest in East Asia because they perceive it risky <u>to</u> do so. If this latter hypothesis is correct, however, a number of questions pose themselves. For example, exactly what are the risks in East Asia which US firms fear? Is it risk of expropriation? No major expropriations have occurred in East Asia since the 1970s. Do US firms fear that there is risk of an end to high growth, to be followed by a period of economic instability, such that there would be no future return on investments made now? If so, it would appear that US investors have, for quite a number of years running, "missed the boat" in the sense that growth in East Asia alone likely would have led to quite satisfactory returns on direct investment in the region.

Another, related hypothesis might be that policy regimes in many of the high performance East Asian nations are restrictive towards FDI and that, although US firms would like to expand their activities there, these firm have faced major obstacles when trying to gain entry into the region. However, there is a problem with this hypothesis: most of these nations have rapidly been liberalizing their policies during the past decade or so. Numerous barriers still remain, but entry is possible.

At the end of the day, perhaps all that can be said is that reasons for the low stocks and flows of USDIA in East Asia remain something of a mystery. Given the economic performances of many nations in the region, one might have expected the US direct investment presence there to be much greater than it is.

C. US firms are investing in new geographic areas, or new industries, in Europe

The possibility exists that US firms are investing in Europe in new sectors, or in new geographic areas, and that this accounts for the large percentage of total US direct investment activity in Europe during the 1990s. Table K7 examines the sectoral issue. As can be seen, the major changes that have occurred are that the percentages of the US direct investment position in Europe accounted for by petroleum slipped significantly and by manufacturing slightly. Other sectors correspondingly gained. Interestingly, however, the percentage of new equity funds flowing into the manufacturing sector actually was higher than the 1992 percentage of the direct investment position accounted for by this sector. Whatever caused the overall drop of the share of the manufacturing sector in the stock of direct investment (direct investment position), it was not lack of new equity investment.

Table K7 US Direct Investment Position in Europe at Year End 1992 and 1994, with New Equity Flows 1992-94, by Major Sector, as Percent of Total

Sector	Direct Investment Position, end-of-year 1992	Direct Investment Position, end-of-year 1994	Percent of Equity Flow, 1992-94
Petroleum	9.8	8.4	0.5
Manufacturing	37.8	36.1	45.3
Wholesale trade	11.8	12.1	7.9
Banking	4.3	4.5	5.3
Other Finance	29.2	31.3	20.4
Other Services	4.6	4.9	10.8
Other Sectors	2.5	2.5	9.9
Total	100.0	100.0	100.0

Source: Same as for Table K1

Overall, US direct investment in Europe did not grow in any sector fast enough for rapid sectoral expansion to account for the continuing dominance of Europe as a destination for US direct investment overall.

Table K8 indicates the direct investment position of the United States by country in Europe as a percentage of the total direct investment position for 1992 and 1994. As can be seen, the relative investment positions of some countries, notably Luxembourg and "all others" (mostly the nations of Eastern Europe comprise this last category), increased dramatically. However, the total magnitude of investments going to these areas is just not great enough for the rapid investment in them to account for the continuing dominance of Europe in US direct investment activity.

Table K8 US Direct Investment Position in Europe by Nation, as Percent of Total Direct Investment Position in Europe, 1992 and 1994

	Direct Investment Position, end-of-year 1992	Direct Investment Position, end-of-year 1994
Austria	0.6	0.5
Belgium	4.6	4.7
Denmark	0.7	0.7
Finland	0.1	0.2
France	10.1	9.3
Germany	13.3	13.3
Greece	0.1	0.1
Ireland	3.1	3.4
Italy	5.2	5.0
Luxembourg	0.8	1.9
Netherlands	8.3	8.0
Norway	1.5	1.4
Portugal	0.5	0.5
Spain	3.5	2.7
Sweden	0.8	0.9
Switzerland	11.5	11.5
Turkey	0.3	0.4
United Kingdom	34.2	34.1
Others	0.7	1.4
Total	100.0	100.0

Source: Same as for Table K1

D. US firms and European Firms are Reacting Strategically to Moves made by their Transatlantic Rivals

This possibility has been raised by this author elsewhere.[4] The essence of the argument is that firms that are strategic rivals (i.e., whose own decisions with respect to price, quantity, and investment in physical capital, human capital, and technology development both affect and are affected by similar decisions by competing firms) will mimic each other's moves. For example, if firm A decides to invest in the development of a particular new technology that could, were the investment to prove successful, embody that firm with attributes giving it competitive advantages over its rivals, other rival firms might make similar investments even if, in the absence of such a move by firm A, these rivals would not choose this particular investment alternative. This assumes a great deal of oligopolistic interdependence among these rivals in markets, but lack of out-and-out collusion. If firms actually colluded, in the example above they might agree to cross-license new technologies so as to exploit these jointly.[5] If the rival firms have headquarters in different national markets, they might be expected to invest quite heavily in each other's "home" markets, thus generating substantial FDI between those markets.

One naive test of this hypothesis is simply to examine European direct investment in the United States as a percentage of total such investment. Table K9 just below compares some results already presented in Tables J1 and J2 with comparable information pertaining to direct investment in the United States. What can be seen is that Europe is even more dominant as a source of direct investment in the United States as it is as a destination of US direct investment abroad when one looks at the total stock (direct investment position) but is somewhat less dominant when one looks at equity flows for 1991 to 1994. In spite of this diminished dominance, however, Europe is the major source of direct investment equity flows to the United States, accounting for over 43% of the total from all sources worldwide. This seems consistent with the proposition that US and European firms react strategically to each other, although these data are far from proving the proposition definitively.

A further naive test of this proposition is to examine US outward direct investment and to compare it with US inward direct investment on a sector-by-sector basis. This is done in Table K10. Unfortunately, what is depicted in this table is not the US direct investment position in Europe nor the European direct investment position in the United States. The US Commerce Department, purveyor of the data, does not publish detailed sector-by-sector data just for Europe. However, given this limitation, even a cursory examination of Table K10 suggests that there is some positive relationship between US outward and inward direct investment when broken down by manufacturing sector. A simple regression of the outward and inward positions gives a coefficient of 0.48, with a t-statistic of 3.02, indicating that the estimated coefficient is statistically significantly from zero in the 99% confidence interval.

US outward direct investment thus does appear concentrated in the same sectors as US inward direct investment, a result that suggests that there is indeed strategic rivalry among US-based multinational firms and their non-US rivals. This conclusion is, of course, a global one: it does not apply only or even particularly to rivalry between US and European firms.

Table K9 US Direct Investment Position and New Equity Outflows to and from Europe and the World

$US billions or percents, position figures for 1994, flow figures for 1991-94

	US Direct Investment Position in	Equity Outflows from US to	Direct Investment Position in US from	Equity Inflows to US from
European Union	251.1	30.78	273.7	59.0
as % of world	41.0	63.3	54.3	43.2
United Kingdom	102.4	11.19	113.5	25.9
as % of world	16.7	23.0	22.5	19.0
Germany	39.9	4.07	39.6	9.8
as % of world	6.5	8.4	7.8	7.2
World	612.1	48.61	504.4	136.5

Source: Bureau of Economic Analysis, US Commerce Department.

Table K10 US Outward and Inward Direct Investment Position by Major Manufacturing Industry

$US billions, 1994

Manufacturing Subsector	US Outward Direct Investment Position	US Inward Direct Investment Position
Food and kindred products	28.796	20.88
Industrial chemicals	19.796	29.06
Pharmaceuticals	15.472	21.063
Soaps, detergents, etc.	8.836	9.003
Agricultural chemicals	1.615	1.469
Other chemical products	5.919	6.708
Primary metals	2.454	7.385
Fabricated metal products	8.52	6.941
Office and Computing Machines	20.583	1.783
Other Machinery	9.842	9.911
Electronic components	10.518	5.535
Other electrical and electronic	10.404	14.628
Motor vehicles	26.641	3.492
Other transportation equipment	1.416	1.546
Textile products and apparel	2.442	2.474
Lumber and wood products	1.669	0.809
Paper products	11.942	3.832
Printing and publishing	2.153	11.673
Rubber products	4.581	3.671
Misc. plastics products	3.779	1.876
Glass products	1.85	2.042
Stone, clay, and other related products	2.956	8.891
Photographic equipment and supplies	4.237	0.084
Medical instruments	4.854	4.621
Other instruments	2.281	3.935
Tobacco manufactures	4.667	NA

Source: Bureau of Economic Analysis, US Commerce Department.

3. Conclusions

Overall, then, the evidence seems to be consistent with the notion that continuing US direct investment in Europe results, at least in substantial part, from strategic rivalry among US-based multinational firms and their European-based rivals.

Consistent with this hypothesis is the observation that continuing direct investment by European multinational firms in the United States is similarly motivated. This rather general proposition, while far from proven, seems to this author to be more reasonable than often-heard claims that both European direct investment in the United States and US direct investment in Europe are motivated by continuing fears of protectionism.

If this hypothesis is correct, the prediction would follow that US firms will continue to devote a substantial portion of their direct investment activity to Europe (and, correspondingly, European firms will continue to invest heavily in the United States). Overall, the effects of this should be positive. Rivalry among firms tends to promote innovation and dynamic growth and, indeed, this rivalry might help to explain the paradox of "how can the United States have grown as fast as it did during the past fifteen years while saving and investing so little?"

Endnotes

1 The United States is also the largest host nation to FDI, and the EU is the largest source of direct investment in the United States. The term "US direct investment abroad" is favored by the US Commerce Department, keeper of US data pertaining to FDI, in order that it not be confused with "foreign direct investment in the United States" (FDIUS).

2 The word "seem" is used because the two data series "capital expenditures by majority controlled affiliates of US firms" as published by the Bureau of Economic Analysis (BEA) of the US Department of Commerce and "gross fixed capital formation" as published by the Organisation for Economic Cooperation and Development (OECD) are constructed somewhat differently and hence are not strictly comparable. However, the two series do measure approximately the same thing, notably investment in fixed capital (e.g., machinery and structures).

3 This finding has also been reported by a number of other authors whose work is cited and summarized in GRAHAM (1996).

4 See GRAHAM (1978, 1990). See also DUNNING (1996) for a somewhat different perspective on this issue.

[5] They might also agree to develop the new technologies jointly.

References

DUNNING, J. H. (1996), "The International Development Path Reconsidered," in DUNNING, J. H. and NARULA, R. (eds.), *Foreign Direct Investment and Governments: Catalysts for Economic Restructuring*, Routledge, London.

GRAHAM, E. M. (1978), "Transatlantic Investment by Multinational Firms: A Rivalistic Phenomenon?" *Journal of Post Keynesian Economics*, Vol. 1, No. 1, 82-99.

GRAHAM, E. M. (1990), "Exchange of Threat between Multinational Corporations as an Infinitely Repeated Noncooperative Game," *The International Trade Journal*, Vol. 4, No. 3, 259-277.

GRAHAM, E. M. (1996), "On the Relationships Among Direct Investment and International Trade in the Manufacturing Sector: Empirical Results for the United States and Japan," to appear in ENCARNATION, D. (ed.), *Does Ownership Matter: Japanese Multinationals in East Asia*, Oxford University Press, Oxford and London, forthcoming.

Comments on
US Multinationals and Europe: An Update

Rolf Jungnickel

I feel a bit uneasy to comment on Edward Graham's excellent presentation since there is no major disagreement on the points he made. The only problem I have with the paper is that Graham raised many more questions than he answered. While this may be a result of the complexity of the issue, it leaves us with little information about how he believes US foreign direct investment (FDI) affects economic growth in the EU in practice, and it leaves me with few pegs for comments on Graham's views. In the following, after a general remark about the effects of (US) FDI, I concentrate on some structural aspects of US investment in Europe and in Germany in particular.[1]

Graham rightly emphasized the problem of measuring the effects of FDI on growth. One always has to have a perception of what would have happened were there no or less FDI. This issue of the "alternative position" has kept generations of economists busy, with not much progress so far. With increasing age and volume of FDI and with an increasing share of M&A as a mode of expansion abroad, detailed assumptions as to the alternative position become increasingly speculative and hence irrelevant. It seems to me that even the most sophisticated regression analysis Graham referred to cannot overcome these principal problems. When discussing the effects of US FDI on European growth we have to keep in mind these reservations.

Indeed, I hesitate to go along with the reasoning of the large scale study on the trade effects of US FDI Graham referred to. The result "FDI promotes US exports to Europe" has to be interpreted with caution:

- Generally, doubts are raised since one can hardly speak of export promoting effects if US production in Europe exceeds US exports to Europe by more than the factor 4. The local production/exports ratio has remained rather stable in recent years.

- What is identified as FDI effect, may have been the stimulating effect of a lower Dollar value on US exports - the value of the US$, expressed in European currencies, almost halved from the mid-1980s to the early 1990s.

While it is extremely difficult to determine "the" growth effects of US FDI, one can get an idea by looking at the volume, development, and structure of US affiliates in Europe.

1. Has US FDI Stimulated European Economic Growth?

Graham starts out with showing that the share of US multinational enterprises (MNEs) in European fixed capital formation dropped considerably from 5% in the early 1980s to around 3% ten years later. According to this yardstick, US FDI has to be considered rather unimportant for recent growth in Europe - a fundamental change since the late 1960s. However, the importance of US affiliates becomes more obvious if we look at absolute figures, at other indicators (which may be better comparable with national statistics of the host region) such as production, employment, and foreign trade, and at the structural dimension of US involvement in the European economy.

There are almost 2.5 million people working with US investors in western Europe, almost half of all foreign employment of US MNEs. Their share in the west European industrial workforce is about 5%. European manufacturing takes place to over 8% in US affiliates. These shares increased in the 1980s and have been rather stable since then. Thus, one can hardly speak of a generally reduced importance of US MNEs for European economic development. Europe has increasingly come into the limelight for US investors in the 1980s and early 1990s.

However, in my view, the main effects of US MNEs do not depend on the **volume** of their activities in Europe. The **structural** dimension is of greater importance. We have to consider the "quality" of American production in Europe and take into account the regional dimension. In the following, as an addition to Graham's paper, I therefore briefly deal with the question whether US investors contribute to European productivity growth by intensifying specialization and the international division of labor and thus promote structural change.

One could expect that US investors play a significant role for European economic development by **deepening the international division of labor**: They are more flexible in their locational decisions than their European counterparts since they are less bound to a traditional home market in Europe. Modern communication, information, and transportation technologies have drastically reduced distance costs and increased the possibility to split up the value-added chain and organize production processes on a wider regional scale according to locational advantages and scale economies. Investment and productivity have become more mobile. The reduction of barriers to trade and investment in the Internal Market supports this process. One should, therefore, expect a development towards fewer and more specialized production units which show above average and increasing export quotas. Production networking (PNW) is the catchword here. It should lead to structural change and increases in productivity and growth.

The PNW hypothesis was developed especially in various World Investment Reports (UNTCMD, 1992; UNCTAD, 1994). There is a lot of evidence on production networking by American multinationals in Europe (Ford, IBM etc.) which have often been regarded as institutions that most efficiently push forward European integration of production. However, the total picture is mixed. On the one hand, the export quota of slightly over 40% clearly surpasses the European average (about 33%) - American MNEs are thus an important factor for the development of a deeper international division of labor. On the other hand, there are substantial qualifications to be made:

- Exports of manufacturing US affiliates in Europe are largely of an intra-regional nature (according to the latest Benchmark Survey, about 90% are destined for other European countries - US DEPARTMENT Of COMMERCE, 1992). The affiliates account for about 18% of all intra-European trade in manufactures. While this helps to **intensify the intra-European division of labor**, US affiliates contribute little to the integration of Europe into the **worldwide** division of labor. "Globalization" of production goes along with regionalization of sales.

- Above average export quotas have increased only slightly as the Internal Market was implemented in the late 1980s (see Table k1). The jump between 1989 and 1992 (from 41% to 45%) probably was a result of diverging business cycles and, more particularly, the import boom of the united Germany. The quota fell back to 43% in 1993.

Table k1 Manufacturing Affiliates of US MNEs in the European Economy 1982-1993

US affiliates	absolute figures		p. c. of all foreign manufact. affiliates of US firms		p.c. of total manufact. in western Europe	
	1982	**1993**	**1982**	**1993**	**1982**	**1993**
Employment (1000)	1628	1516	49	47	5	5
Production ($bn)	145	356	54	57	7	9
R&D outlays ($bn)	2.3	6.6	74	72	8	7

Source: US Department of Commerce; OECD; own calculations.

Production networking, therefore, apparently is a more recent development. It is but one element of the FDI strategy of US firms. The other - still dominating - element is market orientation. The majority of sales of US-owned firms is still realized on the local market of the host countries. The FDI boom in the late 1980s was primarily driven by the desire to capture market positions rather than exploiting locational advantages opened up by the EC'92 program. This view is supported by empirical evidence:

- The FDI boom set in long before most EC'92 measures were realized;

- The mode of investment more often than not was acquisition rather than greenfield ventures;
- The FDI boom was characterized by cross investments rather than inter-sectoral specialization of subsidiaries in the individual countries.

US FDI in Europe thus has a **strong strategic element**. This is not to say that such investment is necessarily not as "good" for economic growth as cost-motivated investment. The problem is, however, that an assessment of the growth effects is much more difficult since effects on competition are extremely hard to be taken into account. The age of an investment certainly plays a role in this respect - Graham rightly pointed out that one can expect more pro-competitive effects the more recent an investment is. In my view, this question can only be assessed for individual markets on the basis of individual cases.

Two other structural elements of US affiliates are of relevance for economic growth: (1) **productivity advantages** and (2) **high R&D intensity**. Both can be seen from Table k1. The share of US affiliates in total European manufacturing output (sales) is much higher than the employment share, and of all R&D undertaken abroad, almost ¾ are performed in European affiliates. They show an R&D intensity of slightly less than 2% (this compares with 9% for affiliates outside Europe. However, whether productivity lead and high R&D in full can be regarded as an effect of US FDI remains an open question. One has to assess whether European firms became more productive and increased their level of technology after being acquired by US firms. As mentioned above, this can only be done for individual markets and firms.

2. The Case of Germany

From a national perspective, the overall role of US FDI for European economic growth is only of limited importance. Rather, the central issue is: to what extent does the individual country profit from the growth potential of inward FDI? In the case of Germany it is often feared that US FDI, as well as international FDI in general, has increasingly passed the country by as a consequence of diminished quality of German business locations.

This view is based on the observation that net inward FDI flows have come down to minimal values in recent years. There were even negative inflows at times. Foreign investors take out their capital rather than invest it in Germany. This holds true especially for US MNEs. They disinvested several billion DM in the early 1990s according to German statistics.

However, this is only one side of the coin. FDI flow data are not very reliable. The picture gets brighter (from a German perspective) when we, again, take a closer look at employment and production data and at the "quality" of US production in Germany:

- Germany, along with the UK, still is the number 1 location in Europe for US MNEs. Her position in total foreign production of US firms has not changed dramatically since the early 1980s. Even in 1993, the most recent year covered by the statistics and a recession year for Germany, no substantial falling behind was reported. US investors account for almost 5% of manufacturing employment and over 7% of manufacturing production in Germany (Table k2). If one considered only enterprises with a workforce of at least 20, the US share in production comes up to about 10%.
- **High income activities** are obviously **concentrated in Germany**. US affiliates show a clear productivity lead over indigenous firms. Compensation per employee is second only to Switzerland but 10% higher than in France and almost 50% higher than in the UK. Over one quarter of the US MNEs' foreign R&D takes place for German subsidiaries. This could lead to spillovers and productivity gains in the German economy.

Table k2 Manufacturing Affiliates of US MNEs in the German Economy

US affiliates in Germany	absolute figures		p.c. of all manufacturing affiliates abroad		p.c. of total manufacturing in Germany[a]	
	1982	**1993**	**1982**	**1993**	**1982**	**1993**
Employment (1000)	404	375	12	12	5	5
Production ($bn)	38	95	14	15	6	8
R&D outlays ($bn)	85	2.4	27	27	8	8

[a] German figures taken from OECD database. According to German statistics which exclude small firms, percentages are slightly higher. In a survey of the top 500 companies in Germany, the Stifterverband estimates the share of those foreign-controlled firms which are included in the top 500 at about 15% of all R&D in German manufacturing. US affiliates account for 6.3% of the R&D personnel (NIW et al., 1996).
Source: U.S. Department of Commerce; OECD; Stifterverband; own calculations.

Compared with indigenous firms, however, US subsidiaries (and foreign-controlled firms in general) show average R&D intensities (NIW et al., 1996; DÖRRENBÄCHER and WORTMANN, 1991). This is not surprising in view of the fact that many of the affiliates are acquisitions of existing firms. It gives rise to the assumption that foreign investors do not produce particular technological impulses and that their main economic effects result from their strong competitive position.

Furthermore, there are signs of a worsening in the locational quality: other European locations and Japan have apparently improved their relative attractiveness for R&D recently. An increasing share of what is reported as "R&D outlays" in German subsidiaries (Table k2) is bought from the MNEs' R&D facilities in other countries. This does not necessarily mean that US production in Germany is falling behind technologically. However, there is an obvious risk that new clusters of high-income activities are being developed in neighboring European countries (or overseas, e.g. in Asia-Pacific) rather than in Germany. Growth effects would then pass Germany by. In this context, it is interesting to note that US FDI is no longer particularly prominent in the growth sectors of the German economy. High and increasing market shares are mostly achieved in average-growth sectors. US FDI (and FDI in general) can no longer be considered a growth engine in the German economy.

This development is unsatisfactory if one considers the political and economic conditions for inward FDI: (1) Germany is the largest market in the EU, closely located to the transition economies in central and eastern Europe (CEE), (2) there are virtually no formal barriers to inward investment. Instead, massive subsidies are given to foreign (as well as domestic) investors in order to attract entrepreneurial resources to east Germany and to establish a certain countervailing power against west German firms.

The results of the promotion policies are not overwhelming. US investors, as well as investors from other countries, hesitated to engage in east Germany for a long time after unification. After they started to invest, they largely concentrated on regional markets which are less exposed to international competition (e.g. services, construction, energy, food, stone and earthen industries) and on crisis sectors where entry costs were particularly low (e.g. shipyards, mining, metal). Foreign investors contributed little to the re-establishing of an internationally competitive industrial basis. Opel's (i.e. General Motors') modern plant in Eisenach does not reflect a trend. FDI usually does not initiate economic dynamism. It rather follows it and reinforces existing trends. The conclusions from this for the CEE countries in transition are: the best way to attract FDI and take advantage of it as an agent of growth is to create a dynamic economic environment from domestic resources.

Endnotes

1 The following is mainly based upon HÄRTEL, JUNGNICKEL and KELLER et al. (1995).

References

HÄRTEL, H. H., JUNGNICKEL, R. and KELLER, D. et al. (1995), "Grenzüberschreitende Produktion und Strukturwandel - Globalisierung der deutschen Wirtschaft", Mimeo, Hamburg (to be published in spring 1996).

DÖRRENBÄCHER, C. and WORTMANN, M. (1991), "The Internationalization of Corporate Research and Development", *Intereconomics*, May/June.

NIW et al. (1996), "Zur technologischen Leistungsfähigkeit Deutschlands", Erweiterte Berichterstattung, (Mimeo), Hannover et al. (to be published in 1996).

UNCTAD (1993), *World Investment Report 1993*, New York.

UNTCMD (1992), *Worl Investment Report 1992*, New York.

U.S. DEPARTMENT OF COMMERCE (1992 and 1987), *U.S. Direct Investment Abroad. Benchmark Survey*, Washington, D.C.

U.S. DEPARTMENT OF COMMERCE (1995), *U.S. Direct Investment Abroad*, (Diskettes), Washington, D.C.

L. Multinational Investment and Economic Growth in Eastern Europe

Jan Stankovsky

1. Introduction: Volume and Growth of Foreign Direct Investment in the East

This paper deals with the contribution of foreign capital, especially foreign direct investment (FDI), to economic growth in the transition countries. The analysis concentrates on the situation in central eastern Europe (CEE: Hungary, Poland, the Czech Republic and Slovakia) and south eastern Europe. The situation in the former Soviet Union is treated only occasionally.

As an introduction, some figures about FDI in the East may be helpful: The flows of new investment peaked in 1993 with \$7.2bn, and fell slightly in 1994 to \$7.0bn. They recovered in 1995 but fell again - according to preliminary statistics in 1995. These data include investment in kind. Other statistics report slightly different figures.

In CEE the flow of FDI peaked in 1993 (\$4.8bn) as well. New investment of \$3.4bn was reported in 1994 and \$10bn in 1995. The highest increase in the flows up to now occurred in 1991 (+\$2bn) and in 1995 (\$9.8bn). In 1992 and 1993 the increases amounted to some \$1bn. In 1993 and 1995 the increase was mainly due to the huge Telecom privatization in Hungary. Balance of payments statistics record lower levels for most countries (notably Poland), but also show similar tendencies[1].

The stock of FDI in the East at the end of 1995 can be estimated at \$43bn, in central eastern Europe at \$28bn.

Hungary has up to now been the most successful among the eastern countries in attracting foreign investment. The stock of FDI in Hungary by the end of 1995 amounted to $13.3bn, followed by Poland ($6.8bn) and the Czech Republic ($5.9bn). For Russia an estimate of $5.5bn is reported.

The high attractiveness of Hungary has recently diminished a little, whereas Poland (especially since a settlement for the London club debts was reached) and the Czech Republic are becoming more attractive. The stocks of FDI per capita are highest in Hungary, followed by Slovenia, the Czech Republic and Estonia.

Though the size of flows and stocks of FDI in the East is remarkable, it is significantly lower than expected. The capital flows are concentrated on very few countries of the region.

2. The Role of FDI in the Transformation of Eastern Europe: Expectations

FDI have long been seen as one of the most important instruments for securing and promoting the transformation of the East. Initial estimates of the capital needs of the East were, for various reasons, very high. First of all, a quick catching-up process, requiring high investment, was expected. The capital stock from the previous system was seen as more or less useless. In addition to this, it was assumed that during the transformation period the domestic savings of all sectors of the economy (public, enterprises and private households) would be reduced. Saving ratios would therefore not be high enough to finance the countries' investment needs.

The estimates of the capital needs of the East were based on different approaches, for example, a target growth approach, a labor productivity approach, or an approach that uses the Marshall Plan aid after World War II as a point of reference. The estimates are as high as $16trillion during a period of 10 years ($1,600bn per year). Naturally, a high share of this capital was earmarked for the former Soviet Union. But even the more cautious projections for eastern Europe (excluding the former Soviet Union) assumed a capital need ranging from $70 to 100 billion per year for a longer time period.[2] These high estimates caused concerns that capital flows might be diverted from the South to the East, and more generally, that restructuring of the East would result in a sustained increase of the real interest rates in the world economy.

The capital need discussion has been influenced by the enormous amounts of capital transferred from west to east Germany after reunification. For the "other" eastern countries, however, a different model of financing has been targeted: after a short period of (mostly humanitarian) aid, the economy of these countries should have been stabilized and put on a growth path with the financial support of international organizations. This would create a climate appropriate for private foreign capital flows, which should become the main source for the financing of the East.

Eastern countries were expected to be very attractive for western investors due to the extremely cheap but mostly skilled and experienced labor force. The proximity to the West and the expected high domestic demand also helped to make these countries highly attractive for western investors. An abundance of energy and raw materials makes Russia an attractive place to invest.

From a macroeconomic perspective foreign capital can substitute for domestic savings. It is used for financing deficits of the current account and/or of the budget (in the case of insufficient public saving). Equally important is the function of FDI in channeling managerial, marketing and other skills towards eastern Europe. FDI can contribute to the process of privatization.

Extremely important is the "demonstration" effect of FDI: at the macro level, high flows of private long term capital are seen primarily as an indicator of the degree of success in the transformation process. Enterprises with foreign participation usually enjoy a better rating on the stock exchange and have easier access to cheaper credits from abroad. After integration into multinational enterprises, eastern firms can utilize the international sales organization of the parent company. Multinational enterprises with subsidiaries in eastern Europe are probably the most powerful lobbies against protectionist tendencies in western countries.

An important issue in this connection are the - real and psychological - aspects of security: the higher the capital invested in the East, the higher the expectation that the country of the investor will support the eastern country in the case of a foreign threat.

Numerous empirical studies of the role of FDI in developing countries support the expectation that FDI will foster growth in eastern Europe. This impact has been analyzed by BORENSZTEIN et al. (1995) "in a cross-country regression framework, utilizing data on FDI flows from industrial countries to 69 developing countries over the last two decades." ... "Our results suggest that FDI is an important vehicle for the transfer of technology, contributing relatively more to growth than domestic investment" (p. 1).

<u>Contribution of FDI to economic growth</u>

"The contribution of FDI to economic growth could result from two effects. First, FDI could add to capital accumulation, and thus to economic growth. And second, FDI could contribute to economic growth if it is more productive, or efficient, than domestic investment" (p. 14). ... "Our results suggest that FDI is in fact an important vehicle for the transfer of technology, contributing to growth in larger measure than domestic investment. Moreover, we find that there is a strong complementary effect between FDI and human capital, that is, the contribution of FDI to economic growth is enhanced by its interaction with the level of human capital in the host country. However, our empirical results imply that FDI is more productive than domestic investment only when the host country has a minimum threshold stock of human capital" (p. 3). "The value of the point estimates place the total increase in investment at between 1.5 and 2.3 times the increase in the flow of FDI. Thus, in addition to its effect on technological progress, it appears that FDI contributes to economic growth by increasing total capital accumulation in the host economy" (BORENSZTEIN et al., 1995, p. 3).

3. Economic Growth and Investment in Eastern Europe: Recent Developments

All countries in eastern Europe recorded positive economic growth rates in 1993. Growth accelerated in 1994 in most countries of the region and was be maintained in 1995 and 1996. The highest growth rates were achieved by Poland and Slovenia. Slovakia has excellent results, as well. In Poland, the Czech Republic, Slovenia and Slovakia, growth rates from 4 % to 6 % are expected in 1996 and 1997. Only Hungary will show modest results.

Despite different conditions in the various eastern countries some generalizations are possible. Growth was induced in a "classical" way by exports ("export as an engine of growth"). The upswing of the business cycle in western Europe in 1994 contributed to growth in the East. Internal factors were important, too. In 1993, a period of deep recession in western Europe, Poland recorded a high growth rate, and the Czech Republic was rather successful in exports.

Growth in the East was usually accompanied by an increase in investment, which can be seen as an important precondition for sustained growth in the future.

4. Second Thoughts Concerning the Role of FDI in Eastern Europe

Though the importance of FDI for the successful transformation in eastern Europe is undisputed, it should not be accepted without question. Reservations about the contribution of FDI to the catching-up process in eastern Europe might be based on the following facts:

- The investment flows to central eastern Europe peaked in 1993. They stagnated in 1994, despite better conditions: in the eastern countries the institutional framework for investments improved, in western Europe the economy recovered from the 1993 recession.

- The contribution of FDI to the actual upswing in eastern Europe was limited. A significant negative correlation between the amount of FDI/head and the growth rates in eastern Europe could be constructed (STANKOVSKY, 1996)
- References to negative secondary effects of FDI in eastern Europe are increasing.

5. Importance of FDI for Eastern Europe

FDI played an important but not a decisive role in the transformation of eastern Europe. The resource transfer to eastern Europe on an expenditure basis - a broad definition, which includes FDI and other capital - has been, according to UNECE calculations, slightly negative every year since 1990. The only exception was 1993 with a positive net resource transfer of $5bn.[3]

Only in Hungary did FDI (including other capital) contribute significantly to the financing of the current account and budget deficit. There, FDI in percent of GDP reached 4½ to 6½ percent. Comparable figures for other east European countries range from only 1 to 3½ percent (STANKOVSKY, 1995). Similar results are shown by SHEEBY (1994), who calculated FDI in relation to GDP at purchasing power parities. The FDI stock corresponds in 1993 to 10.4 percent of GDP in Hungary, 5.7 percent in Czechoslovakia, 2 percent in Poland and Romania and to 1 percent in Bulgaria. The corresponding figures for new investment in 1993 were 2.6 percent, 1 percent and 0.1 to 0.2 percent.

The level of FDI has to be seen in relation to the level of gross investment, and especially to that of private investment of enterprises (corporate investment). According to the calculations of UNCTAD (1995), the "investment ratio" of FDI was rather high in eastern countries: 6.7 percent in 1991 and 8 percent in 1992. These figures were higher than in developing countries (3.2 percent and 4.9 percent, respectively).[4]

HUNYA (1995) has calculated the share of FDI (excluding privatization income) in business investment in Hungary. This share peaked in 1991 with 29 percent and continued falling to 17 percent in 1994. According to the new OECD report on Hungary the share of FDI in total gross investment in 1993 was significantly higher (47 percent; "Europe", No. 7301, 15 September 1995). A simple calculation for other eastern countries (including also the privatization revenues) shows investment ratios for the Czech Republic, Poland and Slovenia of some 10 percent, and for Slovakia 4 percent in 1992 and 1993 (STANKOVSKY, 1995). NESVERA (1995) summarizes his very detailed analysis of the investment finance in the Czech Republic as follows: "the contribution of foreign capital to the real creation of new investment property ... did not exceed 10 percent in 1993-1994 ..." (p. 22).

The increase in corporate investment in the reform countries during the last upswing was financed - according to the studies of the European Union and the UNECE - by the enterprises themselves through an improved profitability. "The recovery of fixed investment in Eastern Europe ... has been largely financed by the resources of the enterprises themselves, not by the intermediation of domestic savings or by foreign investors. The growth of enterprises' own resources was in turn a function of large productivity gains, a moderate growth of wages, and increases, although moderate in general, of producer prices. Thus increased profit margins were an important source of funds for enterprises wishing to invest." (UNECE, 1995, p. 3).

The European Union has released a study on recent trends, prospects and policy issues of saving and investment in transition countries (EU, 1995). According to this study, external capital is playing and will continue to play an important role in the future in the transition process. The experience of other countries suggests that the future recovery of investment ratios in eastern Europe is likely to be mostly financed by an increase in domestic saving, particularly corporate saving.[5] This conclusion "is consistent with the fact that the recent recovery of corporate investment in the most advanced Central European countries (Czech Republic,

Poland and Hungary) has been largely self-financed through an improvement in enterprise profitability."

"The low current rates of saving in the transition countries reflect to a considerable extent the recession and the initial difficulties linked to the process of systemic transformation. As transition economies gradually strengthen and enterprise and financial sector restructuring proceeds, domestic saving ratios are bound to increase. This is particularly clear in the case of corporate saving, since enterprise profitability is likely to improve quickly with the cyclical conditions of the economy. Other things being constant, economic recovery and structural progress will also tend to increase public saving, both by increasing revenues and by reducing unemployment benefits and (explicit and implicit) subsidies to loss-making enterprises and banks."

"Furthermore, TC may be able, at least during an initial period, to sustain high rates of growth with relatively moderate ratios of investment to GDP. The inefficiency of past investment patterns, and the fact that a considerable fraction of the capital stock inherited from the socialist period will be of little value under a market economy, mean that there is a relative shortage of useful productive capital in TC. This will tend to make investment in TC very productive."

6. Are There Negative Secondary Effects of FDI in Eastern Europe?

After the initial euphoria, in which FDI was sometimes seen as a panacea for almost all problems of eastern countries, a more realistic assessment is gaining ground. In addition to the question about the real size of the contribution of FDI, possible secondary effects are also being discussed. The whole issue is rather sensitive, as it easily becomes a question of ideology. On many points the "leftist" criticism is in accord with "rightist" (national) objections against FDI.

Most reservations against foreign direct investment stem from the fact that the inflow of foreign capital restricts the room for maneuver of national economic policy making. This argument is certainly true, but it can be interpreted in two alternative ways: as a reduction in economic policy choices or as a healthy force in strengthening self-discipline.

New aspects of this question emerged in connection with the globalization of the world economy and the increasing power of multinational enterprises (MNE). An interesting viewpoint on this issue is presented in the latest publication of DUNNING (1995): "As this century draws to a close, it is clear that MNE activity - which comprises a composite of FDI, collaborative agreements and trade - can be divided into two categories. The first is traditional value added activity designed to exploit the existing resources and capabilities of firms" ... "The second kind of MNE activity ... main impetus is to protect the existing market shares of the investing firms by cost reducing and innovation, and also to gain access to new markets. We have called such MNE activity strategic assets seeking. ... Strategic asset acquiring crossborder activity poses new challenges for national governments and supranational agencies as they seek to better understand the causes and effects of FDI. The key issue is whether such activity promotes static and dynamic efficiency ... or, whether it reduces competition by increasing the concentration of economic power and inhibiting a country's dynamic comparative advantage".

Due to their strong bargaining power, big investors in the East were successful in securing their markets by erecting artificial trade barriers. This happened mostly in the first years of the transition and can be illustrated by a number of examples, such as in the car industry, in former Czechoslovakia, Poland and Hungary, or in the tobacco industry in the Czech Republic. The EBRD (1994) summarizes its analysis of these problems as follows: "Some of the largest investments have been at least partly enticed by selective, 'tailor-made' protection from imports".

The latest UNECE Survey (1995) reads as follows: "It is in countries where economic and social institutions are relatively weak, where the structures of the state are weak - that this more predatory behavior by the enterprise is both more apparent and least restrained. The transition economies are, by definition, characterized by still imperfectly functioning markets, embryonic institutions." ... "Where markets are not competitive or the state lacks effective regulatory powers, there can be no presumption that the activities of foreign companies will automatically contribute to a more efficient use of resources" (p. 14 ff).

From this perspective the initial reluctance of former Czechoslovakia (Czech Republic) to allow foreign capital to participate in privatization can be seen as a carefully thought out measure.

These investment strategies of multinational enterprises greatly account for the limited contribution of foreign direct investment to the export performance of the eastern countries. The initial expectations of high capital flows toward the East were based on the assumption, that cheap labor would motivate multinational enterprises to transfer production into this area. This, however, has not yet been the case. The EBRD analyzed all surveys on motives for FDI in eastern Europe. The results were the following: "Most striking perhaps is the predominance of market access among factors of importance to investor decision." ... "Factor cost advantages are clearly rated as less important than market access in all the surveys." ... "Most studies explicitly play down the role of cheap labour" (EBRD, 1994, p. 132). This conclusion can be illustrated by surveys of the OECD and of the Austrian National Bank.

Data showing the contribution of FDI to foreign trade of the reform countries are scarce. An interesting illustration is offered in statistics released by the Austrian National Bank on intra-firm trade between Austrian parent companies and their subsidiaries in eastern Europe. Austrian intra-firm exports were approximately three times as high as imports (1993 S4.3bn compared with S1.6bn).[6]

These findings leave open the possibility of an overall positive impact of Austria's direct investment on the current account of the eastern countries, for instance through import substitution or exports of the subsidiaries to unrelated companies. Such a development could at least be expected in the future.

Nevertheless, these results underline the decisive impact of internal factors of the eastern countries on the development of exports.[7]

The attitude of the management and owners of eastern enterprises toward western capital is changing, too. At the beginning of the transformation, the (often inexperienced) management saw western money and advice as the only possible way out of the crisis. Western investment was accepted under almost any conditions. After five years the learning curve shows some results. Western capital is still seen as important, but not as the decisive factor. Some examples in this respect are quoted in an interesting article in the September 1995 issue of Business Central Europe.

7. Absorption Capacity of Eastern Europe for FDI

The rather small amounts of foreign capital flowing to the East can also be seen from another perspective. The original estimates of the capital needs were based on the assumption of high growth rates of the region - rates, necessary to rapidly close the income gap to the West. The old and new Tigers in the Far East have shown that sustained growth at 8 percent to 10 percent p.a. is not impossible. Eastern Europe has the additional advantage of being highly endowed with human capital.

The models predicting high growth rates in the East, however, have not taken labor force problems sufficiently into account. In the Far East the labor force for new factories is recruited almost exclusively from the (poor) agricultural sector, whereas in eastern Europe workers must be drawn from the oversized (and mostly privileged) "socialist" industries. High growth would therefore require a radical structural adjustment. After 40 years of "politics of entitlements", the labor force can only cope with limited amounts of painful change. In this respect the situation in eastern Europe is far more similar to the situation in western Europe than to that in the Far East. Therefore, sustained growth rates of more than 5-6 percent are probably feasible only under very favorable conditions.

A more dynamic economic development could possibly be achieved with a model of "Singapore democracy". Such a model is based - at least from my point of view - on two pillars. First, there must be an authoritarian but not too corrupt political leadership, which imposes a moderate income policy and intervenes in the economic policy rarely, and if so, competently. Second, the country needs a functioning market economy. It is questionable, however, whether such a concept can be realized in central eastern Europe at the present time.

8. A Short Conclusion

The previous analysis of the contribution of foreign capital to economic growth in the East can be summarized as follows. Foreign capital (including FDI) plays an important role, directly and indirectly, in the process of transformation. Its quantitative contribution to economic growth and to the financing of investment has been rather limited. The only exception being Hungary.

Especially in the first stage of the transformation, some investors used their market power and the weak bargaining position of their eastern counterparts to establish barriers for competition which eventually could have negative economic consequences.

In the future, foreign capital will contribute significantly to economic growth only in those countries which have mastered the transformation and have embarked on a path of growth. The danger of negative secondary effects of FDI could be kept at bay by economic and political stabilization, but also by participation of the eastern countries in the competition regulations of the European Union.

Such a conclusion may be satisfactory from an economic point of view, but certainly not in the realm of security. A failure of economic transformation could cause political destabilization which could endanger western Europe as well. Private capital flows will certainly not contribute to a reduction of this risk. The political interest of the west would therefore require efficient transfers of public funds to the less successful countries of the region. This in turn would imply that the donor countries would have influence on the economic policy of the recipient countries and that the taxpayers in the west would be willing to make financial sacrifices. Neither the first nor the second preconditions are realistic. Therefore the only way to support the advancements of the successful transformation countries is to integrate them into the security alliances of the west.

Appendix

Table L1 Direct Investment in the East 1993 and 1994: New Investment

	1991	1992	1993	1994	1995	1994	1995
			$ mn			Shares in percent	
Czech Republic	494	1,004	654	569	2,562	8.1	17.2
Slovak Republic	0	0	135	185	181	2.6	1.2
Hungary	1,700	1,641	2,550	1,300	4,570	18.5	30.7
Poland	247	900	1,479	1,342	2,511	19.1	16.9
Central Eastern Europe	2,441	3,545	4,818	3,396	9,824	48.4	66.0
Albania	0	18	48	140	65	2.0	0.4
Bulgaria	39	56	171	196	101	2.8	0.7
Romania	156	269	227	627	323	8.9	2.2
Former Yugoslavia	352	575	444	673	524	9.6	3.5
Slovenia	340	165	139	395	196	5.6	1.3
Croatia	0	408	288	268	320	3.8	2.2
Macedonia	12	2	17	10	8	0.1	0.1
South Eastern Europe	547	918	890	1,636	1,013	23.3	6.8
Eastern Europe	2,988	4,463	5,708	5,032	10,837	71.7	72.9
Former USSR	300	695	1,460	1,987	4,037	28.3	27.1
Baltic countries	0	0	113	275	237	3.9	1.6
Estonia	0	0	66	118	97	1.7	0.7
Latvia	0	0	47	82	121	1.2	0.8
Lithuania	0	0	0	75	19	1.1	0.1
CIS	300	695	1,347	1,712	3,800	24.4	25.5
Russia	300	378	668	637	2,017	9.1	13.6
Ukraine	0	170	200	91	420	1.3	2.8
Belarus	0	7	264	23	44	0.3	0.3
Other countries	0	140	215	961	1,319	13.7	8.9
East	3,288	5,158	7,168	7,019	14,874	100.0	100.0

Source: WIFO database.

Table L2 Direct Investment in the East 1993 and 1994: Stocks

	1991	1992	1993	1994	1995	1994	1995
			$ mn			Shares in percent	
Czech Republic	595	1,556	2,153	3,191	5,916	11.6	13.9
Slovak Republic	0	231	366	552	733	2.0	1.7
Hungary	3,150	4,850	7,400	8,700	13,270	31.6	31.1
Poland	600	1,500	2,979	4,321	6,832	15.7	16.0
Central Eastern Europe	4,345	8,137	12,898	16,764	26,751	61.0	62.6
Albania	0	18	77	130	200	0.5	0.5
Bulgaria	14	65	195	429	530	1.6	1.2
Romania	264	533	761	1,244	1,595	4.5	3.7
Former Yugoslavia	854	1,481	1,601	2,274	2,798	8.3	6.6
Slovenia	827	1,044	859	1,254	1,450	4.6	3.4
Croatia	0	408	696	964	1,284	3.5	3.0
Macedonia	27	29	46	56	64	0.2	0.1
South Eastern Europe	1,132	2,097	2,634	4,077	5,123	14.8	12.0
Eastern Europe	5,477	10,234	15,532	20,841	31,874	75.8	74.6
Former USSR	1,854	3,002	4,642	6,661	10,826	24.2	25.4
Baltic countries	0	460	668	867	1,110	3.2	2.6
Estonia	0	250	316	434	531	1.6	1.2
Latvia	0	210	258	264	378	1.0	0.9
Lithuania	0	0	94	169	201	0.6	0.5
CIS	1,854	2,402	3,541	4,423	6,821	16.1	16.0
Russia	1,854	2,232	2,900	3,650	5,527	13.3	12.9
Ukraine	0	170	370	461	881	1.7	2.1
Belarus	0	0	264	287	331	1.0	0.8
Other countries	0	0	7	25	82	0.1	0.2
East	7,331	13,236	20,174	27,502	42,700	100.0	100.0

Source: WIFO database.

Table L3 Direct Investment in the East 1993 and 1994: Number

	Stocks 1994	Stocks 1995	Growth 1995	Stocks 1994	Stocks 1995	Growth 1995
	Number			Shares in percent		
Czech Republic	23,005	32,946	9,941	13.4	16.3	32.4
Slovak Republic	7,207	9,092	1,885	4.2	4.5	6.1
Hungary	23,557	27,900	4,343	13.8	13.8	14.2
Poland	19,737	24,086	4,349	11.5	11.9	14.2
Central Eastern Europe	73,506	94,024	20,518	43.0	46.6	66.9
Albania	208	400	192	0.1	0.2	0.6
Bulgaria	3,087	4,806	1,719	1.8	2.4	5.6
Romania	43,100	49,206	6,106	25.2	24.4	19.9
Former Yugoslavia	11,892	12,477	585	7.0	6.2	1.9
Slovenia	3,604	4,007	403	2.1	2.0	1.3
Croatia	6,840	6,900	60	4.0	3.4	0.2
Macedonia	1,448	1,570	122	0.8	0.8	0.4
South Eastern Europe	58,287	66,889	8,602	34.1	33.2	28.1
Eastern Europe	131,793	160,913	29,120	77.0	79.8	95.0
Former USSR	39,280	40,812	1,532	23.0	20.2	5.0
Baltic countries	19,486	19,722	236	11.4	9.8	0.8
Estonia	9,592	9,400	-192	5.6	4.7	-0.6
Latvia	5,419	5,419	0	3.2	2.7	0.0
Lithuania	4,475	4,903	428	2.6	2.4	1.4
CIS	19,794	21,090	1,296	11.6	10.5	4.2
Russia	13,300	14,276	976	7.8	7.1	3.2
Ukraine	3,500	2,969	-531	2.0	1.5	-1.7
Belarus	2,070	2,645	575	1.2	1.3	1.9
Other countries	924	1,200	276	0.5	0.6	0.9
East	171,073	201,725	30,652	100.0	100.0	100.0

Source: WIFO database.

Table L4 Direct Investment in the East 1993 and 1994: Per Capita

	Stocks				New investment	
	1994	1995	1994	1995	1994	1995
	$ per capita		Number per 1 mn inhabitants		$ per head	
Czech Republic	309.8	574.4	2,233.5	3,198.6	55.2	248.7
Slovak Republic	102.2	135.7	1,334.6	1,683.7	34.3	33.5
Hungary	852.9	1,301.0	2,309.5	2,735.3	127.5	448.0
Poland	111.9	177.0	511.3	624.0	34.8	65.1
Central Eastern Europe	259.9	414.7	1,139.6	1,457.7	52.7	152.3
Albania	38.2	58.8	61.2	117.6	41.2	19.1
Bulgaria	51.1	63.1	367.5	572.1	23.3	12.0
Romania	54.8	70.3	1,898.7	2,167.7	27.6	14.2
Former Yugoslavia	95.5	117.6	499.7	524.2	28.3	22.0
Slovenia	627.0	725.0	1,802.0	2,003.5	197.5	98.0
Croatia	200.8	267.5	1,425.0	1,437.5	55.8	66.7
Macedonia	26.7	30.5	689.5	747.6	4.8	3.8
South Eastern Europe	69.9	87.9	999.8	1,147.3	28.1	17.4
Eastern Europe	169.7	259.6	1,073.2	1,310.4	41.0	88.2
Former USSR	22.8	37.1	134.3	139.9	6.8	13.8
Baltic countries	109.7	142.3	2,466.6	2,528.5	34.8	30.4
Estonia	271.3	331.9	5,995.0	5,875.0	73.8	60.6
Latvia	101.5	151.2	2,084.2	2,167.6	31.5	48.4
Lithuania	45.7	54.3	1,209.5	1,325.1	20.3	5.1
CIS	15.5	24.0	69.6	74.3	6.0	13.4
Russia	24.6	37.3	89.7	96.5	4.3	13.6
Ukraine	8.9	17.2	67.7	57.9	1.8	8.2
Belarus	27.6	31.8	199.0	254.3	2.2	4.2
Other countries	0.3	1.1	12.5	16.2	13.0	17.8
East	66.2	103.0	411.9	486.7	16.9	35.9

Source: WIFO database.

Table L5 Foreign Direct Investment and Import Protection in Hungary and Poland

	All Sectors	FDI-intensive sectors	Examples Non-FDI-intensive Chemicals	Examples FDI-intensive Transport equipment	Examples FDI-intensive Beverages
Hungary			In percent		
Average Tariff[1)]	15.0	24.9	9.9	17.4	48.5
Maximal Tariff[1)]	35.8	62.5	40.0	50.0	150.0
Non-Tariff Barriers[2)]	13.4	21.1	7.0	20.0	17.0
Poland					
Average Tariff[1)]	19.8	37.6	14.3	45.0	45.8
Maximal Tariff[1)]	21.3	49.4	20.1	35.0	145.0

1) Simple average.
2) Number of Non-Tariff Barriers at 2-digit level.

Source: EBRD, Transition Report 1994.

Table L6 Prime Reasons for Attractiveness of the East as Investment Locations

	All investors	Austrian investors
	Shares in percent	
Market oriented motives		
Access to large domestic market	43.8	35.3
Market share	25.9	26.5
Market "potential"	11.1	5.9
Resource oriented motives		
Low cost production	9.3	5.9
Source of raw materials	6.8	5.9
Others		
Geographical location	5.6	20.6
To follow clients	4.3	2.9

Source: OECD, Assessing Investment Opportunities in Economies in Transition, Paris, 1994.

Table L7 Motives of Austrian Enterprises for Foreign Direct Investments 1993: East and the EU

	Hungary	Czech Republic	EU	Total
Measured by the number of subsidiaries		Shares in percent		
Market access (sales guarantee)	77.5	80.9	80.0	79.3
Labor cost	6.4	5.2	0.5	2.6
Purchasing security	2.4	0.9	1.8	2.4
Tax considerations	0.7	0.0	3.3	2.2
Others	13.0	13.0	14.4	13.6
Total	100.0	100.0	100.0	100.0
Measured by the nominal capital				
Market access (sales guarantee)	86.0	87.4	54.7	66.5
Labor cost	3.9	1.1	0.1	1.4
Purchasing security	1.7	1.2	4.3	3.6
Tax considerations	0.1	0.0	10.0	5.7
Others	8.4	10.3	30.9	22.7
Total	100.0	100.0	100.0	100.0

Source: Austrian National Bank.

Table L8 Intra-Firm Trade of Austrian East-Multinational Enterprises 1992 and 1993

	Austrian exports			Austrian imports		
	Total	Intra-firm		Total	Intra-firm	
	ATS bn		In percent of total	ATS bn		In percent of total
1992						
Hungary	15.56	2.53	16.3	11.96	0.32	2.7
Czech Republic	9.52	0.27	2.8	7.75	0.11	1.4
Slovak Republic	4.28	0.13	3.0	3.35	0.02	0.5
Slovenia	5.64	0.65	11.5	3.00	0.82	27.3
Specified Eastern countries	35.00	3.58	10.2	26.06	1.27	4.9
East	56.50	3.58	6.3	43.54	1.27	2.9
World	487.56	20.01	4.1	593.92	5.79	1.0
East in per cent of world	-	*17.9*	-	-	*21.9*	-
1993						
Hungary	16.55	2.68	16.2	10.83	0.42	3.9
Czech Republic	11.34	0.50	4.4	9.13	0.19	2.1
Other Eastern countries	31.46	1.13	3.6	23.07	1.01	4.4
East	59.35	4.31	7.3	43.03	1.62	3.8
World	467.17	20.95	4.5	564.91	6.09	1.1
East in per cent of world	-	*20.6*	-	-	*26.6*	-

Source: Austrian National Bank.

Endnotes

1 Statistics of FDI in eastern countries are discussed in detail in BREWER (1994) and in STANKOVSKY (1995).

2 For a detailed survey of the different estimates of the capital needs of the East, see HANDLER, KRAMER and STANKOVSKY (1992), HANDLER and STEINHERR (1993), STEINHERR (1993).

3 The net resource transfer on expenditure basis is calculated as follows: trade balance plus non-capital services and private transfers (i.e. the current account excluding (net) investment income payments and official transfers), which measures the combined change in domestic absorption (i.e. consumption and investment) and foreign reserves (UNECE, 1995).

4 This comparison is flawed, however, as the definition of direct investment according to balance of payments statistics differs from that of gross investment in the system of national accounts (direct investment includes also property transactions).

5 In the empirical literature a high correlation between national saving and investment rates is generally found.

6 Similar relationships hold for intra-firm trade between Austrian parent companies and their subsidiaries in Germany. In trade with Switzerland, however, imports of Austrian parent companies are higher.

7 A different conclusion is drawn in the OECD report on Hungary: Hungarian enterprises with foreign capital contributed 50 percent to the total exports of Hungary.

References

AGARWAL, J. P. (1994), "Impact of 'Europe Agreements' on FDI in Developing Countries," Kiel Working Paper, No.640.

BALDWIN, R. E. (1994), "The Effects of Trade and Foreign Direct Investment on Employment and Relative Wages," OECD Economic Studies, 23.

BORENSZTEIN, E., DEGREGORIO, I. and LEE, I. W. (1995), "How Does Foreign Direct Investment Affect Economic Growth?" NBER Working Paper No. 5057.

BREWER, T. L. (1994), "Indicators of foreign direct investment in the countries of Central and Eastern Europe: a comparison of data sources," *Transnational Corporations*, Vol. 3, No. 2.

DUNNING, J. (1995), "The Role of Foreign Direct Investment in a Globalizing Economy," Banca Nazionale di Lavoro, Quarterly Review, No. 193.

DUNNING, J. H. (1993), *Multinational Enterprises and the Global Economy*, Addison - Wesley.

EBRD (1994), *Transition Report*, London.

EC (1995), "Saving and Investment in Transition Countries," *European Economy*, No. 7, Supplement A.

GABRISCH, H. (1994), "Ausländische Direktinvestitionen in Mittel- und Osteuropa werden überschätzt," IWH.

HANDLER, H., KRAMER, H., STANKOVSKY, J. (1992), "Debt, Capital Requirement and Financing of the Eastern Countries," WIFO, Vienna.

HANDLER, H. and STEINHERR, A. (1993), "Capital Needs and Investment Financing in Eastern Countries," WIFO Working Paper No.55.

HINDLEY, B. and MESSERLIN, P. (1994), "Attracting Foreign Direct Investment by Trade Policy," Mimeo.

HUNYA, G. (1995), "Foreign Direct Investment in Central and Eastern European Countries - Why is Hungary Attractive?" WIIW, Mimeo.

HUNYA, G. (1995), "Foreign Direct Investment. The Case of Hungary", Seminar Paper.

IMF (May 1995), *World Economic Outlook, Foreign Direct Investment and Macroeconomic Performance*, Washington D.C.

NESVERA, K. (1995), "The Development of Investments in 1991-1994 and Prognosis for 1995," Investicni a Postovni Banka, Newsletter for Foreign Investors, No. 2.

OBLATH, G. (1995), "Economic Growth and Fiscal Crisis in Central and Eastern Europe," WIIW, Research Report No. 218.

OECD (1994), *Assessing Investment Opportunities in Economies in Transition*, Paris.

SACHS, J. (1995), "Postcommunist Parties and the Politics of Entitlement", *Transition*, Vol.6, No.3.

SCHMIDT, K. D. (1994), "Foreign Direct Investment in Central and East European Countries: State of Affairs, Prospects and Policy Implications," Kiel Working Paper No. 633.

SCHMIDT, K. D. (1995), "Motives of Large Multinationals Investing in Small Transition Countries: A Literature Review," Kiel Working Paper No. 668.

SHEEBY, J. (1994), "Foreign direct investment in CEEC's," *European Economy*, No. 6.

STANKOVSKY, J. (1994), "Österreichs grenzüberschreitende Direktinvestitionen," WIFO-Monatsberichte, 67(2).

STANKOVSKY, J. (1994), "Förderung von Direktinvestitionen in Osteuropa," WIFO-Monatsberichte, 67(10).

STANKOVSKY, J. (1995), "Direct Investment in Eastern Europe, Factors, Extent and Industry Structure," WIFO, commissioned by Bank Austria, Wien.

STANKOVSKY, J. (1995), "Österreichische Direktinvestitionen in Osteuropa," in BUSCH G. and WALTERSKIRCHEN E. (Koord.), *Auswirkungen einer EU-Osterweiterung auf Österreich*, WIFO, Wien.

STANKOVSKY, J. (1996), "The Role of Foreign Direct Investment in Eastern Europe," WIFO, Austrian Economic Quarterly, No. 2.

STEINHERR, A. (1993), "Capital Needs in Eastern Countries," *Empirica*, Vol. 20.

UNCTAD (1994), *World Investment Report 1994, Transnational Corporations, Employment and the Workplace*, New York and Geneva.

UNCTAD (1995), *Recent Developments in International Investment and Transnational Corporations*, TD/B/ITNC/2, Geneva.

UNECE (1994), *Economic Bulletin for Europe*, Vol. 46, New York and Geneva.

UNECE (1995), *Economic Survey of Europe in 1994-1995*, New York and Geneva.

WELFENS, P.J.J. (1992), "Foreign Investment in the East European Transition," *Management International Review*, 3.

WELFENS, P.J.J. (1993), "The Growth of the Private Sector: Privatization and Foreign Direct Investment in Eastern Europe," in SIEBERT, H. (ed.), *Overcoming the transformation crisis*, Tübingen.

Comments on
Multinational Investment and Economic Growth in Eastern Europe

Gábor Hunya

Economic Development under Foreign Penetration in Hungary

1. Introduction

Mr. Stankovsky gives a correct picture of the basic facts and problems related to the inflow of direct investment capital in CEECs. He concentrates on the act of investing, its motivation and consequences, but leaves many questions concerning the behavior of foreign firms unanswered. The contradictory quotations concerning the impact of FDI on fixed investments reveals that the literature on such issues is not yet very developed. I intend to focus on the preliminary findings of ongoing research which confronts economic results of domestic and foreign investment enterprises in Hungary based on their tax declarations. This seems to be a reasonable method to get a realistic picture of the activities of FDI. Further comments will refer to differences between Hungary and the Czech Republic and the possible role of FDI in EU eastern enlargement.

2. The Foreign Sector in Hungary

2.1 Contribution to GDP

In 1993 the foreign sector contributed 14.6% to the value added in the non-financial corporate sector and its share in GDP can be calculated as 9% (see Table 11). We lack information concerning international comparison for the moment, but among the CEECs Hungary shows the highest level of foreign penetration. A partial and preliminary comparison of Austria in 1989 and Hungary in 1993 reveals that private (63%) and foreign (30%) shares in industry were very similar in the two countries. Estimating the shares in total GDP, Austria's level of privatization in 1989 was about 70% and the share of the foreign sector about 15%, which is very close to the Hungarian level expected by the end of 1996.

Increasing efficiency and profitability of economic activities can duly be expected from foreign investments. According to the Hungarian national accounts statistics, operating surpluses (value added minus compensation of employees plus net taxes and subsidies) of all non-financial corporation made up 23% of value added in 1993, but in case of foreign companies 35%. Foreign companies generated 22% of the total operating surplus. As foreign companies also had an over-proportional share (21%) in retained earnings, they must have had a higher investment propensity than the domestic sector.

Part of the income from direct investments, mainly in the form of dividends, are a loss to the country if transferred abroad. Foreign companies paid HUF18bn net dividends (7.4% of value added) which made up 41% of the total dividends paid in 1993. Gross dividends paid by all companies amounted to HUF70bn, of which 24bn was paid by foreign companies. This amount could have been transferred abroad. Companies with foreign investments, including minority foreign-owned firms (i.e. foreign investment enterprises, FIEs) paid dividends in the value of HUF34.3bn of which 15.7bn were reinvested in the company. 46% or HUF18.5bn were transferred abroad. Profit transfers seem to be a relatively small part of value added in foreign companies, although these figures are three times as high as those reported in the current account. Transfer pricing widely used in trade within multinational enterprises is also used to transfer profits.

2.2 Invested Capital in FIEs

In 1993 the total invested capital in companies providing tax declarations (in foreign investment enterprises) amounted to US$6,583mn.[1] The presence of foreign investments is negligible in agriculture as foreigners are not allowed to buy agricultural land. Also the energy sector, a state monopoly expecting partial privatization soon, is almost free from foreign investors, just like public services. In other branches 25-45% of the statutory capital is in FIEs (Table 13). The share of foreign capital in the total statutory capital ranges from 14% to 31%.

FIEs control more than 40% of capital in financial services, manufacturing, hotels and catering, around 35% in construction, trade, transport and telecoms. The highest share of FDI in statutory capital is in manufacturing (31%), hotels and catering (28%), construction (26%) and trade (22%). The difference between the share of FIEs and FDI is marked in branches where foreign capital is confined to minority shares, such as in transport and telecoms as well as financial services.

Half of the FDI in Hungary was invested in manufacturing. The second most important investment target is trade, with 13.6% of invested capital. Transport and telecoms, financial services and consulting services attracted 7-8% of FDI each.

2.3 Employment

FIEs employed 20% of thc companies' workforce, majority foreign-owned companies only 11% (all data refer to 1993, see Table 12). FIEs operate with lower labor intensity than domestic firms in all branches of production, except financial services, and in all sub-branches of manufacturing. Lower labor and higher capital intensity of FIEs in comparison to domestic companies seems to be the result of different company strategies. One can assume that foreign firms are faster in restructuring, they lay off redundant workforce sooner and employ more labor-saving technology than domestic firms. Data on investment activity (see below) supports the idea that FIEs have more recent capital stock than domestic companies. Company surveys and press reports refer to higher efficiency but also higher work intensity in foreign-controlled companies than in domestic ones.

Employment in manufacturing companies was on the decrease in 1992 and 1993. Non-financial corporations with double-entry book-keeping lost 500 thousand people from 1992 to 1993 and employed 2 million people in the latter year. All the decrease in employment (518 thousand) took place in the public sector, but the domestic private sector also lost 22 thousand. The only sector with expanding employment was the foreign sector (majority foreign-owned companies), with a 33 thousand increase. The employment level of foreign companies increased in all branches of the economy in 1993. It is obvious that employment problems can hardly be tempered by foreign investments. Foreign companies only have a positive influence on the availability of workplaces in very specific regions where they are concentrated (Budapest, Northern-Transdanubia). If we consider, that the expansion of the foreign and domestic private sector took place in part due to privatization and the job transfer from the public to the private sector, genuine job creation by the foreign sector must have been negligible.

Low labor intensity and efficient use of labor lead to high sales and value added per employed person. Foreign investment enterprises reported 59% higher per capita net sales than the average of companies and the difference in the case of wholly foreign-owned firms was 2.5 times. The latter category turns out to be a special type of firms, mainly greenfield investments with more modern technology.

2.4 Foreign Trade of FIEs

Export sales of FIEs account for half of the total exports of Hungarian companies, and the share is even higher in the case of the most important export branch, manufacturing. Two thirds of machinery exports and almost 60% of exported food-industry products are from FIEs. In 1993 companies exported 12.5% of their sales, foreign investment enterprises 20%, both less than in the previous year. The decline in export intensity reflects the overall decline in Hungary's exports in the wake of shrinking demand by the most important trading partners.

Highest export shares were registered in manufacturing: 23.2% for all companies and 30% for FIEs. Within manufacturing machine building had an average export share of 35%, in the case of FIEs 47%. The difference is even higher for textiles, 39% on average and 58% in the case of FIEs. In these branches producing for exports is the dominant motivation of investors. The food industry on the other hand was highly domestic oriented. The relatively low export intensity, 16% of FIEs' output, reveals that foreign investment in this branch was motivated by access to the domestic market. Nevertheless, FIEs delivered almost 60% of the food industry's export sales.

Important discrepancies appear between the export sales of companies and exports leaving the country. The method of data collection and the range of companies involved make such discrepancies unavoidable. The difference is most marked in the case of foreign investment companies whose export sales are significantly higher than the actual exports. One reason is the performance of duty-free-zone (offshore) companies, all foreign owned, which are not covered by customs statistics.

FIEs tend to import more than they export, thus they have an unproportionately high share in the foreign trade deficit. In 1993 and 1994, when Hungary accumulated dangerously high deficits in its foreign trade, FIEs generated 40% and lately 56% of this deficit. Several specific conclusions can be made concerning the role of FIEs in foreign trade:

- The high foreign trade intensity of FIEs points to the fact, that many of them are engaged in export processing activities with low domestic value added.
- Unproportionately high imports can be interpreted as a sign of a low level of integration into the domestic economy. Some of the foreign companies behave like enclaves, receive their inputs from abroad but sell some of their products

domestically. The question for the future is to what extent they will develop spill-over effects.

- The high import intensity of foreign companies is also due to their premature stage of development. In the build-up period companies import their own machinery and more components than at a later stage.
- The smaller decline of FIEs' exports in the recession year 1993 shows that foreign companies rely more on secure foreign markets than domestic companies.
- FIEs engaged in trade and commerce have a higher import intensity than domestic companies. Some of them, especially in wholesale and car distribution were established with the straight forward aim to penetrate the Hungarian market with foreign-made products. Foreign-owned retail networks, when operating in the higher price echelons, have also high import rates.

2.5 Gross Fixed Capital Investments

The share of foreign investment enterprises in business sector investments was 26% in 1992 and 34% in 1993. In 1993 investment of domestic companies without foreign capital remained constant, the whole increase being due to FIEs. The share of majority foreign firms was 17% in both years, i.e. the increase occurred in FIEs with a domestic majority. The explanation lies in the telecom investments made by MATAV which received minority foreign shareholders during the year and was also a major investor. The shift of previously Hungarian companies to the foreign sector seems to have been more important than the increase in investments by old FIEs.

FIEs invested less than average in buildings, more in machinery, two thirds of which was imported. FIEs' share in machinery investment was 45% in 1993 and half of imported machinery was invested by FIEs. The contribution of FIEs to economic modernization through machinery investment and the import of hopefully modern technology seems to be outstanding. On the other hand, the deterioration in the current account can also be partly attributed to the investment activity of foreign firms.

3. Economic Performance in the First Half of 1995: Clear Signs of Duality

This year the Hungarian economy shows a clear duality of performance. Economic growth can be estimated to have been about 2% annually in 1994-1995.[2] The slow rate of growth is due to the curtailment of private and public consumption in the wake of the stabilization policy, which aims to cure the deficits on the current account and the government budget.

Some activities show remarkable growth rates in the first half of 1995 compared to the same period of the previous year and continuing the trend of 1994: manufacturing production +10%, engineering +32%, export sales of engineering +57%, gross capital investments of corporations +14% (government initiated investments -3%), export payments +47%, import payments +8%. Clearly, an important segment of the economy, most notably the one dominated by foreign investment enterprises has been expanding considerably.

Foreign direct investments inflow amounted to US$100mn per month at a time of complete standstill of privatization. More investment goes into existing ventures than in setting up new ones. FDI has become a self-generating process. The more dynamic FIEs seem to be those operating in export processing, while domestic market oriented ventures face difficulties imposed by the austerity policy.

Foreign companies have changed not only the structure of the economy but also the composition of Hungary's foreign debt. Public foreign debt in real terms is at the level of 1990, the increase of US$5.7bn in total net debt was generated by the corporate sector. The best and biggest debtors are the subsidiaries of foreign companies which receive credits below the interest rate implied by Hungary's country risk.

There are some signs of spill-over effects of FDI, but the strengthening of an economic duality within Hungary still is the main trend. The foreign sector concentrates in specific industries, regions and demands only the younger and more educated workforce. Education is pushed towards elite training with foreign language skills while general public education is under organizational and financial distress. The duality of the Hungarian economy will partly be cured by spill-over and spread effects in the wake of economic growth, and by regional and industrial policies. Budgetary means for correcting expenditures are missing however.

4. The Hungarian Way of Transformation Compared to the Czech

No country is a clear case, but in many respects the Hungarian way of transformation and structural change differs from the Czech way. The latter is characterized by Vladimir Benacek as "capital hoarding, postponed bankruptcies, missing financial capital for restructuring". Under such conditions the chances for preserving old structures are higher, restructuring seems to be slower but less painful. Production remained competitive because capital costs are low due to written-off assets. In privatization voucher holders bought assets for nothing and have no capital related costs. Export revenues can be increased by selling low unit-value products. Czech exports to the EU are dominated by capital and energy-intensive products, Hungarian exports have a higher share of skill and labor-intensive products. As the pressure for investing is not very strong in the Czech case, most of the economy can survive in domestic hands. (Our interpretation differs from the one implied by Dr. Stankovky's remark on Czech privatization.)

The question for the future is what is more beneficial for a country: somewhat outdated firms and industries selling under their own trademark and leaving little capacity and labor idle - the case of the Czech Republic, or the Hungarian counterpart with very modern islands engaged in outward processing and offshore assembling while suffering of high unemployment and redundant capacities? Worldwide developments in the last few decades support the Hungarian way: intra-industry and intra-multinational company trade are the more successful and dynamic specialization. But too abrupt changes increase the need for imports and external finances so that the need for stabilization blocks economic growth in Hungary and pushes it towards duality.

5. Relevance of FDI for the EU-CEE Capital Transfer

The last paragraph in Dr. Stankovsky's paper provokes discussion about EU eastern enlargement. I think, the role of corporate integration may be a more positive one in the accession process.

About 70% of the invested capital in Hungary originates from the EU-15. Corporate integration of Hungary into the EU is more rapid than institutional integration. Benefits for EU firms do not only consist of repatriated profits, but also of benefits through trade. Trade benefits arise both from increasing volume and high surpluses. They should finally increase incomes and tax revenues in the FDI-source EU countries. The terms of accession of Hungary and other CEECs to the EU should stimulate the recycling of these gains. Increasing transfers must cure some of the problems that emerged partly through the activity of FIEs and summarized above as economic duality.

Hungary, like other associated countries, reckons with (or dreams of) high transfers from the EU when it gets access to the agricultural and regional funds. Present member countries consider these would-be transfers as a price for political stability at their eastern borders, not as an investment compensating for past benefits and stimulating future economic growth in the enlarged EU as a whole. They do not acknowledge the economic benefits they may receive if transfers are efficiently invested. I think this is a mistake. One should see the transfers as a recycling of revenues earned by EU firms through their presence in eastern countries. Transfers should contribute to overcoming duality and encourage economic growth.

Regionally and socially unbalanced economic development would promote social controversy and in this respect transfers contribute to political stability. Regionally balanced economic growth would promote investment opportunities for foreign firms.

The foreign control already achieved over much of the Hungarian economy promises that transfers, which enhance economic growth and as a consequence consumption, would benefit EU firms by providing a growing market at their doorstep. Understanding the relation between transfers from the EU budget and the corporate profits of EU firms benefits the case of CEE accession.

Table 11 Gross Value Added of (GDP) Non-Financial Corporations by Sectors of Ownership in Hungary

	1992		1993	
	HUF bn	%	HUF bn	%
Public	791.4	56.5	715.7	42.8
Foreign	129.9	9.3	244.4	14.6
Domestic private	479.4	34.2	712.2	42.6
Total	1400.5	100.0	1672.3	100.0

Source: KSH (1995a), p. 98-99.

Table 12 Number of Employees in Non-Financial Corporations in Hungary

	1992		1993	
	in '000	%	in '000	%
Public	1330.3	53.0	821.1	41.0
Foreign	192.1	7.7	225.4	11.3
Domestic private	986.4	39.3	964.3	48.2
Total	2508.8	100.0	2001.8	100.0
FIE, non-fin. co.	359.6	14.3	399.9	20.0
FIE, all companies	...	...	435.6	20.0

Source: KSH (1995a), p. 171-173, for FIEs KSH (1995b), p.12.

Table 13 Share of Foreign Investment Enterprises in the Whole Hungarian Economy[1] by Branches, 1993

	Employment	Capital total[2]	Capital FDI[3]	Sales	Exports	Investment[4]
A,B Agr.	0	5.2	0	0	22.4	0
C Mining	11.5	25.2	19.0	12.1	21.1	35.0
D Manuf.	30.6	45.0	31.2	40.2	51.7	61.8
E Energy	0	0.6	0	0	0	0
F Constr.	14.6	35.9	25.8	24.7	34.5	35.5
G Trade	21.0	34.6	22.1	32.3	50.4	37.0
H Hotel	22.5	40.3	28.3	27.3	37.0	41.7
I Transp	12.0	35.3	13.8	36.0	52.9	54.6
J Finance	47.4	46.1	14.9	79.6	94.3	0
K Real.	14.2	24.7	16.7	29.8	42.2	38.6
L Admin.	0	0	0	0	0	0
M Educ.	0	0	0	0	0	0
N Health	0	0	0	0	0	0
O Other	0	0	0	0	0	0
Total	20.1	26.6	15.9	30.9	50.0	34.0

0 denotes less than 5%
A to O denote activities by NACE classification
[1] All companies providing tax declaration.
[2] Statutory capital of foreign investment companies.
[3] Foreign direct investment in statutory capital.
[4] Gross capital investment.

Source: KSH (1995b, 1995c).

Endnotes

[1] By the end of 1993 cash inflow through the banking system as registered in the balance of payments amounted to US$5,576mn, including investments in kind the foreign investment stock was US$7,400mn. By mid-1995 cash investments increased to US$8,142 and the total amount to some 9.5bn.

[2] The 1994 GDP growth rate was revised recently to almost 3%. Our forecast for 1996 is 2%.

References

HAVLIK, P. (1995), "Transition countries: consolidating economy in 1995," The Vienna Institute Monthly Report, No. 10.

HUNYA, G. (1992), "Foreign Direct Investment and Privatization in Central and Eastern Europe," *Communist Economies and Economies in Transition*, No. 4.

HUNYA, G. (1995), "Foreign Direct Investments in Central and Eastern European countries - Why is Hungary Attractive?" *Südosteuropa*, No. 9.

KORNAI, J. (1995), "Transformational Recession: the example of Hungary," in SAUNDERS, C. (ed.), *Eastern Europe in Crisis and the Way Out,* Macmillan in association with WIIW.

KSH (Central Statistical Office) (1995a), *National accounts Hungary 1991-1993*, Budapest.

KSH (Central Statistical Office) (1995b), *A külföldi müködötöke Magyaroszágon 1993 (Foreign direct investments in Hungary 1993)*, Budapest.

KSH (Central Statistical Office) (1995c), *A beruházások alakulásának fö tendenciái 1991-1994 (Main tendencies of the development of investments 1991-1994)*, Budapest.

RICHTER, S. (1995), "Transformation der ungarischen Wirtschaft," in CZERNY, M. and PALME, G. (eds.), *Wirtschaftsentwicklungsprogramm für die ungarische Region Nógrád*, WIFO, Vienna

ROJEC, M. (1995), "Foreign Direct Investment and Privatization in Central and Eastern Europe," ACE Project Final Report, Ljubljana.

SZANYI, M. (1994), "Efforts at Adaptation by Hungarian Industrial Firms During the Transformation Crisis," Institute for World Economics, Hungarian Academy of Sciences, Working Papers No. 46, December.

ZEMPLINEROVA, A. and BENACEK, V. (1995), "Foreign Direct Investment - East and West: The Experience of the Czech Republic," Mimeo, ACE Project Workshop, Prague, 6-8 April

ZEMPLINEROVA, A., LASTOVICKA, R. and MARCINCIN, A. (1995), "Restructuring of Czech Manufacturing Enterprises: An Empirical Study," CERGE-EI Working Papers, No. 74, Prague.

Part III

Panel Discussion

The Banks' Role in Financing Economic Expansion in Eastern Europe

Recent Developments in the Hungarian Financial Sector

Rezsö Nyers

The developments in the international financial markets are characterized by huge and quick changes. The previously separate national markets have been integrated into a global market and are more and more international. The last decade has seen an explosion in the volume of international financial flows. The main contributing factors to this development have been the removal of exchange controls, domestic financial liberalization and rapid advances in financial technology.

Besides globalization the fundamental feature of financial sector development has been widespread universalization. Strict and dividing institutional and legal walls, which existed between the individual elements of the financial sector, have gradually been abolished by comprehensive and fine tuned regulations. Globalization and universalization of the financial sector has been accompanied by an explosion like development in financial technology and financial instruments. These developments create great challenges both for monetary policy and supervisory institutions. Countries which intend to integrate in international financial markets are forced to adjust to these processes. This challenge is extremely difficult in the case of countries in transition, because the tasks of setting up the legal and institutional framework of a market oriented financial sector and of catching up with the recent developments in the international financial have to be solved simultaneously.

Liberalization and the development of an effective and modern financial sector in Hungary started already in the mid-80s. In a relative short time significant progress has been made in the creation of a financial sector. This is reflected in the following facts:

Since 1987 a two tier banking system has been operating in Hungary, the tasks of the central bank have been reduced to the classical central banking functions. Commercial banks are operating in the form of independent joint stock companies. The number of commercial banks has doubled compared to 1987, and now 44 banks are operating in Hungary, 20 of which are partly or fully owned by foreign financial institutions. Besides the commercial banks savings- and credit cooperatives are also participants in the financial sector. At present 250 savings and 4 credit cooperatives are operating in the Hungarian financial sector.

In the process of building up a developed financial sector specialized financial institutions have also been created, for example the state-owned Export-Credit Insurance and Guarantee Institution, and the National Deposit Insurance Fund.

According to the legal regulations in force commercial banks are not allowed to take part in security trading. The main actors in the security market are the security trading companies. While in 1987 there were no independent security trading companies, there now are 85 companies operating in the Hungarian market. However, the overwhelming majority of the security trade **turnover** is carried out by the 5 to 10 largest security trading companies.

At present there are 14 insurance companies operating in the Hungarian insurance market, the overwhelming majority of which are joint ventures.

Supervisory organizations have also been set up. The main responsibility of supervisory organizations is the control and supervision of banks, the security market and the insurance sector.

During the financial sector reform restrictions concerning different activities were abolished gradually: restrictions on retail activity and corporate finance were abolished between 1987-1989, followed in 1989-1991 by practically all restrictions referring to the foreign exchange operations of commercial banks.

In recent years the legal and institutional framework for the basic financial markets was set up: money market, interbank foreign exchange market, capital market and the futures market.

The financial sector is operating within a legal framework, which enforces and transmits international standards in the Hungarian financial sector. The last among the financial acts, the Act on Foreign Exchange, came into force in October this year. According to this law the Hungarian currency - the forint- became practically convertible in current operations and at the same time the regulation on capital operations became more transparent and flexible.

Although the financial sector is developing at a rapid pace, the approach to the unified single financial market of the European Union presents a considerable challenge not only in further adjustment of regulations and in the development of the institutional framework, but also in the field of strengthening competitiveness and capital base of the financial sector and in improving the efficiency of financial intermediation.

The present state of the Hungarian financial sector can be characterized by weaknesses deriving from recent macroeconomic developments, which are a more or less necessary phenomenon accompanying the transformation to a market economy.

For the time being the extent of financial intermediation lags significantly behind that in developed countries. In the case of European Union members the total assets of the financial sector is equal to or exceeds the value of nominal GDP, while this indicator amounts only to 60 % in Hungary. The relatively low volume of financial intermediation can be explained - among other things - by the inadequate capital base of institutions, the insufficient choice of financial instruments and the lack of deepness of domestic financial markets. The most sensitive problem from the above mentioned imperfections is the relatively low level of capital and as a consequence the limited risk-taking ability of financial institutions, the limited ability of banks to extend credit, and the fragility of the financial sector.

The low capital base can be partly explained by the "artificial" establishment of the two tier banking system. The major part of commercial banks, especially the three large ones, established at the launching of the banking reform in 1987, began their activity with an inadequate capital base. But at the same time precisely these banks took over the corporate finance, the enterprises as clients together with the hidden risk and earlier accumulated hidden losses of large state-owned companies.

The measures aiming to bail out the banking sector were implemented in three phases. The bailing out process of banks focused on increasing the capital base to strengthen the banks' risk-taking and lending ability and on strengthening management skills and supervision. As a result of the credit and bank consolidation scheme the capital and provisions of the concerning banks have been raised, with the overwhelming part of the consolidation scheme's cost being covered by the state budget.

At present Hungarian banks meet the international capital requirements, with the capital adequacy ratio of the banking sector on average exceeding the 8 % minimum level. However, approaching international standards requires further efforts: catching up with the rapid development of the financial intermediation system, increasing the competitiveness of financial institutions, strengthening the cost sensitivity of institutions, introducing new financial instruments and deepening the financial markets. In this context the following aspects have to be underlined:

- The Hungarian financial sector is strongly segmented and concentrated. This dates back to previous regime. The situation is changing only slowly. While the market share of the two leading banks in household savings amounts to 60-70 %, in corporate finance another three to four banks have a share of 40-50 %. The overwhelming part of securities trading is carried out by 4 to 5 leading brokers. Traditional market leaders dominate also the insurance sector. The strong concentration and segmentation of the financial markets weaken the competition, decline the efficiency of financial intermediation and disturb the interest transmission mechanism of monetary policy.

Table The Weights of Bank Groups in the Total Assets of the Banking System (in %)

	1987	1988	1989	1990	1991	1992	1993	1994	1995. 1st half
Large banks	93	91	90	84	77	75	75	73	72
of which: **National Savings and Commercial Bank, Postbank**	35	38	38	36	35	35	38	39	39
Medium-sized banks	5	6	7	14	22	23	24	25	26
of which: **banks with joint ownership**						16	17	17	17
Specialized financial institutions	2	3	3	2	1	2	1	2	2

- To improve the health of the financial sector state ownership in the sector needs to be further reduced and the legal and regulatory framework further developed. Like most other Central European Countries, Hungary has opted for universal banking, thereby permitting banks to invest in non-financial companies. While universal banking has many advantages, it exposes banking institutions to a number of risks, and places ***additional demand on bank management.*** These risks can be contained by segmenting banks according to risk level and applying differential licensing, capital and management requirements to different groups of institutions. Although the banking supervision issued regulations covering capital adequacy, loan classification and liquidity requirements, the regulations need to be upgraded to international standards, including classification of off - balance - sheet items, capital adequacy of credit and trading books.
- The effective operation of the financial sector is weakened to a great extent by the unsuitable information system and insufficient independent supervision. Owing to the inadequacy of statistical information supervisory bodies have no reliable facts and figures, hindering them from drawing up a reliable and transparent picture of the performance, risk, and efficiency of the financial

intermediation. For this reason regulation usually occurs after the event and as a consequence systemic risk is increasing. The coordination between the state, as the main owner, the supervisory bodies and the central bank should be fundamentally strengthened.

The institutional framework, targets and instruments of monetary policy are characterized by rapid changes in the period of transition. The increased independence of monetary policy, that is of the central bank, the gradual separation of non-central bank activities, that is the separation of commercial bank and fiscal functions, allow monetary policy to concentrate on its final goal. The change of the institutional framework is connected with the transition from direct to indirect instruments in monetary policy.

Interest rate ceilings (e.g. in retail banking), restrictions on commercial bank activities and credit rationing by the central bank played a decisive role at the beginning of the transition period. The main instrument of liquidity control was the refinancing credit by the central bank for both long and short maturity. This direct instrument was inefficient and often led to serious disturbances in the financial intermediation or to disintermediation. By now, the direct instruments have largely been substituted by indirect instruments. i.e. mainly by repo and open market operations of the central bank. The role of direct tools is small, it is practically restricted to domestic channeling of special foreign credit facilities.

Simultaneously with the adoption of indirect instruments and with the gradual withdrawal of the central bank from the capital market, the central bank can concentrate more and more on the money market, focusing on its influence over money market liquidity and interest rate levels. For this reason the central bank concentrates on the shortest maturities of the money market. The third, probably the most decisive and most difficult change of the transition is the gradual withdrawal of the central bank from lending to the state.

Institutional changes, the clear distinction between monetary and fiscal policy, the increasing liberalization and openness of the economy - all of these changes are contributing to the transformation of the targets of central bank policy.

The target system of central bank policy has become more consistent and more comprehensive. Curbing inflation and improving the balance of payments had been the two ultimate goals of monetary policy in a more closed and less liberalized economy. By now, because of large-scale liberalization, openness and a pegged exchange rate regime, the direct possibilities for monetary policy to influence the balance of payments are limited (at the same time the role of fiscal and income policy has become decisive). Thus, price stability has become the single ultimate goal of monetary policy.

The intermediate targets of monetary policy have, in connection with the change of ultimate goals, also changed. At the beginning of the transition period the intermediate targets of monetary policy consisted of quantitative targets for various monetary aggregates - mainly net domestic credit - and the stability of the real exchange rate. With an open economy and open money and capital markets as well as a fixed exchange rate regime quantitative intermediate targets can no longer be followed. In these circumstances the only intermediate target is to keep the nominal exchange rate on the path assigned by the crawling peg system introduced in 1995. Hence, money market interest rates can only be regarded as operative objectives and the short run open market and repo operations of the central bank are used to influencing money market interest rates.

The switch in monetary policy from direct to indirect instruments and the transformation of the target system are perhaps the most important pre-requisites for monetary policy to help the development of the economy and for making financial the intermediation more effective. The effect of monetary policy in the transitional period largely depends on

- whether institutional reforms are sufficiently comprehensive and deep.

- whether the long-run goal of monetary policy has been harmonized with the short-run orientation of governmental economic policy and the coordination of monetary and fiscal policy is successful. In economies of transition, including Hungary, the central bank plays a very important macroeconomic advisory role in questions of economic policy. Thus, monetary policy advocates and pushes for macroeconomic stabilization and economic policy which concentrates on curbing inflation, promoting sustainable economic growth and implementing further long run structural and institutional reforms.

The specific dilemmas of the central bank in the period of transition derive from the changing environment and from the changing behavior of economic agents, and as a consequence the uncertainty of about the transmission mechanism in the transitional period. The most important dilemmas of monetary policy are the following:

- The level of domestic savings, saving ratio was extremely low in centralized planned economies, with the behavior of households, enterprises and institutions oriented to spending and consumption. The modernization and catching up with the developed economies requires a substantial increase in accumulation, the propensity to save. At the same time, after the immense changes accompanying the transition public confidence needs to be re-established and credibility rebuilt. However, establishing credibility takes a long time while rapid change is needed because of the requirements for equilibrium.
- The great and strongly fluctuating volume of capital flows associated with liberalization poses a particular challenge to the economies in transition. Hungary belongs to those central European economies in transition where 70-80 % of capital inflows is in form of foreign direct investment or long term investment loans. The danger of capital flight in the case of diminishing credibility is, therefore, not even high. However, the danger of unfavorable consequences of excessive capital inflow is higher: capital inflows may decrease domestic interest rate level thereby discouraging domestic savings. That is why monetary policy has had to face the question on how to deal with a liquidity

increase caused by large capital inflows. What are the tools for conducting sterilization? What is the price of sterilization? Is sterilization really necessary? What could be the consequences of sterilization? So far, the rapidly increasing capital inflow has not resulted in a too rapid decrease in interest rates in the Hungarian money market. The high - and this year increasing - effective reserve ratio and the money market operations of the central bank neutralized a substantial part (approximately half) of the capital inflow. The slight decline in money market rates was associated with the decline in the financing needs for the budget. Another important point is that the increasing liquidity of the banking system has not revived the "moral hazard" phenomenon. Lending activity of the banking system can be regarded even now as prudent. The further demand for sterilization, however, may be difficult to meet. A further increase in effective reserves is not possible, since due to the present 17% compulsory reserve requirement domestic banks are at a substantial competitive disadvantage compared to foreign banks. An increase in sterilization needs a higher proportion of marketable government papers in the portfolio of the central bank and continued budget adjustment.

- The low level of domestic savings was accompanied in the past by a continuously large and increasing fiscal deficit. Perhaps the most decisive reason for the fiscal deficit has been the excessively high level of social, welfare and cultural expenditures which is not in harmony with the true maturity of the economy. This is one reason why it is inevitable to create a long-run program to build a new and smaller-sized social welfare system based on other principles. Even in Hungary monetary policy faces the question as to what kind of role the central bank should assume in the management of government debt. The balance sheet of the central bank is characterized by serious imbalances. Most of them derive from the centralized planned economy and the monobank system. Before the transition the central bank was the only foreign borrower and it covered the budget deficit out of foreign credits. The role of the central bank in raising foreign capital is decreasing due to the liberalization of the financial sector and direct central bank financing of the budget deficit is also limited. However, because of the past, a large scale potential so-called quasi-fiscal deficit piled up in the balance sheet of the central bank because the budget did not pay the real cost to the central bank of loans which were covered by foreign credits. (Devaluation losses.) Managing the potential losses and cleaning up the central bank balance sheet can support the improvement of the current account and establish the pace for increasing private borrowing. This also requires the re-shaping of the role of the central bank as the government's fiscal agent. The central bank should assist in building up an institutional system which would increase the transparency of the government securities market and enable the government to finance itself securely and continuously. (Primary dealership.) Simultaneously to this, money market operations of the central bank would really need to be confined to open market operations supporting the targets of monetary policy.

Principles, instruments and implementation of Hungarian monetary policy do not very much differ from the norms in member countries of the European Union. This also helps our association and the catching up process. However, several great tasks are still ahead, in regulation as well as in market-building and fine-tuning of the monetary policy implementation. The total opening of the financial sector to international markets in the future poses a serious challenge, e.g. establishment of foreign branch offices in Hungary and vice-versa, liberalization of capital transactions, complete opening of the securities market. So far, the risks of complete opening are still too great. Some segments of the financial sector are too fragile to compete with the institutions of more developed countries without any support. Therefore, in the period of transition the regulation of financial markets cannot do without a few protective, helping instruments.

Linking the securities and banking markets more comprehensively still lies ahead - both in market-building and in regulation. Development of banking supervision with special regard to management of various risks and assets is also needed in connection with the above mentioned task.

Withdrawal of the central bank as monetary authority from all activities outside the management of monetary policy also lies ahead. In our case it means the abolition of its activities in channeling foreign credits and providing other kinds of long term credits, the abolition of the presence of the central bank in the capital market, the re-definition of its role as fiscal agent of the government.

Hungarian society perceives immense tensions which derive from economic transformation and macroeconomic imbalances hindering the catching up process. We are not over the worst in the process of stabilization and modernization. If society is ready to assume the burden, implied by further comprehensive reforms and adjustment measures, and if policy makers do avoid making the inevitable decisions, Hungary will not miss the train of the European Union heading towards dynamic and stable development.

The Present Situation of the Banking Sector in the Transition Countries

Werner Varga

The central European transition countries were surprisingly fast in implementing the reform of the finance sector - one of the basic conditions for a modern monetary sector. With the central banks divesting themselves of their commercial bank operations, the previous single-tier system was transformed into a two-tier banking system. The savings banks were left untouched by the process and continue to offer their services. In the wake of the separation of commercial business from the central banks, all the transition countries established the "large", initially state-owned banks. With the aim of promoting competition within the banking system from the very beginning, the authorities also chartered private banks. Especially the admission of foreign private banks was meant to further competition and to help introduce the know-how required in this sector more rapidly. This policy gave rise to a veritable boom of new bank establishments in the central and eastern European transition countries (WYCZANSKI, 1993).

In fact, the central and eastern European countries have achieved secular changes in their organizational structures and the money and capital markets are swiftly evolving, proving that from an organizational point of view developments are "right on course" (BONIN and SZEKELY, 1994; PIEPER and SCHRÖDER, 1995).

While admittedly there are great differences in the course the individual countries are taking, they still share a number of features due to the historic development of their economies:

- In all of these countries, savings deposits - a liabilities item of the aggregate balance sheet of the banking sector - are still predominantly held by the "old-type" savings banks. In many of the CEECs, savings banks continue to hold a market share of some 80% in this segment.

- Lending to the corporate sector, a line of business originally administered by the central bank, was passed on to the "new" banks when they were separated from the central bank. However, during the transformation process the financial situation of many enterprises turned from bad to worse and today a great number of these loans fall within the category of "bad debts", a much-discussed problem, which has been partially solved only in Hungary and the Czech Republic.
- The enthusiasm which fueled the "establishment of new banks" has waned. In many cases the banks were founded by private residents (sometimes supported by foreign capital) on inadequate capital requirements. Today they are more and more becoming a burden on the entire banking system. In their initial stages of existence, they extended loans to the corporate sector on relatively liberal conditions, but these loans have meanwhile turned into doubtful or irrecoverable debts. At present, the banks are trying to collect savings deposits for refinancing purposes by promising high interest rates. However, a collapse of the small banks might well undermine the population's trust in the entire national banking system - this all the more so because in most of the CEECs there is still no deposit insurance for these banks.
- With the initial enthusiasm ebbing off, the central banks have been modifying their licensing policy. The more restrictive stance also comes to bear vis-à-vis foreign banks. Though wooed in the beginning, foreign banks now find it hard or even impossible to obtain a license. In many cases, as in Poland, the Czech Republic, but also in Hungary, a banking license can only be obtained by acquiring one of the small banks.
- The banks' competition policy has become highly selective. Especially foreign banks or their subsidiaries mainly promote blue-chip enterprises in CEECs

Undertakings with less than first-class ratings, on the other hand, find it rather difficult to raise the funds they need.

- The privatization of banks is being delayed not only because their assets contain a huge amount of bad debts. Politicians in the transition countries have also realized that a certain scope of influence on the banking system may improve their room for maneuver in economic policy issues. Moreover, the CEECs' leading banks, which to some extent have to bear the burdens of the past, have recently been venting concern with regard to the growing influence of foreign banks.
- A Continental-type universal bank system appears to be gaining ground on the American-type system of functional separation in the financial services sector. For the time being, broker houses and commercial banks are still separate, but otherwise the banks quite legitimately designate themselves as universal banks. A consensus on eliminating even this last fire wall appears to be emerging in Hungary.
- The banks are fulfilling their service functions ever more efficiently. The money market (interbank market) is performing up to par. Developing this function proved especially important in the face of the liquidity overhang of savings banks and the high demand on the part of commercial banks - a systemic imbalance due to the above-described historic developments. The capital market generally still is in a more or less embryonic stage, but especially in Hungary, Poland and the Czech Republic it has already been put on a sound footing. All the CEECs have already developed payment transactions to a point that there is no noticeable difference to western market economies in terms of the speed bit which payments are handled.
- In monetary policy, the countries are gradually attaining the professional standards required. The CEECs' central banks have a grip above all on inflation rates. Turning to exchange rate policy, in only six years of time the countries achieved the standards which our western market economies took up to 36 years

to attain: the Czech Republic, Poland, Slovenia as well as Hungary have already reached convertibility according to Article VIII of the IMF Articles of Agreement.

- In conclusion, the reforming countries obviously have the intellectual and cultural capacity not merely to adjust to western economic standards but beyond that, to adapt the system to their individual needs where necessary. After all, the highly developed western market economies are not a single homogenous system. In fact, the different countries may take their bearings from many models to find their own individual path. The basic framework for the new system has been defined and the evolution leading up to an independent economic system can now progress step by step.

References

BONIN, J. P. and SZEKELY I. P. (1994), *The Development and Reform of Financial Systems in Central and Eastern Europe*, Edward Elgar, Brookfield.

PIEPER, B. and SCHRÖDER, K. (1995), *Unbewältigte Reformen des Osteuropäischen Bankensystems: Sechs Transformationsländer im Vergleich*, Ebenhausen, SWP-S 404.

WYCZANSKI, P. (1993), *Polish Banking System 1990-1992*, Friedrich-Ebert-Foundation Poland, Warsaw.

List of Tables

List of Figures

List of Contributors

Stanley W. Black
American Institute for Contemporary German Studies (AICGS)
Johns Hopkins University
Washington D.C. and
University of North Carolina

Jozef M. van Brabant
United Nations, New York

Miroslaw Bojanczyk
formerly Polish Ministry of Finance
currently Citibank (Poland) S.A., Warsaw

Volker Clausen
Institut für Wirtschaftspolitik, Universität Kiel

Georg Erber
Deutsches Institut für Wirtschaftsforschung (DIW), Berlin.

Evgeny Gavrilenkov
Center for Economic Analysis, Moscow

Edward M. Graham
Institute for International Economics, Washington D.C.

Thomas Gries
Universität-Gesamthochschule Paderborn

Daniel Gros
Center for European Policy Studies (CEPS), Brussels

Peter Hertner
Universität Halle-Wittenberg, Halle (Saale)

Gábor Hunya
Wiener Institut für Internationale Wirtschaftsvergleiche (WIIW), Vienna

Stefan Jungblut
Universität-Gesamthochschule Paderborn

Rolf Jungnickel
HWWA Institut für Wirtschaftsforschung, Hamburg

Hans Kernbauer
formerly Österreichische Bundesfinanzierungsagentur, Vienna,
currently GiroCredit Bank, Aktiengesellschaft der Sparkassen, Vienna

Sydney J. Key
Board of Governors of the Federal Reserve System, Washington D.C.

Elmar B. Koch
Bank for International Settlements, Basle

Timothy Lane
International Monetary Fund, Washington D.C.

Heinrich Matthes
European Commission, DG II (Economics and Finance), Brussels

Rezsö Nyers
National Bank of Hungary, Budapest

Johannes Priesemann
European Monetary Institute, Frankfurt/Main

Albert Schweinberger
Universität Konstanz

Jan Stankovsky
Österreichisches Institut für Wirtschaftsforschung (WIFO), Vienna

Werner Varga
Creditanstalt, Vienna

Uwe Vollmer
Universität Leipzig

Paul J.J. Welfens
Universität Potsdam and European Institute for International Economic Relations (EIIW), Potsdam

Holger C. Wolf
World Bank, Washington D.C., and New York University

Index

MIX
Papier aus verantwortungsvollen Quellen
Paper from responsible sources
FSC® C105338

If you have any concerns about our products,
you can contact us on
ProductSafety@springernature.com

In case Publisher is established outside the EU,
the EU authorized representative is:
Springer Nature Customer Service Center GmbH
Europaplatz 3, 69115 Heidelberg, Germany

Printed by Libri Plureos GmbH
in Hamburg, Germany